Fractures in Knapping

Are Tsirk

Archaeopress

Archaeopress
First and Second Floor
13-14 Market Square
Bicester OX26 6AD, UK

www.archaeopress.com

ISBN 978 1 78491 022 8
ISBN 978 1 78491 023 5 (e-Pdf)

© Archaeopress and A Tsirk 2014

All rights reserved. No part of this book may be reproduced, stored in retrieval system, or transmitted, in any form or by any means, electronic, mechanical, photocopying or otherwise, without the prior written permission of the copyright owners.

This book is available direct from Archaeopress or from our website www.archaeopress.com

Contents

List of Figures vii

List of Tables x

Preface xi

PART I: ELEMENTS OF KNAPPING

1. Knapping Past and Present 1
   Introduction 1
      Traditional Crafts and Industrial Society 1
   Prehistoric Knapping 3
   Recent and Remnant Knapping Traditions 4
   Some Specialized Knapping Traditions 7
      Gunflints 7
      Threshing Sledges 10
      Ceramic Industry 10
   Modern Knapping and Recent Explosion Of Interest 11
   Knapping Studies 14
      Archaeological Record 14
      Ethnography 14
      Knapping Experiments 14
      Living Archaeology 14
      Mechanics, Fracture Mechanics and Fractography 15
      Contemporary Crafts 15

2. Knapping Tools and Techniques 16
      Antler and Wood Billets 16
      Hammerstones 16
      Punches 18
      Pressure Flakers 18
      Holding and Fabricating Devices 20
      Anvils and Supports 21
      Hides 21
      Grinding and Abrading Stones 21
      Nontraditional Tools and Acessories 21
      Use-Wear Indicators 23
      Direct Percussion 23
      Anvil Technique and Anvil Percussion 24
      Bipolar Percussion 25

  Indirect Percussion 25
  Pressure Flaking 26
  Pecking, Grinding, Polishing.. 27
  Edge and Platform Preparation... 27
 Some Rules of Thumb.. 28
 Knappers' Wisdom, Folklore and Dilemmas 28
  Softer Percussors and Slower Blows 29
  Follow-Through with Forces 29
  Ridge Abrasion 29
  Wetting and Soaking... 29
 Learning to Knap... 29

3. Raw Materials... 31
 Material Selection and Use 31
  Obsidian.. 31
  Flint and Chert.. 32
  Other Materials 33
 Physical and Mechanical Properties... 35
  Microstructure and Physical Properties 35
  Homogeneity and Isotropy 35
  Elasticity, Ductility, Brittleness 36
  Elastic Constants 37
  Constants for Thermal Effects 39
  Strength and Fracture Toughness.. 39
  Mirror Constants... 40
 Workability... 41
 Alteration of Properties And Behavior... 44
  Hydration and Vesiculation of Obsidian.. 44
 Cortex and Patina on Flint and Chert 45
  Thermal Cracking... 45
  Thermal Alteration and Heat Treatment 47
  Environmental Effects 48
 Procurement 49
 Nontraditional Uses of Obsidian, Flint and Chert.. 50

PART II - FRACTURE MARKINGS: THE TOOLS OF FRACTOGRAPHY

4. An Overview.. 54

5. Hackles and Hackle Scars 63
 Twist Hackles and Single Tails.. 64
 Multiple Tails 69
  Parabolic Double Tails... 70
 Hackle Scars... 73
  Hackle Scar and Hackle Flake.. 73

	Bulbar Scar and Proximal Scar	73
	Ripple Scars	74
	Ridge Scars	74
	More on Hackle Scar Formation	75

6. Ripples 76
    Ripples 76
    Wallner Lines 79
        Normal Wallner Lines 80
        Anomalous Wallner Lines 84
    Stress Changes Causing Ripples 86
        Static Effects 86
        Specimen Vibration 87
        Stress Pulses 87
    Experimental Ripples 88
        Ultrasonic Modulation 88
        Sonic Modulation 89
        Exploding Wire Experiments 90
    Terminology and Interpretations by Others 90

7. Mirror, Mist, Hackle, Branching 92
    Mirror 92
    Mist and Velocity Hackle 92
    Branching, Incipient Branching and Lateral Wedges 95
    Velocity and Energy Considerations 96
    Mirror Constants and Stresses 97
    Markings Related to Mist and Hackle 98
        Wallner Mist-Hackle Configuration 98
        Mist Suppression Configurations 99
        Mist Lines 100

8. Miscellaneous Markings 103
    Material Interface Markings 103
        Material Interface Ridges and Ripples 103
        Material Interface Hackle 103
        Material Transition Ridge 105
    Split Marks 106
    Dividing Lines 107
    Ruffles 107
    Liquid-Induced Fracture Markings (Lifms) 108
        Effects of Moisture and Liquids 108
        Conditions for Manifestation of LIFMs 110
        Occurrence of LIFMs 110
        Significance of LIFMs 112
        Basic Kinds of LIFMs 112

    A Catalogue of LIFMs and Patterns 114
    Observation of LIFMs 116
    Variability with Liquids 123
    Variability with Lithic Materials... 123
    LIFMs with Sonic Modulation 124
    LIFMs Observed with Condensation 124
    Some Surface Patterns 124

PART III - FRACTURES IN KNAPPING

9. Introduction **126**
    Elements of a Mechanical System And Knapping.. 126
    Stresses, Stress Waves and Vibrations 128
    Some Fundamentals in Fracture Mechanics 128
    Catastrophic and Subcritical Crack Growth... 130
    Research on Fractures in Knapping 131
    Other Research 134

10. Flake Initiations, Proximal and Surface Features..................................136
    Flake Initiations 136
        Some Definitions 136
        Hertzian Cone Fractures 136
        Contact Initiations.. 140
        Non-Contact Initiations 147
        Initiations with Multiple Blows 148
        Effects of Cortex and "Layering" 150
        Environmental Effects 151
        Percussor Softness and Speed... 151
    Proximal Flake Features.. 152
        Platform Characteristics 152
        Dorsal Ridges and Curvatures 153
        Interior Platform Edge 154
        Wing Flakes 157
        Bulbs.. 157
        Popouts and Stepouts 159
    Flake Surface Features 159
        Fracture Directions 159
        Ripple Configurations and Fracture Fronts 160
        Ripple Concavity 160
        Ripples Related to Flake and Core Geometry 161
        Ripples at Inhomogeneities 162
    Why Ridges Guide Flakes.. 163
    Fracture Velocities.. 164
        Mist and Related Markings... 164
        Hackle Scars 165

    Ruffles 165
    Split Marks 165
    Tails and Incipient Tails 165

11. Crack Paths and Flake Profile Features 167
    Criteria for Crack Paths... 167
    Crack Paths and Core Geometry 167
    Crack Paths and Forces Applied 168
    Popouts and Related Fractures 168
    Compression Lips, Curls and Compression Wedges... 168
    Step-In and Step-Out Fractures 171
    Incipient Breaks... 175
    Popout Fractures.. 175
    Ripple Profiles and Kinks 181
    Wavy Crack Paths 182
    Flake Terminations 183
    "Jacked" Flakes 185

12. Forces in Knapping 186
    Non-Contact Flake Initiations 187
        Edge Angle and Core Geometry 188
        Location and Direction of Force Application 189
        Platform Characteristics 189
        Flaw Distributions 189
        Flaker Properties 190
    Contact Initiations 190
        Location of Force Application 190
        Direction of Force Application 190
        Edge Angle and Core Geometry 191
        Platform Characteristics 191
        Flaw Distributions 191
        Flaker Properties 192
    Contact and Non-Contact Flake Initiations: Comparisons.. 192
    Subsequent Detachment 192
    Direct Percussion... 195
        Percussor Characteristics 195
        Velocity of Blows 195
    Indirect Percussion 195
        Punch Characteristics 195
        Striker Characteristics... 197
    Core Mobility 198
        Percussion Flaking 198
        Pressure Flaking 198
    Supports... 198
        Distal... 198
        Dorsal.. 199

Bipolar Percussion..199

13. Breakage of Blades, Flakes and Bifaces..**201**
　　Axial Loads, Bending, Shear, Torsion and Their Effects 201
　　Clues from Fracture Markings and Other Features 201
　　Some Fractures with Blades and Flakes 202
　　　　Splitting of Blades and Flakes 202
　　　　Step-In and Step-Out Fractures 202
　　　　Incipient Breaks 202
　　　　Popouts 203
　　Some Fractures with Bifaces 207
　　　　Overshots and Edge-to-Edge Flakes 208
　　　　Amputations 210
　　Transverse Breakages 211
　　　　Fracture Origins 211
　　　　Fracture Directions 214
　　　　Compression Lips, Curls and Compression Wedges 215
　　　　Mist and Related Markings 216
　　　　Branching and Lateral Wedges for Blades and Flakes 223
　　　　Fracture Velocities 224
　　　　Location of Force Application 224
　　Some Special Breaks 224
　　　　Bowties 224
　　　　Slices 226
　　　　Segmentation 228
　　Aztec Appreciation of Mechanics 230

Concluding Remarks **232**

Glossary **234**

References **243**

Index **259**

List of Figures

Fig. 1.2 A Solutrean laurel leaf from Volgu, France. ... 3
Fig. 1.3 A Paleoindian Clovis Point from Blackwater No.1 Site. ... 4
Fig. 1.4 Replica of an Egyptian Predynastic Gerzian knife. ... 4
Fig.1.5 Type IV-E Danish dagger. ... 5
Fig. 1.6 Type IC Danish dagger. ... 6
Fig. 1.7 Replicas of Neolithic square section axes of Denmark by Thorbjorn Petersen. ... 7
Fig. 1.8 An exhausted blade core on the gunflint knappers work floor at Brandon. ... 8
Fig. 1.9 Threshing sledges in Turkey. ... 9
Fig. 1.10 Knapped blocks at Eben-Emaël for porcelain industry. ... 11
Fig. 3.1 Callahan's proposed lithic grade scale (Callahan 1979, reproduced with permission) ... 42
Fig. 3.2a Workability vs. K_{1c} ... 43
Fig. 3.2b Fracture Toughness vs. Lithic Grade ... 43
Fig. 3.3 Potlid fractures. ... 46
Fig. 3.4 A frost pitted nodule of Cobden chert. ... 47
Fig. 3.5 Sinuous fracture of a chert biface. ... 48
Fig. 3.6 A modern Normanskill chert quarry in Greene County, New York. ... 51
Fig. 3.7 Use of flint for houses in Brandon, England. ... 52
Fig. 5.1 Tails (as at A and B) and twist hackles as persistent tails (black arrow) in obsidian. ... 63
Fig. 5.2 Formation of twist hackles ... 64
Fig. 5.3 Twist hackles at the edge of an obsidian flake. ... 65
Fig. 5.4 Twist hackles at and near the edge of a biface thinning flake ... 65
Fig. 5.5 Twist hackles and incipient twist hackles in a coarse variety of Normanskill chert ... 66
Fig. 5.6 Twist hackles (arrow) and incipient twist hackles (especially in b) in Esopus chert. ... 67
Fig. 5.7 Tails in obsidian often persist as twist hackle. ... 68
Fig. 5.8 Tails at irregular inclusions in obsidian ... 68
Fig. 5.9 Parabolic double tails. ... 71
Fig. 5.10 Parabolic double tails and many mist lines on the surface of a flake. ... 72
Fig. 5.11 Parabolic double tails in a mist region. ... 73
Fig.5.12 Convergent tails with trailing mist line.. ... 74
Fig. 5.13 Hackle scars at the edge of an obsidian flake ... 75
Fig. 5.14 An overshot hackle flake and its scar on an obsidian flake. ... 75
Fig. 6.1 Stress changes associated with ripple formation. ... 76
Fig. 6.2 Ripple profiles and associated changes in shear stress. ... 77
Fig. 6.3 Gull wings at numerous inclusions on a flake.. ... 82
Fig. 6.5 Formation of gull wings ... 83
Fig. 6.6 "Knappers' Speedometer" ... 83
Fig. 6.7 Wallner wake formation. (From Tsirk 1988) ... 85
Fig. 6.8 An obsidian flake detached by percussion with ultrasonic modulation at 175 kHz ... 88
Fig. 6.9 Sonic modulation (at 183 Hz) used on an obsidian pressure flaker. ... 89
Fig. 7.1 Breaking stresses and mirror radii ... 92
Fig.7.2 Mist (dashed arrow) and hackle (solid arrow) on an accidental break of a biface ... 93
Fig. 7.3 Fracture surface of an accidental break from an internal flaw ... 94
Fig. 7.4 A mist-hackle configuration (arrow) in a mist region in obsidia ... 99
Fig. 7.5 Mist line in obsidian Fracture direction downward. ... 100
Fig. 7.6 Mist and hackle patterns. ... 101
Fig. 8.1 Material interface ridges. ... 104
Fig. 8.2 Formation of a material interface ridge. ... 105
Fig. 8.3 Split marks on a flake ... 106
Fig. 8.4 Ruffles on the inner surface of an obsidian flake ... 108
Fig. 8.5 Variation of fracture velocity V_f ... 109
Fig. 8.6 The basic LIFM type called an escarpment scarp. ... 112

Fig. 8.8 The basic LIFM type called linear band features 113
Fig. 8.7 The basic LIFM type called a liquid-induced hackle 113
Fig. 8.9 The basic LIFM type called a cavitation scarp 114
Fig. 8.10 Two unusual encounter-depletion scarps. 115
Fig. 8.11 Sierra scarps in a soda-lime glass plate 116
Fig. 8.13 Miscellaneous scarps. 121
Fig. 8.12 An encounter scarp (arrow) manifested as a hackle scarp. 121
Fig. 8.14 Depletion scarps manifested as irregular fingerlets 122
Fig. 8.15 Occurrence of scarps with distance from the fracture origin 122
Fig. 8.16 The very many inclusions of variable sizes 124
Fig. 8.17 The very many inclusions of variable sizes 125
Fig. 8.18 Sonic modulation at 183 Hz was used for this obsidian pressure flake. 125
Fig. 10.1 Hertzian cone fracture. 138
Fig. 10.2 Force vs. time for several impact velocities and sphere radius R = 5.1 cm.. 139
Fig. 10.3 Flake initiation by wedging in Normanskill chert 141
Fig. 10.4 Flakes with Hertzian initiation in Normanskill chert 142
Fig. 10.5 Flake with Hertzian initiation. 143
Fig. 10.6 Combined wedging-Hertzian initiations 144
Fig. 10.8 A wing flake can drastically alter the edge angle for subsequent flaking 146
Fig. 10.7 A flake with a wing flake that was detached to the left side 146
Fig. 10.9 Flake initiation by unzipping. 149
Fig. 10.10 Grinding over pecking on a platform of an Aztec blade from Otumba site in Mexico. 151
Fig. 10.11 Schematic outlines for cross-sections of a square section axe 153
Fig. 10.12 Mist and hackle at the lip by the right edge of an obsidian biface 155
Fig. 10.13 Proximal region of the same flake.. 156
Fig. 10.14 A hackle scar on a bulb, with the associated overshot hackle flake. 159
Fig. 10.15 Variations of flake thickness in transverse direction 161
Fig. 10.16 These ripple configurations relate to the variations in flake thickness i 162
Fig. 10.17 Material interface markings 163
Fig. 10.18 Split marks. 166
Fig. 11.1 Popout and related fractures 169
Fig. 11.2 Nominal stress trajectories for bending o 170
Fig. 11.3 Effect of shear on the direction of the compression lip 171
Fig. 11.4 Regular popout fractures with and without a roll-in from a hackle scar 172
Fig. 11.5 Formation of a stepout fracture 173
Fig. 11.6 Schematic profiles and fracture directions for popout and stepout fractures observed ... 174
Fig. 11.7 Incipient, quasi-stepout and quasi-popout fractures 176
Fig. 11.8 Partial profiles of obsidian blades with dorsal concavities 176
Fig. 11.9 Regular but unusual popout fractures from percussion 178
Fig. 11.10 Reverse (a and c) and compound popouts. 179
Fig. 11.11 Double popouts 179
Fig. 11.12 Formation of popout fractures. 180
Fig. 11.13 Popout fracture on an obsidian biface thinning flake 180
Fig. 11.14 Comparison of intrusive hackle scars... 181
Fig. 11.15 Flake terminations 184
Fig. 12.1 Wedge loaded at its tip 186
Fig. 12.2 Wedge with a force applied in an arbitrary direction at distance e from its tip. 187
Fig. 12.3 A two-dimensional model for analysis of blade detachment forces............................. 193
Fig. 12.4 Variation of forces with lengths of the detached part of the flake. 194
Fig. 13.1 Broken bifaces from the Caradoc Site 206
Fig. 13.2 A Normanskill chert biface broken accidentally during manufacture 207
Fig. 13.3 Overshot (white arrow) flakes on a Clovis preform 208
Fig. 13.4 Biface with a laterally overshot flake 209
Fig. 13.5 Biface with a longitudinally overshot flake 209
Fig. 13.6 Schematic illustration of an amputation from direct percussion................................... 210

Fig. 13.7 Blade detachment 212
Fig. 13.8 Stresses in a blade with triangular cross-section from a bending moment M 212
Fig. 13.9 Geometrical properties of triangular, trapezoidal and rectangular sections 213
Fig. 13.10 Examples of fracture fronts 215
Fig. 13.11 Mist and hackle at a transverse biface break 219
Fig. 13.12 Mist and hackle (arrows) on a section of a prehistoric flint blade 220
Fig. 13.13 Mist and hackle at a transverse biface break from bending 221
Fig. 13.14 Some types of mist patterns 222
Fig. 13.15 Mist patterns at the downstream faces of the slices seen in Fig. 13.16 222
Fig. 13.16 Multiple blade breaks with two slices. Obsidian 223
Fig. 13.18 A pair of lateral wedges on a Cobden Chert biface 225
Fig. 13.17 Bowtie from blade breakage 225
Fig. 13.19 Slice formation with loss of contact 227
Fig. 13.20 Slice in biface breakage 229
Fig. 13.21 Moment reduction vs. blade geometry when starting a crack from the outer face ... 231

List of Tables

Table 3.1 Major Constituents in Obsidians 33
Table 3.3 Constants for Thermal Effects 40
Table 3.4 Examples of Fracture Toughness 41
Table 4.1 Fracture Markings Terminology 55
Table 4.2 Occurrence of Fracture Markings 57
Table 4.3 Utility of Fract ure Markings 58
Table 4.4 Clues from Fracture Markings 60
Table 4.5 A Catalogue of Fracture Markings 60
Table 6.1 Errors (%) in V_F/V_S due to rotation of fracture plane 84
Table 8.1 Basic Types of LIFMs (by Appearance) 111
Table 8.2 Liquid-Induced Fracture Markings (LIFMs) 117
Table 10.1 Flake Initiations 137
Table 10.2 Hertzian Cone Fractures and Hertzian Flake Initiation 141
Table 12.1 Normalized Force Variations with Wedge Angle 188
Table 12.2 Force Variations with Distance from Edge 189
Table 12.3 Comparisons for Contact and Non-Contact Flake Initiations 191
Table 12.4 Properties of Some Woods 196
Table 13.1 Dimensions (mm) of flakes with popout fractures 203
Table 13.2 Nondimensional popout characteristics 204
Table 13.3 Biface breakages considered 207
Table 13.4 Lateral Wedges and Branching Cracks on Biface Tensile Surface 217
Table 13.5 Observation of Mist, Hackle, Mist Lines and Parabolic Double Tails 217
Table 13.6 Observed obsidian slices 226

Preface

The book is for students and practitioners of not only knapping, lithic technology and archaeology, but also of fractography and fracture mechanics. At the conferences on fractography of glasses and ceramics, I have been asked to demonstrate knapping as well as provide overviews of fractography learned from it. The first part of the book is intended to stimulate such interests further, in order to solicit contributions from a largely untapped pool of experts. Such contributions can advance significantly our understandings of knapping as well as fractography. In Part II of the book, fracture markings as the tools of fractography are introduced, with their formation, meaning and utility explained. Observations on the presence or absence of the markings in knapping are considered in Part III, along with a number of interpretations of fracture features.

The basic principles and concepts of fracture mechanics and fractography apply to fractures produced in any cultural context. It is therefore prudent to address most questions on fracture in a generic sense, independent of cultural contexts. In general, understanding of fractures provides a sounder basis for lithic analysis, and use of more recent scientific tools opens new avenues for lithic studies.

For stimulating my interest in archaeology, lithic technology and even fractography, I thank Ralph Solecki. Part II of this book is an expanded version of my lectures at Columbia. It was a pleasure to have many useful discussions on knapping with Jack Cresson, Scott Silsby, J.B. Sollberger, Errett Callahan and others

I am indebted to Don Crabtree for stimulating my interests in flintknapping, and putting me in contact with V.D. Fréchette to whom I am deeply grateful for many inspiring and enlightening discussions over 22 years. During my earliest years of pursuing knapping fractography, I had many fruitful discussions with Stephen W. Freiman. I am grateful for his insights and for his kindly pointing me in in the right direction with many ideas. Herbert Richter encouraged my attempts at fracture mechanics approaches to knapping, and Kouichi Yasuda occasionally steered me from the wrong paths in these attempts.

I gratefully acknowledge the receipt of some unusual industrial glass from Ernest Chrisbocker, the preparation of obsidian test specimens by Mark Green and the testing on obsidian by Kouichi Yasuda. I thank Ene Inno for editorial assistance and Sushant Singh for his help with the electronic version of the manuscript.

PART I: ELEMENTS OF KNAPPING

1. Knapping Past and Present

Introduction

Many species of animals not only use but also manufacture tools (Angier 2001, Beck 1980). For example, chimpanzees remove twigs from branches to "fish" for termites. They have also been observed to manufacture sharpened wooden spears, carrying them around and spearing bush babies in tree hollows. Tool manufacture by humans is vastly more complex, characterized by a greater anticipation of future needs and longer curation of the tools. So we humans see the difference.

For at least 99.5% of prehistory, artifactual remains consist primarily and often only of lithic remains. Archaeologists are greatly interested in extracting all relevant information from lithic artifacts. Understanding of flintworking (knapping) along with material properties can provide insights to functioning of prehistoric societies..

Knapping refers to the manufacture of artifacts by detachment of flakes. There are lithic artifacts whose manufacture involved significant pecking, grinding and polishing. Knapping by humans is not limited to manufacture and re-shaping of stone tools. It has also been used for shaping other, non-utilitarian artifacts (Fig. 1.1).

An understanding of knapping helps to distinguish characteristics of use-wear from those of manufacture on lithic artifacts. The principles involved in use-chipping are similar to those in flake production in knapping. But there are major differences in the scales involved, the manner of force application and the control of geometry.

Traditional Crafts and Industrial Society

At home I have lithic raw materials from five continents, including many states in the U.S. All transported by car or plane. Some mined with metal hammers and mining tools. My favorite hammerstones for obsidian are from Sun Valley, Idaho, some 3300 km away. Often I use antler from New England, the Midwest, Estonia or Sweden, as well as a zoo. I usually prepare antlers billets with a machine grinder, antler tines with a steel file. It requires little reflection to imagine how mind boggling the differences often are in practicing a traditional craft in an industrial as compared to a prehistoric society.

But that's not all. Watching TV or using a keyboard, telephone or pen does not provide the manual dexterity or sense of craftsmanship useful for learning to knap and use proper precautions. At an obsidian conference in Pachuca, Mexico, a number of knappers were working with obsidian from large nodules. When a couple of small Mexican kids showed up to hammer at the nodules, I quickly asked the conference organizer to stop them,

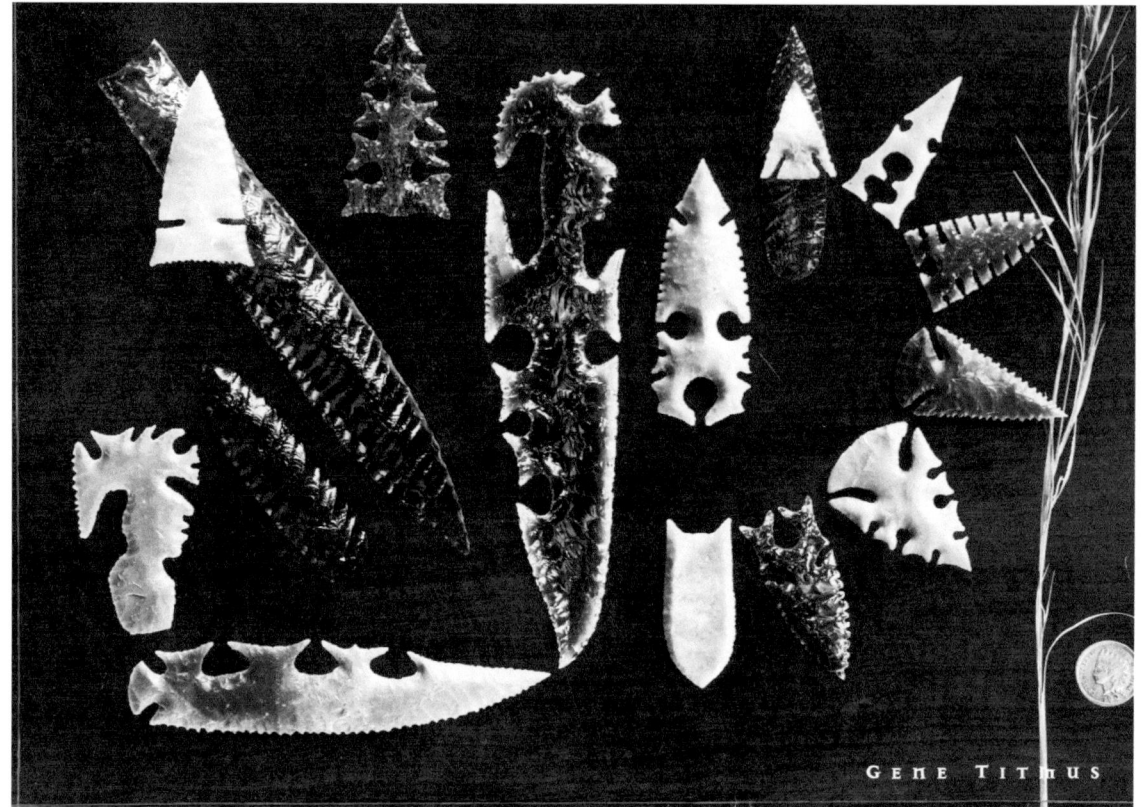

Fig. 1.1 Replicas of some utilitarian and nonutilitarian artifacts by Gene Titmus (Photography ©mcleandesign.com; Reproduced with permission.)

fearing they might get hurt. Knowing better, he left them alone. Sure enough, they did not cut themselves. They had grown up in an environment where manual dexterity is more commonplace. A number of today's best knappers are also good with other manual skills, such as woodworking.

Today our apprenticeship in knapping may come not only through observation of other knappers, but also through reading or watching knapping videos, even on the Internet. Many contemporary knappers practice the craft after working hours with limited time. François Bordes once observed an Australian aborigine scrutinize a nodule some 45 minutes before striking the first blow. The meaning and organization of time in that society was very different.

Information on knapping in its broadest sense obtained from contemporary practice of the craft is necessarily limited, devoid of comparable cultural contexts. An old Spanish ethnographic description of some special blade production in Mexico noted that the knapper had to fast for five days. To the accompaniment of a chant, the blades were then pressed off. If a blade broke, it indicated the knapper did not fast properly. Such information can hardly be obtained from archaeological evidence or contemporary knapping experiments.

Prehistoric Knapping

Flintknapping has been practiced for at least a couple of million years, known from the Hadar and Gona sites in Ethiopia (Semaw et al. 1997). In the Old World, knapping in some form or other was still practiced during the Neolithic period and later. It was practiced by the American Indian after the European contact period, with some remnants considerably later. In a few societies in the world, it is still practiced today.

Interesting observations from prehistoric knapping can be made on the efficiency of material utilization. For obtaining a certain length of cutting edge per unit weight of material, blades (long, roughly parallel-sided flakes) are by far the most efficient. In one experiment, 2.1 cm of cutting edge per gram of the preformed polyhedral obsidian core was obtained with pressure flaked blades (Sheets and Muto 1972). Blade production at a high level of skill was practiced, for example, by a number of Upper Paleolithic and Mesolithic cultures. The changes in flintknapping technology during the Lower and Middle Paleolithic are evident even to the nonspecialist, as reflected in the changes from the crude choppers to thick bifaces to thinner bifaces. Some of the very finest flintworking craftsmanship ever, such as some of the Solutrean laurel leaves, is from the Late Paleolithic in France (Fig. 1.2).

FIG. 1.2 A SOLUTREAN LAUREL LEAF FROM VOLGU, FRANCE. THE CAST IS 27.4 CM LONG AND ABOUT 7 MM THICK. (THE PHOTO IS OF A CAST FROM THE MUSEUM OF MAN IN PARIS.)

In the New World, some of the finest flintworking is from the Paleoindian period (Fig. 1.3). Some very fine craftsmanship in the New World can also be seen much later, at times with wide trade networks for nonutilitarian goods. These also suggest knapping craftsmanship beyond utilitarian needs. A word of caution, though: Extremely fine craftsmanship in itself does not imply a nonutilitarian function, as demonstrated by some Paleoindian points. Perhaps we tend to prejudice our hypotheses by our own notions of time and its organization. Examples of extremely fine craftsmanship can also be seen in the Gerzian flint knives from Egypt (Fig. 1.4) and the flint daggers from Denmark (Fig. 1.5). For the Gerzian knives, as well as for the Type IC Scandinavian daggers (Fig. 1.6), surfaces were ground in order to achieve best control in flaking. On the Egyptian knives, only one face was flaked. A nonutilitarian function is suggested for these artifacts.

A specialized technique was used for the manufacture of the Neolithic square section axes of Denmark (Fig. 1.7 and Vang Petersen 2008). After flaking to a square cross-section, they were ground. The axes as well as the daggers were traded very widely (Apel 2001). Not all of the axes were utilitarian. Some exceptionally fine ones, probably prestige items,

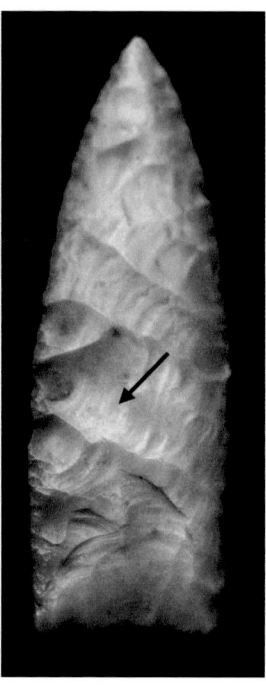

FIG. 1.3 A PALEOINDIAN CLOVIS POINT FROM BLACKWATER NO.1 SITE. 10.6 CM LONG. THE ARROW INDICATES A FRACTURE MARKING KNOWN AS A SPLIT RIDGE (CHAPTER 8), SEEN POORLY. (PHOTO IS OF BOSTROM'S PLASTIC CAST BY KRISTIAN METS.)

have been found in caches. There is a specimen 46.5 cm long at the Danish National Museum in Copenhagen. This could not have been utilitarian.

There are numerous other examples of nonutilitarian flaked stone artifacts from prehistory. From the New World these include flaked animal representations and the Mesoamerican, Hohokam and other eccentrics (Clements and Reed 1939) (Fig. 1.1). From Vietnam, there are two unusual examples of "lithophones" (lithic xylophones), with extremely large bifaces of variable sizes to produce the different notes. The longest of the bifaces measures about 90 cm.

From prehistory there are numerous examples of ground and polished implements of obsidian, flint and other stone materials. From Mesoamerica, unusual examples from obsidian include large mirrors, extremely delicate earspools (Thomsen and Thomsen 1971) and an exquisite vase with a monkey for decoration. Both in the New and Old Worlds, the decline in prehistoric flintworking reflects changing lifeways and a shift in emphasis to other crafts and activities. Many examples of prehistoric knapping are illustrated in Bordes (1968) and Bordaz (1970).

Recent and Remnant Knapping Traditions

The last American Indian to retain (until 1911) traditional lifeways, as a lone survivor of his tribe, was Ishi, a Yahi Indian (Holmes 1919, Heizer and Kroeber 1979). Remnants of some knapping among American Indian include the Maya in Guatemala (Hayden 1987) and the Xêtá Indians in Brazil (Miller 1979). Hayden discovered use of flaked basalt chopping tools in making of metates (grinding stones). Miller reported on use of flint flakes among the Xêtá, a tribe with only six survivors at the time.

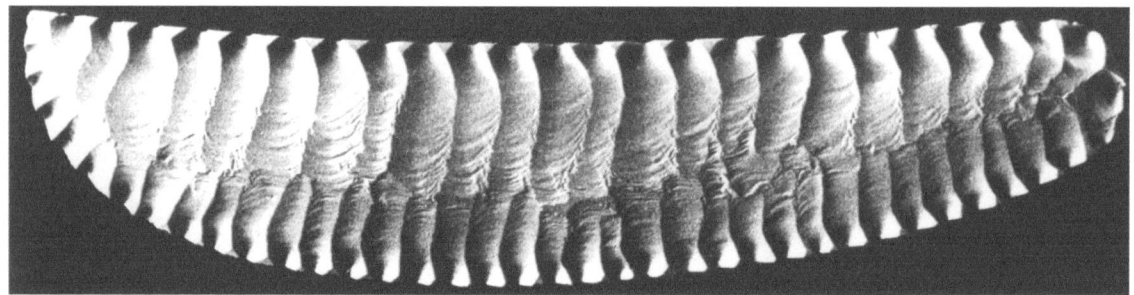

FIG. 1.4 REPLICA OF AN EGYPTIAN PREDYNASTIC GERZIAN KNIFE. FLINT, 25.2 CM LONG. (KELTERBORN 1984. REPRODUCED WITH PERMISSION)

Fig.1.5 Type IV-E Danish dagger. Errett Callahan's replica of the famous Hindsgavl Dagger. Flint, 29.3 cm long. (Callahan 1999, reproduced with permission)

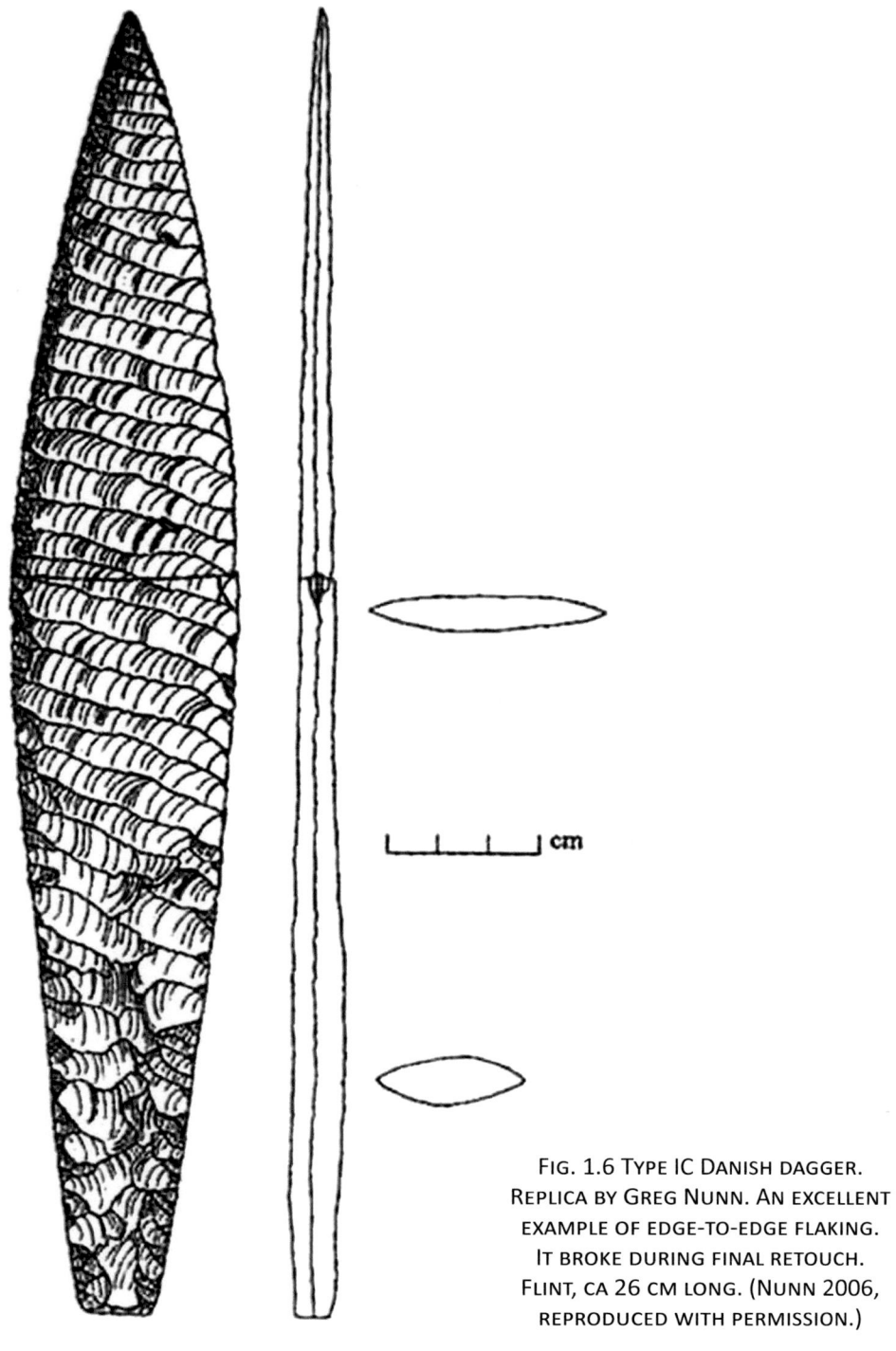

Fig. 1.6 Type IC Danish dagger. Replica by Greg Nunn. An excellent example of edge-to-edge flaking. It broke during final retouch. Flint, ca 26 cm long. (Nunn 2006, reproduced with permission.)

Knapping Past and Present

FIG. 1.7 REPLICAS OF NEOLITHIC SQUARE SECTION AXES OF DENMARK BY THORBJORN PETERSEN (COURTESY OF ERRETT CALLAHAN. PHOTO BY JACK CRESSON).

Knapping has been observed among aboriginal tribes in Australia (Tindale 1985, Hayden 1979) and New Guinea (Blackwood 1950, White 1967). Use of traditional knapping in New Guinea has also been observed very recently (Schick and Toth 1993, Hampton 1999). Flaked stone axes were made, utilizing the flake biproducts for miscellaneous other tasks for which they happened to be suitable.

Recent uses of modern glass as tools have been reported for many parts of the world, including Australia, Africa, the U.S., Greece, France and Great Britain. Use of teeth in edge chipping of obsidian blades has been observed in Africa.

Some Specialized Knapping Traditions

Three specialized knapping industries – which may be viewed as traditions – are noted here. The youngest of these is the production of flint blocks for liners in ceramic industry. Gunflint manufacture as an industry is some 400 years old. The production of flint inserts for threshing sledges dates back thousands of years, to Roman and earlier times.

Gunflints

Gunflints are thought to have been used first in the 15th century. Leonardo da Vinci illustrates a flintlock mechanism in his *Codex Atlanticus,* dated 1490 (Shepherd 1972). With inventions of new flintlock mechanisms, use of gunflints became more significant from the early 17th century on, peaking during the Napoleonic Wars. The British army abandoned the use of flintlock rifles around 1850.

The need of gunflints in flintlock arms brought to life a new flintknapping industry. The most extensive gunflint manufacture was in England and France, with manufacturing centers also elsewhere.

Production of gunflints in England involved three specialists. A "cracker" would "quarter" or break a nodule with a large metal hammer to get a flat platform, and remove preliminary flakes and blades to prepare the cores. A "flaker", the most skilled craftsman, would use a small metal hammer to produce blades – the larger ones about 15 cm X 2.5 cm. An expert knapper could produce 5000 to 7000 blades a day. Finally, a "knacker", later called a "knapper", would break and trim the blades into segments for use as gunflints. For this task, one family in the 19th century is reported to have used a specially tempered cast steel file for a hammer and a square rod of soft iron, covered with leather, set in a wood block at an angle (Shepherd 1972). From good blades, an expert "knacker" produced some 300 gunflints in an hour. Finally, gunflints were sorted and then counted, sometimes at the rate of 20 000 an hour!

In England, the tradition still survives as a part-time occupation to produce gunflints for antique arms and hunters using flintlock rifles. The last gunflint knapper at Brandon, Fred Avery, died in 1996. In France, the tradition lasted at least until 1920. More recently, the son of Fred Avery has taken up knapping for gunflints.

In mid-1800s just before the Crimean War, 36 knappers at Brandon shipped 11 million gunflints in one year to Turkey alone. Brandon gunflints were still used by Abyssinians against Mussolini in 1935, and at least until the 1960's in West Africa because of a prohibition on firearms except flintlocks (Shepherd 1972).

The productivity at Brandon can be appreciated from the following (Forrest 1983):

- During 1880 – 1885, one shop produced over 23 million gunflints.
- In 1813, the quota ranges placed on individuals were from 60 000 to 156 000 per month.
- About the same time during the Napoleonic Wars, 14 Brandon masters were called upon to produce 1,500,000 musket flints a month in a national emergency.

A 75 year old knapper recalled in 1950 that his apprenticeship started at the age of eight. Many knappers died at an early age of lung disease due to inhaling silica dust (Kalin 1981).

In 1983, I visited the pub Flintknappers Arms in Brandon. It used to belong to a gunflint knappers family. There was a workshop with a shed and a vast amount of knapping debris in its backyard. Several exhausted blade cores (Fig. 1.8) were seen along

FIG. 1.8 AN EXHAUSTED BLADE CORE ON THE GUNFLINT KNAPPERS WORK FLOOR AT BRANDON.

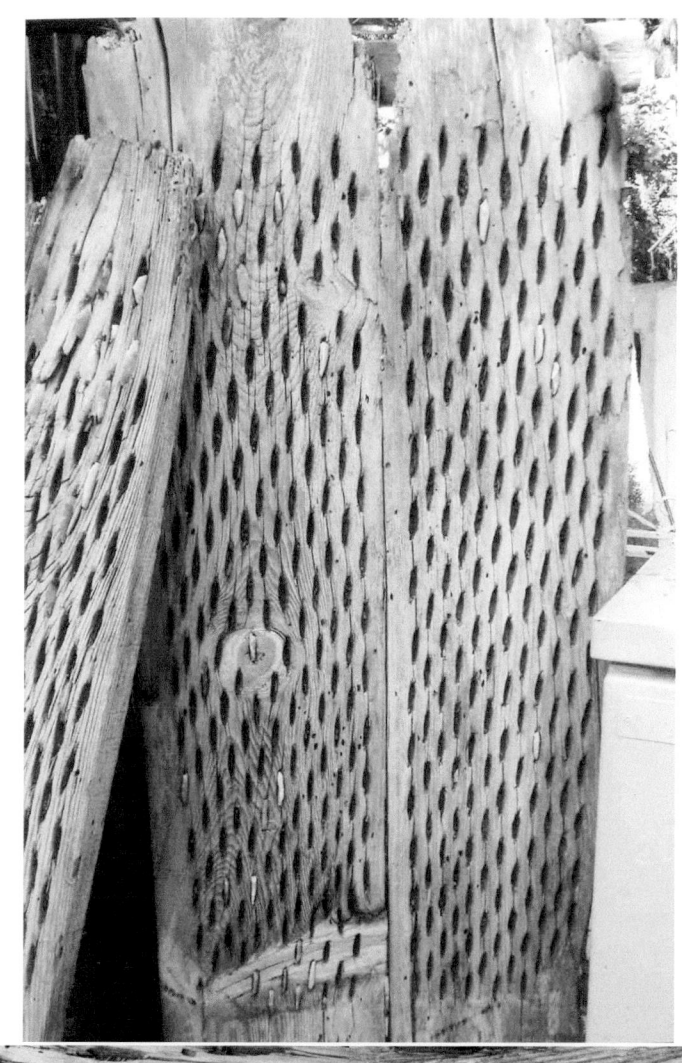
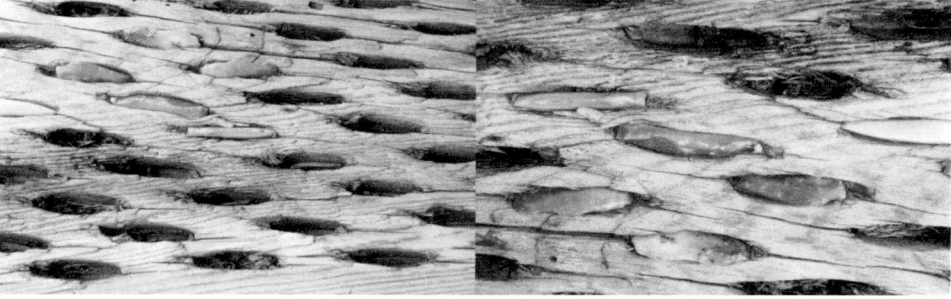

Fig. 1.9 Threshing sledges in Turkey. The one at the right, as well as the partly seen sloping one at the left, has two wide blanks. The lower two photos show the details of the flint blade inserts. These were in a "coffee shop" in the tourist section of Antalya.

with a number of proximal and distal blade sections as well as a few blades, all unsuitable for gunflints.

Threshing Sledges

Bordaz (1969) and others (Gebel 1980, Weiner 1980, Whittaker 1996, Whittaker et al. 2009) have reported on a recent or contemporary flintknapping industry in Turkey associated with threshing sledges. The sledges are usually made of two or three blanks side by side with flint inserted on their underside (Fig.1.9). They are used after a harvest to separate the grain and to chop up the stalks to facilitate winnowing. Professional knappers use soft steel hammers near the mines to produce the flint blades and flakes that are then transported to a village to be trimmed and retouched with metal hammers into forms suitable for inserting in a sledge. One knapper reported producing 4000 blades a day. Such threshing sledges were still made in Turkey in 2000.

A threshing sledge industry of recent times was widespread in the Mediterranean region. It has been reported most extensively for Cyprus, where it disappeared about 50 years ago as a viable occupation. Threshing sledges are still used extensively in Morocco. Many threshing platforms can be seen today in Southeast Morocco.

In recent years, threshing sledges have appeared for sale in antique stores in Paris and the U.S. The use of threshing sledges with flint inserts is an old tradition. A threshing sledge was known as a tribulum to Romans. They are also referred to in the Bible (Whittaker 2008: 5).

Ceramic Industry

Until the beginning of the 20th century, there was a knapping industry in Eben-Emaël, Belgium, for producing flint blocks for liners in steel drums used mostly in the porcelain industry (Fig. 1.10). The description here is based on Slotta (1980) and Callahan (1985).

The drums were used as mills for pulverizing the kaolin for making porcelain, or for other milling. The liners served to prevent discoloration of the kaolin by contact with the metal. The drums were cylindrical, with either flat or cupped ends.

Large flint nodules were "chopped" into sections by a sledge hammer, and little flaking was then used to dress the blocks with a smaller steel hammer having a very hard tungsten steel insert. It is quite remarkable how the production was optimized to use a minimum effort to yield finished blocks of almost identical shapes and sizes, mostly with rectangular or trapezoidal cross sections. One knapper at Eben-Emaël estimated working a ton of flint daily.

In the "chopping" of the nodules as well as the flaking to dress the blocks, the fractures had wedging initiations (also known as "split cones" or "shearing fractures") characteristic with a very hard percussor or flaker. Similar fracture initiations are encountered in the production of flint blocks for buildings.

Fig. 1.10
Knapped blocks at Eben-Emaël for porcelain industry. Squared blocks for end of the mill. (Callahan 1985. Reproduced with permission.)

The flint liner blocks in Eben-Emaël have been produced for a number of countries in Europe, as well as Africa and the U.S. It was reported in 2000 that the Eben-Emaël industry would close very shortly, because ceramic materials were replacing the flint as liners. At that time, there were similar industries still operating in the former Yugoslavia and China.

Modern Knapping and Recent Explosion Of Interest

A slow revival of flintknapping began with experimentation going back to the 19th century (Lewis Johnson 1978). In the 3rd quarter of the last century, especially since the 1960's in the U.S., there was a significant resurgence in the craft of flintknapping. The last quarter of the century saw an explosive expansion in the practice of knapping. It is too early to assess its impact, but it may very well be drastic, with positive as well as negative implications for archeology (Whittaker and Stafford 1999, Whittaker 2004).

"Modern knapping" is used here for all contemporary and recent knapping in industrialized societies. It is removed from the context of traditional lifeways, subsistence activities and value systems of a pre-industrial society. In that sense, all modern knapping is non-traditional with respect to the societies in which it is practiced. However, I will use the terms "traditional" and "non-traditional" in quite a different sense subsequently.

Why is knapping practiced today? For many reasons, including the following (Whittaker 2004: 136-146): for understanding how prehistoric tools were or could have been made; as a source of income by the production of "replicas" (and occasionally forgeries) or other artifacts not resembling any prehistoric ones; as a hobby for just the pleasure of practicing the craft, with its technical and esthetic aspects, as part of "living archeology" experience; for survival in nature interests; for the purpose and satisfaction of re-creating and practicing "primitive technology", meaning pre-industrial technology. The above reasons are often overlapping for particular individuals. As Bruce Bradley, after some 40 years of experience aptly put it, "I do it for fun, art and science."

Until recently, most modern knapping has been experimentation to understand prehistoric stone tools and lithic industries. Some experiments have involved replication of only the end product, or attempted replication of the whole process of tool manufacture with the intermediate stages and by-products or only some aspects of the manufacturing process. The first scientist to give a public flintknapping demonstration was Sir John Evans in 1868 (Lewis Johnson 1978). He had observed the Brandon knappers, read ethnographic descriptions on knapping, and experimented personally. A number of scholars as well as others, mostly in England, experimented with knapping in the last quarter of the 19th century, with forgeries already a problem.

For 19th century knapping, reference must be made to the tragic tale of Edward Simpson, better known as Flint Jack, born in 1815. He was an extremely talented flintknapper with great curiosity about flint fracture and ancient implements - how they were made. He also considered good craftsmanship in flint an art, and took pride in some of his fine work ending up at the British Museum (without being identified as such). Flint Jack gave demonstrations to distinguished societies and scholars. He loved flintknapping above everything else, and refused to pursue a more comfortable occupation. Homeless and to avoid starvation, he stole and was jailed. Flint Jack's talents were appreciated by only a handful of scholars. But even they viewed him as a curiosity, oblivious to the potential scientific significance of his work. Flint Jack's tragedy, it seems, was being born ahead of his time (Blacking 1953).

Reference is made in Lewis Johnson (1978) to many knappers in the last quarter of the 19th and the first half of the 20th century. From the U.S., the names Havlor Skavlem (Pond 1930) and W. Holmes Ellis (1944) stand out. The former primarily because of Pond's extensive reporting, and the latter because of his landmark experimentation on a great variety of knapping techniques.

One must, of course, recall the knapping of L.S.B. Leakey and François Bordes. Because of their great fame as scholars, they also created much world-wide interest in knapping. The first films of flintknapping were made of Leakey and L. Coutier of France.

As discussed in Lewis Johnson (1978), a great impetus to flintknapping experimentation came by the archaeologist Earl Swanson "discovering" Don Crabtree, both of Idaho. Born in 1912, Crabtree had been knapping since the age of 7, but had never published. This led to the establishment of the Flintworking School sponsored by the National Science Foundation, to the 1964 Les Eyzies Conference, to numerous publications and films by Crabtree (1967a, 1967b, 1968, 1972), and the establishment of the *Newsletter of Lithic Technology*, later *Lithic Technology*. The Les Eyzies Conference brought a number of archaeologists together with the three most renowned knappers of the world: Don Crabtree and the archaeologists François Bordes and Jacques Tixier (Tixier 2012). The conference not only led to greater international communication and cooperation on knapping but, more importantly, to communication between archaeologists and non-archeologist knappers.

Among the contemporary French knappers is the master knapper and archeologist Jacques Pelegrin. The best students of Don Crabtree are the archeologists and master knappers Jeffrey Flenniken and Bruce Bradley. It can be said there are three knapping "traditions" in the U.S.: the Idaho tradition of Don Crabtree (1912-1980), the Virginia tradition of Errett Callahan, and the Texas tradition of J. B. Sollberger (1914-1995). By now, the influence of these traditions has spread across the U.S. and internationally (Whittaker 2004). Sollberger was a master knapper in Dallas, Texas. He had a lasting influence, mostly through personal contacts, but also publications (Whittaker 1994). Among the master knappers was the late Gene Titmus of Idaho.

The work of the master knapper Errett Callahan of Virginia has had the greatest impact on international communication among knappers and archeologists interested in knapping. He is an archeologist, artist, expert on survival skills, and has experimented on "just about everything" related to archeology or "primitive" lifeways, including ceramics, bows and arrows, and housing. He started the *Flintknapper's Exchange* and has conducted "living archeology" as well as flintknapping schools. He is the founder and, until 1996, was the president of the Society of Primitive Technology. Callahan is not only a scholar, but has also earned his living through flintknapping. Some of his commercial products represent a level of craftsmanship in flintworking never achieved in prehistory.

Among the professional knappers in the U.S. is D.C. Waldorf of Branson, Missouri. He has taught numerous flintworking schools, published perhaps the best beginner's guide, *The Art of Flintknapping*, and edits *Chips* for communication among knappers. Among other accomplished professional knappers are Chris Miller of Ohio, Jim Redfearn and Tim Dillard, both of Missouri, and Dan Theus of Texas.

Since 1970's, a great many "knap-ins" or workshops on flintknapping and "primitive technology" for anyone interested have been organized in the U.S., and some also in Europe. The number of such knap-ins has greatly increased in the past 25 years and is still growing. In other words, we still seem to be in the middle of an explosion of interest in the craft of knapping. The number of knappers in the U.S. has increased perhaps by a factor of 50 to 100 in the last 30 years. This has brought much talent to the craft, and may become increasingly more significant for information and potential experimentation, if utilized by archaeologists. However, it also has its negative aspects. For one, the sources of raw material are being depleted. In 1996, about 20, 000 kg of flint from Brandon were imported by one enterprising individual, and about 23,000 kg from Belize by another. Comparable quantities of mookite (a.k.a. mook jasper) have been imported from Australia. Great numbers of knappers procuring flint have become a nuisance to landowners.

The scarcity of raw material has led commercial knappers to sawing a nodule to slabs, and then flaking it into a finished product. Especially the commercial aspects have stimulated increasing use of the so-called "copper boppers" for expediting their work. It conserves antler that is becoming scarce as well. Making stone tools from slabs with the so-called "copper-bopper" is not flintknapping in the traditional sense, but it does conserve raw material. A "copper bopper", incidentally, is really a lead plug with a thin copper shell casing.

What will the future see? On the one hand, experimentation and the practice of knapping may be expected to continue (or decline) along the more conventional paths, but at a more skilled level and perhaps with greater use of industrial tools and materials for learning and experimentation. On the other hand, we are witnessing the growth of a "modern knapping tradition" in flintworking with metal and other non-traditional tools. For archeology, its relevance may be akin to that of the manufacture of gunflints or blades for threshing sleds. Several opposing categories have been used for modern knapping – such as academic vs. non-academic and commercial vs. non-commercial knapping.

Knapping Studies

Lucy Lewis Johnson (1978) provides a survey on flintknapping studies from 1838 to 1976.

Archaeological Record

Evidence on prehistoric knapping comes from the archaeological record. This does not mean that information or supporting evidence of some kind cannot come from other sources.

Ethnography

Ethnography can suggest possible hypotheses. The probability of the hypothesis being correct depends on a number of factors, including the similarities in context.

Knapping Experiments

Knapping experiments can also suggest possible hypotheses for prehistoric studies. In one sense, they are less useful because of the great contextual differences. On the other hand, they are more useful because the experimenter can change the focus and objectives of his study at will. Knapping experiments and ethnographic observations can point to questions of interest and to some relevant data that may not have been thought of by studying the archaeological data alone.

Lewis Johnson (1978) provides valuable references to research by Bordes, Bradley, Callahan, Crabtree, Ellis, Newcomer, Sollberger, Tixier and others. Recent and past experimental work includes that of Clark, Flenniken, Kelterborn, Titmus (Hirth et al. 2006) and others (Apel and Knutsson 2006, Ellis 1944).

Living Archaeology

To overcome the limits posed by the context of knapping experiments, experiments in "living archaeology" and survival were conducted by Errett Callahan in the 1970's.

Experiments in "living archaeology" can provide information to archeologists that other sources can not. They can pose questions and point to relevant data that may not be apparent otherwise. "Living archaeology" has also been used in a very different sense (Gould 1971 and 1980) to refer to ethnoarchaeology or ethnography.

Mechanics, Fracture Mechanics and Fractography

While "living archaeology" takes knapping experiments to broader contexts for the purpose of representing more relevant situations, application of mechanics, fracture mechanics and fractography as science does the opposite. With the former, the number of variables increases, their relationships become more complex, and the meaning of experimental control becomes more fuzzy. The opposite is true for application of mechanics to flintworking. Mechanics is a relatively "hard" science. Theories and their empirical bases change with time in all sciences, but less so in the "harder" and more mature sciences. In other words, establishing relationships in mechanics, if useful, could provide a firmer basis.

Flintknapping is not a mechanical process. Some of its elements however are. To make use of mechanics in flintknapping, the key is to recognize what these elements are and what the field of mechanics can do. For this, interdisciplinary communication is important. The application of mechanics can pose questions and point to relevant data not apparent otherwise. It is possible to apply the body of knowledge already available in mechanics to improve our understanding of flaking, and to perform controlled testing for particular purposes.

Contemporary Crafts

Observations from contemporary crafts and industrial practices can occasionally provide clues to knapping. While observing a mason pointing a masonry chimney with a steel chisel and hammer, he occasionally hit his knuckles. Yet he would not use a longer chisel, he said, because he would then need to use a heavier hammer. In the past, bricks were split by first chiseling a groove all around, for the crack to run flat across. In the rejuvenation of prehistoric obsidian cores, a section of the core by its platform was sometimes removed by first pecking around the core (Trachman 1999). Experiments by Gene Titmus confirmed the feasibility of doing this (Trachman and Titmus 2003).

Fire has been used in quarrying and breaking up larger blocks or boulders of rock in contemporary and prehistoric societies (Cresson 2005, personal communication) as well as recently in New Guinea (Hampton 1999).

During a flintknapping demonstration I was tapping an obsidian nodule to check for cracks., A lady in the audience said that she also does that – tapping a loaf of bread in the oven to see if it is ready. A roofer may also tap a piece of slate to check for cracks. In the first half of the last century, welds were sometimes checked by tapping with a hammer and listening with a stethoscope. When asked about the significance of sounds in knapping, Gene Titmus said, "I don't think I could knap if I couldn't hear."

2. Knapping Tools and Techniques

The basic types of knapping tools and accessories described here for contemporary knappers were available at least to some prehistoric knappers in some form, shape and perhaps similar material. For describing the techniques, much reliance is basewd oncontemporary knapping.

Antler and Wood Billets

Hammerstones and antler billets are the most common tools used in direct percussion. Some knappers also use billets of wood such as boxwood, dogwood, live oak or some other hardwood. Antler and wood billets are sometimes also referred to as soft hammers.

Wood billets work particularly well with many of the toughest materials, including quartzite, argillite, felsite, rhyolite and quartz. With these materials there is rapid wear and potential damage to the antler. According to Jack Cresson (2001), most of the eastern hardwoods with a specific gravity of 0.60 or more will work as a percussor. Examples with their approximate specific gravity include

White oak	(Quercus alba)	0.68
American hornbeam	(Carpinus caroliniana)	0.70
Dogwood	(Cornus florida)	0.73
Pignut hickory	(Carya glabra)	0.75
Live oak	(Quercus virginiana)	0.80

Live oak tends to splinter, especially when used as a punch.

Moose, elk, white tail or mule deer antler have been used by knappers in America today (Fig. 2.1). In contrast to elk and deer, moose antler is usually solid and dense throughout for at least a considerable distance from the basal end. It does not wear out as fast as elk or deer and for this reason, as well as its density, is treasured by most knappers.

The shape of the striking end of an antler billet is relevant in knapping. Rounded and relatively flat ends each have their advantages and disadvantages. For example, less accuracy is needed with a flatter end when striking an isolated platform in biface thinning. For removal of regularly spaced flakes in biface thinning, on the other hand, most knappers would prefer a well rounded end. Tom Dillard has masterfully thinned bifaces with an antler having its end in the shape of a frustum of a cone.

Antler billets of various lengths and overall weight are used by knappers. A greater velocity may be needed with a lighter billet. Antler and wood billets may also be used in indirect percussion to strike a punch.

Hammerstones

For various knapping tasks and raw materials, a range of hammerstone hardnesses, sizes and shapes is desirable. Except for quartering or removal of extremely large flakes from a

FIG. 2.1 KNAPPING TOOLS: ANTLER BILLETS, PUNCHES, A PRESSURE FLAKER, AN ABRADER AND HAMMERSTONES (CM SCALE).

cobble or a boulder, hammerstones not exceeding 10-12 cm in size are usually used. For smaller flakes, as in thinning a biface, smaller hammerstones are convenient.

Hammerstone hardness is extremely important for working different raw materials as well as for different tasks with the same material. For removing long thinning flakes from an obsidian biface, for example, medium-soft hammerstones work well. On the other hand, for detaching very short flakes in thinning or beveling the edge of a biface during platform preparation, a harder hammerstone is preferred by some knappers.

Hammerstones can range from very hard, such as diorite, flint, quartz or quartzite, to medium-hard such as many sandstones, to soft such as some sandstones and some limestones. Hard and medium-hard hammerstones are relatively easy to find in most regions. Medium-soft to soft hammerstones are more difficult to come by. The modulus of elasticity and density of a hammerstone are expected to be important.

Although it is possible to use hammerstones of various shapes for some tasks, most knappers prefer rounded forms - say, oval or spherical shapes, or "flattish" shapes with rounded edges. The shape of hammerstones can be much more important than that of the ends of antler billets. Most knappers usually strike with a hammerstone so that contact is made at or near its rounded end or edge. Some knappers prefer to strike instead with a relatively flat, slightly rounded portion, using "sliding blows."

The shape of hammerstones can change significantly from use-wear. Rounded portions tend to become bevelled. In my earliest knapping, I wore some spherical quartzite hammerstones to cylindrical ones with rounded ends from knapping chert. Hammerstones may also become softer or harder due to use. The softer outer layer seen on some hammerstones may be simply worn away to harden them. Some harder hammerstones, on the other hand, will have their surface layer softened from multitudinous impacts.

There are several ways of using stone and antler percussors. A long antler billet may be used by holding one end and swinging the other end for impact. A shorter piece of antler may be used instead more like a hammerstone is usually used, impacting near its end or even on the side. An antler billet or a shorter piece of antler may be used in yet another manner, without the rotation of the antler about one end. Namely, it can be used just as a hammerstone as if to "drop it" against a core or a biface, say, by just swinging the arm and perhaps also the wrist.

The surface texture of hammerstones is important, especially for some tasks. A rough surface allows the hammerstone to "grab" better. A smooth surface, as on a water-worn quartz or other nodule, will not permit that. Use of a hammerstone will roughen its surface. Hammerstones are discussed more extensively in Crabtree (1967b) and Nunn (2007).

Punches

Punches most commonly used for indirect percussion are made of antler tines (Fig. 2.2). Other materials such as wood, stone, ivory, and copper (Crabtree 1967a), as well as composite punches (as a copper bit in antler) have also been used. Punches of dogwood or boxwood, for example, work well on obsidian and cherts that are not too tough. The ends of punches and pressure flakers are usually rounded. However, flat ends have also been used by contemporary as well as prehistoric knappers.

Pressure Flakers

Antler and copper bits are most often used in pressure flaking today (Fig. 2.3). Use of pressure tools of bone, wood, ivory, shells, stone pebbles, chert flakes and other materials has been reported (Crabtree 1967b, Titmus 1985). Pressure flakers may be of a single material - such as antler tine, wood or bone (Crabtree 1970) - or they may be composite (Fig. 2.3). Pressure flaking tools are discussed in Callahan (1999). The frequency of required maintenance is an important consideration with wood pressure flakers. Fire-hardening the tips, though it did not appear to help.

Pressure tools are usually simply hand held. Sometimes a longer tool is used such as a longer piece of antler or a copper or antler tip mounted in a longer handle. The latter kinds are referred to as Ishi sticks, named after the last Yahi Indian who used such an implement (Kroeber 1969).

Sometimes a pressure flaking tool with a longer staff and a cross-piece at the far end is convenient for highly controlled blade production (Crabtree 1968, Inizan et al. 1999). Variants of such implements have been referred to as a shoulder, chest, pectoral or abdominal crutches.

Fig. 2.2 Chert core and blades, moose antler punches and a striker (billet, a.k.a. a paddle, 33 cm long) of oxel wood of Sweden. (Courtesy Peter Viking)

Antler tines are excellent for pressure flaking, but require time for reshaping the tip. To avoid this disadvantage, copper is excellent for learning and some experimental work. Since it is possible to have smaller contact areas with copper than with antler, the forces required can be different.

Use of copper in prehistoric pressure flaking has been reported from New York State, the Midwest and India-Pakistan region. The "Iceman" recently found in the Alps had a pressure flaker of antler mounted in a wooden haft.

Holding and Fabricating Devices

Various holding devices are used by modern knappers. For example, a device such as the one in Fig. 2.4 can serve two functions for a knapper. It can assure that the dorsal flake surface is free and it helps to prevent rotation of the preform during flake detachment. Various vices and other devices have been used for holding a core in blade production or a point to be fluted (Crabtree 1968, Pelegrin 1984). Sollberger (1985) has used a fluting device for holding the point and applying the force by means of a lever. By now, the use of variants of many such devices has spread across America. These devices enable exercise of an extreme measure of control in the removal of very long channel flakes in fluting.

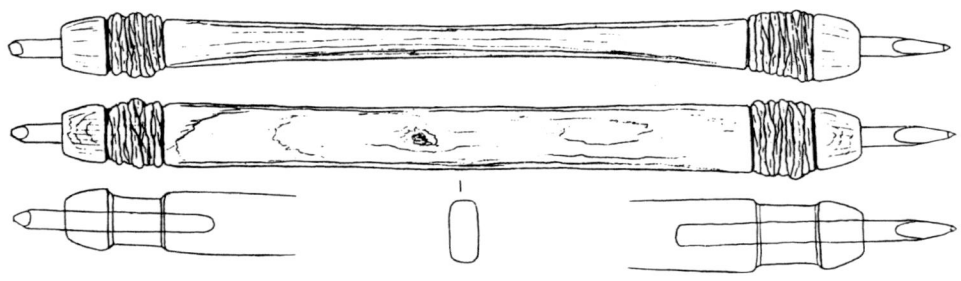

FIG. 2.3 EXAMPLE OF A LONG MODERN COMPOSITE PRESSURE FLAKER. ANTLER TIP ON LEFT, COPPER TIP ON RIGHT, FLEXIBLE WOOD GRIP, RAWHIDE BINDING. 36 CM LONG. (FROM CALLAHAN 1999 WITH PERMISSION.)

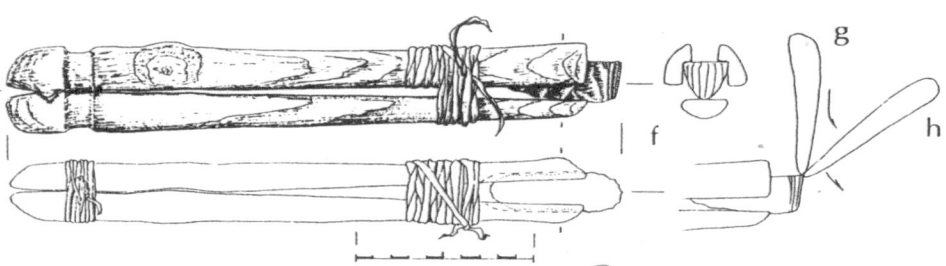

FIG. 2.4 A HAND-HELD CLAMP (32 CM LONG) FOR PRODUCTION OF MICROBLADES. (FROM CALLAHAN 2000 WITH PERMISSION)

Anvils and Supports

A right handed knapper may simply hold a specimen to be flaked by pressure or percussion in the left hand (free hand technique), or support against a leg (Fig. 2.5). The object to be flaked may also be supported against an anvil of wood, antler, stone or a leather pad resting on a leg.

It is sometimes convenient to support a sizable nodule to be flaked against the side of the thigh, to dampen the shock or vibration of the stone and to prevent bruising the leg. To remove large flakes from large nodules, it is convenient to support the nodule on the ground. Holding the nodule on another massive rock, concrete floor, or even a tree stump can lead to excessive "shock" and unintentional breakages. Should a hard support be used nevertheless, it is usually preferable to direct a blow in such a way that the applied force is not aimed directly to the hard support (Fig. 2.6), except in bipolar percussion (Fig. 2.7).

Hides

Hides or leather pads are useful with percussion flaking and other techniques (Fig. 2.5). When holding a preform to be pressure flaked against the palm of a hand, a leather pad serves as protection.

When an object to be percussion flaked is supported on or against a thigh, single or multiple hide layers serve to prevent cuts, and potential bruising from impact. Multiple layers of hide are also useful to provide lateral support to the flake being detached or "axial" support to avoid overshots.

Grinding and Abrading Stones

Grinding or abrading stones are needed in knapping for several tasks, as for edge grinding in "platform" preparation for flaking. Sandstones of several hardnesses, and even some flakes of quartzite are suitable. It is wasteful to use difficult to find hammerstones for this purpose. Abrading tools are also useful for preparation and reshaping of antler flaking tools.

"Materials for abrading tools can be of any substance with loosely adhering grains of sand or of volcanic tuff. The substance must be soft enough to allow the grains to loosen as the abrasive becomes dulled. This prevents the pores of the abrasive material from clogging and glazing. This is most important when grinding antler, bone, ivory, or tooth enamels" (Crabtree 1967b: 69). Slight abrasion of the prospective ridges of flakes or blades is used by some knappers. This was sometimes done in flaking Clovis and Solutrean bifaces, as well as in some biface work later in the New World. Heavy abrasion has often been used with crested blades, as with Clovis blades (Collins 1999).

Nontraditional Tools and Acessories

For preparation of wood or antler billets, punches and pressure flakers, most knappers today make use of metal saws and motorized grinding wheels. Metal files are commonly used for resharpening copper or antler tips for pressure flaking, and perhaps for reshaping

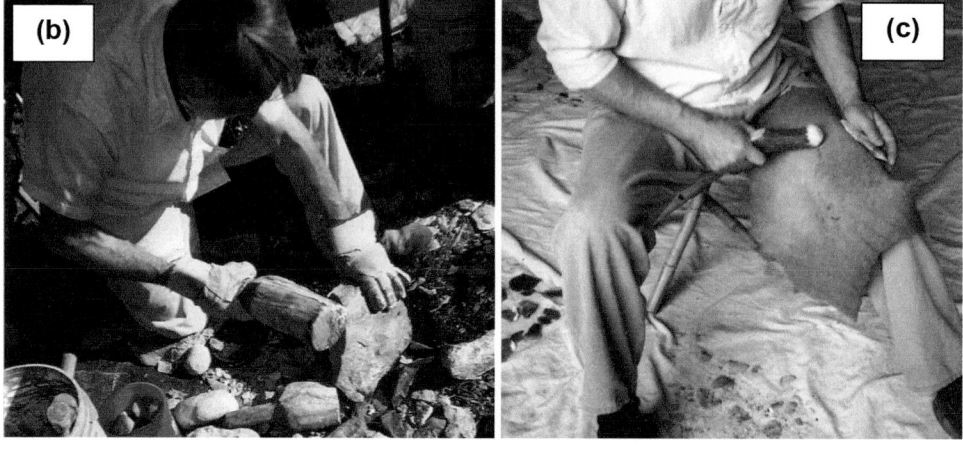

Fig. 2.5 Flaking by direct percussion with a hammerstone (a), wooden billet (b) and moose antler (c). Jack Cresson in (b); Hugo Nami and Errett Callahan in (a).

antler billets and punches. Industrial abraders are often used by contemporary knappers for edge grinding in "platform" preparation on bifaces.

Especially in the last 20 years, the use of short copper billets and so-called "copper boppers" has spread across America, especially among commercial knappers having the primary aim of getting a beautiful end product regardless of the nontraditional aspects involved. Such practices are not flintknapping in the traditional sense. It is conceivable that copper percussors were sometimes used in prehistory. But this is not the case for "copper boppers", which consist of a copper shell enclosing a lead plug. Some knappers doing masterful work use instead a short solid copper rod with an end slightly rounded.

Use-Wear Indicators

All fabricating tools and accessories used in knapping today show some use-wear consistent with the manner of their use. It is educational to study such use-wear patterns, which can occasionally be quite surprising.

Direct Percussion

In direct percussion, flakes are detached by striking the object to be flaked with a percussor (Fig. 2.5). The main advantage of this technique is that a great force can be applied. A disadvantage is the reduced amount of control. That is, the placement of the

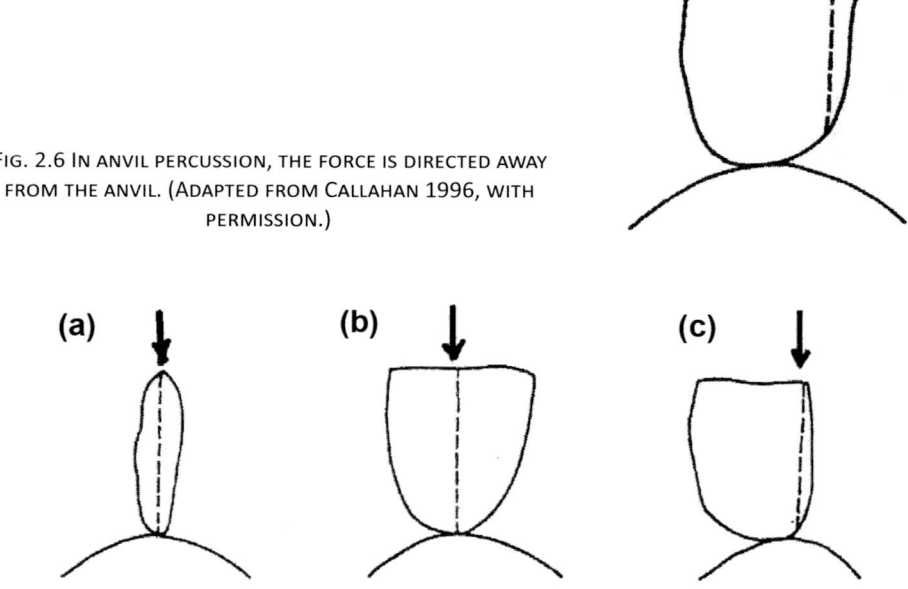

FIG. 2.6 IN ANVIL PERCUSSION, THE FORCE IS DIRECTED AWAY FROM THE ANVIL. (ADAPTED FROM CALLAHAN 1996, WITH PERMISSION.)

FIG. 2.7 IN BIPOLAR PERCUSSION, THE FORCE IS DIRECTED INTO THE ANVIL. (A) AND (B) INVOLVE SPLITTING FROM CENTER OUT, WHILE (C) INVOLVES SPALLING FROM OUTSIDE IN. (ADAPTED FROM CALLAHAN 1996 WITH PERMISSION.)

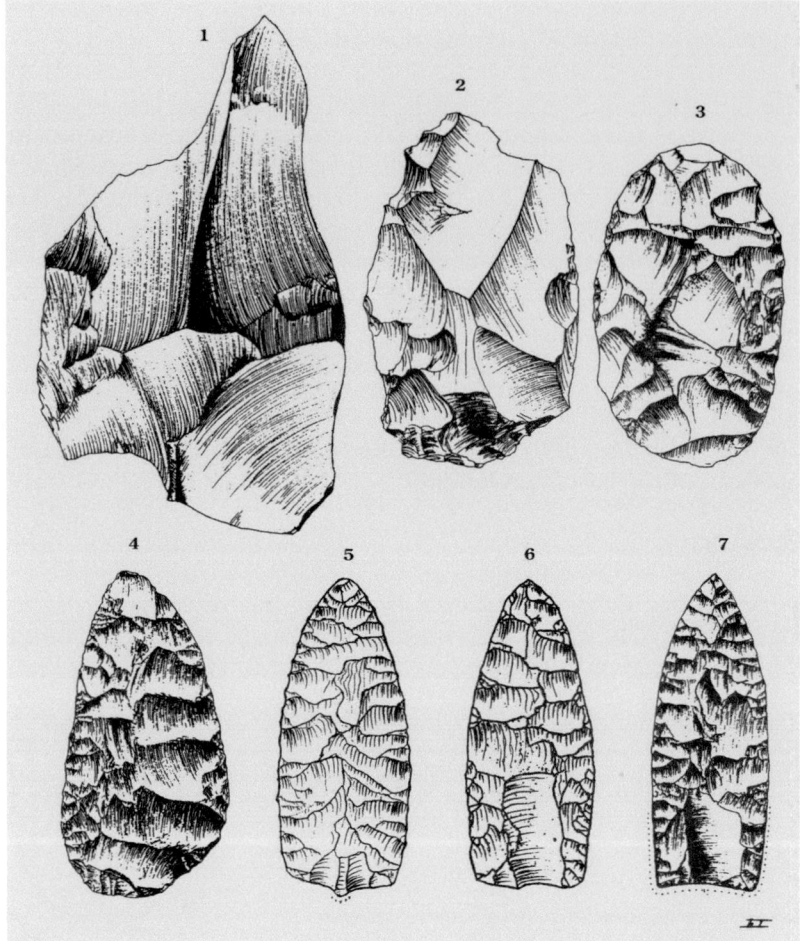

Fig. 2.8 Errett Callahan's stages in the replication of a Clovis point, mostly by direct percussion. (Callahan 1996, reproduced by permission.)

blows is not always as accurate as in indirect percussion and pressure flaking. Also, the amount and direction of the force applied is not as easily controlled as in pressure flaking. For the earliest stages of point manufacture, for example, most knappers today use direct percussion (Fig. 2.8).

Anvil Technique and Anvil Percussion

In the anvil technique, the object to be flaked is held in one or both hands and struck against an anvil to detach a flake. It is probably among the techniques that have been used the least. In the anvil percussion technique, on the other hand, a core is struck when it is held on an anvil, as shown schematically in Fig. 2.6.

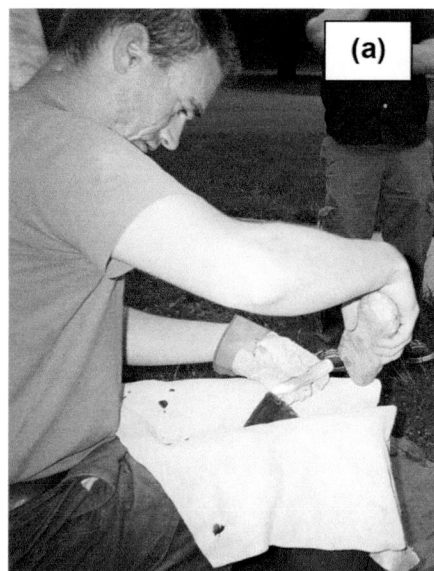

Fig. 2.9 Peter Viking (a) produced the chert blades in (b), maximum length of about 10 cm, with the moose antler punch shown and a wood "paddle" as a striker. (Courtesy Peter Viking)

Bipolar Percussion

In bipolar percussion, a nodule or a core to be fractured or "flaked" is placed and held on an anvil and then struck in such a way that the force is directed through the core and directly into the anvil (Fig. 2.7). It is more appropriate to refer to "splitting" or "spalling" rather than "flaking" in at least some such cases. The bipolar percussion technique is not to be confused with anvil percussion (Fig. 2.6). An advantage in bipolar percussion, when used with hard anvils and hard percussors, is that for given core and hammerstone geometries and percussor velocities, a high contact force can be developed for initiating a fracture (See Chapters 12 and 13). In particular, it can be used to break up round nodules that cannot be broken by other techniques. A disadvantage of bipolar percussion is the relatively poor control.

Bipolar percussion has been used, for example, on quartz and quartzite in Sweden (Callahan 1987, Knutsson 1988), on quartz in Olduvai Gorge (Dies-Martin et al. 2012), as well as other materials in the New World. It is often used by contemporary knappers on rounded, oval-shaped quartz nodules.

Indirect Percussion

In indirect percussion, a punch is usually placed and held against the object to be flaked, and the opposite end of the punch is struck with a striker – a billet or a hammerstone (Fig. 2.9). An advantage of this technique is the accuracy of the contact with the object flaked. A disadvantage is that, for a single individual, it is more awkward to hold the object flaked while using a punch and a striker. In this technique, a greater force can be applied than in pressure flaking.

The French archaeologist and knapper Jacques Tixier has used an unusual kind of indirect percussion, termed the "sous le pied" ("under the foot") technique, without a punch (Tixier 1972). An antler billet is placed against the core to be flaked that is held under a foot. The billet is then struck with another percussor such as another antler billet. There is a reference to a combined pressure and indirect percussion flaking tool in Holmes (1919: Fig. 182). The chest crutch pressure flaker has a branch segment protruding from the staff to be struck with a striker.

Pressure Flaking

In this technique, the tip of the pressure tool is placed against the object to be flaked and a force is then applied on the flaker (Fig. 2.10). The advantages of pressure flaking include the great amount of control that can be used, the accuracy of the placement and the magnitude and direction of the force applied as well as the "follow through" force after a fracture has already started. An overview of blade production by pressure is given in the 19 articles in Desrosiers (2012).

A disadvantage of pressure flaking is obviously the limitation on the amount of force that can be applied. A lever device used as a pressure flaker by some knappers helps to overcome this (Sollberger 1985). To remove a long channel flake in fluting a Cumberland type point with a chestcrutch, the late Gene Titmus had his wife on his back. As the flake came off, he dropped his wife on the couch.

Another unusual method of pressure flaking involves the use of teeth. Edge retouching with teeth has been reported for four American Indian tribes, for Australian aborigines

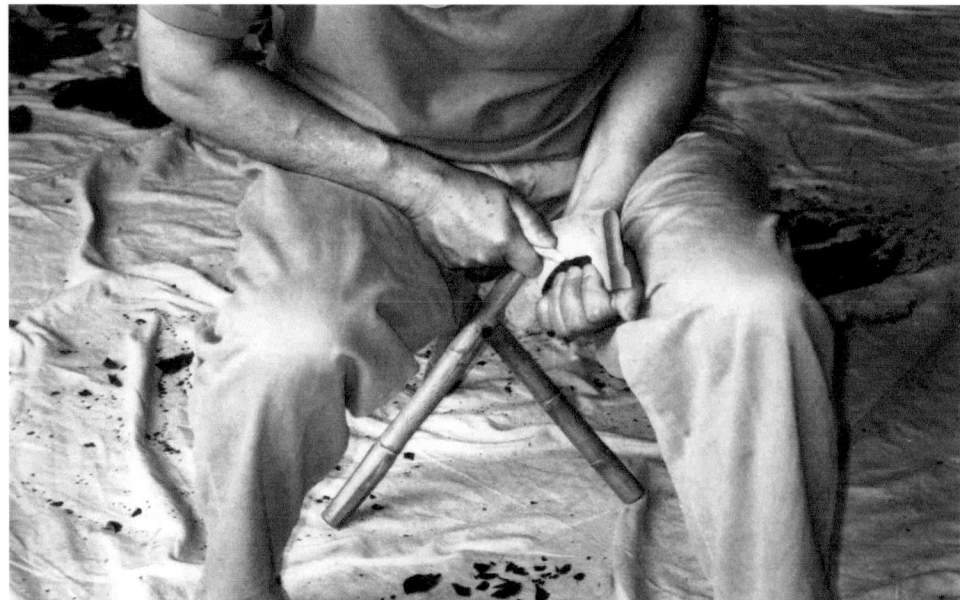

FIG. 2.10 PRESSURE FLAKING A BIFACE WITH AN ANTLER TINE.

and for Africa, at least for retouching the edges of projectile points or blades. Tiny chips of obsidian and chalcedony in coprolites at one American site suggest it may have been practiced in prehistory (Hester 1973). The late J.B. Sollberger experimented with this technique.

Pecking, Grinding, Polishing

Except for occasional grinding or abrasion, these techniques are normally not used in the process of knapping. However, they may still be associated with manufacture of artifacts. For example, flaked stone axes (or adzes and celts) may later be ground and polished partly or completely (Hampton 1999, Vang Petersen 2008). As already noted, grinding was used to smooth the surfaces of Gerzian knives (Fig. 1.4) and some Danish Type IC daggers (Fig. 1.6) to permit extreme control over subsequent pressure flaking. Pecking has also been used, for example with Mesoamerican blade cores, for platform preparation or rejuvenation (Trachman 1999, Trachman and Titmus 2003, Flenniken and Hirth 2003).

Unlike grinding and polishing, pecking involves repeated impacts. An extreme form of pecking can be seen on the back sides of large obsidian mirrors in the form of curved "slabs", from Mesoamerica. The back faces of these mirrors are covered with amazingly large cones at close spacing. Protruding from the back sides are four large legs, monolithic with the mirror. One expects that the "pecking" for these cones was probably done before the "slabs" were removed from an obsidian boulder by some unknown sawing process. Pecking and grinding on a polyhedral core platform can reduce the forces required for blade production.

Edge and Platform Preparation

The platform on a conical core may have a single facet or it may be multi-faceted. It may be concave, flat or convex. Rejuvenation flakes may be detached from the platform to achieve the desired flatness or slight concavity. Repeated removal of rejuvenation flakes from near the platform edge leads to a platform convex in the overall sense or else a higher island near the middle. Pecking and grinding may be used to achieve the desired flatness as well as surface roughness. Pecking reduces the force needed for blade detachment. Pecking and grinding also increases the friction between the core and the flaking implement.

Preparation at the edge of a core may also be used, by abrasion or removal of tiny flakes from the sides of the core or its platform. This may involve isolation of a platform to an extent desired, or it may be used to improve the alignment of a platform protrusion with a ridge. Platform isolation with the removal of tiny flakes from the platform tends to lead to an undesirable convex platform, as noted above.

A biface edge to be flaked may be prepared by flaking, abrasion and occasionally even pecking. Tiny flakes may be detached for edge beveling as well as for the elimination of an undesirable longitudinal concavity near the edge. Grinding (or pecking) of an edge may serve to strengthen or weaken an edge. A platform with a very acute angle may be strengthened by abrasion normal to the edge, possibly followed by abrasion along the edge. A heavily abraded edge may be weakened by use of a coarser abrader along the edge. Platform isolation on bifaces is highly desirable for obtaining controlled flake patterns, and for production of very thin bifaces.

Some Rules of Thumb

Some knappers' principles, best viewed as "rules of thumb", are noted here briefly. They are based on the intuitive understandings of flintknappers. Prehistoric knappers certainly had an intuitive understanding of the principles involved in knapping. These are not hard rules that can never be violated. However, following them facilitates knapping.

Ridges guide flakes: A flake tends to follow the ridges or the topographically higher locations on the prospective dorsal surfaces.

Longitudinal geometry: A slightly convex or at least a flat surface of a core in the longitudinal direction of a prospective flake is desirable.

Edge angle: The edge angle of a core platform should usually not exceed 90^0.

Force direction: The direction of a blow and a force are usually not the same. The force applied should be directed away from the center of the core mass, except in bipolar percussion. By changing the direction of the force, it is possible to change the flake length.

Force location: More force is needed when applied further from the edge of a core.

Edge location and center plane: The location of an edge of a biface relative to its center plane is important, especially in edge-to-edge-flaking. By changing the edge location, it is possible to change the flake length. Also, keeping the edge location at a sufficient distance below the center plane will reduce the risks of accidental biface breakage.

Platform isolation: Platform isolation reduces the amount of force required. It also facilitates more accurate application of the force and is useful for improving the regularity of a flaking pattern on a biface, and for producing very thin bifaces.

Transverse geometry: The transverse geometry at a platform location relates, in effect, to having platform isolation or not. The transverse geometry away from a platform location relates to the width of a flake.

Supports: Supporting the far end (or the opposite edge) helps to prevent overshot flakes.

Knappers' Wisdom, Folklore and Dilemmas

There are notions or ideas held by some knappers that may or may not make sense. These are referred to here as "knappers' folklore". There are also a number of dilemmas in knapping. the things that work out well in knapping that are either not understood or even appear to contradict what is known in mechanics or fracture mechanics. There is a thin line between such dilemmas and "knappers' folklore", expected to shift over time.

Softer Percussors and Slower Blows

It is counterintuitive that softer percussors and slower ("softer") blows work better with tougher materials, for detaching a flake and even initiating its detachment.

Follow-Through with Forces

Since a flake detachment may require less than a millisecond, it seems to make no sense to talk about follow-through forces in knapping. Yet experienced knappers will not question the significance of a follow-through in knapping.

Ridge Abrasion

With Solutrean and Clovis bifaces, as well as later ones in the New World, the ridges of the prospective flakes were sometimes slightly abraded. Several knappers have given different reasons for this,. another dilemma or just part of "knappers' folklore".

Wetting and Soaking

Effects of moisture and liquid in enhancing fracture propagation in obsidian are well known and expected for flint and chert. In fractography, these effects are known for cracks propagating very slowly, less than about 10 cm/s. But the experimental results of Sollberger with soaking of flint, and the dunking of felsite in water by Bonnichsen just before knapping, suggest the effect is also present for faster fractures. In light of similar observations by others, this is seen as a dilemma requiring an explanation. More surprising but also plausible is the effect of spraying water on the external surface of a biface about to be flaked, at the location of the flake to be detached (Jack Cresson 2002).

Learning to Knap

Anyone involved with lithic technology will benefit from hands-on experience in knapping. Nowadays archaeologists dealing with stone tools learn to knap at least at a basic level. Anyone with ordinary hand coordination can learn to knap. To become an expert knapper, much time is needed. There are, however, a number of archaeologists who have also been expert knappers. These include François Bordes, Jacques Tixier, Bruce Bradley, Jack Cresson, John Fagan, Jeff Flenniken, Jacques Pelegrin, and Witold Migal. Knapping as a craft can provide a source of pleasure and satisfaction.

Raw materials and knapping tools can be obtained easily from commercial sources, at increasingly higher prices. Making friends with fellow knappers is useful.

The best way to learn knapping is by watching, at the knap-ins or primitive technology gatherings. Don Crabtree videos are available from the Idaho Museum of Natural History. Good videos are also available of knapping by Greg Nunn, Bruce Bradley, D.C. Waldorf and others. YouTube has many demonstrations.

The time required for learning to knap is reduced drastically by watching experienced knappers work, by getting some lessons from them or by attending knap-ins or a flintworking school. Several flintknapping schools are offered in the U.S. by intermediate, expert and master knappers. Some of the schools emphasize or use exclusively certain kinds of raw materials or knapping tools. It is therefore prudent to know who the teacher is and what is involved in the course. Many knapping demonstrations can be seen on YouTube, including those by Bruce Bradley an Jacques Pelegrin. In my opinion, the video of Greg Nunn making a Danish Type IC dagger is one of the best knapping videos made (Nunn 2005). Reading about knapping (Patten 1999, Waldorf 1993, Whittaker 1994) can supplement observation.

The detachment of a flake by percussion produces a cloud of fine silica particles. Some of these are inhaled by the knapper. Over time, this can lead to silicosis or other lung-related problems. The effects are progressive and irreversible (Kalin 1981). Most gunflint knappers at Brandon died of lung disease at an early age. It is best to knap outdoors or, if indoors, then with ventilation. It is, of course, prudent to wear eye protection. Cutting oneself is the most common knapping injury. Cuts can be extremely severe, especially with novice knappers. A number of knappers have required hand surgery. One master knapper cut off the tip of a finger, and had it sewed back on. The beginning knapper must recognize and appreciate the dangers and proceed with diligence. After all, an obsidian edge is often sharper than a razor blade. Many cuts result when a hand follows through against a sharp edge. With diligence, the potential consequences can usually be predicted and avoided. Even expert knappers are occasionally reminded that most serious accidents occur when trying something new. Extensive and regular knapping can lead to problems with the tendons of the arms, to a tennis elbow, to carpal syndrome, and to a worn out cartiledge.

The end-products from present-day knappers, including debitage, can confuse or even mislead archaeologists (Whittaker and Stafford 1999). It is therefore appropriate to dispose of debitage properly. Discarding it with trash is an alternative. It is not a good idea to knap at or near archaeological sites.

Quarrying stone from a known prehistoric quarry is unethical and often illegal. It disturbs the archaeological site and deprives future generations of their cultural heritage. Procurement of raw material from private property calls for use of common decency. The owner's permission should always be obtained beforehand. Trespassing to remove rock would be illegal. It may violate the privacy of the owner and it shows disrespect for him. Lack of common decency on the part of some knappers has resulted in the owners declaring their properties off limits to all knappers.

Extensive descriptions of flintknapping techniques are available, including publications by Crabtree (1972), Hellweg (1984), Holmes (1919), Inizan, Reduron-Ballinger, Roche and Tixier (1999), Patten (1999), Waldorf (1993), Whittaker (1994) and others.

3. Raw Materials

Material Selection and Use

The raw materials used in knapping must have the desired characterisctics not only for manufacture but also for use and curation of the artifacts. A material must have the appropriate mechanical and physical properties, and be available in the desired quantity, size, sometimes also shape, and occasionally even appearance. A traditional knapper probably had to make compromises. The physical and mechanical properties desirable for manufacture often differ from those for tool use. For cutting meat or hide, for example, a sharp edge is desirable. Obsidian (noncrystalline) and the finer grained materials (such as finer grained flints) would be more suitable for that purpose. Obsidian and finer grained materials are usually also better for flaking.

The esthetic appearance of a material may perhaps relate to the function and length of curation for an artifact. A conspicuous example from the New World is the occasional use of materials with exotic color patterns for manufacture of ground and polished atlatl (spear thrower) weights.

Various materials have been used for flaked stone tools in different parts of the world. They are discussed in Callahan (1979), Crabtree (1967a, 1972), Luedke (1992), Speth (1972), Domanski and Webb (2000), Domanski, Webb and Boland (1994) and many other publications. To a large extent material use depends, of course, on the availability of the raw material and thus the settlement system of a prehistoric society.

Obsidian

Obsidian is a volcanic glass found in many parts of the world, including Hungary, Slovakia, Iceland, Lipari (Italy), Greece, Turkey, parts of Africa, New Guinea, Mexico, South America and some western states in the U.S. It is **amorphous,** noncrystalline and can, therefore, provide a sharper edge than any crystalline material, including a steel razor. Obsidian blades were used for shaving during the 19th century in Mexico and recently by tribesmen in Africa. They have also been used in modern surgery, at least for the initial incisions, with the wound healing more rapidly than one from a steel scalpel. Several knappers have tried to market obsidian blades for the medical profession. The severe demands of the medical profession are informative. Aside from their preferences for certain blade curvatures posing difficulties to a knapper, they do not like to have twist hackles near an edge and they would like blades not older than a few hours because the edge sharpness would deteriorate significantly due to obsidian interacting with moisture. Don Crabtree was once asked to provide a sharp-tipped obsidian blade for experimental surgery on mosquitos! Although an obsidian blade can provide a sharper edge than a steel scalpel, its use may also differ in other respects. Steel is forgiving when a knife or a scalpel is wiggled or bent, whereas an obsidian edge may chip.

Obsidian quality for tool manufacture and use can vary, especially in terms of inclusions of different sizes and shapes. Even for the same source there can be significant differences in quality. Experienced knappers have distinguished at least seven to twelve different flaking qualities of Glass Buttes Obsidian from Oregon. On rare occasions, obsidian is found to have significant residual thermal stresses built in from nonuniform cooling of the lava. Such stresses can make fractures unpredictable.

Although black obsidian is most common, the material can occur in various colors or color combinations, including grey, brown, red, green, blue. I have also seen obsidians that are translucent and colorless or with a slight pinkish color. When viewed at different angles, the colors of some obsidians can change, with exotic color bands resembling a rainbow occasionally seen. When flaked along particular planes, some obsidians may exhibit a sheen of gold, silver or purple color. The above observations may relate to the orientation and shape of microscopic inclusions and the reflection of light. Many obsidians are banded. A Glass Buttes obsidian with grey and black bands is fairly common.

Obsidian can occur as nodules or boulders of various shapes and sizes, as well as in a massive form. Small nodules known as Apache tears are found in Arizona. Contemporary knappers have excavated several "4 and 5 man boulders" at Glass Buttes.

By chemical composition, obsidians resemble some granites, which cool more slowly, permitting crystal growth. Most obsidians contain some 70-78% silica (SiO_2), with various other major and minor constituents, as well as trace elements. Table 3.1 indicates some ranges for the major constituents in obsidians (Takács-Biró 1986 and others). The trace (<0.1%) elements in obsidians are useful for source identification. Because of its highly desirable characteristics, obsidian has been traded widely during prehistoric periods. The International Association of Obsidian Studies has been focused on obsidian sourcing.

Water, and smaller amounts of carbon dioxide, are the "volatiles retained after degassing of the magma during eruption and cooling" (Steffen 2005: 124). Although water content is usually less than 1%, up to 3% has been observed. The nature of the volcanic activity and eruptive history contribute to its variation (Steffen 2005: 135). The water content is relevant to hydration and vesiculation of obsidian.

Flint and Chert

Flint and chert are the materials used most often for prehistoric knapping. They occur much more widely than obsidian. There is much confusion and controversy about what is flint and what is chert. A reasonable approach is to consider the finer-grained, cryptocrystalline varieties flint, and the coarser-grained, microcrystalline varieties chert, perhaps even defining the grain size for the distinction. Sometimes, however, chert is used more generically, with flint considered a finer-grained variety of chert. Either one of these usages seems reasonable. In this book, chert and flint are sometimes used interchangeably. "Flint" is sometimes used for a chert that appears to have a finer texture or simply if there is a tradition for using that word. For example, it is used for English chalk flint and for Flint Ridge (Ohio) flint.

Table 3.1 Major Constituents in Obsidians

	Weight %
SiO_2	70.0 – 77.5
Al_2O_3	11.4 – 16.3
Fe_2O_3	0.1 – 3.3
FeO	0.1 – 2.6
MnO	<0.1 – 0.8
MgO	0.0 – 1.1
CaO	0.2 – 2.5
Na_2O	2.7 – 5.9
K_2O	2.4 – 7.7

Flint and chert occur most commonly in limestone formations. Among the finest flints is that of Brandon, England (especially the black "floorstone") found as nodules or tabular forms that tend to occur as layers in chalk. Near Cobden in Southern Illinois, Clear Creek runs through a limestone formation, with good quality Cobden chert nodules being washed out. Flint and chert can occur also in shale – as Normanskill (near Catskill, NY) and Esopus chert (near Cherry Valley, NY). The latter has sometimes been referred to as a silicified shale.

Some chert occurs as tabular layers rhythmically embedded in limestone, as at the coastal cliffs on the Isle of Portland near Weymouth, England. Normanskill chert and Arkansas novaculite can occur as massive embedments. Nodular forms of chert are commom for English flint, Cobden chert, Indiana hornstone and Mill Creek chert, for example.

Flint and chert consist predominantly of silica (SiO_2). For eleven cherts or flints used in Hungary, Takács-Biró (1986:127) indicates the following ranges for the chemical compositions:

	SiO_2	Al_2O_3	CaO
% by Weight	82.5 – 97.4	0.58 – 1.59	0.17 – 8.11

Flint and chert can have just about any color including black, gray, white, red, pink, brown, yellow, green, and blue. The colors may be uniform, or the material may be banded or mottled. Nodules with concentric banding are quite common for Cobden Chert and Indiana Hornstone.

Cherts may have a large range of grain sizes and flaking qualities, sometimes for the same source. For Normanskill chert, the workability may range from excellent (very fine grained) to extremely poor (very coarse grained). A very fine quality Normanskill chert was rated by the professional knapper Chris Miller to be as good as heat treated Flint Ridge flint. Don Crabtree thought some Normanskill chert to be comparable to Indiana hornstone, and Scott Silsby considers Normanskill chert to be among the very finest in Eastern U.S.

Flint and chert nodules occurring in limestone often have an outer calcareous layer, called a cortex, which may vary in thickness, hardness and flaking qualities. The formation and occurrence of flint and chert are discussed in Luedke (1992) and Shepherd (1972). .

Other Materials

Other materials that have been used in North America include:

| quartz | quartz crystal | chalcedony | rhyolite | jasper |
| ignimbrite | quartzite | argillite | basalt | novaculite |

Quartz, the most abundant mineral, is crystalline silica (SiO_2). It is usually colorless, milky white or grayish, but with impurities can have other colors including pink (rose quartz) or purple (amethyst). In many localities it can often be found as rounded waterworn nodules or large pebbles that tend to be oval. In prehistoric times, quartz was often used in areas where better flint or chert were not as readily available. Quartz usually includes small or large fractures or incipient fractures that tend to render the material unpredictable for much percussion work, with frequent flat and angular fractures. Contemporary knappers often use bipolar percussion to break up quartz nodules. Some resulting smaller pieces relatively free of fractures can be worked well by pressure flaking. Petrographers and some archaeologists distinguish several kinds of quartz.

Quartz crystal, a single crystal of quartz, has been used rarely. Surprisingly large bifaces of quartz crystal were found at the Simon site in Idaho. Jeff Flenniken has experimented extensively with quartz crystal, the Arkansas state mineral.

Quartzite is either sedimentary, known as silicified sandstone, or metamorphosed sandstone, known as metaquartzite. Quartz is the major constituent of quartzites. The flaking qualities of quartzites have a very broad range, with the finer grained varieties being better. Silicified sandstones have been observed to be more workable (Crabtree 1967a, Callahan 1979). There is very fine prehistoric workmanship on bifaces from North Carolina and Virginia, for example.

Novaculite is a metamorphosed chert, with colors including white or light gray and black. Arkansas novaculite, well known in America, is relatively tough, but easier to work than coarser quartzites (Callahan 1979). It responds well to heat treatment, but at relatively high temperatures.

Chalcedony is a cryptocrystalline form of silica having fibrous crystals, usually containing also colloidal silica. It has a waxy luster and is often colorless or white, but has also been observed as yellow, amber, orange, and red, with occasional tints of brown or black from impurities (Crabtree 1967a).

Jasper has been classified in several ways by different authorities, some simply calling it a variety of chert. Yellow, red, brown and green varieties have been observed, with yellowish or brownish varieties known from Virginia and Pennsylvania. It is usually opaque. The latter varieties respond well to heat treatment, with the Pennsylvania jasper turning red.

Argyllite has been called a variety of metamorphosed shale. Used extensively in New Jersey, it tends to be on the tougher side, but can vary significantly in working quality. Local farmers used to refer to it as the blue jingler, since it produces a "ringing sound" when a tabular nodule is tapped with another stone. A wooden billet works well with argyllite.

Basalt is a volcanic rock with gray and black varieties known best. Many basalts are extremely tough or unworkable for knapping. However, a fine-grained variety of gray basalt from Arizona is known to have excellent flaking qualities, worked easily.

Rhyolite, an igneous rock, is often relatively tough to work. It has been used extensively in North Carolina, Maine and Pennsylvania. In composition, rhyolites can resemble granite, but are finer grained. A Pennsylvania rhyolite is strongly anisotropic, fracturing more easily along particular directions. In order to thin a biface, for example, a knapper must make adjustments for this (Silsby 1985).

Ignimbrite is formed by the "welding together" of ash particles produced by aereal volcanic eruptions. It occurs in Idaho, for example, and resembles obsidian in ease of workability.

Physical and Mechanical Properties

Microstructure and Physical Properties

Of the materials used, only quartz and quartz crystals are **minerals** since they have a definite chemical formula (SiO_2). All the others are rocks. The mechanical properties of crystalline rocks depend on characteristics of the matrix, the grains (including size, shape and orientation) and the bonding interfaces. For example, sandstones characteristically differ from quartzites by their weaker matrix and bonding. Fractures in sandstone tend to go around the grains (**intergranular fracture**). In quartzite, they tend to go through the grains (**transgranular fracture**).

In working with mechanics of crystalline materials, the properties of a material are characterized in an average sense over dimensions significantly larger than the grains. That is, the material is considered to be a continuum, discarding the details at the grain level.

Homogeneity and Isotropy

A material is **homogeneous** if it has the same properties throughout, and **isotropic** if it has the same properties in any direction. For knapping, it is the homogeneity and isotropy with regard to the mechanical properties that is of interest. Many cherts are not homogeneous. Highly variable properties are often encountered even in a particular nodule, as in the Normanskill and Esopus cherts of New York. In some chert nodules, fracture toughness can vary significantly for their outer and inner portions, as sometimes with the concentrically banded nodules of Cobden chert. For the English chalk flint from Brandon, it has been reported that the interior of a nodule is of inferior quality.

In a broader sense, most obsidians are homogeneous from a knapper's perspective. However, fractographic evidence from irregular ripple patterns indicates variations in material properties by color in some obsidian nodules. Occasionally residual stresses are encountered in banded obsidians. Highly localized residual stresses may also occur at inclusions in obsidians as well as cherts.

Isotropy refers to the independence with regard to directionality in material properties. For example, wood is anisotropic rather than isotropic. Slate, because of its platy cleavage, is also anisotropic. So is Pennsylvania rhyolite.

Preferential orientation of crystals in a rock may influence their elastic properties as well as fracture behavior. It is conspicuous to experienced knappers that Pennsylvania rhyolite is anisotropic at least with respect to fracture toughness. It does not fracture the same way in different directions. One suspects this to be true also for its elastic behavior, but a definitive statement would require laboratory testing. Expert knappers can work well with the Pennsylvania rhyolite, taking into account its anisotropy.

Some obsidians exhibit at least some anisotropy – as in reference to the directions parallel and normal to the flow planes in some banded obsidians. The presence of residual stress in obsidian can render it both inhomogeneous as well as anisotropic. Knappers occasionally note that some obsidian nodules just do not fracture predictably.

Anisotropy can be associated with the presence of cleavage planes (as in slate) or bedding planes (as in argyllite from New Jersey). Preferential orientation of "irregular" grains, even when fine, can lead to anisotropy in elastic properties as well as fracture toughness. There is an interesting reference to Brandon gunflint knappers looking for "cleavage", in reference to some anisotropy. Such a more subtle kind of anisotropy is discussed by Shepherd (1972: 189) for the Brandon flint (See also Mason 1978: 19). He refers to anisotropy in both the elastic and fracture behavior. He notes that "a flint nodule generally shows a propensity for splitting easily and evenly in certain particular directions", and their disposition is found "by tapping the flint all round and listening for a satisfactory 'ring'." The directionality for fracture of Brandon flint was discussed with Brandon knappers by Hallam Movius. He "found that they operated upon this premise and had apparently good reason for their opinion" (Goodman 1944: 420). Contemporary knappers, however, do not recognize any anisotropy in Brandon flint.

Elasticity, Ductility, Brittleness

All materials, including flint and chert, deform when stressed. Material behavior is **elastic** if the material returns to its original form after deformation, when the forces acting on it are removed (fractures not considered). For practical purposes, all lithic raw materials used for knapping behave essentially elastically at a macroscopic scale during knapping. Copper, wood and antler can behave not only elastically (under low stress) but also inelastically under high stress, as seen by dents from contact with stone. The term "elastic" is used also in another sense, as a measure of flexibility by saying a material is **less elastic** (stiffer) or **more elastic** (more flexible).

If a material behaves only elastically before it breaks, then it is **brittle** (and behaves in a brittle manner). Thus, all raw materials used for knapping are essentially brittle. Copper, on the other hand, is not. Instead, it is **ductile** because it can be stretched inelastically quite a lot.

Some remarks are appropriate. Glass is the most brittle material, said to be the ideal example of a material with brittle behavior. At a crack tip in glass, such as obsidian, there is some inelastic behavior at a very fine scale between the microscopic and atomic levels (Wiederhorn 1967). Also, there is a standard test for glass that is pressed with a small "point" or hard indenter, leaving a depressed region. In this case, the material behavior is far from elastic. In some (normal) glasses including obsidian, this is inelastic behavior; in others, it is called densification instead.

Elastic Constants

For quantitative description of elastic deformations, use is made of elastic constants. Of the many such constants, only two are independent. Others can be calculated from any two of them.

Suppose a solid cylinder with a cross-sectional area A and length L is compressed axially by a force F to get a change in length ΔL. The **modulus of elasticity**, also known as the **Young's modulus**, is defined on the basis of such a uniaxial test as

$$E = \sigma/\varepsilon = (F/A)/(\Delta L/L) \tag{3.1}$$

where $\sigma = F/A$ is the **stress** and $\varepsilon = \Delta L/L$ is the **strain**. The lower the E, the more elastic is the material. This is like compressing a spring with a spring constant equal to $E(A/L)$.

Suppose the cylinder has a diameter D. During compression this will increase by some amount ΔD. The **Poisson's ratio** ν is defined as

$$\nu = |(\Delta D/D)/(\Delta L/L)| \tag{3.2}$$

This is a measure of (the absolute value of) lateral to longitudinal deformation per unit length.

Compare stretching a steel wire and a rubber band. A rubber band is more elastic because it has a much lower modulus of elasticity than steel. The transverse dimension of a rubber band will change much because it has a Poisson's ratio of about 0.5, the highest for any material. For steel it is 0.29, and for some obsidians, flints and cherts, it is often about 0.18 (Table 3.2).

With the above two constants, the **shear modulus** G is

$$G = E/[2(1+\nu)] \tag{3.3}$$

The sounds we hear were transmitted through air by stress waves called **longitudinal stress waves** traveling at about 330 m/s in air. Such waves can also travel through solids with a speed equal to

$$V_p = (E/\rho)^{1/2} \tag{3.4}$$

where ρ = mass density, which can be obtained from the specific gravity or density. Eq. 3.4 is for a longitudinal wave (**P-wave**).

In contrast to air or water, there can also be **shear waves (S-waves)** in a solid traveling at the speed

$$V_S = (G/\rho)^{1/2} \tag{3.5}$$

For some obsidian, $V_S \sim 3500$ m/s and $V_P \sim 5{,}500$ m/s (See Table 3.2).

The last two equations are for a long body such as a rod. The P-wave speed V_P in a plate is slightly faster, and faster yet in a massive solid. The equations for such speeds are given in (Kerkhof 1970).

Suppose a blade is being detached by applying a certain force. By knowing the force and its location of application, E for the material, and the blade dimensions, one can calculate how much it will bend. Such calculations are of interest in relation to the effectiveness of hand supports provided in some pressure flaking. Or if the blade should fly off with a sound, one could predict the note it will produce to a musical ear. E is a constant relevant to mechanical studies on flaking.

The shear wave velocity, V_S, is important in fractographic investigation especially for obsidian, to calculate the speed of fracture propagation relative to the shear wave speed, V_F/V_S (Tomenchuck 1985, Hutchings 1997 and 1999). In percussion flaking, relative fracture speeds V_F/V_S up to at least 0.58 have been observed for a flake surface (Tsirk 1996). Such measurements are not available for flint and chert.

Elastic constants as well as strength properties of some obsidians, flints and cherts have been considered by many investigators (including Speth 1972, Tomenchuk 1985, Luedke

TABLE 3.2 ELASTIC CONSTANTS AND STRESS WAVE VELOCITIES

Material	Density (gm/cm³)	Poisson's Ratio ν	Modulus of Elasticity E (GPa) [10⁶psi]	V_S (m/s)	V_P (m/s)	Reference
Oregon Obsidian (Avg. of 2 methods)	2.36	0.187	71.1 [10.3]]	3,567*	5,745*	Manghnani et al. 1968
Glass Buttes Obsidian	2.36*	0.206	71.8 [10.40]	3,552	5,836*	Yasuda p. c. 2012
Lipari Obsidian	N.A.	0.17	65.3 [9.46]	3,425	5,245	Tomenchuk 1985, Hutchings 1997
Chert (Mean values)	2.59	0.16	67.8 [9.83]	3,393*	5,168*	Speth 1972

* indicates an average value.

1992, Domanski, Webb and Boland 1994, Hutchings 1997 and 1999, Domanski and Webb 2000, Domanski et al. 2009). There are difficulties with some of the results presented, however. What a geologist might call obsidian or chert might not be what we think it is. Also, there are some results that seem to be inconsistent or not credible. Examples of elastic constants and stress wave velocities are given in Table 3.2 based on the average or mean values of E and ν.

Constants for Thermal Effects

Breakage during thermal alteration and other thermal effects in lithic materials depend not only on the elastic constants, but also on the material properties known as the coefficient of thermal expansion, the specific heat and the thermal conductivity. The **coefficient of thermal expansion** α (alfa) is the change in length per unit length for a temperature change of one degree. As an example, suppose a rod of length L has a temperature increase T. Then the length increase is

$$\Delta L = \alpha T L \qquad (3.6)$$

and the strain is

$$\varepsilon = \Delta L/L = \alpha T \qquad (3.7)$$

Table 3.3 lists the constants for the thermal effects for some lithic and other common materials. Essentially no such data is available for the lithic materials of interest in knapping. The coefficient of thermal expansion given for the Ocala chert in the table is from Beauchamp and Purdy (1986).

The **specific heat** of a material, c, is the quantity of heat required to increase by one degree the temperature of a unit mass of the material. It is measured in units of calories per gram per degree centigrade (Cal/(gm °C) or Btu/(lb °F). **Thermal conductivity** k relates to how much heat is conducted through a material. Suppose a plate of thickness L and area A has temperatures T_1 and T_2 at its faces. Then the amount of heat Q flowing through the plate is

$$Q = k A (T_2 - T_1)/L \qquad (3.8)$$

In general, the transfer of heat may occur by conduction, considered above, by convection or by radiation. For practical purpose, only conduction is relevant to the thermal effects in lithic materials. Slight transfer of heat by radiation can occur in materials that are transparent, as some obsidians, but may be neglected. Convection of heat, though relevant to lava flows, is of no interest here.

Strength and Fracture Toughness

Leonardo da Vinci (1452-1519) observed that long wires break more easily than short wires. This relates to material flaws. A longer wire is more likely to have a bigger flaw and therefore a lower tensile strength. The **tensile strength** is expressed as the maximum stress, often in units of psi (lbs./in^2) or MPa (megapascals). The tensile strength already takes into account the flaws in a material. It may vary significantly, depending on the nature of the flaws present. For example, in an experiment with glass rods the tensile strength was observed to vary about 30% for longitudinal and transverse grinding with a diamond wheel (Mecholsky, Freiman and Rice 1977). Tensile strength of cherts has been considered in Speth (1972) and Purdy and Brooks (1971), and also for obsidians in Purdy (1974). In testing for tensile strength of materials for knapping, the appropriate kinds of tests and a sufficient number of them must be performed to allow for variability due to flaws.

TABLE 3.3 CONSTANTS FOR THERMAL EFFECTS

Material	Coefficient Of Thermal Expansion, α $\times 10^{-6}$/°C	Specific Heat C Cal/(g °C)	Thermal Conductivity K Cal/(cm sec °C)
Soda Lime Glass	8.5 - 8.9	0.20	0.002 - 0.0026
Ocala Chert	14.9	---	---
Limestone	7.6 – 9.0	0.22	0.003
Marble	8.0 – 26.0	0.20	0.005 - 0.007
Granite	5.0 – 15.0	0.19	0.005 – 0.006
Sandstone	7 – 12	0.22	0.004 – 0.006
Concrete	9 - 12	0.18 - 0.21	0.004
Brick	9.5	0.20 - 0.22	0.0014 - 0.0024
Copper	14 - 18	0.09	0.9 - 1.1
Aluminum	23 - 24	0.21	0.48 – 0.50
Steel	11 - 12	0.12	0.11

Although tensile strength includes the effects of flaws, it does not explicitly take into account the flaws present in a material. **Fracture toughness** K_{IC} also known as the **critical stress intensity factor**, does account for flaws explicitly. It is often expressed in the units MPa m$^{1/2}$. For example, the force required to initiate a fracture for a flake in pressure flaking will depend on factors that include fracture toughness as well as the characteristics of the flaw where the fracture started.

Fracture toughness of some raw materials for knapping is considered in Schindler, Hatch, Hay and Bradt (1982), Beauchamp and Purdy (1986), Quinn, Hatch and Bradt (2001), Domanski, Webb and Boland (1994), Domanski and Webb (2000), and Domanski et al. (2009). Examples of fracture toughness of some lithic materials are provided in Table 3.4, along with soda-lime glass (window glass) for comparison. Fracture toughness obtained from different laboratory tests has been found to vary significantly (Beauchamp and Purdy 1986). It is therefore of practical interest to use the same tests for comparing the results. They are still expected to be meaningful in a relative sense.

Mirror Constants

Mirror constants A_i (Chapter 7) have been used to calculate the fracture stress σ_f from the respective mirror radii R_i by

$$\sigma_f = A_i R_i^{-1/2} \quad \text{(for i = M, H, B)} \quad (3.9)$$

where R_M, R_H and R_B are the distances from the fracture origin to the mirror-mist boundary, the mist-hackle boundary and the branching boundary, respectively (Mecholsky 1994, Quinn 2007). Guidelines for measuring mirror constants are provided in Appendix D of the latter reference. No numerical values for the mirror constants are available in literature for any lithic materials of interest to knapping. However, the cited references provide numerical values for a number of industrial materials. For a soda lime glass (window glass) with $K_{IC} = 0.72$ MPa m$^{1/2}$ and $E = 73$ GPa (10.6×10^6 psi), the mirror constants are (Mecholsky 1994: 45):

$$A_M = 1.8 \quad A_H = 2.0 \quad A_B = 2.3$$

From Eqn. 3.9

$$\sigma_{fN} = \sigma_f / A_i = R_i^{-1/2} \quad (3.10)$$

where σ_{fN} is the normalized fracture stress. The equation is convenient to use for obtaining the relative fracture stresses for a particular material when the mirror constants are not known. The equations are most useful for accidental or intentional breakage by bending. Examples would include bifaces and blades. However, it cannot be applied when the stresses are too low or the specimens are too small, with no mist manifestation. From these equations it is seen that the smaller the mirror radii, the higher the fracture stress. Branching related to R_B does occur with accidental breakages in knapping occasionally, associated with lateral wedges.

TABLE 3.4 EXAMPLES OF FRACTURE TOUGHNESS

Material	Fracture Toughness Without Heat Treatm. MPa m$^{1/2}$	Fracture Toughness With Heat Treatment MPa m$^{1/2}$	Reference
Flint & Chert	1.53 – 2.59	----	Domanski, Webb & Boland 1994
Bald Eagle Jasper	2.07	0.95*	Schindler et al. 1982
Ocala Chert	1.55	1.05*	Mecholsky & Mackin 1988; Beauchamp & Purdy 1986
Obsidian	0.76 – 0.87	----	Domanski, Webb and Boland 1994
Soda Lime Glass	0.72	----	Mecholsky 1994

*Varies with heat treatment temperature.

Workability

By **workability** is meant here the **workability of the parent material.** Callahan (1979) proposed a very useful Lithic Grade Scale for this purpose (Fig. 3.1). In addition to its suitable workability range, to be discussed, it is desirable to have a parent material that is homogeneous, isotropic and brittle.

Ideally, a bulk material should be free of inclusions, flaws, defects, cracks, weathering planes and other irregularities. Since there is practically no such an ideal material, Domanski et al. (1994) have adopted the use of a **uniformity rank** with 15 grades for this purpose. It makes very much sense to do so. It seems reasonable to adopt the use of particular grades based on localized regional circumstances, at least at first.

It has been recognized that particular methods (such as direct percussion and pressure flaking) and techniques (such as freehand support) are more suitable for working some

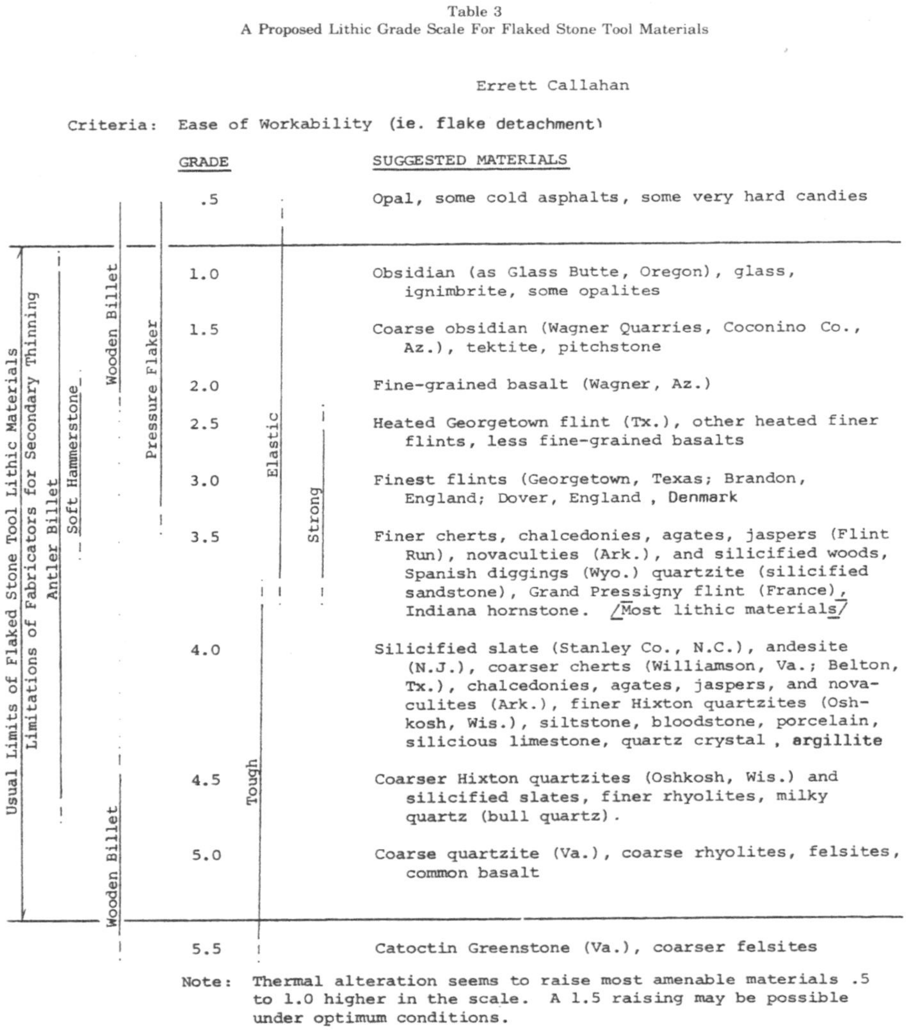

Table 3
A Proposed Lithic Grade Scale For Flaked Stone Tool Materials

Errett Callahan

Criteria: Ease of Workability (ie. flake detachment)

GRADE	SUGGESTED MATERIALS
.5	Opal, some cold asphalts, some very hard candies
1.0	Obsidian (as Glass Butte, Oregon), glass, ignimbrite, some opalites
1.5	Coarse obsidian (Wagner Quarries, Coconino Co., Az.), tektite, pitchstone
2.0	Fine-grained basalt (Wagner, Az.)
2.5	Heated Georgetown flint (Tx.), other heated finer flints, less fine-grained basalts
3.0	Finest flints (Georgetown, Texas; Brandon, England; Dover, England, Denmark
3.5	Finer cherts, chalcedonies, agates, jaspers (Flint Run), novaculties (Ark.), and silicified woods, Spanish diggings (Wyo.) quartzite (silicified sandstone), Grand Pressigny flint (France), Indiana hornstone. /Most lithic materials/
4.0	Silicified slate (Stanley Co., N.C.), andesite (N.J.), coarser cherts (Williamson, Va.; Belton, Tx.), chalcedonies, agates, jaspers, and novaculties (Ark.), finer Hixton quartzites (Oshkosh, Wis.), siltstone, bloodstone, porcelain, silicious limestone, quartz crystal, argillite
4.5	Coarser Hixton quartzites (Oshkosh, Wis.) and silicified slates, finer rhyolites, milky quartz (bull quartz).
5.0	Coarse quartzite (Va.), coarse rhyolites, felsites, common basalt
5.5	Catoctin Greenstone (Va.), coarser felsites

Note: Thermal alteration seems to raise most amenable materials .5 to 1.0 higher in the scale. A 1.5 raising may be possible under optimum conditions.

FIG. 3.1 CALLAHAN'S PROPOSED LITHIC GRADE SCALE (CALLAHAN 1979, REPRODUCED WITH PERMISSION)

particular materials (Callahan 1979). These will not be included in this consideration of workability, even though they do relate to material properties.

Knapping involves the production as well as prevention of (accidental) fractures. These pose opposing demands on the material properties desirable for workability. Moreover, the relationships of these opposing demands may vary for different knapping tasks - for production of thin blades vs. thick flakes for instance. Furthermore, it is of interest to know the mechanical properties relevant to initiation of fractures and to their subsequent propagation.

The most important mechanical property for workability is the fracture toughness K_{IC}. There is an optimum value of K_{IC} for the intermediate ranges, shown by the "highest values" (the best) of workability in Fig. 3.2a. Workability is considered to decrease above and below this range. When K_{IC} is too great, the material is simply too tough to work. When it is too low, it is too susceptible to accidental breakage, including platform

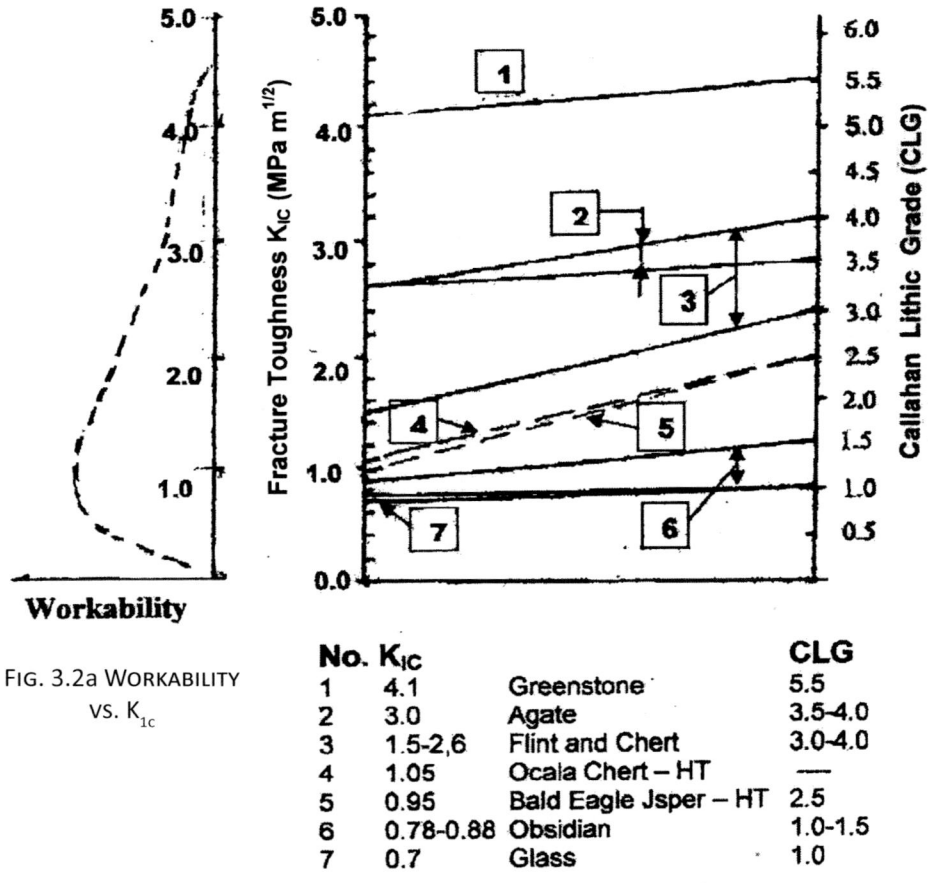

FIG. 3.2a WORKABILITY VS. K_{1C}

No.	K_{IC}		CLG
1	4.1	Greenstone	5.5
2	3.0	Agate	3.5-4.0
3	1.5-2,6	Flint and Chert	3.0-4.0
4	1.05	Ocala Chert – HT	—
5	0.95	Bald Eagle Jsper – HT	2.5
6	0.78-0.88	Obsidian	1.0-1.5
7	0.7	Glass	1.0

FIG. 3.2b Fracture Toughness vs. Lithic Grade

crushing and what Crabtree called end shock or amputation (Crabtree 1972). For all K_{IC}, the susceptibility for accidental breakages depends very much on the knapping task at hand. The changes in workability to either side of the optimum range in the figure are gradual, of course.

The lithic grade scale for "ease of workability" (Fig. 3.1) proposed in the pioneering effort by Callahan (1979) is subjective. An attempt is made here to relate the fracture toughnesses K_{IC} for some materials to this lithic grade scale. K_{IC} is available for a limited number of materials for which the lithic grade scale is not known. A number of assumptions were made to arrive at a rough, tentative correlation shown in Fig. 3.2b. As a preliminary effort, the correlations appear to be meaningful despite the many questions related to the figure. Nevertheless, the correlations do indicate that K_{IC} is indeed a significant mechanical property for workability of lithic materials. It is more meaningful than the tensile strength.

The modulus of elasticity E is relevant to knapping in several ways. Some suggestions are made on its relevance to workability. For considering the effects of E, the basic idea is that a lower E increases the flexibility as well as the deformations and displacements. A partly detached flake will thus be more flexible and will have greater displacements. For example, the desired amount of support provided to the back (dorsal) side of the flake will depend on E. Also, the likelihood of outward buckling of a long thin blade will increase with a lower E.

The modulus of elasticity E can affect control in flaking. In knapping, the fracturing for a flake surface is essentially always subcritical (Tsirk 2012). This is indicated by the fact that very high fracture velocities and the manifestation of mist and hackle is essentially never associated with flaking. One suggested reason for the subcritical fracturing is that the loads in flaking are self-relieving. That is, they are reduced because of the deformations and displacements of a flake during its detachment. They would be less with a higher E. This suggests that the manifestation of mist and velocity hackle is more likely on flakes of such materials. It is of interest to note that the few exceptional cases in which mist has been observed in flaking have been without exception on thick flakes (Tsirk 1996). Mist manifestations by a lip region are excluded here.

There is another aspect of control in flaking, related to the above discussion. Because of the displacements of the flake during its detachment, the ratio of the horizontal to the vertical component of the applied force will decrease as the flake is being detached (Chapter 12). This enables a knapper to achieve control over a flake detachment more easily. Although E is available for a number of materials, it is difficult to draw general conclusions about its significance, even though it was recognized by the master knappers Crabtree (1967a) and Callahan (1979).

Alteration of Properties And Behavior

Hydration and Vesiculation of Obsidian

Obsidian absorbs water from moist atmosphere or water to alter its surface appearance that can look sometimes mat, grayish or whitish. With time, the absorption of water and the chemical-physical alteration of the material penetrates deeper. Factors that can affect the hydration rate include temperature, obsidian composition and water content (Steffen 2005). The obsidian hydration process involves volumetric changes, and therefore leads to mechanical strains. This sometimes leads to microscopic crazing and "spalling". Hydration tends to obscure some subtle, microscopic fracture markings such as mist and scarps. Mist can still be seen on prehistoric artifacts with significant hydration and scarps, though partly obscured, on geological fractures with hydration.

The effects of a forest fire on obsidian has been studied extensively by Steffen (2005). When obsidian has softened due to the heat, the nucleation and growth of bubbles in it leads to vesiculation. It is affected significantly by water content. As observed at the Capulin Quarry in the Jemez Mountains of New Mexico, a flake may be fully or only partly vesiculated. A fully vesiculated flake has its original size increased several-fold, having the appearance of a rigid sponge, but retaining some resemblance to its original morphology. A partly vesiculated flake has a surprising appearance, with part of it completely vesiculated and part of it apparently unaffected, retaining its original size and shape.

Cortex and Patina on Flint and Chert

Weathering of flint and chert is a physical-chemical process that can depend on many factors including the chemistry of the material and its environment, porosity of the material and its microstructure. Patination of flint and chert is a form of weathering at a thin outer layer that can be due to a number of processes (Luedke 1992). Some patina, also called a weathering rind, can form quickly; some others may require considerable time. Some patination may involve surface deposition, others replacement with leaching. White as well as yellow, brown, red, nearly black and translucent varieties of patina have been observed.

Some nodules of cert can develop a significant cortex under certain conditions. For example, a Cobden chert nodule in its limestone formation can have a layer of $CaCO_3$ that can vary in thickness as well as trength. A Normanskill chert nodule in its shale formation has often a thin, strong layer deposited on it. Flaking can be affected in both of these cases.

Thermal Cracking

Thermal cracking is due to temperature variations within a specimen. When the temperature outside a specimen is changed, it will take some time for the specimen to heat up or cool down to the surrounding temperature, to have a uniform temperature thereafter. Until this happens, there will be internal temperature differentials, and therefore also differences in the strains and stresses that may lead to fractures. The internal strains are greater with a higher coefficient of thermal expansion, for a lower specific heat as well as lower conductivity (See Table 3.3). Of course, the rate of cooling or heating amplifies the differential effects. In principle, it may be possible for two different mechanism to produce a similar fracture.

In climates with freezing, exposed flint or chert nodules left outside for years are sometimes observed to fracture or shatter. Such **frost splitting,** frost spalling or **frost**

FIG. 3.3 POTLID FRACTURES: AT THE BOTTOM OF THE CENTER COLUMN IS A POTLID FRACTURE ON WHICH A SECONDARY ONE (SHOWN ABOVE IT) OCCURRED AT ITS INNER SURFACE. A POTLID FRACTURE WITH THE ASSOCIATED POTLID IS SHOWN IN THE RIGHT COLUMN.

shattering can be caused by the freezing of water in the cracks of the nodule. A flint or chert nodule may also be split by frost if it contains water (Shepherd 1972). In at least some cases, **potlid fractures** (Fig. 3.3) may be seen in effect as frost spalls in the above sense. In their appearance, **frost pits** (Fig. 3.4) can be similar to potlids. Shepherd notes (1972: 39) that a nodule covered with numerous potlid fractures is said to be frost-pitted. Contemporary rock dealers note that, in their heat treatment of flint and chert, potlids are always formed during heating, consistent with the observations by Purdy (1975: 136). The fractures noted above may be caused by differential strains from thermal effects, perhaps combined with other factors such as material irregularities.

Shepherd (1972: 38) notes that "flint is readily shattered by heating it in a fire and then plunging it into cold water." According to Purdy (1975: 135-136), the Florida cherts she experimented with exploded at 400°C when heated too fast. Also, there was some explosion or spalling when the rock was removed from the oven at 350°C. She also notes that explosion by cooling seemed to occur at a lower temperature (350°C) than explosion by heating (at or above 400°C). Some obsidian nodules at a quarry site in the Jemez Mountains exhibited heat spalling from being subjected to a forest fire (Steffen 2005: Appendix B). In general, thermal cracking depends on the geometry of the specimen involved.

The fine surface cracking, (a.k.a. **crazing** or shrinkage cracks) is caused by cooling. "Columnar" or "starch" fractures, with column-like forms and sometimes with square or rectangular section, are occasionally manifested with a thick cortex (Shepherd 1972: 39). When a biface or a slab at a higher temperature is cooled too rapidly, it can break with a wavy, sinuous crack. It has been referred to as an oscillating or crenated fracture, and as a meander crack. Wavy crack paths are considered further in Chapter 11. If heating rather than cooling is involved, tension will develop instead in the central part, and the cracks may start there.

FIG. 3.4 A FROST PITTED NODULE OF COBDEN CHERT.

Thermal Alteration and Heat Treatment

Heat treatment can significantly alter not only the physical and mechanical properties, but also the appearance of some flint and chert. It has been used in prehistoric times in the Old World and the New World, and is practiced by many contemporary knappers to improve the workability of the stone (Crabtree and Butler 1964, Domanski and Webb 1992, 2007). There are also ethnographic references to heat treatment.

Heating and cooling during heat treatment must be sufficiently slow, so as not to induce fractures due to excessively nonuniform temperature, and perhaps for other reasons as well. Most contemporary knappers heat treat relatively smaller pieces such as flakes or bifaces for further flaking. But large pieces have also been heat treated with sufficiently slow temperature changes. It has also been noted that slower temperature changes are also needed for some multi-colored cherts.

Heat treating can change the color drastically, slightly or not at all. For example, the yellow Bald Eagle jasper of Pennsylvania can turn bright red (Schindler et al. 1982). Esoteric color patterns appear in some materials. Heat treatment can also lead to a change in texture and luster, but only on fracture surfaces produced after the treatment. In some cases, this may be explained by the mode of fracture being changed from intercrystalline to transcrystalline by the process, but other reasons have also been noted (Luedke 1992, Schindler et al. 1982). Tensile strength and fracture toughness is decreased drastically in some materials by heat treatment (Table 3.4). The workability of many cherts is improved significantly by heat treatment. Callahan (1979) notes that the lithic grade may be improved by 0.5 to 1.5. It is well known to contemporary knappers that heat treatment of Arkansas novaculites improves their workability drastically. In ongoing research, however, an opposite effect is observed for some Arkansas novaculite. In experimental biface thinning by direct percussion, Mandeville and Flenniken (1974) observed that heat treatment led to a reduction of hinge fractures and to thinner bifaces. Temperatures needed for effective heat-treating usually vary for different materials, some requiring as low as about 225 degrees Centigrade (about 440 degrees Fahrenheit) and others up to 375 degrees Centigrade (about 710 degrees Fahrenheit) for "optimum workability" according to Luedke (1992). There may, of course, be thermal alteration of a material without any intent of heat treatment. This can be due to nature or the activities of man.

Environmental Effects

Moisture, water and other liquids can decrease the fracture toughness of glass when the fracture velocity is very low (less than about 5 to 10 cm/s) and stress is present (Schönert, Umhauer and Klemm 1969). These effects are thought to be due to a sharpening of a crack or microcrack. If moisture, water and some other liquid is present with no stress, then a crack is thought to be blunted (Michalske 1984), thereby increasing the strength and fracture toughness. This is known as **aging**.

Based on the cited research, the effects of moisture, water and other liquids on fracture toughness are very significant for industrial glasses, but only when a fracture is starting and propagating extremely slowly, at less than about 5 cm/s. The effects are greater at higher temperatures. When comparing dry air vs. moist air environment, or dry air vs. water, the differences are extremely significant. Similar effects are known for ceramic materials. Comparable effects are expected for obsidian, flint and chert. According to some contemporary knappers, cold obsidian, flint, chert and quartzite do not flake well.

In knapping, wetting the location where a fracture starts (usually the platform) can lead to a decrease in the initial force required to start a fracture. In experimental pressure

FIG. 3.5 SINUOUS FRACTURE OF A CHERT BIFACE DUE TO COOLING TOO FAST. BURLINGTON CHERT FROM CRESCENT QUARRY.

flaking of obsidian, fractographic evidence can be observed for water enhancing crack propagation (Chapters 6 and 8). Such evidence has not been observed in crystalline materials such as flint or chert, because the associated fracture markings have not been observed in polycrystalline materials.

It was noted that water can aid fractures propagating only at very slow velocities. That is because water behind the fracture front cannot follow the crack. But what happens when water from soaking or wetting is already ahead of the crack, in the pores, waiting for the crack to arrive and pass the water filled pore at relatively high velocity? This has not been explored in controlled laboratory experiments. One would anticipate that such water would facilitate fracture propagation. Judgements by contemporary knappers (including Bonnichsen, Sollberger and Cresson) indicates that it does.

A glass cutter knows that glass can be broken more easily right after scoring. This is due to aging, which increases the strength in the absence of stress. Aging is relevant to knapping and use-wear studies. For example, suppose the edge of a biface is ground for flake removal. Less force will probably be required to detach a flake right after grinding than the next day. If done next day, regrinding would be useful.

Aging depends on time, temperature, and the environment. Extremely significant strength increases in glass have been observed over 24 hours, and the process may continue after a month. Aging is definitely significant for obsidian, and is expected to be so also for flint and chert.

Procurement

The procurement of raw materials obviously relates to subsistence and settlement patterns, trade or networks of exchange in a broader sense. The International Association of Obsidian Studies is involved in identifying the sources of obsidian, and Luedke (1992) the sources of flint and chert. Examples are noted here of the methods used to obtain raw materials. Quarrying and mining of raw materials, and their procurement in a broader sense are treated in Holmes (1919) and Shepherd (1980), for example.

Now, as probably prehistorically, some materials in certain localities are easy to obtain. Examples are the waterwarn nodules or cobbles of quartz and quartzite, abundant in some localities. Chert nodules occur in riverbeds and streambeds in Southern Illinois, for example.

However, procurement of the best quality material desired usually involved extensive efforts. The largest and most elaborate flint mining activity known is from the Neolithic times at Spiennes, Belgium and Grimes Graves, near Brandon, England. At both localities, the flint in chalk was mined by use of vertical shafts with radial galleries at the elevation of the best quality flint. Mining of flint in the soft chalk is easy compared to localities where the parent rock is hard and the material of interest occurs in massive form. An example is the obsidian mining at Pico de Orizaba, Veracruz, Mexico. The obsidian flow is in a rhyolite matrix. One of the mine passages extends 70 meters into the obsidian descending 14 meters from the entrance. The mining passages are thought to follow larger fractures in the flow, with chambers used to exploit the higher quality obsidian (Stocker and Cobean 1984).

At Sierra de las Navajas in Hidalgo, Mexico, numerous vertical shafts (some 7 to 9 m deep) are still open from the Aztec time. Ongoing research indicates that radial galleries were extended from vertical shafts.

Mining of rhyolite at Mt. Jasper, New Hampshire in the U.S. required extensive efforts. The rhyolite occurs in a matrix of gneiss or some other hard rock. Open pits and exposures at cliffs were used in some quarrying, but one passage extended 10 m into the side of the mountain, with greenstone hammers and hammering marks found (Gramley 1984).

In the New World, it was common to quarry the raw materials by use of open pits or by exploiting outcrops at a hillside. Both of these methods were used, for example, for the Normanskill chert at Flint Mine Hill (Parker 1925) and other locations in Greene County, New York. The chert occurs in massive form, sometimes broken up into boulders or nodules, within a relatively hard shale formation (Fig. 3.6).

At the Mill Creek Quarries in Illinois, a different situation is encountered (Holmes 1919). The weathering of the limestone strata led to the chert nodules being embedded in clay layers of over 25 ft. (7.6 m) in places. Mining involved vertical shafts in this clay, with some hazardous horizontal tunneling. In 1974, I saw a number of shallow hillside pits at the Mill Creek Quarry as well as the Iron Mountain Quarry for kaolin chert.

At Glass Buttes, Oregon in 1973, nodules up to about a head size were abundant at or near the surface, together with extensive prehistoric debitage. For larger pieces and better qualities of obsidian, excavation was necessary. Recently, some contemporary knappers obtained an 815 kg boulder from a pit at about 5 m depth.

Nontraditional Uses of Obsidian, Flint and Chert

Recent uses of flint for gunflints, threshing sledges and liners in ceramic industry were already considered. Some other uses of knapping materials are noted here.

Flint, chert and quartz were probably used for making fire in prehistoric times. For example, iron pyrites, flint and tinder found at the Mesolithic site of Starr Carr in England are thought to have been used in making fire (Clark 1971). Strike-a-lights with flint and iron were in common use well after phosphorus matches were introduced in 1832 (Mason 1978). Ceremonial use of flint in making fire has lasted into the 20th century in some contexts. In 19th century England, tinder boxes were in common use. They contained steel, flint and tinder of charred cotton or linen cloth. As late as 1947 in Estonia, a man who could not afford matches was observed to light his cigarettes with flint and a steel strike-a-light (Mäesalu, personal communication, 1997). Strike-a-lights with flint are used even nowadays in some regions of the Near East by shepherds because of wind, even though matches and cigarette lighters are available to them.

FIG. 3.6 A MODERN NORMANSKILL CHERT QUARRY IN GREENE COUNTY, NEW YORK. THE CHERT AND THE PARENT SHALE ARE USED IN CONTEMPORARY CONSTRUCTION. THE SCALE OF THE OPERATION IS SEEN BY THE CONSTRUCTION EQUIPMENT IN THE BACKGROUND. THE NODULES AND BOULDERS SEEN ON THE PHOTO ARE CHERT.

To avoid explosions from use of candles, "steel mills" came to be used for lighting in coal mines from the time of their invention, probably around 1740. A mechanism with wheels was cranked by hand so that steel would strike against flint to produce a stream of sparks (Mason 1978, Shepherd 1972). Steel mills were replaced by safety lamps around 1815.

Flint has been used in artwork and jewelry for centuries (Slotta 1980). Flint, jasper, obsidian and other stones are used today as semi-precious gems in pendants, brooches, etc.

Flint has been used extensively for construction in the southeastern part of England where it occurs in great abundance (Mason 1978, Shepherd 1972). It was used already by Romans in Britain for wall and road construction. There are many churches, houses and other buildings constructed with flint (Fig. 3.7). Entire walls were sometimes made of rounded flint nodules and mortar. At other times, flint was used only as decorative facing. Flint has been used as naturally occurring nodules, as partly trimmed, or as very carefully knapped rectangular blocks (Whittaker 2001). Flakes or chunks of flint were sometimes used in the mortar between the nodules of flint – called garreting, garneting or galleting. Elaborate flint designs can be seen on some houses and churches, occasionally within brick walls (Fig. 3.7). Precast panels with flint are sometimes used today for building facades, and flint is being used as coarse aggregate in concrete for roads and structures.

Fig. 3.7 Use of flint for houses in Brandon, England. The Bell on the top left, presently an inn, has untrimmed flint nodules in the wall. The brick house on the right uses trimmed flint as decoration in the brickwork. It used to belong to the gunflint knapper Jim English. The lower photos show details from the "Jim English House".

In some modern road construction in England and Scandinavia, processed flint is used on roadway surfaces to improve light reflection and traction. Small fragments of industrial glass are sometimes used with asphalt, as "glassphalt", to produce some glittering paving on some streets in New York City. Flint was used in the past centuries in England for manufacture of glass, and even more extensively in the ceramic industry since the early 18th century. Use of 800 000 tons of flint annually for ceramics has been reported for the second half of the 19th century in England (Mason 1978). Rounded nodules of flint have been used in the past centuries for grinding grain in "ball mills" in England and

America. Numerous deposits of European flint, used as ballast, have been found along the East Coast of America from Florida to Maine, some dating back to 1534.

Mosaic flooring or pavement of flint in Brandon, England and of obsidian in Pachuca, Mexico has been reported. Decorative use of nodules or chunks of obsidian can be seen in parts of some buildings in Mexico.

There is a sizable tourist industry in Mexico for various objects ground, and occasionally flaked, from obsidian. This includes "Maya style chess sets" of black and brown obsidian, as well as statues, pendants and flaked knives sold at Teotihuacan and other tourist attractions.

PART II - FRACTURE MARKINGS: THE TOOLS OF FRACTOGRAPHY

4. An Overview

Fracture markings are the tools of fractography. If we compare fractography to reading, then fracture markings correspond to the alphabet. Fracture markings may be viewed as the manifestation of unusual events during a fracture that allow us to understand it better. Similarly, it is the variations and unusual occurrences of a fracture marking that render it more meaningful. In general, not only the manifestation but also the absence and paucity of fracture markings can be important for fractographic interpretation.

This overview of fracture markings is provided to help the reader focus in on markings of particular interest. They are considered in greater detail in Chapters 5 to 8. A discussion of liquid-induced fracture markings (LIFMs) with an overview appears in Chapter 8. In these chapters, the formation and meaning of fracture markings are discussed in a generic sense. In Part III of the book, observations and interpretations on their manifestation in knapping are considered.

The terminology used for fracture markings can be confusing. The meaning can sometimes be understood only from the context. The terms adopted here are compared in Table 4.1 with other terms. In this table, the heading "Literature on Knapping" refers to publications dealing with knapping, regardless of whether they appeared in archaeological, fracture mechanics or other literature. "Other Fractography Literature" includes publications not dealing with knapping. Use of these headings recognizes the fact that anyone involved with lithic technology is also a fractographer. Although the terms in the table are not always fully equivalent, the comparison will nevertheless cue the reader in at least approximately to what is meant by any term used.

Many of the fracture markings seen in obsidian are not manifested in other lithic materials such as chert or flint. This is indicated in Table 4.2, along with whether or not the markings can be observed by naked eye, without magnification, based on my personal experience.

The utility of fracture markings, in a generic sense, is noted in Table 4.3. In a broader sense the usefulness of a fracture marking depends on the objectives of a particular study. Table 4.4 indicates which fracture markings may provide clues to various items of interest.

The description and the formation mechanism of fracture markings are briefly noted in Table 4.5. The table does not explain the formation, but it will give the reader an idea of what is involved. The formation of the markings is considered further in the subsequent chapters.

Observations on fractures were made by naked eye, with hand lenses of 20X or lower magnification, and optical microscopy. A binocular microscope was used with 50X, 100X and occasionally 200X magnification. No surface coatings, such as gold, were used. A good discussion on preparation and observation of specimens appears in Quinn (2007).

Table 4.1 Fracture Markings Terminology

Ref. No.	Present Use	Literature on Knapping	Other Fractography Literature
1	**Hackle**	Hackle	Hackle
2	**Twist Hackle**	Twist hackle, hackle, fracture lance, striation, radial striation, fissure, shatter mark, shatter line, tear line	Twist hackle, hackle, hackle mark, shear hackle, lance, fracture lance, tear mark, striation, fracture step, river lines
3	**Tail (Wake Hackle)**	Tail, wake hackle, hackle, short hackle, fracture steps	Tail, wake hackle, wake, fracture step, short ridge, hackle
3a	**(Single) Tail**	Tail, wake hackle, hackle, short hackle	Tail, wake hackle, wake, fracture tail, fracture step, hackle
3b	**Parabolic Double Tails**	Parabolic double tails	Fracture parabola, conic marking, Kies figure
3c	**Multiple Tails**	Multiple Tails	(None)
4	**Hackle Scars**	Hackle scar	(None)
4a	**Bulbar Scar**	Bulbar scar, eraillure	(None)
4b	**Ripple Scar**	Ripple scar	(None)
4c	**Edge scar**	Edge scar	(None)
5	**Ripple**	Ripple, ripple mark, rib marking, compression wave, undulation, compression ring	Ripple, ripple mark, rib, rib marking, undulation, ribbing
5a	**Kinked Ripple**	(Probably included under terms for ripple)	Rib, rib mark, arrest line, dwell mark
5b	**Arrest Line**	(None)	Arrest line, dwell mark, rib, rib mark
6	**Wallner Line**	Wallner line, sometimes included under terms for ripple	Wallner Line

Ref. No.	Present Use	Literature on Knapping	Other Fractography Literature
6a	**Normal Wallner Line**	Normal Wallner Line	(None)
6a-1	**Gull Wings**	Gull Wings	Gull Wings
6b	**Anomalous Wallner Line**	Anomalous Wallner Line	(None)
6b-1	**Wallner Wake:**	Wallner Wake	(None)
Ref. No.	**Present Use**	Literature on Knapping	Other Fractography Literature
7	**Mirror**	Mirror, fracture mirror, mirror surface	Mirror, fracture mirror, mirror zone, polished fracture, polished area
8	**Mist**	Mist, frost, fine hackles	Mist, mist hackle, mist zone, frost, fine ridges, fine hackle, fine roughness (in German)
9	**Velocity Hackle**	Velocity hackle, hackle, coarse hackle	Velocity hackle, hackle, mist hackle, hackle zone, coarse hackle, rough hackle
10	**Incipient Branching**	Incipient Branching	(None)
11	**Branching**	Branching, bifurcation	Branching, crack branching, forking, velocity forking,, velocity branching,
12	**Wallner Mist-Hackle Configuration**	Wallner Mist-Hackle Configuration	(None)
13	**Mist Suppression Configuration**	Mist Suppression Configuration	(None)
14	**Mist Line**	Mist line	Streak
15	**Material Interface Markings**	Material Interface Markings	(None)

Ref. No.	Present Use	Literature on Knapping	Other Fractography Literature
15a	**Material Interface Hackle**	Material Interface Hackle	(None)
15b	**Material Interface Ridge**	Material Interface Ridge	(None)
15c	**Material Transition Ridge**	Material Transition Ridge	(None)
16	**Split Marks**	Split Marks	(None)
16a	**Split Step**	Split Step	(None)
16b	**Split Ridge**	Split Ridge	(None)
16c	**Split Ripple**	Split Ripple	(None)
17	**Dividing Line**	Dividing Line	(In German "Vereinigungslinie")
18	**Ruffles**	Ruffles	(None)

TABLE 4.2 OCCURRENCE OF FRACTURE MARKINGS

Ref. No.	Marking	Observable by Naked Eye	Obsidian	Flint
1	Hackle	Y	Y	Y
2	Twist Hackles	Y	Y	Y
3	Tail	Y	Y	Y
3a	(Single) Tail	Y	Y	Y
3b	Parabolic Double Tails	Y	Y	Y
3c	Multiple Tails	Y	Y	?
4	Hackle Scar	S	Y	Y
4a	Bulbar Scar	Y	Y	Y
4b	Ripple Scar	Y	Y	Y
4c	Edge scar	Y	Y	Y
5	Ripple	Y	Y	Y
5a	Kinked Ripple	Y	Y	Y
5b	Arrest Line	Y	Y	Y
6	Wallner Lines	S	Y	Y
6a	Normal Wallner Line	S	Y	Y
6a-1	Gull Wings	S	Y	N
6b	Anomalous Wallner Lines	S	Y	Y

Ref. No.	Marking	Observable by Naked Eye	Obsidian	Flint
6b-1	Wallner Wake	S	Y	N
7	Mirror	Y	Y	Y
8	Mist	S	Y	Y
9	Velocity Hackle	S	Y	Y
10	Incipient Branching	S	Y	S
11	Branching	Y	Y	Y
12	Wallner Mist-Hackle Configuration	N	Y	-
13	Mist Suppression Configuration	N	Y	N
14	Mist Line	N	Y	N?
15	Material Interface Markings	Y	Y	S
15a	Material Interface Hackle	Y	Y	S
15b	Material Interface Ridge	S	Y	Y
15c	Material Transition Ridge	S	Y	
16	Split Marks	Y	Y	Y
16a	Split Step	Y	Y	Y
16b	Split Ridge	Y	Y	Y
16c	Split Ripple	Y	Y	Y
17	Dividing Line	S	Y	Y
18	Ruffles	Y	Y	Y

TABLE 4.3 UTILITY OF FRACTURE MARKINGS

Ref. No.	Fracture Marking	Utility: Information that May Be Available
1	Hackle	FD (Fracture direction) usually. See exceptions in Table 4.5.
2	Twist Hackles	FD (Fracture direction) FFC (Fracture front configuration) RSD (Relative stress distribution)
3	Tails	FD, FFC, RSD
4	Hackle Scars	FD, indicates relatively higher regions that were removed
5	Ripple	FD, FFC, RSD
5a	Kinked Ripple	Abrupt change in direction of maximum tension along fracture profile
5b	Arrest Line	Abrupt change in direction of maximum tension along fracture profile

Ref. No.	Fracture Marking	Utility: Information that May Be Available
6	Wallner Lines	FD, FFC, RSD, Relative fracture velocity V_F/V_S
6a	Normal Wallner Lines	Stress pulse source at fracture front. V_F/V_S
6a-1	Gull Wings	V_F/V_S
6b	Anomalous Wallner Lines	V_F/V_S
6b-1	Wallner Wake	V_F/V_S
7	Mirror	V_F below practical maximum
8	Mist	V_F near practical maximum
9	Velocity Hackle	V_F near practical maximum
10	Incipient Branching	High stress. State of stress.
11	Branching	V_F at practical maximum
12	Wallner Mist-Hackle Configuration	FD, precursor to general mist region, High V_F
13	Mist Suppression Configuration	An obstruction in fracture path.
14	Mist Line	FD, precursor to general mist region, High V_F
15	Material Interface Markings	Material inhomogeneity, Relative values of material properties
15a	Material Interface Hackle	Relative values of material properties
15b	Material Interface Ridge	Relative values of material properties
15c	Material Transition Ridge	Relative values of material properties
16	Split Marks	On negative flake scar: That the flake was split
16a	Split Step	FD
16b	Split Ridge	FD
16c	Split Ripple	FD
17	Dividing Line	Two independent fracture origins involved
18	Ruffles	On negative flake scar: Had numerous irregularities at flake outer surface

Table 4.4 Clues from Fracture Markings

No.	Item of Interest	Markings May Give Clues
1	Fracture origin	Gull wings and other ripples, twist hackles, tails, mist, velocity hackle, mist lines
2	Fracture direction	(as for Item 1)
3	Fracture front configuration	(as for Item 1)
4	Fracture arrest	Kinked ripples, arrest lines (a misnomer)
5	Extremely high V_F	Mist, velocity hackle, branching
6	Qualitative V_F	(as for Item 1)
7	Quantitative V_F	Gull wings and other Wallner lines
8	Stress patterns	(as for Item 1)
9	Strength & fracture toughness	Mist, velocity hackle, branching
10	Kinds of external forces applied	(as for Item 1)
11	Flake geometry	Ripples, twist hackle configurations

Table 4.5 A Catalogue of Fracture Markings

Ref. No.	Fracture Marking	Description and Formation
1	Hackle	A linear feature in fracture plan, manifested when two partial fracture fronts overlap or form a step. Due to rotation in the direction of the maximum tension about a line in the fracture direction (Mode III participation).
2	Twist Hackle	A hackle in the fracture direction. Due to effects other than those from liquid or material interfaces.
3	Tail (Wake Hackle)	The surface mismatch of this hackle is produced by a fracture front passing around, through or partly through an inclusion or other irregularity. May persist over considerable distance as a twist hackle. Closer and closer to a general mist region, a tail has a trailing mist line and is then completely replaced by a mist line.
3a	(Single) Tail	A tail with a single linear feature, associated with a single surface mismatch of two partial fractures.
3b	Parabolic Double Tails	Two tails extending downstream from the same irregularity, associated with two surface mismatches of three partial fracture fronts.
3c	Multiple Tails	Three or more tails extending downstream from the same irregularity, associated with three or more surface mismatches of four or more partial fracture fronts.
4	Hackle Scars	From an extended lateral breakthrough to one side of the twist hackle.
4a	Bulbar Scar	A hackle scar on the bulb of a flake. Often round, resembling a circle or an oval in fracture plan
4b	Ripple Scar	A hackle scar associated with the higher contour of a pronounced ripple.

Ref. No.	Fracture Marking	Description and Formation
4c	Edge Scars	Hackle scars associated with the higher contour (the ridge) between two flake scars.
5	Ripple	A line or band in fracture plan, usually curved and usually convex in fracture direction. Localized slope change in fracture profile due to the direction of maximum tension rotating about a line parallel to fracture front.
5a	Kinked Ripple	A ripple with an abrupt slope change (a kink) in fracture profile, due to change in the direction of maximum tension.
5b	Arrest Line (a misnomer)	A ripple with an abrupt slope change (kink) in fracture profile. It may or may not represent an actual arrest of the fracture.
6	Wallner Lines	A ripple due to a stress pulse. Its configuration in fracture plan is from the intersection of the stress pulse and the fracture front at successive time instants.
6a	Normal Wallner Line	Having the stress pulse source at the fracture front.
6a-1	Gull Wings	A pair of normal Wallner lines appearing as wings.
6b	Anomalous Wallner Line	Having the stress source away from the fracture front.
6b-1	Wallner Wake	An anomalous Wallner line with a stress pulse source behind the fracture front. At the center portion it is concave in the fracture direction.
7	Mirror (Mirror Region)	An optically smooth region between the fracture origin and the mist region.
8	Mist (Mist Region)	It is between the mirror and a hackle region, Has fine surface roughness. In obsidian, it has a dull misty or frosty appearance. In crystalline materials such as flint and chert, it is characterized by a surface roughness less pronounced than in a hackle region. The surface roughness increases gradually from a mirror to branching
9	Velocity Hackle (Hackle Region)	It has a more pronounced surface roughness than mist. The regular primary fracture front tends to lose its meaning, with fingerlets advancing and interacting. Dynamic interaction of the surface irregularities is a key element in the formation of the hackle as well as mist. When viewed by naked eye or at low magnification, a hackle region in obsidian appears shiny and irregular.
10	Incipient Branching	Incomplete macroscopic branching.
11	Branching	Macroscopic forking of a fracture into two.
12	Wallner Mist-Hackle Configuration	A localized enhancement or manifestation of mist, hackle or both caused by a stress pulse.
13	Mist Suppression Configuration	A band with localized mist suppression or paucity due to an obstruction at a fracture front.
14	Mist Line	A narrow band of mist, hackle or their combination extending in fracture direction. Occurring in a region where the conditions are almost "ripe" for mist in general

Ref. No.	Fracture Marking	Description and Formation
15	Material Interface Markings	Markings manifested at the interface of two materials having different mechanical properties.
15a	Material Interface Hackle	A hackle initiated at and extending along a material interface which is approximately in the fracture direction.
15b	Material Interface Ridge	A ridge or escarpment extending along a material interface
15c	Material Transition Ridge	A ridge or an escarpment along a material interface that is roughly parallel to a fracture front, due to different material properties encountered along a fracture path crossing the interface.
16	Split Marks	Due to the secondary fracture front of flake splitting trying to catch up with the primary fracture front during flake detachment. The fractures of the split parts tend to propagate independently.
16a	Split Step	A split mark manifested as a step along the split line, with each flake part having a different thickness at the step location.
16b	Split Ridge	A split mark formed with the fractures for the two flake parts near the split location propagating along different, partly overlapping surfaces in the distal region.
16c	Split Ripple	A split mark manifested as a ripple on a negative flake scar stopping abruptly or having an irregularity at the split line.
17	Dividing Line	A line where the two fracture fronts of two independent fractures meet.
18	Ruffles (Ruffled Surface)	Numerous irregular dimples, humps and multi-directional undulations. Due to "erratic" directional changes in the maximum tensile stress directions caused by the roughness of flake outer surface.

5. Hackles and Hackle Scars

Twist hackles and **tails** (Fig. 5.1) are linear markings on a fracture surface manifested due to overlapping of two partial fracture surfaces. They are in the fracture direction in their vicinity. Material interface hackles, partition hackles and hackle scarps (Chapter 8) are usually not.

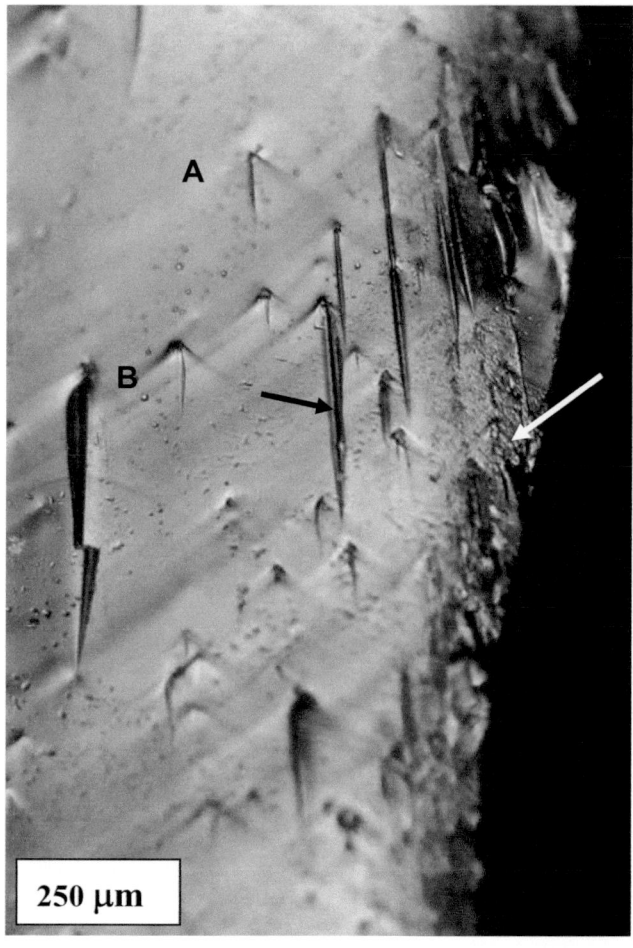

FIG. 5.1 TAILS (AS AT A AND B) AND TWIST HACKLES AS PERSISTENT TAILS (BLACK ARROW) IN OBSIDIAN. THE MIST AND HACKLE AT THE RIGHT (WHITE ARROW) IS AT THE LIP OF A BIFACE THINNING FLAKE. THE GULL WINGS INDICATE A VERY HIGH FRACTURE VELOCITY. AT B, THE APPROXIMATE V_F/V_S = 0.616 AND V_F = 2,200 M/S FOR ASSUMED V_S =3,500 M/S FOR THIS OBSIDIAN. THE FRACTURE DIRECTION ADJACENT TO THE LIP IS ROUGHLY PARALLEL TO IT, DOWNWARD HERE.

64 FRACTURES IN KNAPPING

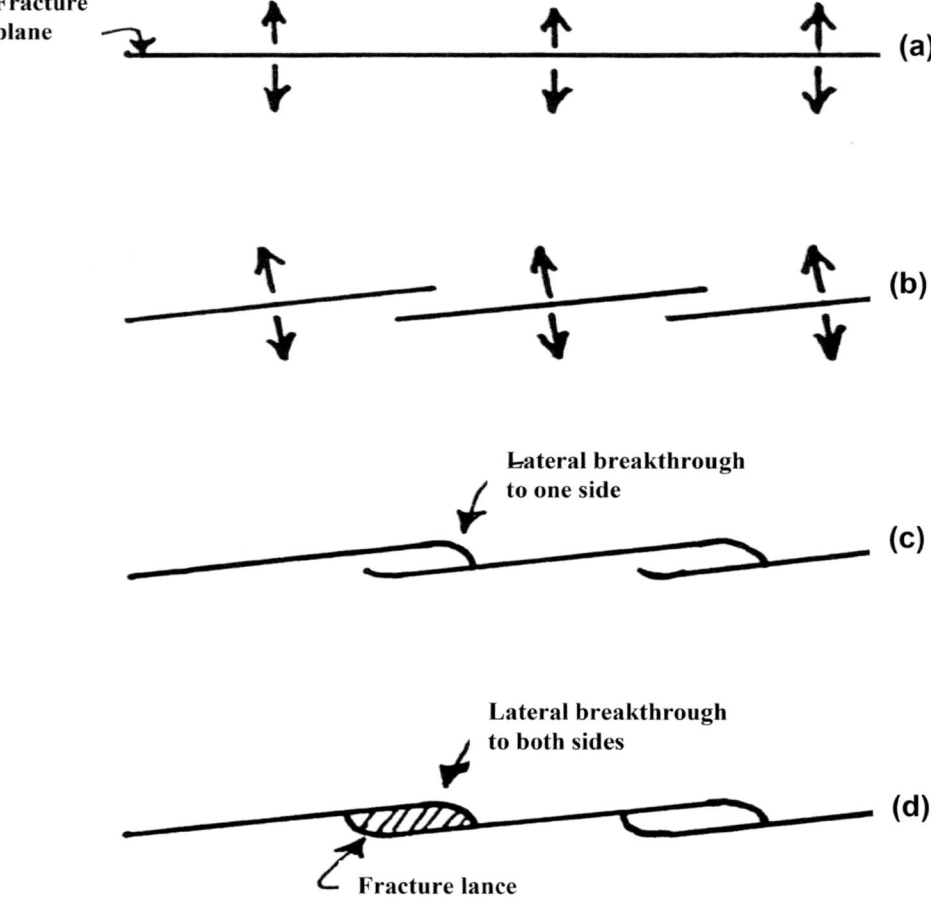

FIG. 5.2 FORMATION OF TWIST HACKLES   Adapted from Fréchette (1990)

The term "hackle", with the meaning velocity hackle, however, is also used for very different fracture markings, namely the hackle of a hackle region. This unfortunate ambiguity, having a long tradition in fractography, can be eliminated by the context or by using instead the terms "velocity hackle" and "twist hackle".

Twist Hackles and Single Tails

A **twist hackle** is a hackle with the overlapping of partial fracture surfaces caused by rotation of the direction of the maximum tensile stress about an axis in the fracture direction. The formation of twist hackles is illustrated in Fig. 5.2, with the fracture running into the paper. When the direction of the maximum tensile stress rotates as from (a) to (b) in the figure, the fracture surface makes a piecewise adjustment to this change to develop the overlapping partial fracture surfaces in (b). As seen in (b), the parts of the specimen to the sides of each partial fracture are not completely separated yet. They are

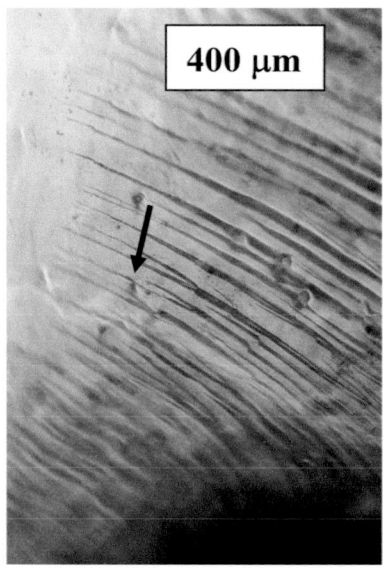 

FIG. 5.3 TWIST HACKLES AT THE EDGE OF AN OBSIDIAN FLAKE. A NUMBER OF SMALLER ONES ARE SEEN TO MERGE INTO A LARGER ONE, AS AT THE ARROW. FRACTURE DIRECTION IS DOWNWARD TO THE RIGHT.

FIG. 5.4 TWIST HACKLES AT AND NEAR THE EDGE OF A BIFACE THINNING FLAKE OF A FINE VARIETY OF NORMANSKILL CHERT. THE GENERAL FRACTURE DIRECTION FOR THE FLAKE WAS DOWNWARD.

still connected by the unbroken ligaments. As the specimen surfaces separate, one or both of these ligaments are broken by lateral breakthroughs to one side as in (c), or in both directions as in (d). In the latter case, **fracture lances** are separated from the fracture surfaces. The lateral breakthroughs occur behind the main fracture front. Some lateral breakthroughs, as to the second side in (d), can occur significantly later, occasionally evidenced by the tinkle heard long after the fracture has been completed (Fréchette 1990: 23). Such a delay relates to the effects of moisture in the presence of the remaining stress. Significant lateral extension may occur with the lateral breakthroughs, as in the case of bulbar scars and other hackle scars on flakes.

The lateral breakthroughs may occur to one side and then, further downstream, to the other side. Such alternate breakthroughs, common to many twist hackles and tails, are manifested as a "flip-flop" in the appearance of the hackles in fracture plan (Fig. 5.1).

Smaller twist hackles may run into a larger one (Fig. 5.3) or diverge from it during later stages, in analogy to river tributaries and deltas, respectively (Fréchette 1990: 23; Hull 1999: 93). The terms "river lines" and "river pattern" are sometimes used for such twist hackle patterns (Bahat 1991; Fréchette 1972, 1984; Hull 1999: 89-119). The noted analogy

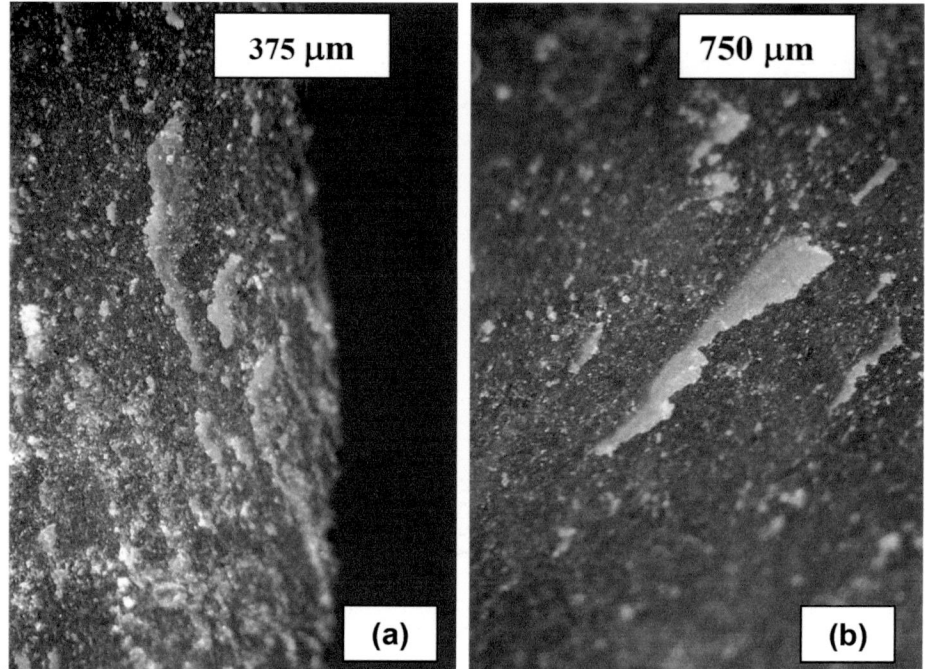

FIG. 5.5 TWIST HACKLES AND INCIPIENT TWIST HACKLES IN A COARSE VARIETY OF NORMANSKILL CHERT. THE CHARACTERISTICS OF THESE MARKINGS ARE INFLUENCED BY THEIR ANGLE WITH THE GENERAL FRACTURE DIRECTION (DOWNWARD HERE) FOR THE FLAKE, AS WELL AS THE SIZE AND NATURE OF THE CRYSTALS. THE COARSER NATURE OF THIS CHERT IS APPARENT FROM A COMPARISON WITH FIG. 5.4.

poses the question regarding the sense of fracture direction parallel to a twist hackle. There are at least two kinds of clues. Firstly, twist hackles are often (usually in obsidian) seen in the context of tails as premature manifestations. In such cases, the presence of the inclusion or other irregularity at the upstream end provides the evidence. Secondly, there are clues from the details of the "tributaries" and "deltas" noted. With "tributaries" there is a greater tendency for them to be normal to the "river", and at "deltas" there is the tendency for the angle between the individual branches to initially increase with distance (Fréchette 1990: 23-24).

In flaking, the lagging of a fracture front contributes to mode III participation. This is at least partly due to the axial or in-plane effect from the forces applied. Twist hackles occur usually at the feathered edges of a flake, where the fracture front is lagging. On a flake with an unsymmetrical cross-section, they are manifested further upstream at the thinner edge (Dauvois 1976, Tsirk 1981). When the fracture front is lagging near the central portion of a flake where it is thinner, twist hackles are occasionally also manifested there.

Twist hackles, along with ripples and tails, are among the most frequent fracture markings, common to obsidian, flint, chert and other materials. The finest ones are manifested only in

FIG. 5.6 TWIST HACKLES (ARROW) AND INCIPIENT TWIST HACKLES (ESPECIALLY IN B) IN ESOPUS CHERT.

obsidian and other glasses. Large ones occur even in coarse-grained rocks, as in sandstone (Fréchette 1990: Fig. 1-1). In flint and chert, for example, regions can be observed with what may be viewed as **incipient twist hackle** manifestation, due to the crystalline nature of those materials. These relate to the irregularities at the crystals, sometimes together with some fracture mode III presence, that enabled the sporadic manifestation of the short features without their persistence as twist hackles. In flint, chert and other crystalline materials, twist hackles are often manifested with an appearance different from obsidian.

The formation of a twist hackle often leads to a highly localized lagging of the fracture front in its vicinity. This relates to the reduction of stress due to the locally increased compliance and the greater energy demands locally for the formation of the two overlapping fracture surfaces.

Twist hackles are frequently encountered in various knapping contexts as well as in use-chipping. They can be due to the external forces applied, as well as geometrical or other effects (Hull 1999: 89-90) in a global or local sense. Occasionally a family of twist hackles is seen with their upstream ends lined up, corresponding to the arrival of a stress pulse. As seen from Figs. 5.4 to 5.6, the lateral breakthroughs in crystalline materials like chert may resemble steps.

Twist hackles are indicators of fracture direction as well as the fracture front configuration perpendicular to them. For curved twist hackles, the fracture velocity is greater on their

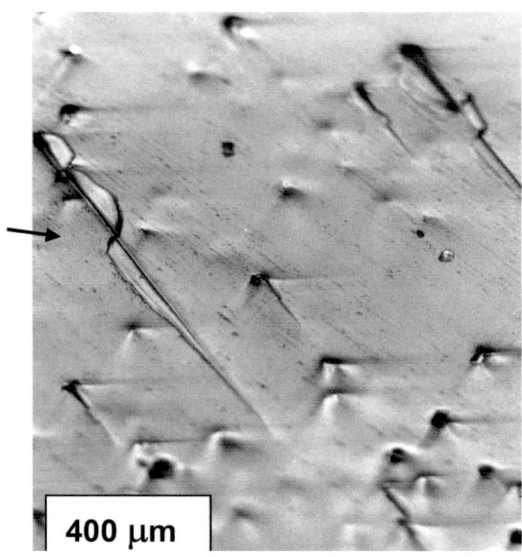

Fig. 5.7 Tails in obsidian often persist as twist hackle. The "flip-flop" by the arrow is due to the lateral breakthrough to one and then the other side. The fracture direction was downward.

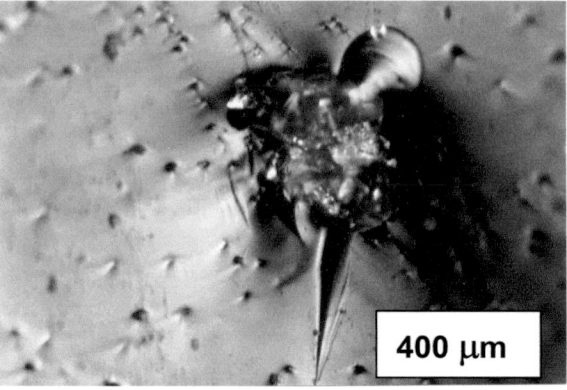

Fig. 5.8 Tails at irregular inclusions in obsidian, formed by the fracture passing around and through the inclusion.

convex side, as noted in Faulkner (1972). Parallel or divergent twist hackles indicate fracture fronts that are straight or concave upstream, respectively. The configuration of the fracture front provides clues to the location of the fracture origin, the relative fracture velocities and stress distributions involved with the fracture. Extremely pronounced twist hackles are thought by some to be an indication of a "high energy fracture" or "shock", as an impact from excessive percussion in knapping. The differences in the characteristics of the manifestation of twist hackles in finer as opposed to coarser cherts can suggest the quality of the raw material involved – that is, fine vs. coarse-grained.

Subsequent to the pioneering efforts of Kies, Sullivan and Irwin (1950), as well as Leeuwerik and Schwarzl (1955), the research by Sommer (1969) was most significant. In his experiments with a glass he showed that the twist hackles were normal to the fracture fronts and that they were formed when the direction of the maximum tensile stress rotated about 3.3 degrees. Twist hackles were first explained in a knapping context in Kerkhof and Müller-Beck (1969), and discussed later by Faulkner (1972). Enlightening discussion related to the terms "river line patterns", "level difference lines" and "steps" is presented by Hull (1999: Chapter 4).

A **tail**, also known as a **wake hackle**, is a hackle with the surface mismatch and overlapping of partial fracture surfaces due to the encounter of the fracture front with an inclusion or other irregularity (Fig. 5.7). This surface mismatch can occur when a fracture passes around, through or partly through an inclusion or other irregularity (Fig. 5.8, and Figs. 1 to 4 in Tsirk 1996). An inclusion may consist of some crystal(s) with preferred plane(s) of cleavage that are not parallel to the fracture plane upstream of it.

Tails or wake hackles are usually very short, but often persist for considerable distances as twist hackles due to the presence of some mode III environment unrelated to the irregularities where the markings originate. Some twist hackles may be viewed as persistent tails or twist hackles with premature manifestation due to irregularities.

A tail, just as a twist hackle, is an indicator of the fracture direction and fracture front in its vicinity, and provides clues to the location of the fracture origin, as well as the relative fracture velocities and stress distributions during the fracture, Single as well as double tails have trailing mist lines within or near general mist regions.

Evidence for the fracture direction is clear from the twist hackles and tails in obsidian, as those in Figs. 5.1. For chert, such evidence is often not clear, especially when the markings are manifested away from a flake edge. To facilitate the recognition of the useful features of twist hackles and the use of the markings as evidence for directionality, it is best to start by observing the markings at the edges of chert flakes.

Multiple Tails

A single inclusion may be associated with more than one tail. **Multiple tails** are linear markings in the fracture direction that are associated with multiple surface mismatches and multiple overlapping of partial fracture surfaces, due to the fracture front encountering an inclusion or other irregularity. They are manifested frequently in obsidians, more so close to general mist regions.

The formation of multiple tails can be understood by recognizing that a surface mismatch can occur when a fracture passes through or partly through an inclusion. With the complex and polycrystalline inclusions encountered in obsidians, multiple surface mismatches should be expected as indeed have been observed (Tsirk 1996: Fig. 1c). Not surprising is the observation of multiple tails in some but not all obsidians. This relates partly to the characteristics of the inclusions or irregularities encountered, but perhaps occasionally also to the nature of the highly localized residual stresses.

Parabolic Double Tails

A double tail may be viewed as a special case of multiple tails. Thus, a **double tail** is associated with two surface mismatches and three partial fracture surfaces produced when a fracture front encounters an inclusion or other irregularity. Some double tails are seen in Tsirk (1996). They often resemble parabolas, as in Fig. 5.9 to 5.11. Occasionally, the arms of a double tail may converge, sometimes having a single trailing mist line (Fig. 5.12).

In knapping context, these markings have only been seen in obsidian and industrial glass. Although they are usually microscopic, very large ones have also been observed in knapping, as those in Fig. 5.10 on a large, thick obsidian flake produced by hardhammer percussion, from a nodule with a very rounded striking platform. The latter rare case is for the markings on a surface of a flake produced in knapping. Parabolic double tails are very common with accidental breakages near general mist regions. Sometimes they can also be seen near or within a mist region by the lip of a bending initiation for a flake (Fig. 5.1).

With the numerous double tails observed in obsidian, there is an inclusion at the head that enabled a partial fracture front to propagate out of the primary fracture plane (Fig. 5.9). Most commonly a double tail is formed with the fracture passing through an inclusion and onto a different plane, which may be tilted or twisted (Fig. 5.9), to form the central partial fracture front. Some large double tails associated with pores in an industrial glass known as "copper ruby" were observed by Silsby.

Some double tails appear with pronounced shoulders, having trailing mist lines (Fig. 5.9a and b) or lines of recurrent hackle (Fig. 5.9c) extending as "arms" from them near general mist regions. Double tails further away from the general mist regions do not have the trailing mist lines. This is also true of single tails. The arms of double tails very close to or within general mist regions may consist entirely of mist lines as in Fig. 5.10. The usual kinds of double tails resembling fracture parabolas occur most commonly in regions close to a general mist region.

In fracture plan, double tails with trailing mist lines can manifest various configurations (Fig. 5.9). In general mist regions, double tails are conspicuous by the absence or paucity of mist in their central region. A reason for this is discussed in Beauchamp (1996).

There is an interesting resemblance of the double tails discussed to the fracture markings known as Kies markings (Fréchette 1990), conic lines (Andrews 1968) and fracture parabolas and related markings (Kerkhof 1970, Kies, Sullivan and Irwin 1950). In less brittle materials such as plexiglass, known as PMMA (polymethylmethacrilate), secondary fracturing is clearly seen to start at an irregularity ahead of the primary fracture front and propagate backwards within the matrix to form fracture parabolas and related markings as

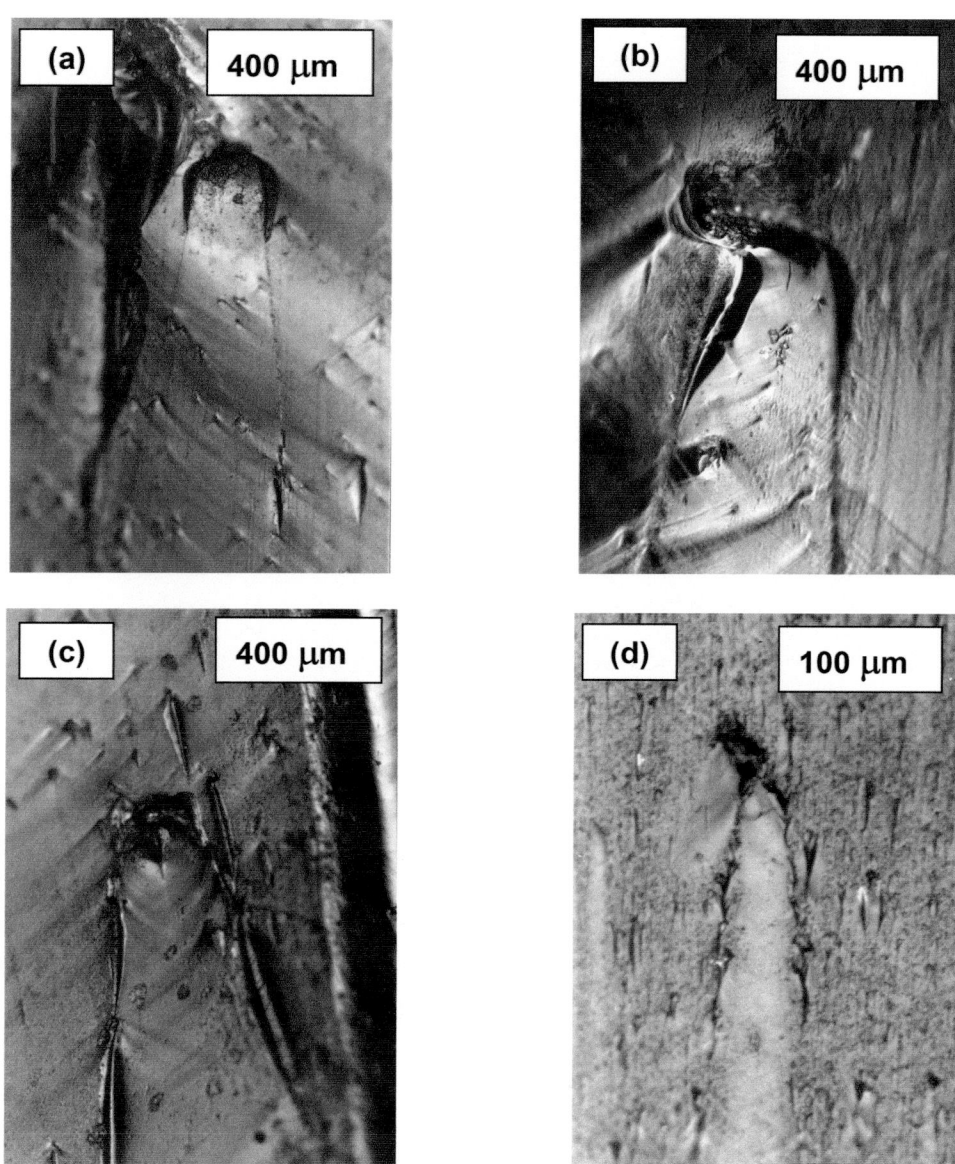

Fig. 5.9 Parabolic double tails, formed as the fracture passes through the inclusion at its head, onto a different plane. Note the third tail in (c). Obsidian. Fracture direction downward.

the primary and secondary fractures meet with a surface mismatch (Fig. 2-35 in Fréchette 1990 for PMMA, and Fig. 7.12 in Kerkhof 1970 for araldite). This, however, is not the mechanism for the double tails observed in obsidian. It is relevant that the modulus of elasticity for plexiglass is very low compared to glasses.

72   FRACTURES IN KNAPPING

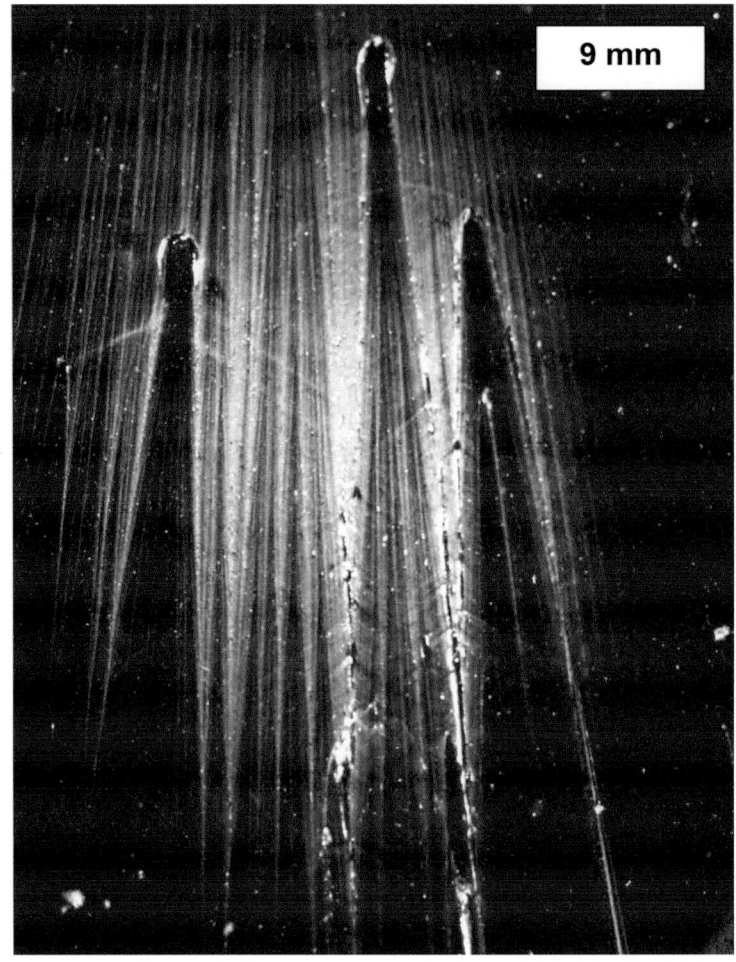

IG. 5.10 PARABOLIC DOUBLE TAILS AND MANY MIST LINES ON THE SURFACE OF A FLAKE. GLASS BUTTES OBSIDIAN. FRACTURE DIRECTION DOWNWARD. (PHOTO BY V.D. FRÉCHETTE; FROM TSIRK 1996)

More intriguing is the resemblance of the double tails to the markings termed fracture parabolas and related markings reported for industrial glass in Kerkhof (1970: Figs 7.10 and 7.11). These very small markings, shown in the cited reference at a magnifications of 890x, each resemble a double tail with mist lines appearing to extend from an inclusion at its head. Surprisingly, the same mechanism discussed for PMMA is ascribed to the formation of these markings by Kerkhof. I have observed a secondary fracture starting ahead of the primary fracture front, and the propagation backwards through the matrix, on a cleavage plane in slate but not in obsidian, flint and similar materials.

The concave side of a double tail configuration is always downstream, with the bisector indicating the general fracture direction in the vicinity of the marking.

Fig. 5.11 Parabolic double tails in a mist region. The fracture in the Jemez Mountains obsidian was caused by a forest fire at an archaeological site (Steffen 2005).

Hackle Scars

Hackle Scar and Hackle Flake

Bulbar scars, also known as éraillures, are among the most common features on illustrations of a flake in archaeological literature. But in terms of the formation mechanism involved, similar features occur also in other contexts in knapping, accidental breakage and use-chipping. The terms "hackle scars" and associated "hackle flakes" are used here for all such features. Bulbar scars have been investigated by Faulkner (1974).

A hackle scar is associated with a twist hackle. Its initiation can be understood as an attempt for the lateral breakthrough of the unbroken ligament associated with the overlapping partial fractures (Fig. 5.2). For the fracture surfaces to be able to separate, some kind of breakthrough must occur. For a piece called a fracture lance to separate, there must be a breakthrough to two sides (Fig. 5.2d).

A **hackle scar** and the associated **hackle flake** are from a secondary fracture due to extended lateral breakthrough of a twist hackle, usually by locally higher contours. This extended fracture propagation occurs behind a fracture front. It has been observed to occasionally break up an inclusion behind the fracture front where the wake hackle (tail) originated (Fréchette, personal communication, 1996).

Bulbar Scar and Proximal Scar

Bulbar scars are associated with the higher contours at or upstream of the bulbar region of a flake. Scars occurring upstream of the bulbar region are here referred to as **proximal scars**. Proximal scars may occasionally extend to the platform of a flake. These should not be confused with the chip scars from the contact of a flaker with the platform near its

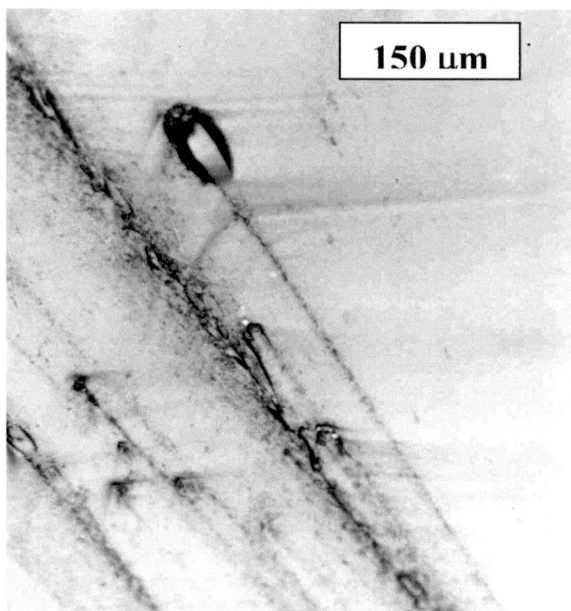

FIG.5.12 CONVERGENT TAILS WITH TRAILING MIST LINE.
OBSIDIAN. FRACTURE DIRECTION DOWNWARD.

edge. Occasionally, two oblique bulbar or proximal scars from opposing sides may run together, sometimes with a noticeable dividing line, and extend subsequently as a single one in downstream direction. It is well known to knappers that a flake tends to follow ridges and other higher contours. This tendency is also present with hackle scars and is seen often with bulbar scars. The latter always initiate in a direction normal to a twist hackle, but may subsequently turn and extend in a different direction. Even 90 degree turns are seen. Wing flakes are seen as special kinds of hackle flakes associated with proximal scars.

Ripple Scars

Hackle scars are sometimes manifested in other than the proximal or bulbar regions of a flake. Hackle flakes and scars, termed **ripple scars**, have been observed at pronounced ripples in the distal portion of a flake. Hackle scars often occur also on accidental breakages.

Ridge Scars

When a flake is detached, as from a core or a biface, ridges are normally left at the edges of the flake scar. When twist hackles occur at these edges, hackle scars extending along the ridge in the downstream direction (on the flake scar) are frequently manifested. These **ridge scars** or **edge scars** (Fig. 5.13), usually very minute but easily visible in obsidian and fine-grained chert, may occur during the removal of large percussion flakes as well as small pressure flakes.

More on Hackle Scar Formation

Why is there extended fracture propagation of the lateral breakthrough that enables hackle scars to form? After all, fracture lances also involve a two-directional breakthrough, but with relatively little fracture extension in the lateral direction. Fracture lances may be viewed as very short hackle flakes. As a secondary fracture extends during the breakthrough to form a fracture lance (Fig. 5.2d), the path of the fracture furthest from the twist hackle makes a sharp turn close to the unbroken ligament at the twist hackle. For the secondary fracturing, there is a significant directional change with fracture lances. But with the secondary fracture tending to run straight in the case of the longer hackle flakes, such a directional change is avoided. The difference must relate to the forces applied at the unbroken ligament in the two cases. The directionality noted can be achieved by a compressive force in the direction of the hackle scar extension. The presence of such compression is seen here to be a necessary condition for the formation of long hackle scars. In a partly detached flake, there is compression in its longitudinal direction. Some of this compression is transferred to the partly detached portion of the hackle scar through the unbroken ligament. This can be understood easily when a twist hackle is transverse or oblique to the long axis of the flake. When a twist hackle extends in the direction of the flake axis, with the lateral breakthrough extending normal to it, the source of the compression needed for the long hackle scar to form is uncertain. It may perhaps come from the Poisson's effect.

Most hackle scars have a feathered termination, but some bulbar scars with a step, hinge and even overshot termination are manifested as well (Fig. 5.14). Occasionally, a bulbar scar can be seen with a very intrusive hinge termination. These appear to transition sometimes to popout fractures. With the usual scales of interest in knapping, twist hackles and hence hackle scars are less likely to be manifested with very coarse materials.

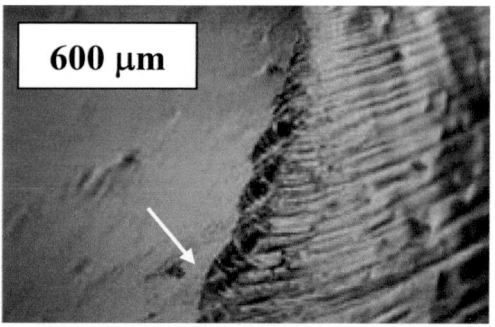

FIG. 5.13 HACKLE SCARS AT THE EDGE OF AN OBSIDIAN FLAKE. ON THE LEFT PORTIONS OF THE FIGURE, THE FRACTURE DIRECTION WAS DOWNWARD.

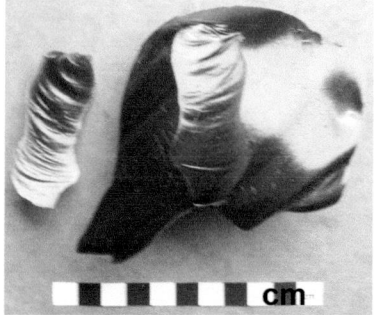

FIG. 5.14 AN OVERSHOT HACKLE FLAKE AND ITS SCAR ON AN OBSIDIAN FLAKE.

6. Ripples

Ripples

A **ripple** or **rib mark** is a more or less regular, curved line or band in fracture plan associated with a change of slope in fracture profile. It is due to the direction of the maximum tensile stress ahead of the fracture front rotating about an axis parallel to the front (Kerkhof and Müller-Beck 1969). That is, it is due to a contribution from fracture mode II (Chapter 9).

The changes in stress causing the manifestation of a ripple are illustrated schematically in Fig. 6.1. In part (a) of the figure, the fracture profile of a ripple is shown with the normals (arrows) to the fracture surface. The fracture direction is downward in (a). The arrows are the directions of the maximum tensile stress. Part (b) shows the sense of the rotations of the normals (maximum tensile stress directions) along the profile, at first counterclockwise (ccw), then clockwise (cw) and finally again ccw. Part (c) shows the sense of fracture mode II contributions causing the directional change in stress. The shear stresses from the mode II contribution are indicated in (d), together with the direction of the tensile stress due to those shear stresses. The directions of the total tensile stress, on which the ripple formation depends, must be between those in (d) and the directions in (a). The variations in shear stress τ (tau) over time, responsible for the ripple manifestation, are shown schematically in (f). In (e) the sections of the curve responsible for the respective changes depicted in (b), (c) and (d) are noted.

The fracture profile in Fig. 6.2a is most common for ripples. This and other fracture profiles can be associated with various changes in shear stress over time. The schematic

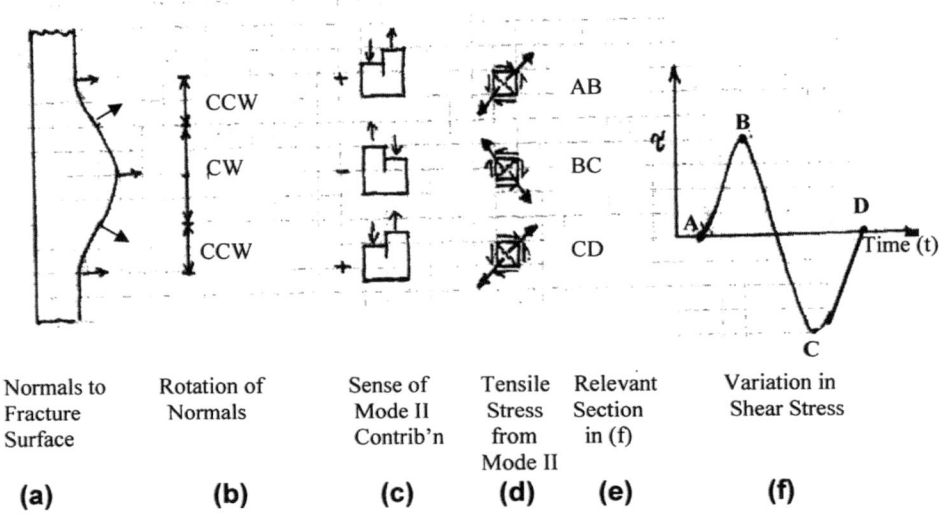

FIG. 6.1 STRESS CHANGES ASSOCIATED WITH RIPPLE FORMATION

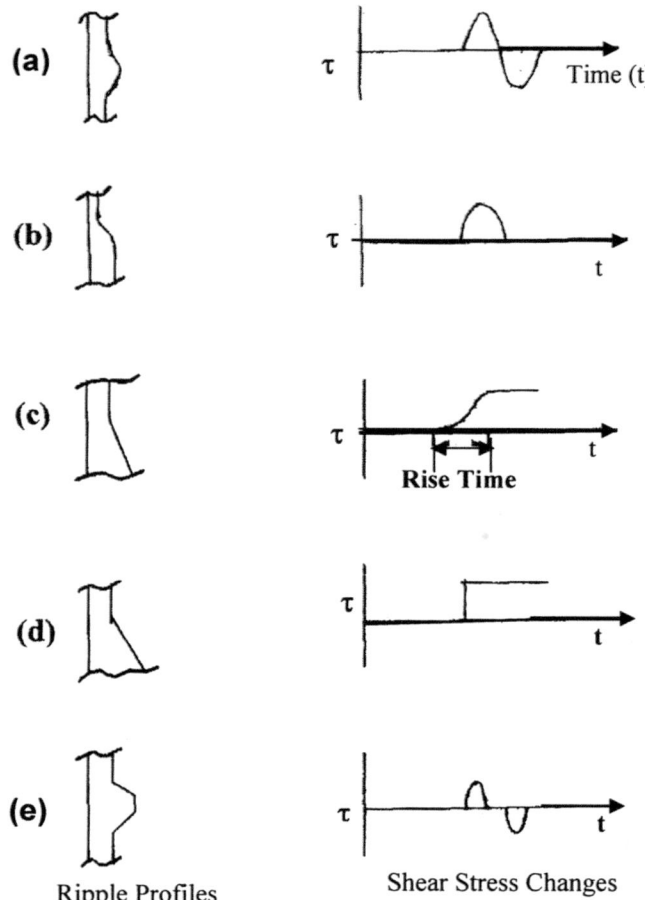

FIG. 6.2 RIPPLE PROFILES AND ASSOCIATED CHANGES IN SHEAR STRESS.

Fig. 6.2 relates the general characteristics of the ripple profiles to the associated stress changes from mode II. They also serve to clarify the meaning of abruptness in a fracture profile and a stress change. The fracture profile clearly relates to both the fracture velocity and the time for the stress change. The abruptness is best thought of in terms of changes along a fracture path rather than over time, especially when a fracture is advancing very slowly or has stopped.

The stress change in (d) is not expected in usual knapping or even in ordinary industrial contexts of fracture, because an instantaneous change in shear stress is not likely in such cases. It can occur, however, with the sudden arrival of a stress pulse and also with a fracture propagating very slowly or if it has stopped. The manifestation of the stress changes in (c) and (d) would look alike for small rise times. In both such cases, the fracture profile would have a kink.

Ripples are meant here to include cavitation scarps due to liquids (Chapter 8), so-called arrest lines, Wallner lines and other ripples considered in this chapter. Scarps other than the cavitation scarp are not included among ripples. Because of their characteristics in fracture plan, ruffles as well as material interface and transition ridges are not included as well.

In fracture plan, ripples may extend across a whole fracture surface or vanish gradually along their length. There may be great variations in the amplitude, width and spacing of the ripples along the fracture path.

Ripples are usually not parallel, not even approximately, to fracture fronts. They are usually concave in the upstream direction, towards the fracture origin. But when the fracture front itself is locally concave in the downstream direction, then so can be the ripples. Such cases can occur due to flake cross-sectional geometry, material inhomogeneity, residual stresses, certain stress wave reflections and, for extremely slow fractures, moisture or liquid effects. Even when the fracture front is concave in the upstream direction, Wallner lines completely concave in the downstream direction are often encountered in the form of Wallner wakes.

The manifestation of ripples depends on the grain size of a material in relation to the characteristic dimensions of the markings. The smallest amplitude of ripples manifested would increase from obsidian to fine grained flints to coarse cherts to sandstone. For the materials of interest to knapping, the finest ripples are seen only in obsidian. Yet very large ripples, measuring tens of meters in fracture plan, are found on sandstone.

It is interesting to observe ripples even on floor slate fractured along a cleavage plane. Not surprisingly, the ripples appear flattened, with a large width to amplitude ratio. The effect of material anisotropy on ripple manifestation can also be observed, for example, in a metarhyolite from Pennsylvania.

Ripples without kinks are among the most common markings on the fracture surfaces produced in knapping, accidental breakage and use-chipping. Some of these may provide clues to the approximate nature of the fracture fronts and directions, the relative stress distributions associated with the production of the fracture, the location of the fracture origin, transverse thickness variations of a flake, relative fracture velocities and material properties, the presence of residual stresses, and the nature of the stress pulses or other stress waves that may have been involved.

Ripples with kinks (**kinked ripples**) are occasionally encountered in knapping, accidental breakage and use-chipping. They may extend across a whole fracture surface, vanish along their length, or revert to a ripple without a kink. An **arrest line,** also known as a dwell mark, is a kinked ripple. The term has traditionally been used as a misnomer. Just as kinked ripples in general, an arrest line may or may not be associated with actual fracture arrest. If an arrest did in fact occur, its duration may have been a fraction of a millisecond, as in some accidental breakages, or it may be months or years, as in geological fractures. Fracture arrest may occasionally occur with no arrest line manifested, when there is no change in the direction of the maximum tensile stress during the arrest.

For actual fracture arrest, an arrest line does not in general represent the fracture front immediately before or after the arrest. Evidence for this is the fact that the directionality indicators twist hackles and tails just upstream or downstream of an arrest line are sometimes not normal to an arrest line. This is understood by the fact that a fracture in general does not stop or restart at the same instant of time all along a fracture front. This is because the stress intensity factor in general varies along a front.

Arrest lines corresponding to fracture arrest are manifested in obsidian, flint, chert and other materials. They occur in the context of knapping, including accidental breakage, as well as use-chipping. However, an arrest line corresponding to actual arrest can never be distinguished from other kinked ripples by its appearance alone. The identification may be made only sometimes by its context. For example, suppose that in flaking a second blow is needed to remove a flake already partly detached. A kinked ripple manifested in the proximal part of this flake would correspond to the arrest known to have occurred.

When a thick flake is removed from a core with a large edge angle using a hard hammerstone (or a steel hammer), a ripple configuration resembling a **stepped cone** in fracture profile is sometimes manifested. The edge of each step is a kinked ripple, probably corresponding to actual fracture arrest. The kinked ripples on the cone-like feature resemble partial concentric rings in fracture plan. Instead of a stepped cone, it is more common to see just ripples without a kink in such context. The cone-like features with ripples are due to the vibration of the partly detached flake caused by the impact from the flaking implement.

On flint nodules broken in geological contexts, ripples resembling concentric rings are sometimes manifested on what are called "frost fractures" (Beuker 1983: 80-81). These ripples may be with or without kinks. Such kinked ripples are probably associated with arrest since the breakages are associated with fluctuating temperatures and thermal stresses.

Wallner Lines

A **Wallner line** is a ripple due to a stress pulse. Its configuration in fracture plan represents the successive intersections of the stress pulse and the fracture front. That a Wallner line is usually not parallel to a fracture front is evident from the fact that they often cross each other. They tend to be closer to fracture fronts for lower fracture velocities, as well as in cases where the stress pulse source is further from the fracture front. When the fracture is very slow, as always with LIFMs (liquid-induced fracture markings), or when the source of the stress pulse is sufficiently far from the fracture front, a Wallner line represents a fracture front for all practical purposes.

In fracture plan, a Wallner line may extend across a whole fracture surface. Just as sound waves in air, stress pulses in a rock attenuate with distance. It is therefore not surprising to also see Wallner lines that diminish in amplitude or vanish altogether with the distance from the stress pulse source. Gull wings, discussed below, are a good example.

The formation of Wallner lines was first explained by Wallner (1939). In knapping contexts, they have been considered by Kerkhof and Müller-Beck (1969), Faulkner (1972), Tsirk (1988) and others.

Wallner lines are among the most common and useful fracture markings in knapping contexts, including accidental breakage. The Wallner lines occurring in knapping contexts range from very small microscopic ripples, appearing as lines, to large ripples exceeding a centimeter in width and appearing as broad bands in fracture plan. The finer Wallner lines are most useful. They can be observed only in obsidian and other glasses, often only with magnification.

On the other hand, Wallner lines manifested as large ripples are frequently observed also in flint and even coarse-grained chert. However, these are usually ill-defined, lacking the crispness of the linear appearance of the finer Wallner lines. For example, a Wallner line is sometimes manifested as a large ripple on a flake when the fracture front encountered a large inclusion.

When a stress pulse source is at a fracture front on a planar fracture surface, only a stress pulse that is a shear wave can produce a Wallner line because of symmetry considerations (Kerkhof 1970). The stress pulses are considered to be shear waves, with velocity V_S, in the following two subsections. However, the basic principles are similar for other types of stress pulses, provided their proper velocities are used. Stress pulses other than shear waves are expected to also produce Wallner lines in knapping and other contexts (Schardin 1950). For example, when a strong stress pulse originates at a fracture front, it may be reflected as a dilatational stress wave to interact with successive fracture fronts to sometimes produce a Wallner line. Such Wallner lines, difficult to identify and interpret in knapping contexts, are not considered here.

Normal Wallner Lines

A **normal Wallner line** is defined here as one caused by a stress pulse having its source at a fracture front. The stress pulses can be generated as a fracture front passes a highly localized irregularity, as an inclusion (Figs. 6.3 and 6.4). Stress pulses producing Wallner lines can also be generated at a fracture front as the fracture itself produces irregularities at the front through secondary fracturing (Fig. 5.33 in Quinn 2007), such as some details in the formation of mist and velocity hackle.

As a fracture front intercepts an internal inclusion or other irregularity, a shear stress pulse may originate there to produce a pair of wing-like, normal Wallner lines known as **gull wings** (Figs. 6.3 and 6.4). The formation of gull wings is illustrated in Fig. 6.5 for straight fracture fronts. The stress pulse source is at O, and it propagates at the velocity V_S. The fracture is propagating downward in the figure with a constant velocity V_F. The dashed and light solid lines represent the successive locations of the fracture front and the stress pulse, respectively, at the same time intervals. The fracture fronts and stress pulses intersect at A, B, C, etc. The bold solid line is the Wallner line. Thus a Wallner line is seen to represent the intersections of the stress pulse with the successive fracture fronts. This is true of all Wallner lines. This illustration was drawn for $V_F/V_S = 0.50$. V_S is constant

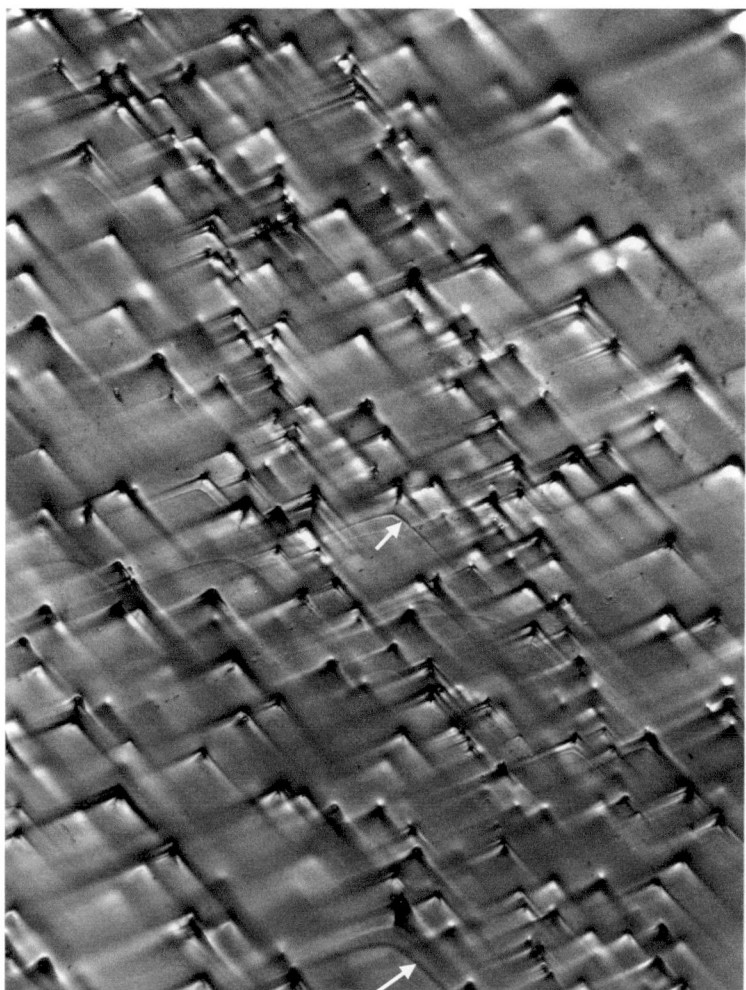

FIG. 6.3 GULL WINGS AT NUMEROUS INCLUSIONS ON A FLAKE. WALLNER WAKES ARE BARELY SEEN AT THE ARROWS. GLASS BUTTES OBSIDIAN. FRACTURE DIRECTION DOWNWARD. WIDTH OF FIELD 1.8 MM. (FROM TSIRK 1988)

for a material (Chapter 3). The formation of other normal Wallner lines is similar to that of gull wings. The relative fracture velocity can be calculated using gull wings from

$$V_F / V_S = \sin \Phi = \cos \theta \qquad (6.1)$$

Fig 6.6 shows the crack velocity variation with the gull wing angle. This "knapper's speedometer" can provide rough estimates of V_F/V_S from gulll wings visually without an actual measurement.

82 FRACTURES IN KNAPPING

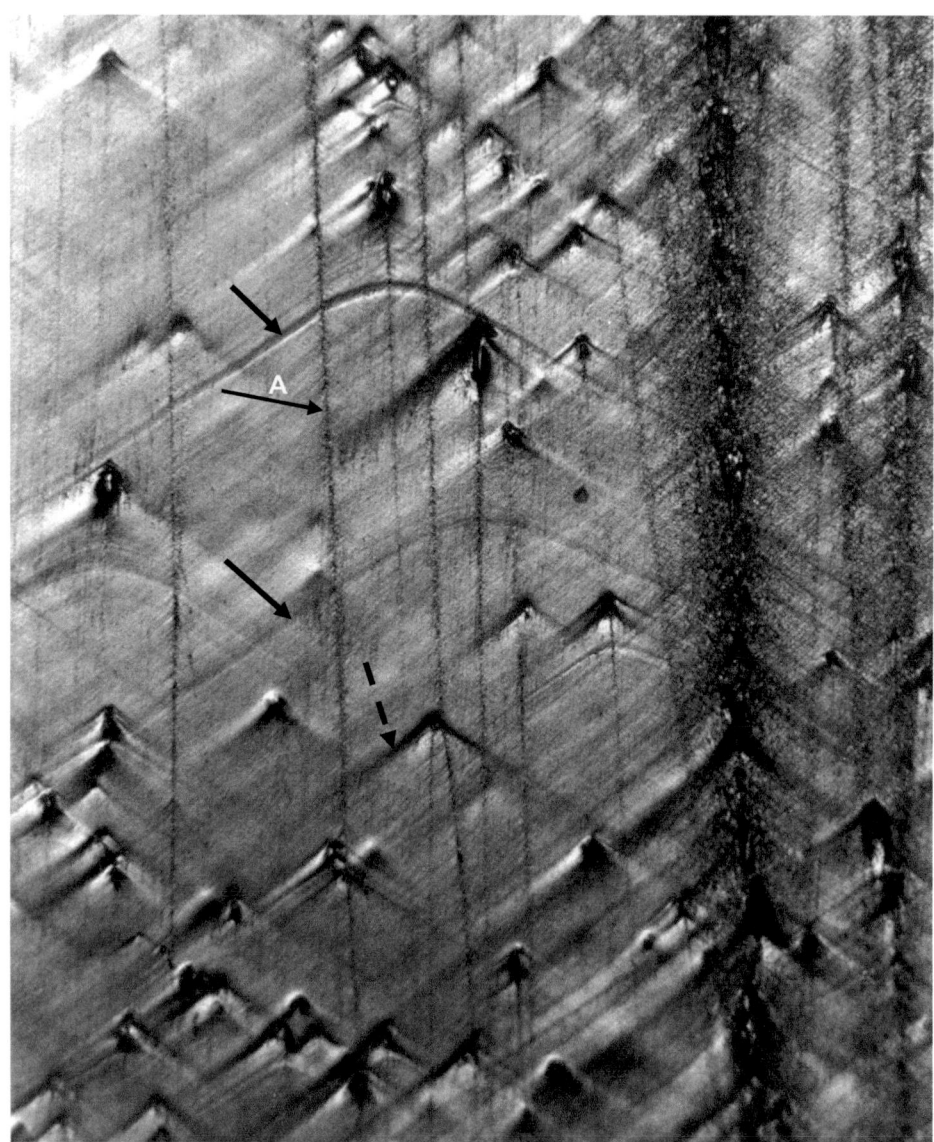

FIG. 6.4 GULL WINGS (DASHED ARROW) AND WALLNER WAKES (BOLD SOLID ARROWS). NUMEROUS MIST LINES (AS AT ARROW LABELED A) ARE ALSO CONSPICUOUS. GLASS BUTTES OBSIDIAN FLAKE. FRACTURE DIRECTION DOWNWARD. WIDTH OF FIELD 1.9 MM.
(FROM TSIRK 1988)

The bisector of the gull wings points in the fracture direction. Gull wings are usually very short due to attenuation of the stress pulse that was weak. Occasionally, though, they may extend across a whole fracture surface. Various equations are available for calculating V_F/V_S for a number of other Wallner line configurations (Kerkhof 1970, Schardin 1950).

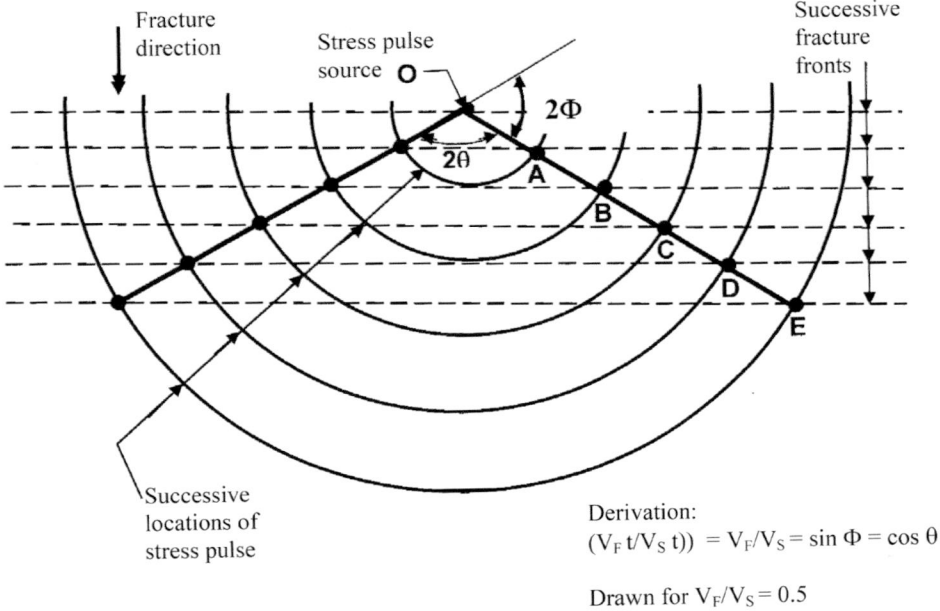

FIG. 6.5 FORMATION OF GULL WINGS

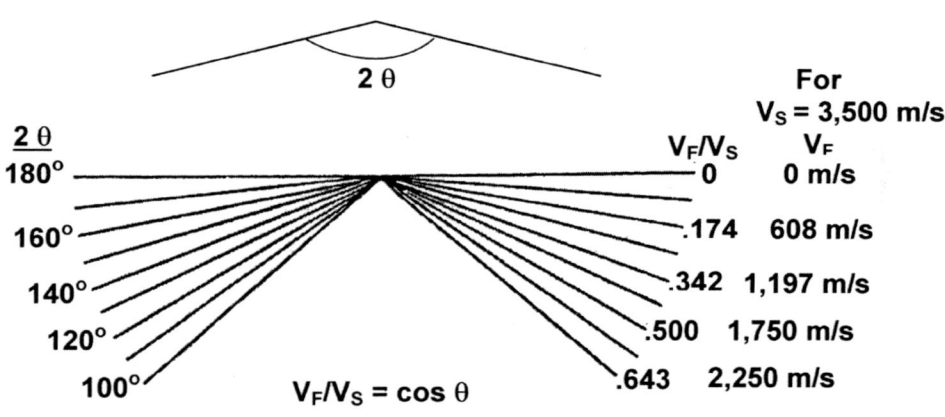

FIG. 6.6 "KNAPPERS' SPEEDOMETER"

Examples of V_F/V_S obtained from gull wings in obsidian for knapping and accidental breaks are considered in Chapter 10.

Gull wings are very common in obsidian. Sometimes, especially when an irregularity associated with the stress pulse source is small, they are manifested in obsidian as clear, crisp lines. At especially larger inclusions or irregularities, they may be poorly defined without any clear line apparent. In even the finer flints, the counterparts of gull wings are manifested, if at all, as some blurry surface irregularities.

To enhance the visibility of Wallner lines, it is often useful to take them slightly out of focus or to rotate the fracture surface. The latter, however, can lead to errors in the angular measurements for the relative fracture velocity. Suppose the fracture surface is rotated by angle α about an axis parallel to the fracture front and by angle β about an axis parallel to the fracture direction. The angle θ measured on the projected plane of measurement will differ from the true angle Φ on the fracture surface, with the following relationship holding:

$$(\cos \theta)/(\cos \Phi) = \{[\sin^2\Phi \, (\cos^2\beta)/(\cos^2\alpha)] + \cos^2\Phi\}^{-1/2} \tag{6.2}$$

For obtaining the relative fracture velocities from gull wings, for example, the value estimated from a projected plane $(V_F/V_S)_P$ compares to the true value V_F/V_S as

$$(V_F/V_S)_P / (V_F/V_S) = (\cos \theta)/(\cos \Phi) \tag{6.3}$$

TABLE 6.1 ERRORS (%) IN V_F/V_S DUE TO ROTATION OF FRACTURE PLANE

Φ	$\alpha = 5°$	$\beta = 5°$	$\alpha = 10°$	$\beta = 10°$	$\alpha = 20°$	$\beta = 20°$
50°	-0.22	+0.22	-0.90	+0.90	-3.67	+3.62
60°	-0.29	+0.29	-1.15	+1.15	-4.63	+4.70
70°	-0.34	+0.34	-1.35	+1.36	-5.38	+5.60

The errors based on the above equations are shown in Table 6.1 for several angles Φ and rotations α (when $\beta = 0$) and β (when $\alpha = 0$), rotations (α and β) and angles Φ. As shown in the table, the errors are not significant for rotations less than about 10°. The errors can be reduced by using a rotation with α and β approximately equal. For $\alpha = \beta$, there is no error since the right hand side of Eq. 6.2 becomes unity.

Normal Wallner lines may be useful for many purposes other than determination of relative fracture velocity and fracture direction. Since they are usually concave upstream, they may provide clues to the location of the fracture origin, general fracture directions, the general fracture front configurations with the leading and lagging parts, and hence the relative stress distributions associated with the fracture. The leading of a part of a fracture front is exaggerated by a Wallner line (Fréchette 1990).

Irregularities of Wallner lines in fracture plan, especially local concavity in downstream direction, may provide clues to the presence of residual stresses, thickness variations along a flake cross-section and relative material properties.

Anomalous Wallner Lines

An **anomalous Wallner line** is defined here as one caused by a stress pulse having its source away from a fracture front. Various secondary and tertiary fractures that may generate such stress pulses do occur behind a fracture front at or near the fracture surface. Examples include the lateral spreading and break-through of twist hackles and tails, as well

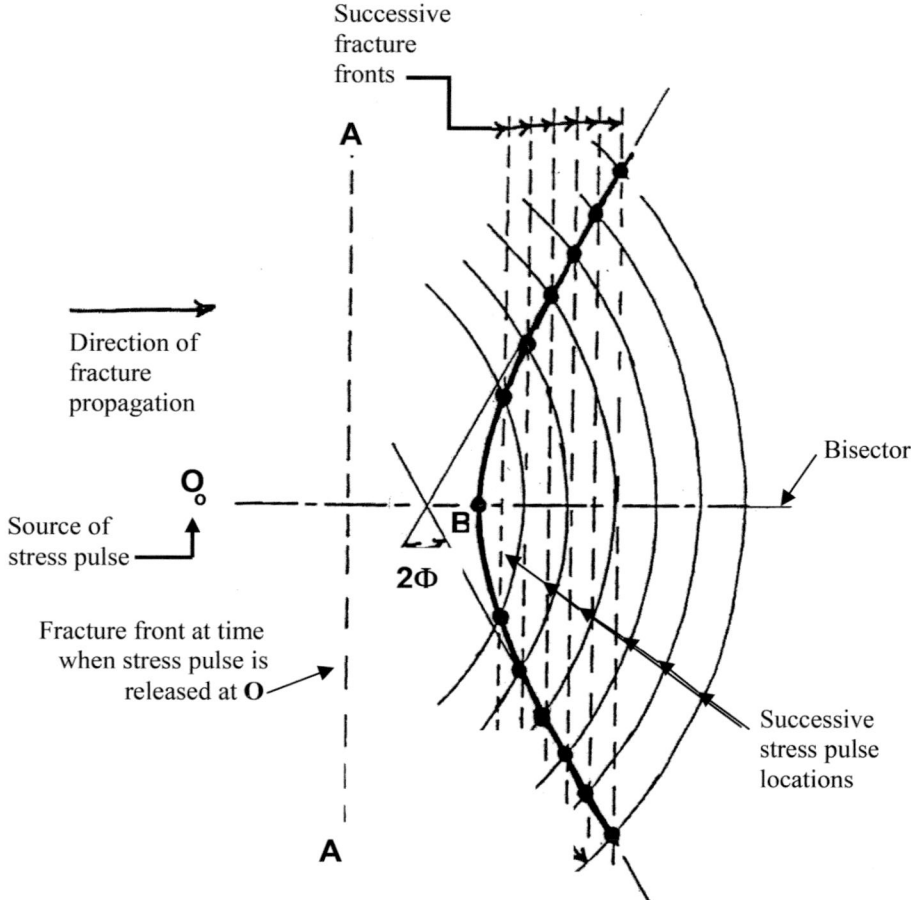

FIG. 6.7 WALLNER WAKE FORMATION. (FROM TSIRK 1988)

as some fracturing in the formation of the mist and hackle regions associated with high fracture velocity. There are other potential, even macroscopic sources of stress pulses that may produce anomalous Wallner lines in flaking and accidental breakages. Of course, the stress pulses originating at the external loading (by the flaking implement in knapping) are of primary interest. Such stress pulses may come directly from the loading due to its variations in time (personal communication, Robert Jackson 2002, and Scott Silsby 2008,), as due to vibrations at the contact region.

A **Wallner wake** (Figs. 6.3 and 6.4) is an anomalous Wallner line due to a stress pulse from a source at the fracture surface behind the fracture front. Its formation is illustrated in Fig.6.7 for fracture fronts straight in its vicinity. It is assumed for this figure that $V_F/V_S = 0.5$. The stress pulse, generated at O at the time instant when the fracture fron is at A-A, first catches up with the fracture front at B. With tedious efforts it is possible to calculate the relative fracture velocity V_F/V_S from these markings, but with reasonable accuracy only in the exceptional cases when they have adequate length (Tsirk 1988). It is much simpler and more accurate to obtain the relative fracture velocity from gull wings whenever they are present. A Wallner wake can easily provide a lower bound estimate of the relative fracture velocity simply as

$$V_F/V_S = \sin \Phi \qquad (6.4)$$

where Φ is shown in Fig. 6.7. The bisector of a symmetrical Wallner wake provides the fracture direction. As a Wallner wake becomes longer, the extremities of its arms tend to become parallel to gull wings.

With curved fracture fronts, the arms of a Wallner wake may have double curvature. Near the tensile surface of a fracture from bending, Wallner wakes are occasionally manifested with the arm nearest the tensile surface having single curvature and the other double curvature.

Stress Changes Causing Ripples

Static Effects

Some ripples in knapping contexts are best understood as due to static (actually quasi-static) effects, without considering inertia. In the production of flakes and blades, such effects can relate to geometry and to changes in the forces applied in flaking (See Fig. 6.2).

Consider the production of a straight blade, for example. For the fracture to propagate straight, there must be a delicate balance in the stresses at the fracture front. This balance is affected by both the vertical forces (parallel to the blade axis) and bending. Fluctuations in one or both of these can lead to the manifestation of ripples.

The very turning away of the fracture from its original plane also affects the stresses of interest. This is because the blade cross-section is changing and, more importantly, because the eccentricity of the applied downward force changes. The ripples considered can be viewed as temporary directional changes with self-corrective adjustments. In hinge formation, there is no such adequate adjustment.

The ripples due to the static effects from changing external forces are particularly apparent when fracture velocities are extremely low, as in some blade production by pressure. Crabtree (1968) has referred to the wobble or quiver of a pressure flaker causing ripples.

Consider a case when the thinning of a blade itself along its length may affect the delicate balance of stresses needed for a fracture to extend straight. The axial stresses in the blade depend on its cross-sectional area, proportional to the blade thickness t. Bending stresses, however, depend on t^2. The effects of a blade thinning along its length, taken together with the self-corrective nature of some ripples, become particularly significant with small thicknesses as in the distal parts of blades or flakes with feathered terminations. It is thus not surprising to often see many ripples at close spacing in such cases. These can be viewed as recurrent directional changes with self-corrective adjustments. The ripples resembling concentric rings on "frost fractures" are probably due to static effects from stress changes.

Specimen Vibration

Static processes discussed above ignore the dynamic effects from inertia. Such effects are included in considering specimen vibrations, necessarily dynamic events. Specimen vibration refers to events such as the vibration of a whole core, a partly detached flake or a biface being broken by accident. Some ripples are understood more easily in terms of vibrations rather than stress waves.

Due to the impact in percussion flaking, the specimen will necessarily be set in vibration, as will the percussor itself. After the flake initiation and some advance of the fracture, there may also be significant vibrations of the partly detached flake. During the detachment of a blade by percussion, both its flexural vibrations and the higher frequency axial vibrations are relevant since they both influence the participation of fracture mode II. The actual manifestation of ripples depends on the fracture velocity together with the frequencies of the vibrations, which change as the fracture advances during a flake detachment. Elementary calculations made for some dimensional characteristics of ripples, a range of realistic fracture velocities in knapping and the natural frequencies of vibration of some partly detached blades lend credence to the explanation offered.

The profile features on stepped cones and the ripples resembling concentric rings on and near a cone-like feature (Crabtree 1972) are examples of ripples interpreted as being due to vibrations.

Stress Pulses

All specimen vibrations in a global sense, as considered in the above section, may be viewed as due to superposition of a number of stress waves with their reflections. For example, the axial vibrations of a partly detached blade are due to the superposition of dilatational stress waves propagating back and forth along its length, with the longest natural period (inverse of the fundamental frequency) of vibration being equal to the time it takes for the wave to travel its length four times. The discrete passage of stress waves is often not considered because it is easier to interpret certain effects in terms of global specimen vibrations. This section will include some brief reflections on the effects of stress wave passage that cannot be interpreted in terms of global specimen vibrations.

A shear wave as well as a dilatational wave incident to a free surface at appropriate angles will each be reflected as a shear and a dilatational wave (Kolsky 1963, Lawn 1993, Speth 1972). It has been demonstrated analytically as well as experimentally that ripples can be produced by not only shear waves but also dilatational waves arriving at the fracture front from certain directions (Kerkhof 1975, Richter and Kerkhof 1994).

Intentionally introduced ripples due to stress wave passages, including various reflections, have been identified in experiments with simple specimen geometry (Richter and Kerkhof 1994). In knapping, because of the complex geometries and various other effects producing ripples, ripples associated with stress wave reflections are difficult to identify. However, ripples from such effects are expected also in knapping. The sources of such stress waves and their reflections may possibly be associated with the impact of the forces applied in percussion flaking and accidental breakage of bifaces as well as bipolar percussion. A range of possibilities in general, relevant to the present discussion, is considered in Schardin (1950).

Experimental Ripples

Ultrasonic Modulation

Introduction of minute ripples, in fact Wallner lines, intentionally by ultrasonic modulation provides an immensely valuable research technique. The artificial ripples are produced by applying external stress pulses to a specimen during its fracture from other causes. The pulses usually used are cyclic, either continuous or intermittent. Single rather than cyclic pulses can also be used with some equipment. Using a predetermined frequency, the time lapse between adjacent ripples is known. The absolute fracture velocities can then be determined by measuring the distance between the ripples when they represent the fracture fronts with the stress pulses applied sufficiently far from the fracture fronts of interest.

The various kinds of equipment that can be used are reviewed in Richter and Kerkhof (1994). Technologies are available to measure fracture velocities in the range of at least 10^{-6} m/s to 2000 m/s.

The method was developed already in the early 1950's, derived from the principles for Wallner lines. Sommer (1969), for example, has used the method to demonstrate that twist hackles are indeed in the fracture direction. For clear interpretations, the specimen geometry should be relatively simple. This poses limitations and challenges but does not preclude application of ultrasonic modulation to knapping experiments.

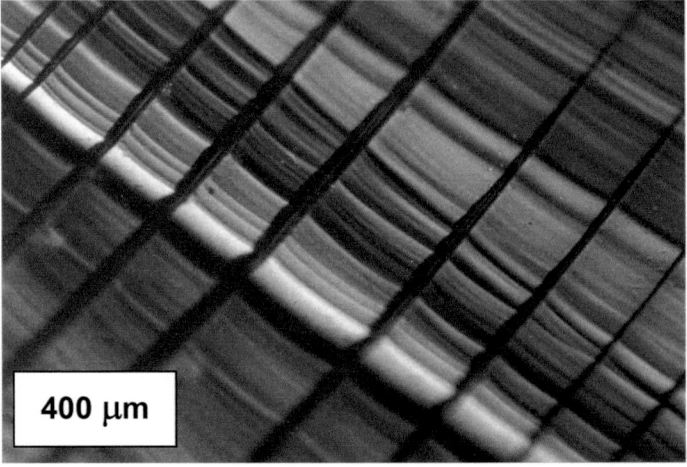

FIG. 6.8 AN OBSIDIAN FLAKE DETACHED BY PERCUSSION WITH ULTRASONIC MODULATION AT 175 KHZ. FRACTURE DIRECTION DOWNWARD. (COURTESY M.G. SCHINKER FOR THE MODULATION)

During my 1978 visit to the Institute for Solid Mechanics in Freiburg, Germany, a couple of flakes were removed by direct percussion while continuous sinusoidal shear waves were introduced at the base of the core at 1.75 kHz by Dr. M. G. Schinker of the Institute. This was an impromptu attempt rather than a planned experiment with simple geometry. The cores used had to be supported on a metal plate, shaking in its own plane, thus being a counterpart of the anvil technique. Reflections from the irregular free surfaces hindered the interpretation of the resulting artificial ripples (Fig. 6.8). Nevertheless, some interesting observations can be made. It is possible to obtain the lower bound estimates of fracture velocities. The fracture front is seen to lag locally at the twist hackles. Another interesting observation from these impromptu experiments is that a localized lag of the fracture front, and hence a slowing of the fracture, occurs at a location on a flake surface where there is a geometric depression (due to a hinge fracture) on the dorsal face. There is much useful information to be learned for knapping from planned experiments with ultrasonic modulation.

Sonic Modulation

Low frequency sonic modulation at 183 Hz was used to study the formation of liquid-induced fracture markings (LIFMs) in pressure flaking from a blade core (Chapter 8). Such a low frequency is suitable only for very slow fractures, propagating at only a few

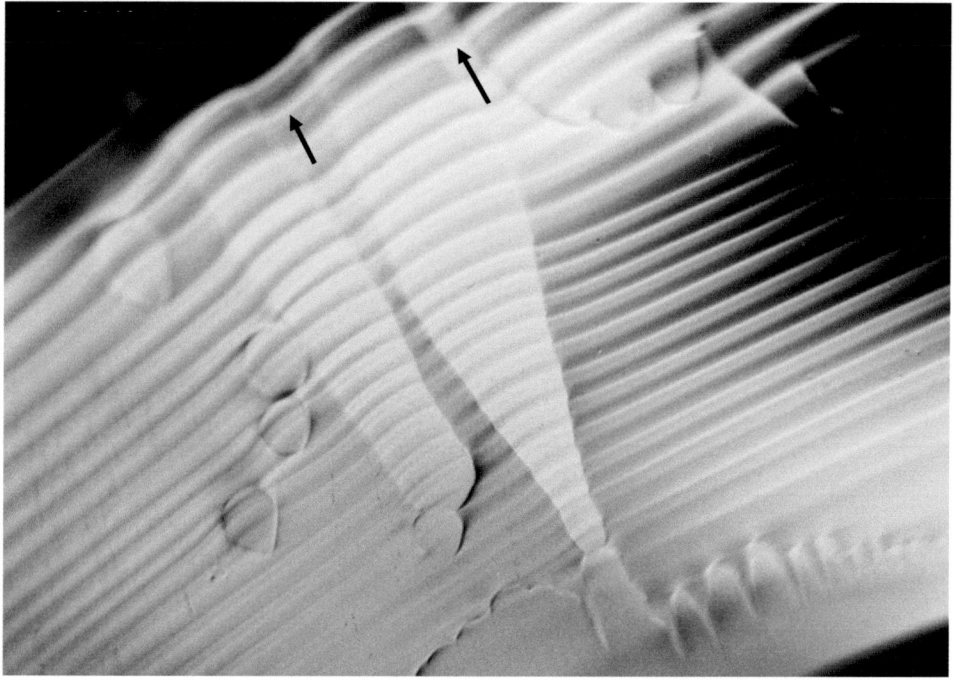

FIG. 6.9 SONIC MODULATION (AT 183 HZ) USED ON AN OBSIDIAN PRESSURE FLAKER. THE FRACTURE IS PROPAGATING UPWARDS AT ABOUT 2 TO 3 CM/S. THE DRY PARTS (AS AT ARROWS) ARE LAGGING BEHIND THE LEADING WETTED PARTS. THE IMAGE WIDTH IS ~2.8 MM.

cm/s. Such low velocities are common with the LIFMs studied, which occur close to a fracture origin. Because of the very slow fracture velocities always involved with the sonic modulation used, the sonic modulation lines here are Wallner lines representing the true fracture fronts. Also, for the same reason, any problems with stress wave reflections from the irregular surfaces of the core are avoided. To introduce the sonic modulation, an off-the-shelf palm sander was used. It vibrates with a circular motion in the sanding plane at 11,000 cpm (183 Hz). The palm sander was applied to the side of a wooden staff of a chest crutch, similar to the one used by Crabtree (1968).

Examples of the sonic modulation lines are shown in Figs. 6.9. For this example, the external surface of the core near the pressure platform was wetted with water. When the water was following the fracture and maintaining a wetted fracture front, fracturing was facilitated. At the partial fracture fronts that were depleted of water, this direct facilitating effect was not present. These effects are seen by the leading and lagging parts of the fracture. In some other examples with sonic modulation, it is seen that near fracture origins the fracture velocity does not increase monotonically but fluctuates.

Exploding Wire Experiments

Experiments have been made (Kerkhof 1970) with a "sharp" elastic pulse introduced by use of an exploding wire placed near the face of a specimen being fractured from another cause. With the simple geometry of a glass plate, the ripples due to the direct shear and compression pulses as well as the reflected waves could each be identified in such an experiment. Some of the ripples exhibited a kink in fracture profile, due to the "sharpness" (small rise time) of the stress pulse (Fig. 6.2d).

The exploding wire and ultrasonic modulation experiments provide a clear and convincing demonstration of the analytical capabilities (Richter and Kerkhof 1994) for predicting the manifestation of ripples from the different stress waves and their reflections.

Terminology and Interpretations by Others

The anomalous Wallner lines of this study are included among the tertiary Wallner lines of Fréchette (1990) and Quinn (2007). The normal Wallner lines fall under their primary and secondary Wallner lines.

In contrast to the definition used here, Schardin (1950) has considered his "normal" and "anomalous" Wallner lines to be associated with stress pulses originating at or away from the fracture plane, respectively.

Kerkhof and Müller-Beck (1969) have interpreted the proximal ripples resembling concentric rings on a flake as due to stress pulses from the percussion impact. A similar explanation, but in terms of "global" specimen vibrations, is offered in Fréchette (1990) for an impact fracture in an industrial context.

Cotterell and Kamminga (1990) consider Wallner lines to be only fine ripples from stress pulses, a view different from that adopted here as well as in Kerkhof and Müller-Beck

(1969), Fréchette (1990) and Quinn (2007). Cotterell and Kamminga do refer to some larger ripples as due to the passage of shear waves. It is reasonable to include such ripples among Wallner lines.

The tertiary Wallner lines of Fréchette (1990) and Quinn (2007), caused by stress pulses from outside the fracture front, were not considered by Wallner (1939). The definitions of the primary and secondary Wallner lines of all the three researchers are in close agreement. Primary Wallner lines are caused by a stress pulse due to the encounter of the fracture front with an inclusion or other singularity in the specimen. Secondary Wallner lines are defined as being caused by a stress "pulse released by a discontinuity in the progress of the crack front" Fréchette 1990: 16). That is, they are associated with the stress pulses from the secondary cracking at a fracture front due to its passage. These definitions were not adopted in this book.

7. Mirror, Mist, Hackle, Branching

Mirror

In a brittle fracture under sufficiently high stress, regions of mirror, mist and hackle, and then branching are manifested at increasing distances from the fracture origin (Freiman 1980). This is shown schematically in Fig. 7.1. Incipient (macroscopic) branching is also manifested in some accidental transverse breakage by bending. In the above context, "hackle" should be taken to mean "velocity hackle". A specimen must be large enough for the above features to be manifested. The relationships given in Fig. 7.1 are empirical.

Closest to the fracture origin is a **mirror** region. Almost all flake surfaces produced in knapping are mirror surfaces. Mist and velocity hackle are manifested on flake surfaces extremely rarely, except by the lip in bending initiations (Fig. 5.1 and Chapter 10). The mirror has a relatively smooth surface, aside from the fracture markings such as twist hackles, tails and ripples, and aside from the material irregularities such as inclusions in obsidian or the crystalline structure of flint, chert and other materials. A mirror surface even in glass has roughness visible with an electron or atomic force microscope (Smekal 1950, Poncelet 1958, Hull 1999).

Mist and Velocity Hackle

A mirror-mist boundary, also known as a mist boundary, separates a mirror from a mist region. More generally, the locations where mist, hackle and branching first occur are

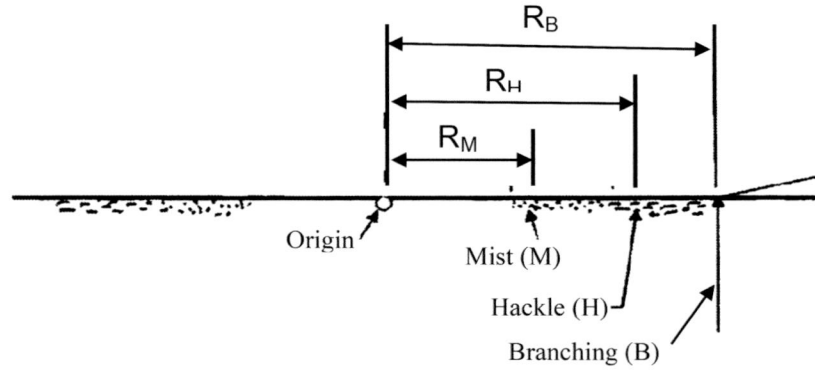

Breaking Stressd = $\sigma = A_i/\sqrt{R_i}$ $i = M, H, B$

where A_i = Mirror constant
R_i = Radius to boundary i

FIG. 7.1 BREAKING STRESSES AND MIRROR RADII

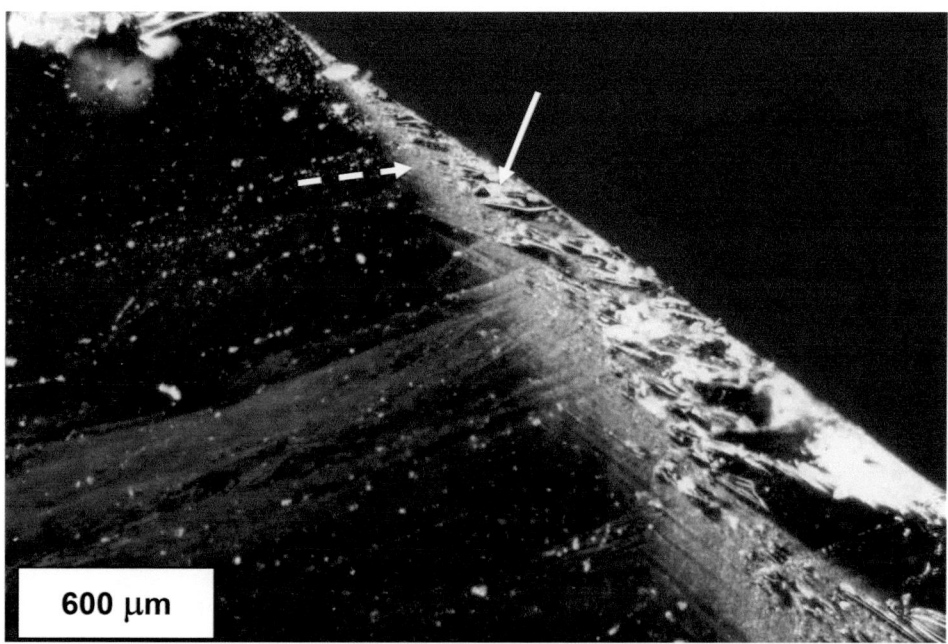

FIG.7.2 MIST (DASHED ARROW) AND HACKLE (SOLID ARROW) ON AN ACCIDENTAL BREAK OF A BIFACE. THE TENSILE FACE OF THE BIFACE IS AT THE RIGHT. MIST LINES AND NARROW, PARABOLIC DOUBE TAILS ARE SEEN IN THE LOWER PART OF THE MIST REGION. GLASS BUTTES OBSIDIAN. FRACTURE DIRECTION IS DOWNWARD TO THE RIGHT NEAR THE TENSILE FACE.

known as the respective boundaries, often designated by R_M, R_H and R_B (Fig. 7.1). For a given material, the appropriate distances to these boundaries relate to the magnitude of the (nominal) stress at which the fracture started. The shape of these boundaries, on the other hand, depends on the distribution of the stresses.

In mist and hackle regions, surface roughness increases with the distance from the fracture origin. The mist region in obsidian and other glasses, with its fine microscopic surface roughness, appears misty or frosty to the naked eye and at low magnification (Fig. 7.2). In early glass literature, it was aptly described as "a dull fracture" having "the appearance of being 'grey'" (Preston 1926). Mist in glass has also been referred to as "fine roughness" (Kerkhof 1970) and "fine hackles" (Fréchette 1972). The constituent markings in a mist region can be described as microscopic deviating cracks gouging the surface (Poncelet 1958), with "a fibrous-appearing structure" in the fracture direction (Fréchette 1990) becoming evident in its downstream portions. Within a mist region, there are significant differences in the size and characteristics of the constituent features (Hull 1999, Bahat et al. 2005). Such differences are amplified by the various microscopic inclusions common in obsidian but not in window glass. In obsidian, some of the individual features are clearly visible at magnifications of 100x and less, while others cannot be resolved at 600x.

A hackle region has coarser surface roughness. It appears as shiny and irregular in obsidian when viewed by the naked eye and at low magnification (Fig. 7.2 and 7.3).

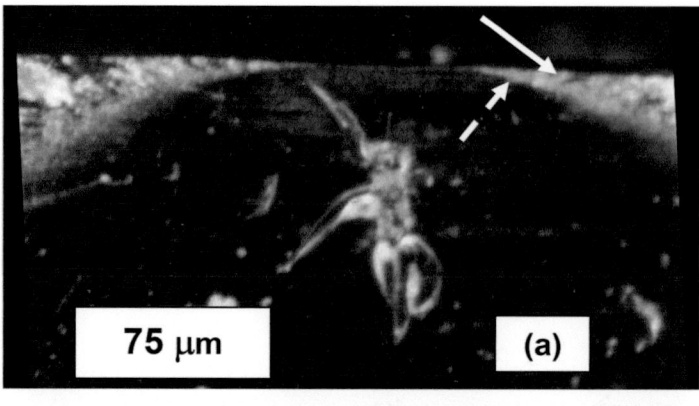
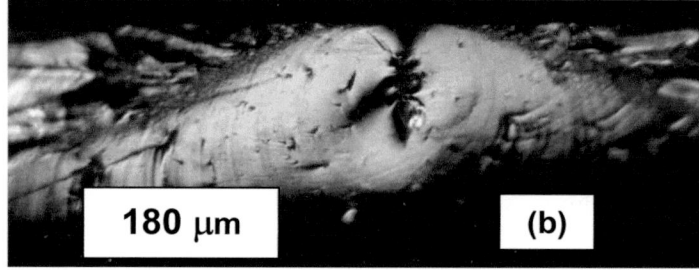

Fig. 7.3 Fracture surface of an accidental break from an internal flaw. Mist (dashed arrow in a) and hackle (solid arrow) are clearly seen in the obsidian.

A hackle region has also been referred to simply as "coarse roughness" (Kerkhof 1970), "coarse hackle" (Fréchette 1965) and "velocity hackle" because of its usual association with higher fracture velocities. The region has been characterized by the fracture front breaking up into a multitude of fingers advancing independently and interacting with other such features (Fréchette 1990). Occasionally, slivers will separate, with the fracture even propagating backwards locally, in the upstream direction. The deviating cracks gouge the surface deeper in a hackle region than a mist region. As a fracture progresses from mirror to mist to hackle, the notion of a general fracture front tends to gradually lose its meaning. Mist and hackle look drastically different in obsidian, but less so in cherts.

The transition from a mist to a hackle region is actually gradual (Hull 1999, Mecholsky 2001, Bahat et al. 2005). For this reason, the term "mist hackle" has been used by Fréchette (1990) for the markings, without separating the two regions. To the naked eye and at low magnification, however, the regions do appear to be distinct, especially in obsidian. A hackle boundary (between mist and hackle) can even be identified in obsidian at low magnification (about 15X to 50X). Because this is of practical significance, the two regions are considered as separate here even though a gradual process is involved.

In knapping contexts, mist, hackle and branching can often be seen in accidental breakage of blades, flakes and bifaces of obsidian and chert, sometimes with recurrent mirror-mist-hackle patterns. Mist and hackle can be observed, though rarely, on the surfaces of thick flakes produced by direct percussion (Fig. 5.10), away from their proximal regions. On percussion as well as pressure flakes associated with bending initiations, mist and hackle often occur also at the proximal ends as the fracture extends laterally (Fig. 5.1).

Mist and hackle regions are associated with localized directional instabilities, involving micro-branching or unsuccessful localized attempts of macroscopic branching. There is no general agreement, however, on the mechanisms responsible for the formation of these regions (Lawn 1993:95-99, Hull 1999: 139-147). The explanations of Poncelet (1958) and Fréchette (1965, 1990) are considered most reasonable here for glass.

Fracture propagation is associated with energy release that may be viewed as stress pulses (stress waves) released at all "points" along a fracture front. The extent to which such pulses are felt by a fracture front away from its source depends on the magnitude and attenuation (with distance) of the pulse, as well as the speed of the stress waves and of the fracture. This is evident in the manifestation of gull wings, for example. The advance of a fracture front without the presence of surface roughness (or other irregularities) includes the effects of the aforementioned stress pulses. As markings associated with surface roughness appear, there is no longer the regularity of the stress pulses released at a fracture front. At low fracture velocity, these irregular stress pulses are felt all along a fracture front near the source, depending on the pulse attenuation. With higher fracture velocities, the stress pulses from each source are felt at only discrete "points" along the successive fracture fronts, thereby producing stress irregularities to promote further surface roughness. The magnitude of the irregular stress pulses increases with the larger constituent markings associated with coarser surface roughness, as well as with greater fracture velocities because of greater energy release. Finally in a hackle region the deviating micro-cracks continue "independently in a stress field thoroughly modified and confused by a host of disordered" stress pulses (Poncelet 1958).

Even in the transition from a mirror to a mist region the submicroscopic roughness of a mirror increases gradually (Hull 1999: 150-155). Nevertheless, a distinct mirror boundary is evident at low magnification.

Clear evidence for the aforementioned role of transient stresses, related to stress pulses or stress wave effects, in the manifestation of the constituent markings of mist and hackle regions is seen in the occasional patterning of mist and hackle as well as their suppression.

Branching, Incipient Branching and Lateral Wedges

The process from mirror to mist to hackle, and up to branching at a macroscopic scale, is a gradual process. It can be visualized most easily by considering what is happening at the tensile face of a biface break (Chapter 13). As the strain energy release rates increase, the individual markings in a hackle region tend to gouge deeper into the surface as aborted attempts of branching with the fracture continuing to propagate along the original surface. At some point, one of these attempts will be successful with the deviating fracture continuing to propagate away from the original fracture surface to produce macroscopic branching. Another deviating fracture, to the opposite side of the original fracture surface, will usually continue to extend into the surface as well, to produce a wedge shape at the branching location.

The branching of a fracture is also known as forking or bifurcation. Velocity branching, velocity forking and velocity bifurcation have also been used (Fréchette 1990) to distinguish it from other kinds of branching. An unrelated type of branching is often seen, for example, in breakage by bending. In knapping, such low velocity branching without mist or hackle is involved with the compression wedges sometimes seen in the breakage of blades and other flakes as well as bifaces.

In everyday life, velocity branching is commonly encountered commonly in the radial fracture patterns of broken window panes. In knapping, it is often seen in accidental breakage of bifaces, flakes and blades. In such contexts, all caused essentially by bending, branching is most readily recognizable by the resulting triangular wedge, termed a **lateral wedge**, occasionally released along one or both edges of the specimen. In biface breakage, for example, incomplete or **incipient branching** can often be seen along the tensile face of the biface along the break, just downstream from the mist and hackle regions.

The branching angle depends on the state of stress. In a plate loaded in its plane, it depends on the ratio of the two principal stresses (Preston 1935, Fréchette 1990) and can serve as an indicator of the stress state. This also applies to the branching angles near the tensile surface of a specimen such as a biface or blade breakage. Branching angles have been investigated by Kalthoff (1973), in complex geological contexts by Bahat (1984) and Bahat, Rabinovitch and Frid (2005). With biface breakage they were considered in Tsirk (2012).

Velocity and Energy Considerations

For a given material there is a theoretical limit on the maximum fracture velocity that relates to the velocity of stress waves, thought to be that of Raleigh waves (Kanninen and Popelar 1985:200). In all practical situations including knapping contexts, however, there is an effective terminal velocity for fracture, well below the theoretical limit. The **effective terminal velocity** for a material is the fracture velocity at which branching occurs, just beyond the hackle region.

When going from mist to hackle to branching, it has been observed for glass that the fracture velocity increase is only slight, but the energy demand increases substantially (Richter, personal communication, 2007), due to the production of the roughening surface. Although more energy is made available to the fracture at higher velocities, increased amounts of it are expended on the surface becoming gradually rougher rather than on acceleration of the fracture.

The effective terminal velocities reported in Kerkhof (1970: 228-229) for 43 industrial glasses range from 700 m/s, for a lead glass with specific gravity of 6.0, to 2155 m/s for silica glass. For soda-lime (window) glass, it is about 1500 m/s. For a Glass Buttes obsidian from Oregon, the highest value measured from gull wings for a thick flake produced by a very hard hammerstone is $V_F/V_S = 0.58$ (Tsirk 1988). For a shear wave velocity V_S =3552 m/s for another Glass Buttes obsidian (Yasuda, personal communication,2012), this corresponds to $V_F = 2060$ m/s. $V_F/V_S = 0.62$ corresponding to $V_F = 2200$ m/s were obtained as approximations near some mist regions on the same obsidian for which the Yasuda measurement was made. For a Jemez Mountain obsidian from New Mexico, the highest value measured for a thermal fracture is $V_F/V_S = 0.63$ (Tsirk 2003, Steffen 2005). For an assumed $V_S = 3552$ m/s, this corresponds to $V_F = 2238$ m/s. The effective terminal velocity for a number of glasses and other materials is given in Quinn (2007: Table 5.1).

Mirror Constants and Stresses

R_M, R_H and R_B in Fig. 7.1 are known collectively as the **mirror radii**. They are the distances from the fracture origin to the first onset of mist, hackle and branching, respectively. Sometimes they are also referred to as the mist, hackle and branching radii. Guidelines for measuring these radii are provided in Quinn (2007).

The term "fracture stress" is used here for what is commonly called the failure stress in engineering applications. It is the nominal stress in a specimen at the location of the fracture origin, without taking into account the stress concentration due to the presence of the flaw at which the fracture originates. For many practical fractures, the fracture stress σ_F is related empirically to the mirror radii by

$$\sigma_F = A_i/\sqrt{(R_i)} \qquad (i = M, H, B) \qquad (7.1)$$

where i can stand for M, H or B corresponding to mist, hackle and branching, respectively. A_M, A_H and A_B are known as the respective **mirror constants** of a material. It is useful to rewrite this equation as

$$\sigma_{Fi} = \sigma_F/A_i = 1/\sqrt{(R_i)} \qquad (i = M, H, B) \qquad (7.2)$$

where σ_{Fi} is the fracture stress normalized by the respective mirror constant. Eqs. 7.1 and 7.2 indicate that the mirror radii increase with decreasing fracture stress. It has been noted that the mirror radii are directly proportional to the flaw size. To calculate the fracture stresses from Eq. 7.1, the respective constants must be known for the material from laboratory tests. However, the normalized stresses for a given material can still be obtained from Eq. 7.2 without knowing the material constants. In dealing with a given material, such normalized stresses provide a useful indication of the relative stresses at failure.

Eq. 7.1 is empirical. But rather good results with surprising consistency have been obtained. The applicability, limitations and reservations for estimating fracture stresses from flaws or mirror radii are discussed in Rice (1984, 1988), Fréchette (1990), and Quinn (2007). Examples of mirror constants obtained for industrial glasses and ceramic materials are given in Mecholsky (1994), Mecholsky, Freiman and Rice (1977) and Quinn (2007). The fracture stress calculated from Eq. 7.1 is the total stress, including any residual stress.

Use of mirror radii with Eq. 7.1 is obviously not possible when the specimen is too small for a mirror boundary to be manifested. Furthermore, the equation is not applicable for low fracture stress (Fréchette 1990), when the mirror boundary is so large as to disturb the overall stress pattern in the region involved. Use of mirror radii for stress calculation, by Eq. 7.1, is ideally applicable for specimens with uniform tension rather than bending, in which case stress gradients are present. With prudence, however, the equation can also be applied to breakage by bending, as noted below. Consistent results have been obtained for uniform tension and uniaxial as well as biaxial bending specimens (Rice 1984, 1988). For circular bending specimens, corrections due to stress gradients have been considered in Johnson and Holloway (1966).

For stone tools, the equations presented can be applicable to intentional snapping of blades and to accidental breakage during knapping as well as tool use. These breakages are essentially always caused by bending. In such cases, best results are expected when the mirror radii are measured at or near a tensile surface that is flat or almost flat in the region where the measurements are taken. The tensile stresses from bending are expected to be constant along such a flat boundary. When an unsymmetrical mirror region is encountered, use of the average of the two mirror radii has been observed to give good results (Quinn 2007). This may also be dictated when a fracture origin cannot be determined. Alternatively, it can be argued that use of the smaller of the two unsymmetrical radii is more reasonable. In general, the equations presented are not expected to be applicable for estimation of stress for flake initiation, even in those rare cases when mist is manifested relatively far on a flake surface. However, the equations may perhaps be applicable to bending initiations of flakes when mist is manifested by the lip.

Markings Related to Mist and Hackle

Wallner Mist-Hackle Configuration

Stress pulses can affect local manifestation of mist and hackle. **Wallner mist, mist-hackle** and **hackle configurations** are lines or bands in fracture plan representing localized manifestation or enhancement of mist, mist and hackle or hackle, respectively, due to stress pulses. Collectively, they are termed here **Wallner mist-hackle configurations** (Fig. 7.4).

It is the energy from the stress pulses that enables the manifestation or enhancement of the localized surface roughness. The formation of the plan configuration of these markings is analogous to that for Wallner lines. The source of the stress pulse for the markings in Fig. 7.4 was behind the fracture front. These markings, in fact, are often associated with the ripple of a Wallner line. Sometimes, however, no such ripple is seen, as in Fig. 3B in Tsirk (1996). The markings discussed can be used for calculating the fracture velocity V_F relative to that of shear stress waves, V_S. The ripple of a Wallner line can affect the appearance of typical mist in a region when optical microscopy is used. Caution is therefore warranted in identification of Wallner mist configurations, and even more so for the mist suppression configurations considered in the next section.

The markings considered in this and the next section are discussed in Tsirk (1996). All of them have been observed in obsidian but not in flint or chert. Andrews (1968) has

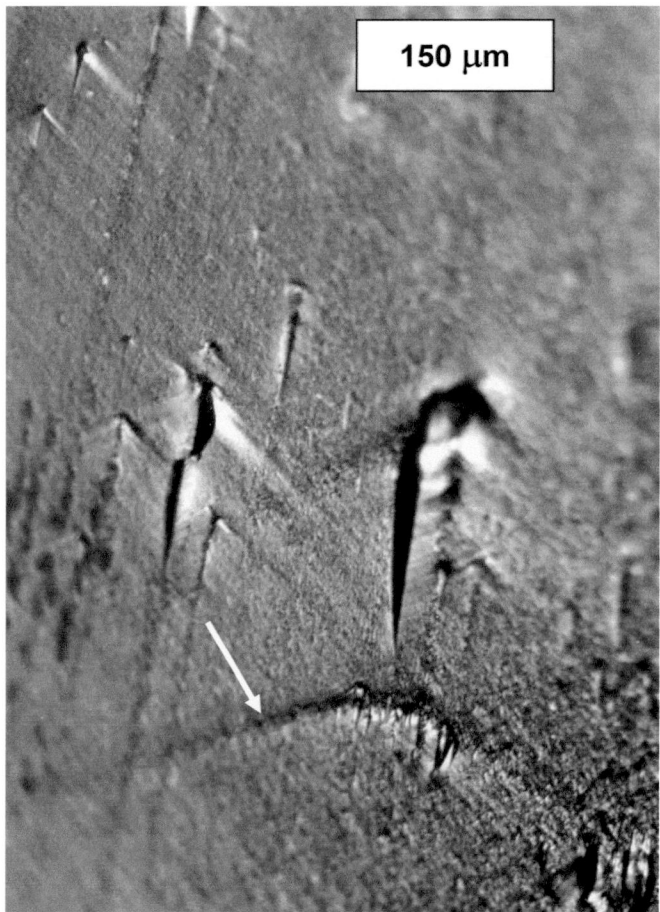

Fig. 7.4 A mist-hackle configuration (arrow) in a mist region in obsidian. Fracture direction is downward.

observed some similar markings in a carbon-filled frozen rubber. Wallner mist and hackle configurations serve as examples of the significance of stress pulses in the manifestation of general mist and hackle regions, as considered by Poncelet(1958), Fréchette (1990) and Beauchamp (1996). It is seen that the stress pulses from a source behind the fracture front can cause the manifestation of relatively small (velocity) hackle as in Fig. 7.4, and much larger hackle as in (Tsirk 1996: Fig. 5).

Mist Suppression Configurations

A localized obstruction at a fracture front is communicated to points along successive fracture fronts downstream that may be manifested in fracture plan as a line or band with mist suppression, in a relative rather than absolute sense. This is referred to as a **mist suppression configuration** here. Its formation (Tsirk 1996) is analogous to Wallner lines and Wallner mist-hackle configurations. During normal fracturing without an irregularity, stress waves or stress pulses are produced at each "point" along a fracture front and felt at successive fracture fronts downstream. When an obstruction is encountered by a fracture front, the release of such a usual stress pulse is suppressed and communicated to appropriate points along successive fracture fronts. If a stress pulse release at an irregularity can produce Wallner mist-hackle configurations, then it is indeed expected that an irregular obstruction at a fracture front will lead to the manifestation of a mist suppression configuration.

Mist Lines

Mist lines (Figs. 6.4 and 7.5).are narrow bands or "lines" of mist or mist and hackle in the fracture direction in their vicinity. Illustrations appear in Smekal (1950), Poncelet (1958), and Tsirk (1988 and 1996). Mist lines have been observed only in obsidian and other glasses. They have also been called "streaks" (Poncelet 1958, Beauchamp 1995 and 1996). The formation of mist lines is discussed in Beauchamp (1995, 1996) and Tsirk (1996). The key aspects in the formation of mist lines are their origin, their persistence over long distances, and the confinement of their constituent features to a narrow band.

FIG. 7.5 MIST LINE IN OBSIDIAN FRACTURE DIRECTION DOWNWARD.

Fig. 7.6 Mist and hackle patterns. Mist lines in lieu of tails and twist hackles are manifested close to the general mist regions. Mexican obsidian. The fracture origin was near the top. The downward fracture direction is indicated by the mist lines.

Mist lines have been observed only near general mist regions or within regions of light mist. That is, they occur only where the general conditions are almost "ripe" for the manifestation of mist in general. Therefore, very subtle perturbations are needed for mist lines to originate and persist over some distance. Various localized perturbations in the nature of irregularities could cause the initiation, but not the persistence of mist lines. Most often the localized irregularities where they originate are observed to be the terminations of tails (or twist hackles) as well as inclusions. The mist lines occurring furthest from general mist regions were observed to originate from the termination of a tail or a twist hackle; and those closest, from an inclusion. That is, very close to general mist regions, mist lines were observed to be manifested in lieu of tails or twist hackles (Fig. 7.6). A case was observed where a twist hackle reverted to a mist line and then back again to a twist hackle.

The persistence of mist lines is seen as due to a self-generating mechanism (Tsirk 1996). The highly localized lagging (or kink in fracture plan) of the fracture front at a mist line leads to an increase in stress and (effective) stress intensity factor K_I as well as effective energy release rate. The greater energy consumption associated with the production of the roughened surface features within the band, in turn, promotes a localized lagging of the fracture front, promoting increase in K_I. At least two reasons are seen for the confinement of the constituent features of a mist line to a narrow band (Tsirk 1996). One of these relates to the mechanism discussed above for the persistence of the mist lines. This contributes to the localization or "pinning" effect near the center of a mist line. Another reason relates to the stress wave effects. The secondary fracturing at a mist line provides sources for the relevant stress pulses. Their effects are greatest near the center of mist lines because of the greater sources there and the attenuation effects with distance from the center.

Mist lines are sometimes seen to become more pronounced along their length as they approach a general mist region. More pronounced mist lines are observed to occur closer to general mist regions, and very faint ones can be barely detected optically at increased distances. A sea of mist lines is seen in Fig. 5.10, and numerous ones in Fig. 6.4.

Mist lines serve as indicators of fracture direction in their vicinity, and of general mist manifestation being incipient, even when a general mist region itself is not manifested. With regard to fracture direction, it is noted that the direction immediately to each side of a mist line is different, neither of which is parallel to that near the center of the mist line. Therefore, judgment must be used in the interpretation of the fracture direction from mist lines. A similar cautionary note applies to tails and twist hackles as well.

8. Miscellaneous Markings

Material Interface Markings

Material Interface Ridges and Ripples

A **material interface ridge**, due to different material properties at each side of an interface parallel or oblique to the fracture direction, is manifested in fracture plan as a linear feature along the interface and as a subtle ridge on a cross-section normal to it. Such markings on flake surfaces are shown in Figs. 8.1. The formation of a material interface marking is considered in Fig. 8.2. In (a) of this figure, A and B are points just above and below the fracture plane along the interface (dashed line) between materials I and II. Suppose that material II has greater fracture toughness K_{IC}, requiring a greater stress intensity factor and stress normal to the fracture plane. Consider an imaginary cut along the interface, normal to the fracture plane. With no stresses at the cut interface (Fig. 8.2b), the deformations would be such that points A and B would be displaced to A' and B' for material I, and to A" and B" for material II. But since A' and A", as well as B' and B", are really the same point, they must move the same amount. Therefore shear stresses, in the sense shown in (b), must exist at the interface in order to equalize the displacements noted, by stretching A'B' and compressing A"B". On the plane of symmetry (the fracture plane), these shear stresses must be zero. Any slight perturbation in the state of stress at the fracture plane, however, would lead to a shear stress increasing with the distance from the fracture plane. These shears are responsible for the ridge. The shear stress causes a rotation in the direction of the maximum tensile stress, and hence a tilt in the fracture plane. The kind of mechanism described is traditionally referred to as an instability. Thus, a localized shear stress combined with instability is seen to produce the material interface ridge in this case. The development of shears in this case is analogous to that in the formation of an escarpment of a scarp (Table 8.2). One only needs to consider partial fracture fronts that are wet and dry in lieu of materials I and II.

Materials I and II were characterized above by different fracture properties. In principle, interface shears can also develop due to a difference in modulus of elasticity E. Fig. 8.2 would still apply, with material II having a lower E. Material interface ridges are usually very subtle. Probably for this reason they have thus far been observed only in obsidian and other glasses with material inhomogeneity.

Wallner lines intersecting a material ridge are sometimes observed to have a very subtle point of inflection, tending to lag on the side of the interface with greater K_{IC} or a lower E. Material interface ridges provide evidence of a difference in the physical properties of the materials relevant to fracture.

Material Interface Hackle

A **material interface hackle**, due to different material properties at each side of an interface parallel or oblique to the fracture direction, is manifested as a hackle, usually extending in the direction of the material interface.

Just as the formation of the material interface ridge, the hackle is manifested due to localized shear stresses, combined with instability, at the interface, in a manner analogous to the formation of partition hackles and hackle scarps. A material interface hackle may be viewed as a special kind of twist hackle.

Although these markings have thus far been observed only in obsidian, they are expected to occur also in some crystalline materials such as fine grained flints. A material interface hackle indicates a difference in the physical properties of the materials relevant to fracture.

As a cautionary note, it is emphasized that this hackle extends in the direction of the material interface. Thus it is an example of a hackle not in the fracture direction. The material interface hackle is in the fracture direction only when the interface lines up with that direction.

It is of interest to ask why sometimes a material interface hackle is manifested instead of a material interface ridge. Sommer's experiments on twist hackles (1969) indicated that those markings are manifested in glass when the maximum tensile stress rotates at least 3.3°. That is, the shear from Mode III had to be sufficiently high for the particular stress environment. A requirement for a similar condition is likely to relate to the manifestation of a hackle instead of a ridge at a material interface. A clarification is in order, however. We recall that a twist hackle may be manifested prematurely as a tail by an inclusion and persist as a twist hackle. Similarly, one can expect that some particular kind of irregularity can enable a material interface hackle to be manifested without the higher shear stress.

FIG. 8.1 MATERIAL INTERFACE RIDGES (SOLID ARROW) AND MATERIAL TRANSITION RIDGES (DASHED ARROW) IN OBSIDIAN.

Miscellaneous Markings 105

Material Transition Ridge

A **material transition ridge**, due to different material properties at each side of an interface roughly parallel to the fracture front, is manifested in fracture plan as a linear feature along the interface and as a ridge or kink in fracture profile. Some such markings appear in Fig. 8.1.

The change in slope in fracture profile is due to change in the direction of the maximum tensile stress. The reason for this directional change is analogous to that for the formation of the kink at a cavitation scarp (Table 8.2). Analogously, it also follows that a material

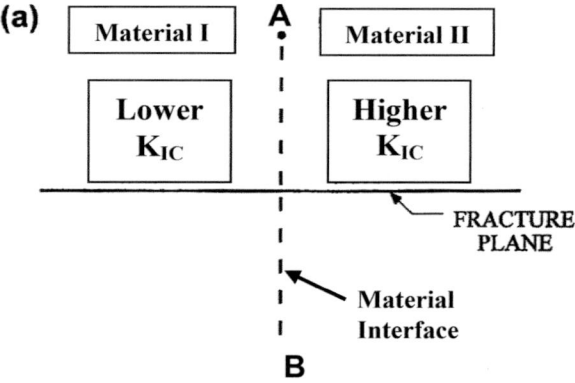

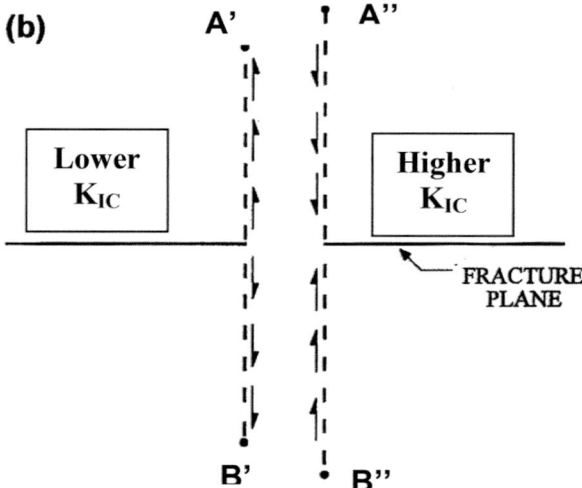

Fig. 8.2 Formation of a material interface ridge.

FIG. 8.3 SPLIT MARKS ON A FLAKE. SPLIT STEP (DASHED ARROW) AND SPLIT RIDGE (SOLID ARROW) ARE SEEN.

transition ridge may sometimes not be manifested at all, even if there are differences in the material properties. But when it does occur at a material interface, it serves as an indication of differences in material properties.

The material interface and transition ridges have been treated as idealized cases in terms of their formation. For a material interface oblique to the fracture direction, the mechanisms discussed for the formation of each of these ridges can be involved.

Split Marks

Longitudinal splitting of a flake often leaves fracture markings termed **split marks** on the flake scar. Fracture markings termed a split ridge and a split step are shown in Fig. 8.3. Split ripples are illustrated in Tsirk (2010a).

The splitting of a flake usually starts at the dorsal (outer) face by the proximal end of the flake. Its initiation is likely to start before the lateral extension of the primary fracture at the proximal end is completed (See Morrell and Gant 2001). The secondary fracture of splitting is due to flake bending in the transverse direction. As the split fracture advances behind the primary fracture front, the "halves" of the partly split flake tend to propagate independently. The split fracture will not be able to catch up with the primary fracture, however. The progress of the split fracture is inhibited by the fact that transverse bending of the flake is not possible at and ahead of the primary fracture front.

XThe split marks are understood by the primary fractures for two flake halves tending to propagate more or less independently. When the "halves" have a different thickness, a **split step** will join them – literally with a step in the transverse direction. When the primary fracture surfaces of the two halves of the flake are not co-planar along the split line, a **split ridge** (Fig. 8.3) can be manifested. **Split ripples** can also be understood as due to the tendency for them to be formed independently for each half of the flake. These ripples can be recognized by their dissimilarity on the two sides of the split line. Sometimes they are offset or kinked in fracture plan. Further variations in split marks and their formation are discussed in Tsirk (2010).

In a sample of 40 flakes with complete longitudinal splits, split marks were seen on 63% of the cases. Split ridges and split steps were manifested on 55% and 20%, respectively. In 28% of the cases, somewhat surprisingly, the split did not start by the proximal end of the flake

Split marks on negative flake scars can indicate that the flake detached was split. This is of archaeological interest for technologies where the flakes were utilized. Split ridges have been recognized on a cast of a Clovis point from Blackwater No.1 Site (Fig. 1.3 and Tsirk 2010: Fig. 4), and a split step or a split ridge is seen on a Clovis biface illustrated in Frison and Bradley (1999: 54-55).

Dividing Lines

When two independent fractures or two partial fracture fronts run together, they often do so leaving a linear feature termed here a **dividing line** or a **junction line** ("Vereinigungslinie" in German). It is often manifested on a flake that had two separate initiations offset in fracture plan. The tails (wake hackles) that are formed by two partial fracture fronts running around an inclusion may also be viewed as dividing lines. Two bulbar scars initiated at twist hackles on opposite sides of a flake often run together at a dividing line, and they may continue with a single fracture front. The split ridge considered in the previous section may also be viewed as a dividing line

A dividing line, appearing as a linear feature in fracture plan, is manifested as a ridge or a hackle. A dividing line is not always manifested when two fracture fronts meet, as sometimes on a flake with two separate origins. The ridges between two flake scars on a biface or other core may also be viewed as dividing lines.

Ruffles

The outside surfaces of obsidian nodules are sometimes pockmarked by multitudinous small cones, cone-like features or their remnants, as well as other irregularities from fractures and weathering effects. **Ruffles** are multitudinous irregular undulations, dimples and humps on the ventral surface of a flake due to highly irregular geometrical features on its dorsal surface (Fig. 8.4).

The formation of ruffles can be understood by recalling that a fracture surface tends to be normal to the direction of the maximum tensile stress. When a flake is sufficiently

FIG. 8.4 RUFFLES ON THE INNER SURFACE OF AN OBSIDIAN FLAKE DUE TO GEOMETRICAL IRREGULARITIES ON OUTER SURFACE. (FROM TSIRK 2012)

thin, the geometrical irregularities at its dorsal surface affect the stresses producing the fracture, causing multitudinous and irregular directional changes in the maximum tension.

If a subsequent, sufficiently thin flake is detached from a core at the location of the ruffles (the **primary ruffles**), **secondary ruffles** may be manifested on the ventral surface of the flake. As expected, the secondary ruffles tend to be less pronounced.

The manifestation of ruffles depends on the thickness of a flake relative to the characteristic dimensions of the dorsal irregularities. Ruffles have also been observed on flint.

Ruffles on the flake scar of a core provide an indication of the nature of the dorsal surface of the flake detached. Those on the dorsal surface of a flake may obviously be interpreted similarly, relating to the dorsal surface of the previous flake. Needless to say, distinction between primary and secondary ruffles on a core is hazardous at best.

Liquid-Induced Fracture Markings (LIFMS)

Effects of Moisture and Liquids

As noted in Chapter 3, very slow fracture propagation in glass is facilitated by water as vapor, liquid or in solution (Fréchette 1990). Some other liquids also have this effect (Michalske and Bunker 1987). It is caused by a chemical-physical interaction of glass with the environment involved in the presence of stress. Not surprisingly, the effects are amplified at higher temperatures (Schönert, Umhauer and Klemm 1969). The terms **stress corrosion** and **static fatigue** have sometimes been used for these effects. Of practical interest to archaeology is the fact that all liquids in nature contain water.

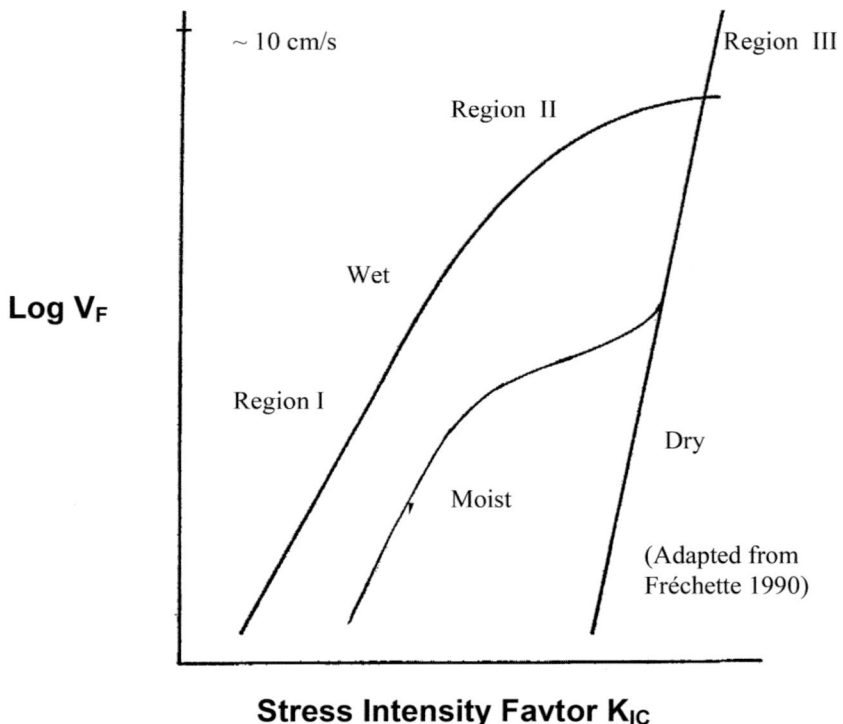

FIG. 8.5 VARIATION OF FRACTURE VELOCITY V_F WITH STRESS INTENSITY FACTOR K_I FOR DRY, MOIST AND WET ENVIRONMENTS FOR A GLASS

In terms of physical behavior, the chemical interaction in the presence of stress causes a fracture front to sharpen and extend (Michalske 1984). In the absence of stress, however, the effect of the moisture or liquid is to blunt the front of an existing fracture or microfracture, thereby strengthening the specimen. This is known as **aging**, first brought to the attention of archaeologists by Bonnichsen (1974).

As seen from Fig. 8.5, a smaller stress intensity factor K_I is required to propagate a fracture at a given velocity V_F in moist air or with water as compared to dry air, and with water compared to moist air. It is also significant to note from the figure that the effects of water can be felt at significantly higher velocities V_F (plotted at a logarithmic scale) than of moisture.

Water cannot follow a fracture at higher fracture velocities. The fracture front will become dry either because of depletion of the liquid or because of cavitation at the front. However, crack propagation can also be facilitated by water (or other liquid) contained in a lithic material from wetting or soaking. No LIFMs are known for such cases.

The liquid behind a fracture front can sometimes have a slight effect in retarding the fracture (Richter 1985). This effect, probably insignificant for lithic technology, is evident to the reader by noting that two plates of glass with liquid in between cannot be pulled apart suddenly without exerting some force.

The effects of water are known to be significant for glasses, including obsidian, and many ceramic materials. This is also expected for chert, flint and other lithic materials of interest to archaeology.

Conditions for Manifestation of LIFMs

When a fracture is propagating with parts of its front dry and wet, or with variable availability of liquid at parts of the front, a local stress irregularity results because water tends to assist in the fracture process. Such localized stress irregularities lead to the manifestation of fracture markings known as **liquid-induced fracture markings** (LIFMs), also termed **Fréchette markings**.

From the previous section, it is evident that the manifestation of LIFMs requires a slow fracture velocity (V_F) and the presence of liquid as well as stress. These are the necessary, not the sufficient conditions.

Stress is always present during the detachment of a flake or a use-chip. For window glass, for example, V_F less than about 5 cm/s is required (Michalske 1979). The velocity required for obsidian is not known, but is expected to be in about the same range. We may assume it to be of the order of 10 cm/s or less. This is extremely slow as far as the fracture velocities in knapping are concerned.

Water vapor can also lead to the manifestation of fracture markings (Varner and Fréchette 1971). However, these markings look very different and are distinguishable from LIFMs. They have been observed only with the vapor diffused to the fracture front laterally from the sides of a narrow specimen but never from behind the fracture front. These markings are not expected in knapping contexts. The markings can occur only at much slower fracture velocities than those normally associated with LIFMs (Fig. 8.5). For window glass, for example, they would have to be of about two orders of magnitude less, say roughly 0.05 cm/s or less. Therefore any such markings in knapping would probably occur so close to the fracture origin that they would not be observable by optical microscopy.

A difference in surface chemistry by environment-assisted and environment-free fractures is demonstrated in Quackenbush and Fréchette (1978). The different fracture surface characteristics are seen by different condensation patterns for the fracture surfaces exposed to 100% relative humidity.

Occurrence of LIFMs

Thus far LIFMs have not been observed in polycrystalline materials such as ceramics, chert or flint because the markings are usually very subtle. However, the LIFMs which are manifested as a hackle (B in Table 8.1; see also the hackle scarp or the partition hackle in Table 8.2) are often not nearly as subtle as other LIFMs. Manifestation and observation of those LIFMs may perhaps be possible for very fine grained crystalline

TABLE 8.1 BASIC TYPES OF LIFMS (BY APPEARANCE)

Desig-nation	LIFM Type	Description	Remarks on Observation	Illustration Figure
A	Escarpment Scarp	Seen as escarpment, a light-dark contrast or both	Seen only with brightfield illumination.	8.6
B	Liquid-Induced Hackle	Looks like a twist hackle except it does not extend in fracture direction	Seen with brightfield as well as darkfield illumination.	8.7
C	Linear Band Features	Fine linear features or linear bands usually in fracture direction	Seen only with brightfield illumination.	8.8
D	Cavitation Scarp	Seen as light-dark contrast, due to slight kink in fracture profile. Usually seen as a smooth arc.	Cannot be identified reliably without other evidence. Can look like arrest lines.	8.9

materials such as some flints, but have not yet been reported. No LIFMs have yet been observed in any prehistoric knapping context on any material. They have been observed on use-chip scars on Aztec blades of obsidian (Tsirk and Parry 2000).

LIFMs have been observed in single crystals. Many varieties of quartzite have been used for prehistoric stone tools in many parts of the world, including Eastern North America. It is conceivable that LIFMs can be manifested on the larger crystals in quartzite.

LIFMs have also been observed on Glass Buttes obsidian nodules fractured in a geological context, as well as on fire-fractured obsidian from Jemez Mountains (Tsirk 2005). They were found just downstream of arrest lines. Most likely, condensation had occurred at the fracture front of a pre-existing crack prior to re-initiation of the fracture from the arrest line. Condensation at a sharp crack is faster than on a flat surface.

In contemporary knapping experiments, LIFMs have been observed usually on 70 to 90 % of the obsidian pressure flakes produced when the platform region was wetted with water or saliva (Tsirk and Parry 2000). Moving a wetted finger across the region is sufficient. In most cases, the markings occurred within 1 mm of the fracture origin.

LIFMs have not been observed in contemporary knapping experiments with direct percussion. Probably this is mostly because the fracture accelerates very rapidly with direct percussion. The markings, which would be anticipated, would probably occur too close to the fracture origin to be observable in the usual optical microscopy, at say 200X and lower magnification. The proximal regions of many if not most direct percussion flakes have extensive damage or scars from secondary fracturing. These would make the observation of any fracture markings that may occur in the proximal region more difficult.

Significance of LIFMs

The presence of a LIFM in a knapping or use-chipping context indicates that external liquid was present to wet the fracture front during the fracture involved. Lack of an observed LIFM, however, does not prove the absence of a liquid. The markings, sometimes extremely subtle, cannot always be found.

When LIFMs are seen in a knapping context, it must be kept in mind that, in principle, the external liquid could be from any possible source. Of conceivable practical interest is the fact that a nodule or piece of obsidian cooled at night can have condensation on it early on a warm morning from air humidity.

Observation of LIFMs on a flake by the usual optical microscopy would indicate the likely use of pressure rather than percussion flaking. LIFMs are often manifested differently due to different liquids. This is of interest to use-chipping.

Basic Kinds of LIFMs

The basic types of LIFMs, by their appearance rather than causal mechanisms, are listed in Table 8.1 along with a brief description, references to illustrations, as well as remarks regarding their observation. For potential applications in knapping, a recognition of just these basic types would usually be sufficient as evidence for the presence of a liquid during the fracture. For use-chipping, as noted, the variability of the markings with different liquids is also of interest.

Various other kinds of evidence, other than just for the presence of a liquid, can be obtained from LIFMs. For this purpose, it is necessary to consider the mechanisms involved with

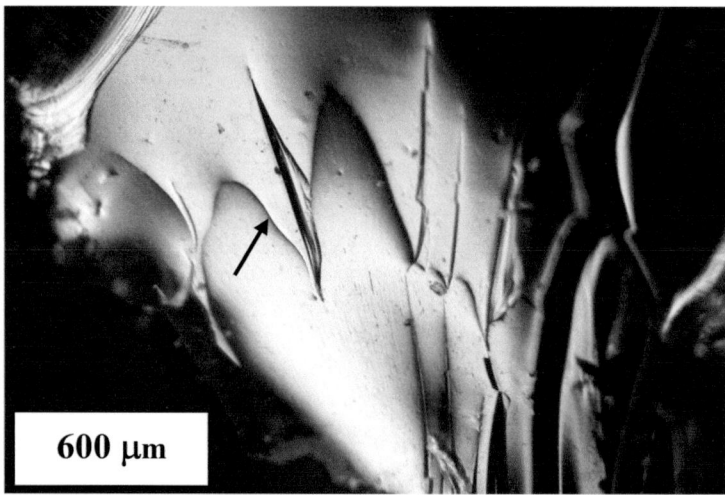

FIG. 8.6 THE BASIC LIFM TYPE CALLED AN ESCARPMENT SCARP (ARROW) ON AN OBSIDIAN PRESSURE FLAKE WITH THE PLATFORM WETTED WITH WATER. FRACTURE DIRECTION UPWARD.

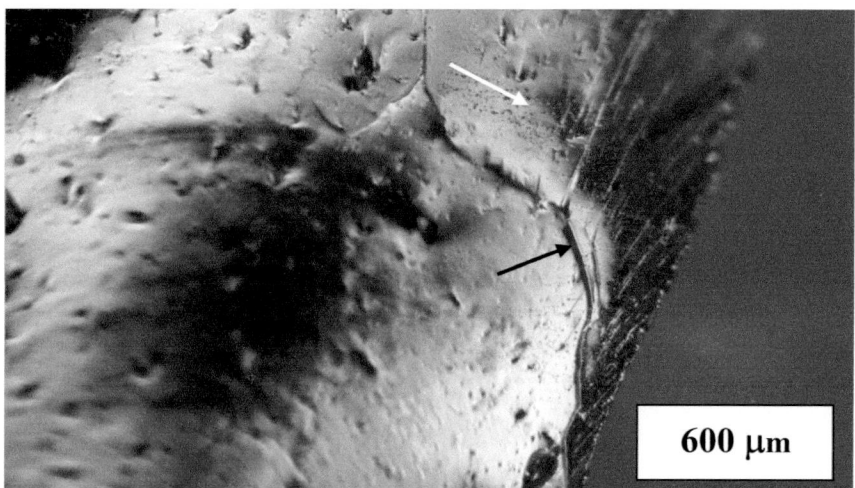

FIG. 8.7 THE BASIC LIFM TYPE CALLED A LIQUID-INDUCED HACKLE (ARROW). THE PLATFORM WAS WETTED WITH SALIVA FOR THE OBSIDIAN PRESSURE FLAKE. FRACTURE DIRECTION UPWARD.

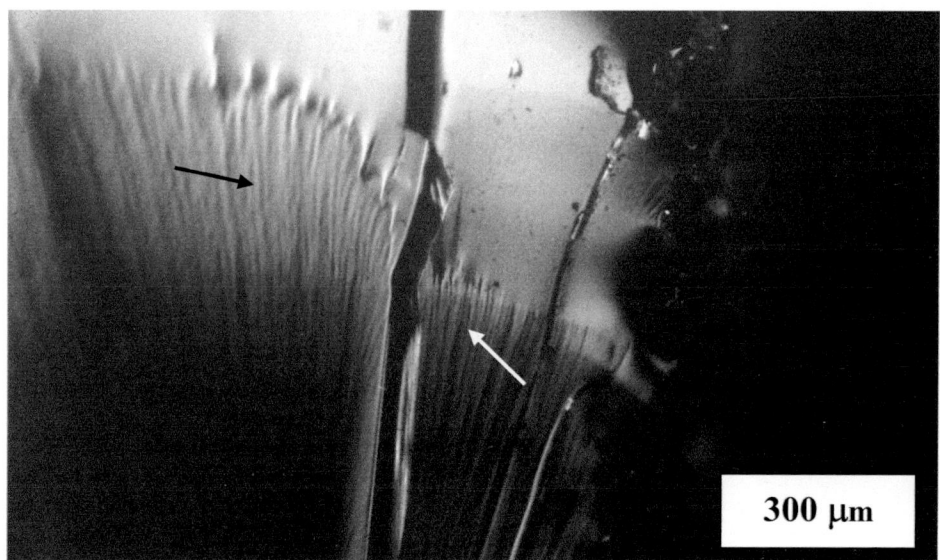

FIG. 8.8 THE BASIC LIFM TYPE CALLED LINEAR BAND FEATURES (ARROWS). OBSIDIAN PRESSURE FLAKE. PLATFORM WETTED WITH WATER. FRACTURE DIRECTION UPWARD.

the various LIFMs. A more detailed description and explanation of of the various kinds of LIFMs is also useful in the positive identification of LIFMs as such when difficulties in their recognition are encountered. Therefore, a catalogue of most of the known LIFMs is presented in this chapter. These markings, listed in Table 8.2, have the appearance of one of the four basic types of LIFMs indicated in Table 8.1.

The escarpment scarp (A in Table 8.1) is manifested as either an escarpment or as a tilt, or as both (Fig. 8.6). Despite the misnomer by appearance, the same term is used for all of these cases because of practical considerations in their distinction.

The liquid-induced hackle (B in the table, and No.1B – Hackle scarp in Table 8.2) can be recognized as it extends in other than the fracture direction (Fig. 8.7). As a cautionary note, however, it should be recalled that a material interface hackle may also not extend in the fracture direction.

The linear band features (C in the table) usually extend in the fracture direction (Fig. 8.8). They may, however, sometimes extend instead in the direction of liquid transport to the fracture front.

A cavitation scarp (D in the table) usually cannot be recognized as such in flaking, unless there is other evidence, because arrest lines can look identical. Such other evidence may consist, for example, of linear band features extending up to and terminating at the cavitation scarp, as in Fig. 8.9. Other kinds of LIFMs contiguous with the cavitation scarp may also enable its recognition as such.

A Catalogue of LIFMs and Patterns

A list of most of the known LIFMs is presented in Table 8.2 with a brief description, and references to illustrations. Rather than explain the formation of the LIFMs, the table

FIG. 8.9 THE BASIC LIFM TYPE CALLED A CAVITATION SCARP (ARROW) ON AN OBSIDIAN PRESSURE FLAKE. PLATFORM WETTED WITH WATER. FRACTURE DIRECTION UPWARD TO RIGHT. (ADAPTED FROM TSIRK 2001.)

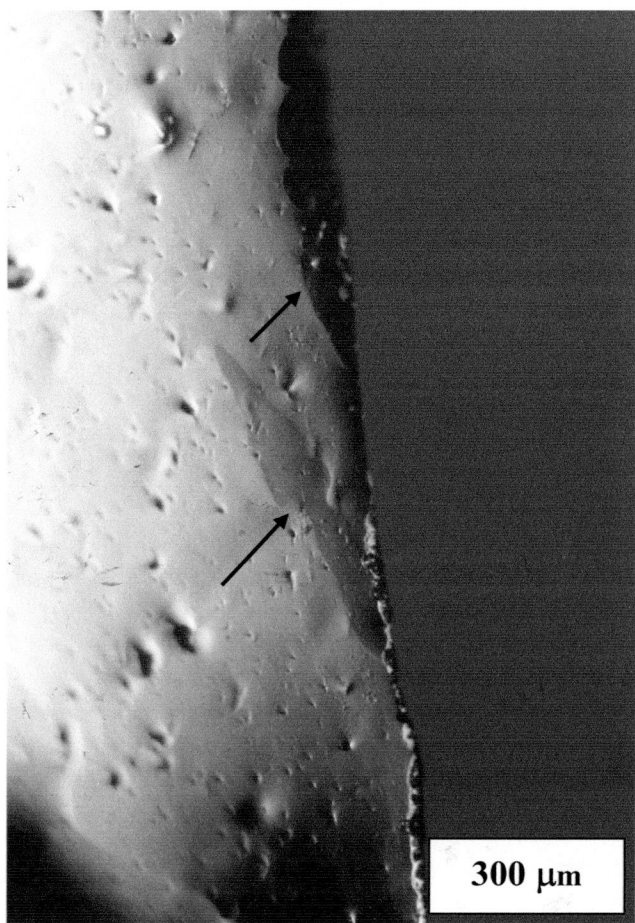

FIG. 8.10 TWO UNUSUAL ENCOUNTER-DEPLETION SCARPS. OBSIDIAN, WETTED WITH SALIVA. FRACTURING UPWARD. THE UPSTREAM PART OF EACH SCARP IS AN ENCOUNTER SCARP (ARROW).

indicates briefly the mechanism associated with their formation. Examples of LIFMs are shown in Figs. 8.6 to 8.14 and 8.16 to 8.18. All but a few of the referenced illustrations are for pressure flaked obsidian. Fig. 8.11 is for an accidental break of a soda-lime glass in the sink. Figs. 8.16 and 8.17 are for an industrial waste glass with many inclusions of variable sizes. The wetting was with water, saliva or blood, except for the single soda-lime glass specimen.

Some terminology in the table differs from that used by others in published literature. A scarp has also been called an intersection scarp by Michalske (1984, 1994) and Fréchette (1984). A cavitation scarp is also known as a transition scarp (Michalske 1979, 1994) and a Michalske scarp (Fréchette 1990). The subcavitation hackle of Fréchette (1990) has also been referred to as transition hackle, hackle ridges, hackle steps and fine hackle by Michalske (1979, 1991, 1994) and as fine wake hackle by Fréchette (1990). The definition of Sierra scarps as well as encounter and depletion scarps as indicated in Table 8.2 was generalized in Tsirk (2007).

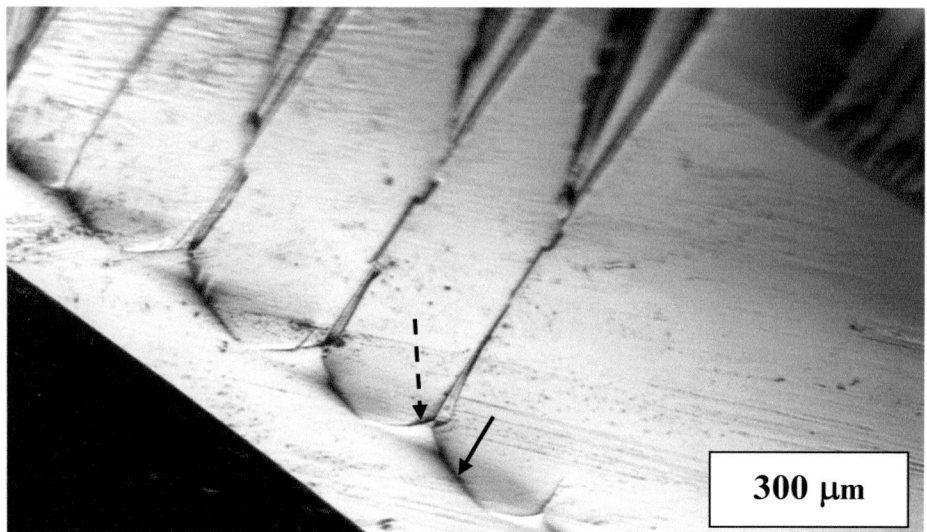

FIG. 8.11 SIERRA SCARPS IN A SODA-LIME GLASS PLATE BROKEN ACCIDENTALLY IN A SINK WITH LIQUID. FRACTURE DIRECTION IS UP TO THE RIGHT. THE UPSTREAM SHOULDERS ARE ENCOUNTER SCARPS, PARTLY WITH ESCARPMENTS (ARROW) AND PARTLY WITH HACKLE SCARPS (DASHED ARROW).

The various types of LIFMs are often not manifested as distinct markings. For example, parts of one continuous LIFM may be an encounter scarp and a depletion scarp, as in Fig. 8.10. As seen from the table, the same overall marking may be viewed as consisting of several types of LIFMs. For example, the upstream shoulders of a Sierra scarp (No. 7A in Table 8.2) may be viewed as encounter scarps and occasionally as hackle scarps (Fig. 8.11).

Observation of LIFMs

Rarely can LIFMs be seen by naked eye. Their positive identification requires magnification. 50X or 100X is adequate. Occasional use of 200X magnification on a binocular optical microscope is helpful. Hackle type LIFM may be viewed with either darkfield or brightfield illumination, but the latter is required for all other types of LIFMs. If the finer Wallner lines cannot be seen, then it is unlikely that LIFMs will be visible. For observing LIFMs on use-chip scars of, say, 0.1 to 0.5 mm in length, 100X together with 200X magnification is preferable. For photography, magnifications of 12.5X to 100X (onto a 35 mm film) are suitable, depending on the particular LIFM features of interest.

Many LIFMs are very subtle. Lighting is therefore critical. Several rotations of a specimen are usually required for the observation. The rotations may sometimes have to be very slight. Stereo microscopes are less suitable for observing LIFMs. Because of the subtle nature of the markings, proper focusing for both eyes is not possible for many if not most of them.

TABLE 8.2 LIQUID-INDUCED FRACTURE MARKINGS (LIFMs)

No.	Marking	Appearance	Definition/ Mechanism	Illustration
1	Scarp	As escarpment scarp, hackle scarp, or cavitation scarp.	Formed between wet and dry partial fracture fracture fronts, caused by liquid.	—
1A	Escarpment Scarp	Usually an escarpment or tilt in section, a line in fracture plan.	A scarp manifested as an escarpment or tilt. Different K_I at the wet and dry partial fracture fronts produce shears in a plane normal to the scarp, at the wet/dry interface.	(Figs. 2-27, 2-28, and 2-30)[3]
1B	Hackle Scarp	Like a twist hackle, but usually not in fracture direction.	A scarp manifested as a hackle. The same interface shears as for No. 1A, when large enough, are responsible for the hackle.	(Figs. 1a, 3c)[4], (Fig. 4)[5], (Figs. 9B, 9C)[6]
2	Cavitation Scarp	Usually a subtle kink in fracture profile, and a smooth arc in fracture plan. Occasionally the kink is absent. May look like an abrupt depletion line..	A scarp formed due to cavitation at an accelerating fracture front at the Region II/III transition. The cavitation may occur at only a part of the marking.	(Figs. 16, 17)[2], (Figs. 2-25, 2-26)[3], (Fig. 2a)[4]
3	Encounter Scarp	An escarpment scarp, a hackle scarp or a combination.	A scarp formed with wet partial fracture front expanding at the scarp location.	Figs. 8.6, 8.10, 8.14 (Fig.2-31, 2-32)[3], (Figs. 13-15)[1]
3A	Deceleration Scarp	A special form of an escarpment or a hackle scarp. Rarely identifiable, by Wallner lines or other evidence.	A scarp formed with gradual wetting of the fracture front when it decelerates through Region III/II transition. Wetting retards and enhances fracturing at its upstream and downstream parts, respectively.	(Figs. 24, 25)[1], (Fig. 2-27)[3]
4	Depletion Scarp	An escarpment scarp; extremely rarely a hackle scarp.	A scarp formed with wet partial fracture front retracting at the scarp location.	(Fig. 1A)[2], (Fig. 2-33)[3], (Figs. 1b, 2, 3a, 3b, 4)[4]

No.	Marking	Appearance	Definition/ Mechanism	Illustration
4A	Pointed-looped Scarp Pattern	A scarp resembling an inverted, multi-looped Sierra scarp. The loops may be regular or irregular, smooth or jagged.	A depletion scarp with the appearance described. Suggested mechanism: Initiation due to an instability; persistence related to energy considerations, with limitation of liquid to a fracture front in an overall sense.	(Figs. 2a and b)[4]
5	Partition Marking	Looks like an escarpment scarp or a hackle scarp.	Formed with liquid at the partial fracture front on each side. A LIFM, but not a scarp, manifested due to different liquid transport at its sides.	—
5A	Partition Hackle	Looks like a twist hackle, but usually does not extend in the fracture direction. Usually the part of a hackle zig-zag or an L-shaped hackle that is not in the fracture direction.	A LIFM manifested as a hackle with different liquid transport at its sides (because lateral liquid transport is prevented before and probably inhibited after the lateral break-through of a hackle). This leads to unequal effective K_I at the partial fracture fronts and to interface shears in a plane normal to the hackle.	(Fig. 1b)[7], (Fig. 9B)[6]
5B	Partition Escarpment	Observed at some boundaries of linear band features (No. 8). Looks like an especially subtle escarpment scarp. May be laterally diffuse, ill-defined.	A LIFM with the formation mechanism suggested to be akin to that for the starvation (No.8A) and depletion bands (No.8B). With forked fingerlet bands, it is associated with enhanced liquid transport in the bands.	(Fig. 3A and 3B)[7]
6	Zig-zag and L-shaped Hackle Patterns	A hackle with a zig-zag or a L shape. The part not in the fracture direction is a hackle scarp or a partition hackle, with the remaining part of the hackle being a twist hackle.	The turn or turns of the hackle relate to competition of two mechanisms – those for the twist hackle and those for the liquid-induced hackle.	(Fig. 1B)[7], (Fig. 9C)[6], (Fig. 1b)[4]

MISCELLANEOUS MARKINGS   119

No.	Marking	Appearance	Definition/ Mechanism	Illustration
7	Sierra Marking	Various forms of escarpment or hackle scarp or their combination. Usually concave in the fracture direction.	Formed when liquid from behind a dry (or starving) fracture front catches up with it, to affect parts of the fracture front gradually.	—
7A	Sierra Scarp	Manifested as multiple loops, usually contiguous, concave in the fracture direction.	Formed with the liquid behind a dry fracture front, as fingerlets due to Taylor instability, catching up to wet the fracture front gradually. Manifested usually without cavitation upstream.	(Figs. 2-28, 2-30)[3], (Fig. 2)[5]
7B	V Marking	Manifested in the form of a V opening in the fracture direction. Each side may be an escarpment or hackle scarp or a combination of these.	A V-scarp is formed with the liquid front, resembling a V opening in the upstream direction, catching up from behind the dry fracture front. Perhaps other V-markings could be formed when liquid from behind a starving rather than dry fracture front catches up with it.	(Figs.2C and 5)[4]
7C	Y Pattern	Looks as if a twist hackle splits into a V, with one side of the V being a hackle and the other an escarpment	Liquid from behind a dry (or starving) fracture front catches up with it preferentially at and to one side of the twist hackle upstream of the V.	(Fig. 5)[4]
7D	Ψ Pattern	As a Y-pattern but with a tiny twist hackle, appearing to split the V, extending from the twist hackle upstream of the V.	As a Y-pattern, with the mechanism related to the liquid transport at the tiny twist hackle splitting the V unknown.	(Fig. 1d)[4]
7E	Slurp Scarp	The hackle offset part of a hackle zig-zag with a miniscule escarpment scarp adjacent to and downstream of the offset.	Liquid from behind a dry fracture front is sucked in to the fracture front preferentially within or at only one side of a twist hackle, causing it to turn as a hackle scarp and to manifest the escarpment scarp.	(Fig. 1c)[4]

No.	Marking	Appearance	Definition/ Mechanism	Illustration
8	Linear Band Features	Valleys and ridges appearing as lines or bands in the direction of fracture or liquid transport.	LIFMs having the appearance described. Their onset is suggested to relate to instability in liquid transport leading to "channels" of different liquid transport, which produce shear stresses in a plane normal to the band, causing the valleys and ridges.	Figs. 8.8
8A	Starvation Bands	A linear band feature with liquid depletion usually at a scarp or an abrupt depletion line directly downstream of it.	Linear band features with limited liquid supply to the fracture front within the band.	(Fig. 1A, 2 and 3)[7], (Figs. 3a, 4c)[4]
8B	Depletion Bands	Linear band features with no liquid depletion at a scarp or other fracture marking directly downstream of it.	Linear band features with liquid being completely depleted in the band.	(Figs. 2 and 3)[7], (Figs. 3a and 5)[4]
8C	Forked Fingerlet Bands	Bands usually resembling escarpment scarps in the form of forked fingerlets, appearing as a "sparse" or "dense" population. Some shoulders of the bands can be partition hackles.	The bands are associated with enhanced liquid transport. Suggested manifestation: due to different liquid supply within and outside a band. At least some of the parts resembling escarpment scarps are suggested to be partition escarpments (No. 5B), the counterparts of partition hackle.	(Fig. 3)[7]
9	Wake Scarp	A scarp downstream of an irregularity such as an inclusion, a twist hackle or wake hackle.	A scarp due to an irregularity affecting liquid transport to the fracture front downstream of it.	(Fig. 9A)[6]

Table references: 1 = Michalske 1979;   2 = Michalske 1991;   3 = Fréchette 1990;
4 = Tsirk 2001;   5 = Tsirk and Parry 2000;
6 = Tsirk 1996;   7 = Tsirk 2007   (Adapted from Tsirk 2007)

MISCELLANEOUS MARKINGS 121

FIG. 8.12 AN ENCOUNTER SCARP (ARROW) MANIFESTED AS A HACKLE SCARP. OBSIDIAN, WETTED WITH WATER. FRACTURE DIRECTION UPWARD.

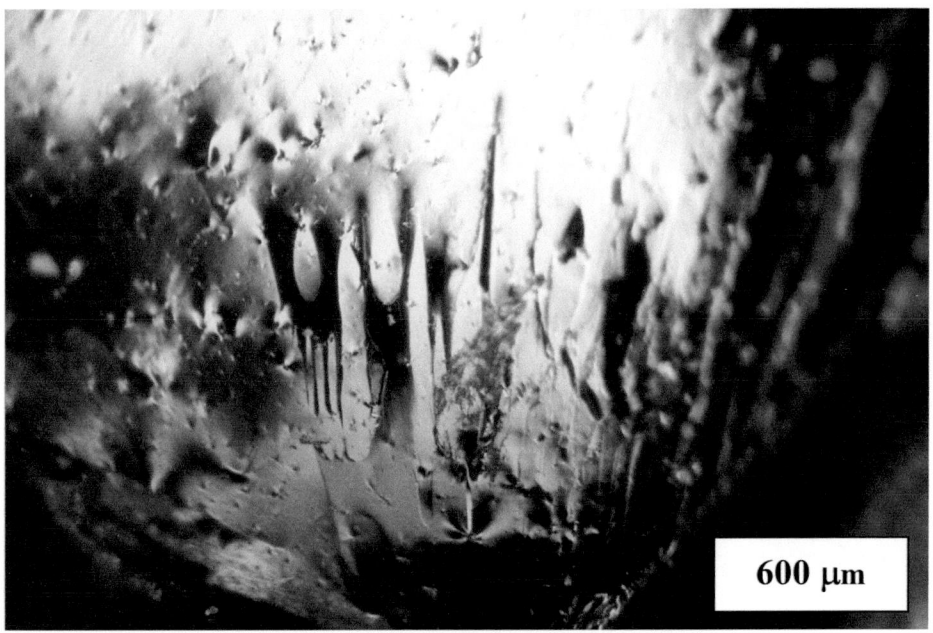

FIG. 8.13 MISCELLANEOUS SCARPS. MOST PROMINENT ARE THE ENCOUNTER-DEPLETION SCARPS MANIFESTED IN THE FORM OF FINGERLETS. OBSIDIAN, WETTED WITH SALIVA. FRACTURE DIRECTION UPWARD.

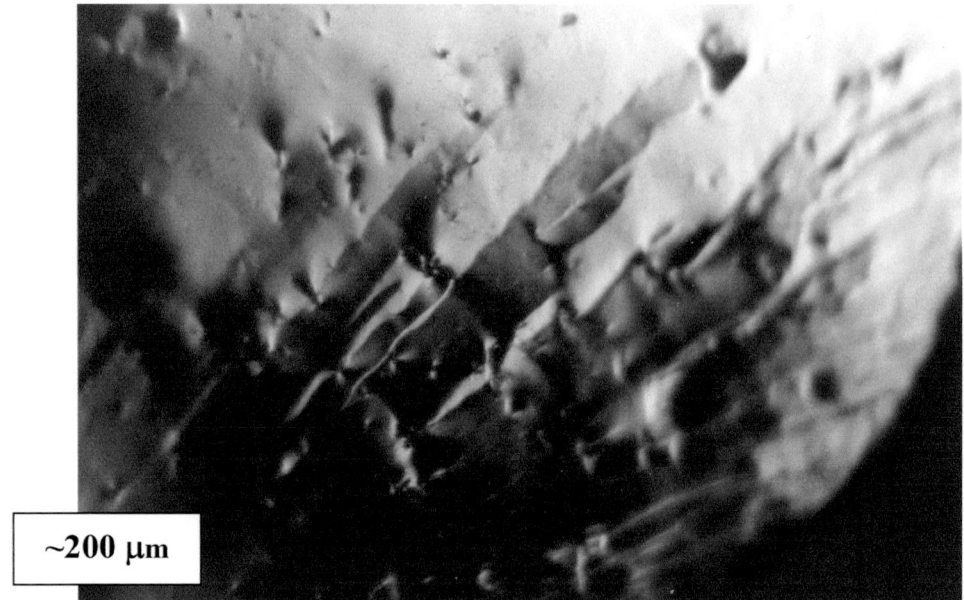

Fig. 8.14 Depletion scarps manifested as irregular fingerlets. Obsidian, wetted with blood. Such irregular fingerlets were never seen with water or saliva. Fracture direction upward to the right (Adapted from Tsirk 2001.)

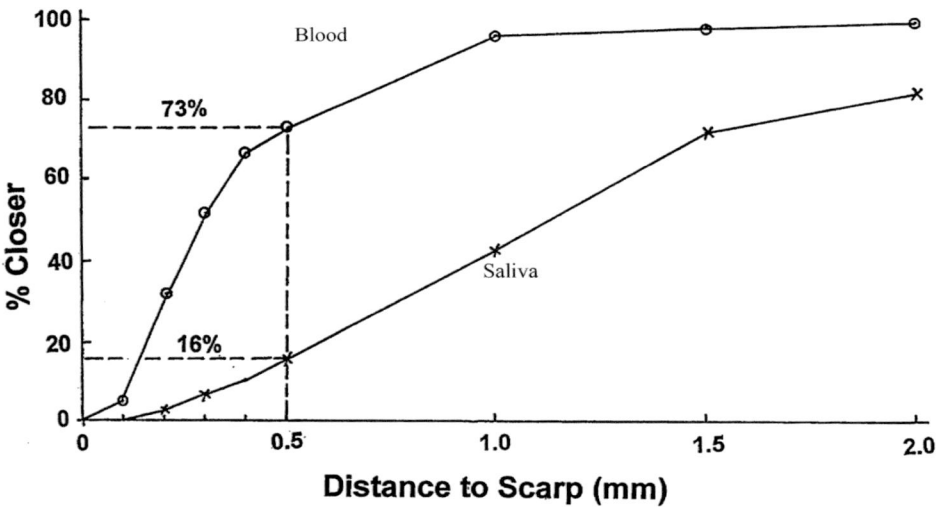

Fig. 8.15 Occurrence of scarps with distance from the fracture origin on pressure flakes of obsidian.

Since LIFMs can occur only with very low fracture velocity VF, they are found at the proximal end of a flake, usually within 0.1 to 3.0 mm from the fracture origin. In use-chipping on Aztec blades they were observed on flake scars as small as 0.1 mm. It is useful to note that whenever gull wings are seen, the fracture velocity is already much too high.

For the purpose of studying various kinds of LIFMs, it is most convenient to produce pressure flakes (say ~1 cm or larger in size for convenience of handling) by wetting the platform region and then flaking while it is still wet. For example, moving a finger across the tongue and wetting the platform with the finger will suffice.

Variability with Liquids

Differences in the manifestation of LIFMs have been observed (Fig. 8.14) sometimes for blood vs. water or saliva, and usually for a 1:1 honey-water mixture vs. the other liquids noted (Tsirk and Parry 2000, Tsirk 2001). Such differences with regard to various liquids are of interest to use-wear studies on stone tools.

LIFMs from blood tend to occur closer to the fracture origin than with water or saliva (Fig. 8.15). This relates to viscosity.

Variability with Lithic Materials

Hydration of obsidian can hinder or obscure the observation of LIFMs. Scarps have been observed, however, on some obsidian specimens from a geological context that have a fair amount of hydration. Identification of these LIFMs as to their specific kind was not possible, however.

Residues, deposits, as well as coatings and sandblasting from weathering can also make the observation of LIFMs difficult or impossible. For example, my inspection of numerous Folsom channel flakes of obsidian from New Mexico was useless because of some coating or sandblasting. In this case the finer Wallner lines and twist hackles could not be seen at all.

With some residues and deposits present on Aztec blades of obsidian, however, some LIFMs were still observed (Tsirk and Parry 2000). There is no doubt that more LIFMs would have been observed without the residues and deposits. With regard to cleaning the residues or deposits, there is the dilemma of destroying evidence on use.

Presence of many inclusions in obsidian can also hinder the observation of LIFMs. It is of interest to note, however, that very many inclusions of different sizes in an industrial waste glass (received from E. Chrisbocher) rendered some of the markings more conspicuous (Tsirk 2001). In this unusual material, at least two kinds of LIFMs were observed that have not been encountered in other lithic materials (Figs. 8.16 and 8.17). Such markings were encountered on each and every pressure flake when the platform was wetted with water.

The unusual band features seen have also been observed with water in soda-lime glass by Richter and in a sintered glass by Fraboulet.

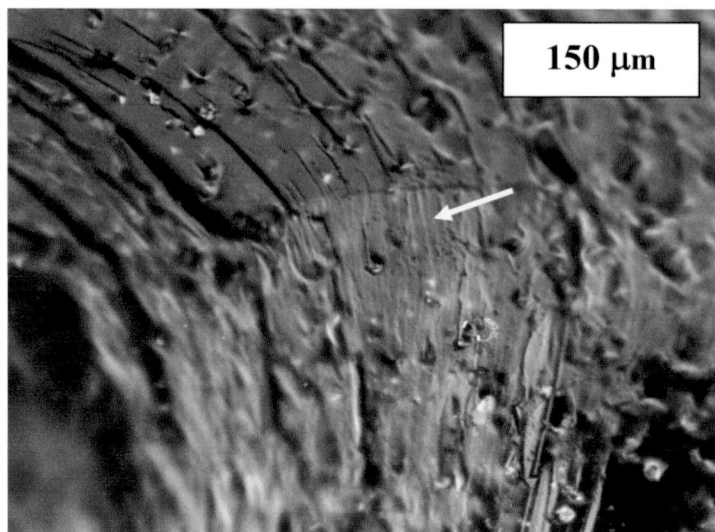

Fig. 8.16 The very many inclusions of variable sizes in this pressure flake of industrial waste glass rendered the LIFMs (arrow) particularly conspicuous. Water used for wetting. General fracture direction upward.

LIFMs with Sonic Modulation

Low frequency sonic modulation and high frequency ultrasonic modulation are discussed in Chapter 6. Examples of LIFMs with sonic modulation at 183 Hz are shown in Figs. 6.9 and 8.18.

The 183 Hz frequency used was adequate for V_F up to about 2 or 3 cm/s. Unfortunately, it was too low for the V_F range in which cavitation scarps are manifested.

LIFMs Observed with Condensation

Fracturing with moisture or liquids involves physical-chemical processes. It is therefore not surprising that a fracture surface produced with wetting differs from one produced when dry. As already noted, such differences have been made visible by the patterns of condensation introduced on the surface. Such patterns may indicate a LIFM configuration (Bauer 1981, Quackenbush and Fréchette 1978: 405-406).

Some Surface Patterns

Fractal analysis has indicated differences for the fracture surfaces of Ocala Chert of Florida that were fractured with and without heat treatment (Mecholsky and Mackin 1988). In particular, the fractal dimension was different for these cases. It is anticipated that fractal analysis will also ahow differences for flint fractured when relatively dry as opposed to having significant internal water. For example, a good candidate for such an investigation would be Brandon flint when fresh out of chalk as compared to it having the fracture surface dried out.

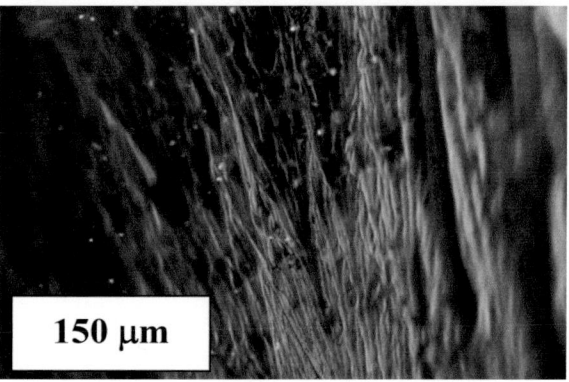

Fig. 8.17 The very many inclusions of variable sizes in the industrial waste glass led consistently to manifestation of very unusual and conspicuous LIFMs over the whole surface. Water used for wetting. General fracture direction upward.

Fig. 8.18 Sonic modulation at 183 Hz was used for this obsidian pressure flake wetted with water. The encounter scarp (arrow) is formed when water becomes available from the right side. From the configurations of these Wallner lines, it is seen that water facilitates crack advance.

PART III - FRACTURES IN KNAPPING

9. Introduction

After introducing the elements of knapping and the tools of fractography, these tools are applied here to interpret some fractures in knapping. But it is first appropriate to ask what, if anything, is unusual about fractures and fractography in knapping. In contrast to the interests in most other fields, such as industrial applications, it is usually production rather than prevention of fractures that is of greatest interest in knapping as well as in intentional breakage of lithic artifacts. Prevention of fractures is also of vital interest in knapping to prevent accidental breakages. Knapping aside, edge chipping is of great interest to use-wear studies (Hayden 1979, Keeley 1980). A fracture surface may be altered significantly after the breakage. For prehistoric and contemporary fractures, such alterations may be quite different. Particularly significant can be patination of flint and hydration of obsidian specimens. These changes may render the interpretation of fracture markings difficult or impossible. Applications of fractography, as in industry and lithic technology, rely on theoretical and experimental research as well as intuitive understandings from experience. Limited theoretical background is more evident in lithic technology applications. These depend less on theoretical and empirical research and rely more on the vastly greater intuitive understanding. Fractography has been practiced over 2.5 million years. Lithic analysts often deal with over 10,000 fracture specimens from a single site, and a master knapper produces over a million fractures in his lifetime. Such fractures involve a great variety of specimen geometries, loadings and boundary conditions, as well as material properties and flaw characteristics. Such a variety of fractures is not encountered in other fields. Therefore, the interpretation of fractures in knapping poses unusual challenges. The variety and complexities involved makes the investigations intellectually rewarding to anyone interested in understanding fractures in general and knapping in particular.

Elements of a Mechanical System And Knapping

The concepts considered in the book are from the fields of study known as statics, strength of materials (a misnomer), theory of elasticity, fracture mechanics and fractography. A system in mechanics is characterized by variables in the following four categories:

- Geometry;
- Material properties;
- Loading (forces or thermal effects);
- Support conditions.

All the variables on which the behavior of a mechanical system depends fall in the above four categories. However, some of the variables in these categories may or may not be significant for practical purposes, even if theoretical dependence is evident.

Before considering these variables, it is necessary to define what constitutes a mechanical system. For different questions asked, it is often useful to consider different systems. The kinds of idealizations used for the systems of interest will also depend on the questions of interest. Formal fracture mechanics analysis of the detachment of a flake is impractical because of the complexities involved. Such analysis is not attempted in this book. Numerical three-dimensional analysis for the production of a single flake is theoretically possible when assumptions are made, for example related to the nature of the loading involved. Such analyses could, in effect, be considered numerical experiments. For formal but practical fracture mechanics analysis of even some aspects related to flake production, significant simplifying assumptions must necessarily be made (for example, Fonseca, Eshelby and Atkinson 1971; Thouless et al. 1987; Tsirk 1979,1981). Much useful understanding can be gained from simplified fracture mechanics analyses, but it is important to recognize the limitations implied. Use of the results from many such analyses is made in this book.

It is still of interest to reflect on some of the questions encountered in attempting to define mechanical systems for the detachment of a single flake in knapping. There are a number of alternatives. Each of these would pose its limitations and present its particular questions or difficulties. For example, a core alone or together with a hammerstone could be considered a mechanical system. For a core alone, the difficulties would include defining the loading (the forces applied) as well as the support conditions. Both of these may vary in space and time. For a mechanical model of a core together with a hammerstone, the difficulties would include defining the motion and/or the forces on the hammerstone and, again, the support conditions. Analysis with such a model could provide the temporal and spatial variations in the forces at the contact, but even numerical analysis would be analytically rather complex .

Without dwelling further on the impracticalities of formal fracture mechanics analysis, it is of interest to reflect on the meaning of the variables that are, at least theoretically, of interest for knapping. The geometry and material properties of not only the core but also of the flaking implement are relevant. These include fracture toughness K_{IC}, modulus of elasticity and mass density. With thermal effects, additional material properties are relevant.

The loading in knapping consists of the forces applied by a flaking implement. This loading varies spacially and over time. Both the magnitude and the direction of the forces usually vary over time. At the same time, the contact area between the core and the flaking implement changes. The definition of a force between a flaking implement and a core, together with the associated contact area, constitutes a **geometrically nonlinear** problem in mechanics. Such analysis, though complex (Zukas et al. 1982), would permit bypassing the assumptions of some simplified Hertzian contact.

Support conditions in knapping can be of utmost importance. This is particularly evident, for example, in the bipolar technique, the anvil technique or in edge-to-edge flaking as used with some Clovis and Solutrean bifaces. On the other hand, they can be only slightly significant or even unimportant for the detachment of small pressure flakes on a large biface, for example.

Stresses, Stress Waves and Vibrations

All fractures are caused by stresses. The stresses in knapping can be viewed as being due to static or dynamic effects (See Chapter 6). For the essential aspects in pressure flaking, it is usually adequate to consider only static or quasi-static effects, ignoring inertia. However, for gull wings and other Wallner lines in pressure flaking and other contexts, consideration of stress waves, with inertia effects, is essential. The relevance of inertia effects is evident from the fact that the speed of a stress wave depends on the elastic properties and the mass density of the material.

Dynamic effects can be studied in terms of stress waves, vibrations or both. Inertia effects are always relevant for understanding vibrations. The wobble of a pressure flaker can introduce vibrations to a flake part already detached. When a blade is completely detached in pressure flaking, it may "fly off" making a sound, produced by vibrations of the blade. Inertia effects may also be relevant in considering the bending and straightening out of a pressure flaker staff during a blade detachment.

But inertia effects are most significant, and most often recognized by knappers in percussion flaking. For example, a biface break known as an amputation (Chaper 13) may occur when it is struck at an end while allowing the far end overhang freely. This is due to axial effects and bending, which can most conveniently be considered in terms of stress waves and vibrations, respectively. An accidental transverse biface break may also occur when a long biface is flaked from the side while allowing too much of its tip overhang freely. The breaking near the tip relates to the inertia effect of the overhanging part.

Stress wave effects are very significant to all knapping by percussion. As a specimen is struck, stress waves from the force application are transmitted to and reflected from the various specimen surfaces and its internal material interfaces at wave speeds ranging from about 3000 to 5000 m/s. The discussion of stress changes causing ripples in Chapter 6 is relevant here.

Some Fundamentals in Fracture Mechanics

Stresses may be applied on a planar crack in three different modes. This is best visualized in terms of the respective movements depicted in Fig. 9.1. **Mode I** is the **opening mode.** Due to application of tensile stresses normal to the plane of the crack, it is associated with displacements of the crack surfaces normal to that plane. **Mode II**, the **sliding mode** (a.k.a. the **shearing mode**), is due to stresses applied parallel to the crack plane and normal to the crack front. The crack surfaces will be displaced accordingly, as shown by the arrows in the figure. **Mode III** is known as the **tearing mode** (a.k.a. the **anti-plane shearing mode**). It is due to stresses applied parallel to the crack plane as well as the crack front. The resulting displacements of the crack surfaces are shown in the figure. The stress distributions and displacements for each of the three modes are given in Lawn (1993:23-28). They are expressed in terms of the elastic constants and the stress intensity factor K for the respective mode.

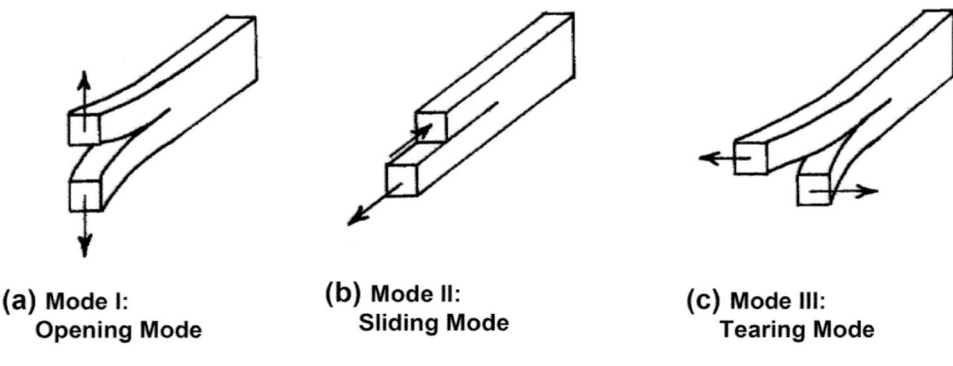

(a) Mode I: Opening Mode
(b) Mode II: Sliding Mode
(c) Mode III: Tearing Mode

FIG. 9.1 FRACTURE MODES

Viewed in fracture profile, a fracture tends to propagate in a direction normal to the maximum tensile stress (Broberg 1999: 603-605). "There is always a tendency for a brittle crack to seek an orientation that minimizes the shear loading" (Lawn 1993: 23). For practical purposes, a strict **normality rule**, rather than a tendency, may be assumed here (Richter and Kerkhof 1994: 75) for brittle materials that are isotropic. The maximum tensile stress is always normal to the maximum compressive stress. Lines parallel to the maximum tensile and maximum compressive stresses are referred to as the **principal stress trajectories** for tension and compression. It can thus be said that a fracture tends to propagate normal to the tensile stress trajectories and parallel to the compressive stress trajectories. The normality rule implies that $K_{II} = K_{III}$.

The term **nominal stress** is used for the stress at a location that would exist in the absence of a flaw or irregularity there. The expression "far field stress" is sometimes used instead, usually with an equivalent meaning. In contrast, the **stress intensity factor** defines the intensity of a localized stress in the presence of a flaw. It depends only on the loading and the specimen geometry. It is a very useful notion for describing the distribution of stresses (Lawn 1993: 25). K_I is used to indicate the stress intensity factor for fracture mode I (the opening mode), and subscripts II and III are used for the second (sliding) and the third (tearing) fracture modes. Fractures in knapping are primarily in fracture mode I. However, all of them involve the other two fracture modes as well. Contributions from fracture modes II and III are associated with the formation of ripples and twist hackles, respectively. The **crack extension force**, usually designated as G with the appropriate subscript for the fracture mode, refers to the **energy release rate** associated with a crack extension. G has the units of energy per unit area. It is useful to note that G_I is proportional to K_I^2 for a mode I fracture.

A fracture does not necessarily initiate where the tensile stress is greatest. It starts where the tensile stress together with a material flaw creates the worst or critical situation. Using the notions from fractography, a fracture in a brittle, isotropic material initiates at the location of the **critical stress intensity factor** $K_I = K_{IC}$ for mode I. K_{IC} is also known as the **fracture toughness**. In a moist or wet environment, a crack can extend when $K_I < K_{IC}$ (Chapter 8).

Catastrophic and Subcritical Crack Growth

At a conference on fracture back in 1978, I met the late Henry Kirchner, a foremost expert in fractography and especially on mist patterns in glass. Upon mentioning my interest in knapping, he immediately said that what you have is **subcritical crack growth**. I had to go back to literature to see what is actually meant by that. In the usual occurrence of brittle fracture in most other fields, such as industrial failures, crack growth is almost always **catastrophic** rather than subcritical. After a critical stress intensity factor K_{IC} is reached in such cases, the situation worsens as the crack grows and accelerates, with the fracture propagating catastrophically. The stress intensity factor K_I usually increases with crack length.

Is the crack growth in knapping really subcritical? If so, then why? Is it always subcritical or does catastrophic crack growth ever occur in knapping? To address these questions, consider first the practical meaning and the recognition of **catastrophic vs. subritical crack growth**. In catastrophic crack propagation, the fracture velocity V_F gradually increases, leading to manifestation of mist, velocity hackle, and perhaps to crack branching if V_F is sufficiently high. For the transition from mist and velocity hackle region to branching, the increase in V_F can be very small, but the increase in the energy required to advance the fracture is substantial. Except by the lip on flake initiations by bending, mist or velocity hackle is manifested extremely rarely, essentially never on the surfaces of flakes produced in controlled knapping. A rare exception is shown in Fig. 5.10. This serves as evidence that the propagation of fractures in flaking is essentially always subcritical, not catastrophic. Crack branching has only been reported for breakage but not the detachment of flakes.

The exceptions, though rare, are of interest. Mist and velocity hackle over an extended portion of a flake surface were observed only once (Fig. 5.10). The very thick flake or "spall" was produced when using a very hard, quartzite hammerstone on a very rounded platform on an obsidian nodule. On a few smaller obsidian flakes especially thick at one side, a small mist region has been observed near the thicker side. In a similar context, mist lines have been observed instead, but also in only a few cases. These can be viewed as precursors of a general mist region. On the surfaces of obsidian flakes with bending initiation (Fig. 5.1 and Chapter 10), mist is seen frequently by the lip at the proximal end of a flake. This has been observed on percussion as well as pressure flakes.

In all of these cases with mist manifestation, the crack propagation was not subcritical locally. That is, it tended to be catastrophic temporarily at some locations or in certain directions. The fracture was not completed catastrophically because of some constraint becoming effective. In the case of the mist at the proximal sides of a flake with bending initiation, when the crack had advanced laterally to release the proximal flake end, the fracturing was still subcritical for the crack advance in the longitudinal direction. In the cases with the very localized mist manifestation along a thicker edge of a flake, it is the other, thinner portions of the flake that constrain the whole width of the crack from accelerating further (Tsirk 1981). In the case of the very thick flake with an extended overall mist-hackle region (Fig. 5.10), it is not clear why that region did not extend all the way to the distal end. It is likely that it related to a sudden reduction in the loading (the force applied). This might not have happened if a blow with more follow-through, and perhaps a larger hammerstone, had been used. It is also not clear how significant a role was played by the reflections of stress waves from the distal portion of the nodule.

The rare exceptions aside, it can nevertheless be said that the propagation of fractures involved in the production of flake surfaces in knapping is essentially always subcritical. In contrast, many of the accidental fractures occurring in knapping are not. Mist and hackle are not rare in accidental breakages, and even branching occurs occasionally. In the breakage of bifaces and blades due to bending, the occurrence of mist-hackle at or near the edge of the tensile side is fairly common, and even fracture branching occurs, with or without the manifestation of lateral wedges. Accidental breakages are discussed in Chapter 13.

Why in knapping is the fracture propagation essentially always subcritical? Two primary reasons are suggested here. In knapping, first of all, an attempt is made to use the least amount of energy for the fracture that is sufficient to detach a flake. Excessive forces are ideally avoided in pressure as well as percussion flaking. In percussion flaking, use of a proper platform, avoiding unnecessarily high impact velocities and use of hammerstones that are not too hard are helpful for this purpose. The second primary reason relates to what may be called the "self-relieving" nature of the loading. That is, the applied forces are automatically reduced as the fracture advances and the partly detached flake becomes more flexible.

Research on Fractures in Knapping

A brief review of research on fractures in knapping is presented here. Only those investigations are considered that relate the study to the disciplines of mechanics, fracture mechanics or fractography.

There is much literature on replicative studies and what have been referred to as knapping experiments by archaeologists and knappers (Lewis Johnson 1978). With rare exceptions, these are not controlled laboratory experiments. Many studies such as those by Callahan (1979), Crabtree (1968), Flenniken (1978), Pelegrin (2003), Sollberger and Patterson (1976), Titmus and Woods (2003), Inizan, Reduron-Ballinger, Roche and Tixier (1999) and many others have made significant contributions to the understanding of knapping and lithic technology. But because these kinds of studies do not, and were not intended to relate the fractures involved to the scientific disciplines noted, they are not considered here. Though important, they are not the focus of this book. Such studies deserve a thorough, extensive and time-consuming review of what has been concluded, rightly or wrongly, about knapping. Research on the properties of lithic materials of interest to knapping is considered in Chapter 3.

A highly significant pioneering effort for the study of fractures in knapping is the co-operative effort of the archaeologist Hans-Jürgen Müller-Beck and Frank Kerkhof (Kerkhof and Müller-Beck 1969), the great expert on brittle fracture (Kerkhof 1970). They discuss Hertzian contact fractures as well as Wallner lines, other ripples, and twist hackles.

The research by Swaminathan Vaidyanathan (1969) is rather unusual. This engineering dissertation on shaping of brittle solids deals primarily with erosion and abrasion, relating the latter to load and grit sizes. Many of the aspects discussed are relevant to knapping. The thesis includes discussions on prehistoric knapping.

A rather unusual and analytically sophisticated, two dimensional analysis is performed by Fonseca, Eshelby and Atkinson (1971) to compare the efficiencies in pressure and percussion flaking. By efficiency they mean the fraction of the work done by the applied forces that goes to actually extend the fracture. To make the theoretical analysis tractable, the authors use what they call anti-plane or fracture mode III analogue. It is not clear what effect this and some other assumptions have on real flaking situations. In a discussion of fracture mechanics of knapping, Bilby (1980: 549-551) relies on the analysis by the above authors as well as his own previous research to reach consistent conclusions.

Aside from the above analytical efforts, a fracture mechanics analysis undertaken specifically to understand knapping is that by Cotterell, Kamminga and Dickson (1985). They investigated the crack paths together with the magnitude and direction of the forces by using a two-dimensional model with a downward and outward force for a "blade". Two of the authors discuss their results in subsequent publications (Cotterell and Kamminga 1987 and 1990: 125-159), together with information on flake initiations and terminations, as well as some fracture markings and fracture velocities in knapping. The study would have been enhanced by some hands on knapping experience by the senior author, to avoid drawing unwarranted conclusions. These studies were preceded by Cotterell and Kamminga (1979), in which the three fracture modes, the stress trajectories near cracks, and Wallner lines are discussed. It is relevant to note that Cotterell is a fracture mechanics specialist; Kamminga, an archaeologist.

A rather unusual research effort is that by Horace Bertouille (1989). With its superb diagrams and figures, it has seen wide international distribution as *Cahiers du Quaternaire* No. 15. The work would have benefitted from greater use of fracture mechanics and fractography as well as hands on knapping experience.

Faulkner (1972) investigated fracture velocities with a high-speed camera, studied the flaking forces by using laboratory loading equipment, and used photoelasticity to investigate stress patterns. Relying on the research of Poncelet (1958), Fréchette (1965) and Kerkhof and Müller-Beck (1969), his discussions of fracture markings were the first in English language literature on knapping.

Speth (1972) researched percussion flaking by considering Hertzian cones, some dynamic aspects of impact, stress wave reflections and spalling. Though not mentioned by the author, it provides a good background for understanding bi-polar percussion. Some properties of lithic materials are also reviewed. Subsequently, Speth (1974, 1975 and 1981) made controlled experiments to study the production of flakes by dropping steel balls onto glass prisms. By varying the ball diameter, the drop height and the edge distance he obtained significant relationships for the flakes. These experimental studies of Speth are of lasting value.

Lawn and Marshall (1979), eminent authorities on brittle fracture, discuss the general scientific understandings on contact fractures for large surfaces away from a specimen edge. The contact fractures are related to what are often called Hertzian and wedging initiations in knapping (Chapter 10). Although intended for use-wear studies, the article provides useful scientific background also for flake initiations in knapping.

Tsirk (1979) presents an analysis for the stress distributions in a two-dimensional wedge loaded at or near its apex. Theory of elasticity solutions from Timoshenko and Goodier (1951) are adapted for the cases with various force directions and locations, with the fracture origin away from the load. The analysis is of particular interest for bending initiations in knapping. Aside from being limited to a two-dimensional case, the study unfortunately does not present a comparison with fractures having a contact initiation (Chapter 10). Tsirk (1989), in the proceedings of a 1981 conference, presents some observations by others from fractography on flaw characteristics, environmental factors and fracture markings. In lieu of using the oversimplified results presented for the effects of water and moisture, it is better for the reader to go directly to the original source (Schönert, Umhauer and Klemm 1969). The effects of flake cross-sectional geometry on the fracture front configuration are discussed in Tsirk (1981) by considering a double cantilever beam model to make the problem analytically tractable.

Pelcin (1996) made an extensive study of percussion flaking with the use of a swing hammer. Steel ball bearings and antler were used as what the author calls "indenters." The aim was to relate a number of the independent variables to the flake attributes of interest to archaeology. Because the latter are difficult to relate to the variables in mechanics, the results are at best difficult to interpret for understanding the mechanics and fracture mechanics of flaking. Pelcin's doctoral dissertation (1996) is closely related to some previous work (Dibble and Whittaker 1981) and subsequent related publications.

Bonnichsen (1974) constructed a machine, termed the "stainless steel Indian", to study various fracture features, including radial fractures, with direct percussion. The machine has a swing arm and capability for attaching "impactors" of different materials. His discussions include fracture markings and various other features of flake morphology. He is the first one in English language lithic technology literature to note the relevance of moisture or liquids (1974: 97), with reference to static fatigue and aging. Bonnichsen's interests included relating various flake morphologies to their causal factors.

Kelterborn (2003) constructed a clever device for the production of pressure blades and other flakes that enables him to make various assessments, including measurement of the peak forces in knapping and evaluation of the effects of flaker stiffnesses. He has used the term "measurable flintknapping."

Tomenchuk (1985) and Hutchings (1997 and 1999) used Wallner lines to study fracture velocities in knapping by different techniques. Their results are significant for understanding knapping. One wonders about the accuracy and hence the meaning of some of the very low fracture velocities, with V_F as low as 0.03 V_S, the shear wave velocity (Hutchings 1997). Also, one is puzzled by a comparison for some results from Wallner lines and gull wings (sic), referred to as fracture wings (Tomenchuk 1985: Fig.2.6a), since gull wings are also Wallner lines. From his discussion it is apparent, however, that the author does have a correct understanding. Hutchings (1997 and 1999) makes use also of gull wings in flint, with limited illustration. Since these markings are rather fuzzy in flint, one wonders about the accuracy of the results.

Tsirk studied fracture markings from liquids in obsidian in (1996, 2001 and 2007) and other markings in (1981, 1988, 1996 and 2010a). He also investigated various fracture features in (2009 and 2010b). In the latter effort, he discusses the formation of popout fractures (a.k.a. nacelle fractures) and relates them to stepout fractures, compression lips and compression wedges. In Tsirk (2009), the relevance of the monumental work of George Quinn (2007) to knapping and lithic technology is noted. Some fractography lessons from knapping, relevant to other fields, are pointed out in Tsirk (2012).

Other Research

Studies on knapping have extended into the fields of fractography and theoretical fracture mechanics. Much other research on fractures and fractography, though not addressing knapping in particular, is relevant to knapping. Some of this work is noted here. The intent is not to provide an extensive coverage of such work. Rather, the emphasis is to point out some areas of research and some specific studies that are relevant. Most of this work is intended for industrial applications, and involves materials not used in knapping. But because of industrial applications, much greater research efforts have been expended on fracture of ceramics than on the lithic materials of interest for knapping. Much of this research, as well as that on industrial glasses, is relevant to the lithic materials. Many of the kinds of fractures encountered in knapping are also of interest in industrial applications, and vice versa. The first conference on Fractography of Glasses and Ceramics at Alfred University in 1986 even included a flintknapping demonstration in the program (Varner and Fréchette 1988). The fourth one of this conference series had a session on edge chipping, with half of the presentations related to archaeology and the other half to industrial applications. All the proceedings of the six conferences in this series have something of interest to knapping. Lawn's historical review of Hertzian fractures in ceramics (1998) is highly relevant to knapping. So is some of the other research related to dental ceramics, which has seen greater research efforts in recent years. The NIST Recommended Practice Guide *Fractography of Ceramics and Glasses* is an excellent, monumental effort by George Quinn (2007) that synthesizes the recent research in fractography. Though intended for industrial applications, it is also of interest for knapping. Obviously, the principles in fractography are the same regardless of the field of application. Therefore, a number of journals have published articles of interest. These include the *International Journal of Fracture*, the *Journal of the American Ceramic Society*, and the *Journal of Materials Science.* number of review papers in *Fractography of Glass* edited by Bradt and Tressler (1994) are also relevant to knapping.

Edge chipping is of great interest also for industry. Research in this area includes Thouless et al. (1987), Thouless and Evans (1990), Chiu, Thouless and Endres (1998), Quinn and Mohan (2005), Morrell and Gant (2001), Danzer, Hangl and Paar (2001), McCormick and Almond (1990), and Morrell (2005). More general treatises on fractography are provided by Fréchette (1990) and Hull (1999). Despite its age, the book of Frank Kerkhof (1970) is still an authoritative and invaluable source on fractures and fractography. Some of Kerkhof's research has been continued by Herbert Richter (Richter and Kerkhof 1994). It is of interest to note the historical "lineage" through professional, personal contact from Smekal to Schardin to Kerkhof to Richter. Many geological fractures are relevant to knapping. Excellent discussion of these is in Bahat (1991) and Bahat, Rabinowich and Frid (2005). *Fracture of Brittle Solids* by Lawn (1993) provides an extensive and authoritative coverage of its subject. Although the book does not lack theoretical rigor, it can also be read meaningfully without delving into all the equations. This is also true of the book by Broek (1978). In contrast, the books by Anderson (1995), Broberg (1999) and Kanninen and Popelar (1985) are among the more advanced texts for the more ambitious readers on fractures.

Of historical interest are the publications of de Fréminville (1914), Preston (1926, 1935) and Poncelet (1958). De Fréminville (1914) described many types of glass fracture and mentioned small undulations, explained later by Wallner (1939). Preston was the great pioneer of brittle fracture in the first half of the last century. Poncelet discussed a number of fracture markings and other fracture phenomena. For example, his explanation of mist formation (1958) is plausible even today.

10. Flake Initiations, Proximal and Surface Features

Flake Initiations

Some Definitions

A **flaw** is a material irregularity. All materials have flaws. A **fracture origin** is a location where a fracture starts. All fracture origins have one or more flaws. But not all flaws, of course, lead to fracture origins. A **flake initiation** is defined here as the release of the proximal end of a flake, including its full lateral extension. All flake initiations have one or more fracture origins. Not all flake initiations lead to the detachment of a flake, since a fracture sometimes stops – much more often near the proximal than the medial or distal part of a flake.

With a **contact initiation** the fracture origin is at or near the contact area between the flaking implement and the core. A **Hertzian initiation** has the origin just outside the area of contact. Several kinds of Hertzian initiation are noted in Table 10.1. A **Hertzian cone fracture** refers to the classical case of a Hertzian fracture in which the applied force acts normal to the surface of a sufficiently large specimen, away from free surfaces and their effects. They are essentially never encountered in knapping. The Hertzian initiations in knapping may be with or without a cone-like feature. By a **cone-like feature** is meant a feature resembling part of a cone. Flake initiations are considered in Table 10.1. Flake initiation by unzipping, associated with multiple blows, is not included in the table.

Hertzian Cone Fractures

There are useful lessons to be learned from Hertzian cone fractures. Since the development of the theory in 1880s, Hertzian cone fractures have been discussed extensively in literature. The foundation for the theory is considered in the theory of elasticity books by Timoshenko and Goodier (1951) and Love (1944). Hertzian cone cracks were introduced to the literature on flintknapping by Kerkhof and Müller-Beck (1969), and considered further in Speth (1972). Brief references to Hertzian cone cracks appear in Lawn and Marshall (1979) and Cotterell and Kamminga (1987, 1990). Lawn (1993) provides a more general treatment of Hertzian cone cracks. The most extensive and authoritative, centennial review of Hertzian cone fractures is in Lawn (1998). Some rare prehistoric Hertzian cone fractures are considered in Bahat (1977).

Static Loading

Consider the contact between a sphere of radius R and the flat surface of a large elastic body (a "half space"), with a normal load P in Fig. 10.1. The solutions for this case are available from the references cited. The radius of the contact circle is

$$a = K P^{1/3} R^{1/3} \qquad (10.1)$$

where

$$K = [(1-v_1^2)/E_1 + (1-v_2^2)/E_2]^{1/3} \qquad (10.2)$$

ν and E are the Poisson's ratio and the modulus of elasticity, with subscripts 1 and 2 for the sphere and the elastic body, respectively. The mean contact pressure is

$$p_o = P/(\pi a^2) \tag{10.3}$$

The maximum contact pressure is 1.5 times the mean value. The maximum tension is the radial stress at the contact circle equal to

$$\sigma_m = (1 - 2\nu_2)\, p_o = (1 - 2\nu_2)\, P/(\pi a^2) \tag{10.4}$$

With Eqs. 10.4 and 10.1

$$\sigma_m = (1 - 2\nu_2)\, K^{-2}\, R^{-2/3}\, P^{1/3} \tag{10.5}$$

TABLE 10.1 FLAKE INITIATIONS

Single Blow		
"Non-Contact"	Contact	
	Single	Multiple
Bending	Wedging	
Non-Contact, no Significant Bending	Hertzian with a Cone-like Feature	With multiple cone-like features
Snap	Hertzian without a cone-like feature	Without multiple cone-like features
Wing flakes	Wedging & Hertzian Combination	
Quartering: Breaking a nodule at a distant location	"Multiple Flakes"- Concentric	"Multiple Flakes," with lateral offset

With this classical Hertzian fracture, a cone crack extends downward only when the force P exceeds a critical value given by

$$P_c = k R \tag{10.6}$$

where k is a material constant (Kerkhof and Müller-Beck 1969: 443). This is known as the Auerbach law. The base of a Hertzian cone has a diameter

$$S = n\, P^{2/3} \tag{10.7}$$

where n is a material constant. The cone angle, independent of R, is a material characteristic (Speth 1972: 40, Kerkhof and Müller-Beck 1969: 443-4). Its variation with Poisson's ratio is considered in Finnie and Vaidyanathan (1974).

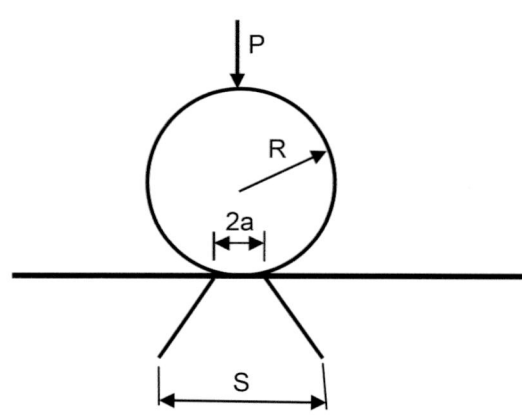

FIG. 10.1 HERTZIAN CONE FRACTURE.

Dynamic Impact

The impact of a sphere on a half-space can be treated as a quasi-static problem with good approximation (Tsai and Kolsky 1967:33). Thus the equations presented for the static case also hold here when the interaction force is taken to be the inertia force equal to the mass of the sphere times its deceleration. The maximum value of the interaction force can be obtained from Speth (1972) as

$$P^5 = \pi^3 (5/3)^3 \rho^3 K^{-6} V^6 R^{10} \quad (10.8)$$

where ρ is the density of the sphere and V its approach velocity relative to the half-space. The maximum tensile stress at the contact circle can be obtained by using P from this equation in Eq. (10.5).

The contact duration for the impact is

$$T_c = 2.94 \, C_1 \, R \, / \, V^{1/5} \quad (10.9)$$

where

$$C_1 = \{(5/4) \, \pi \, \rho \, [(1-v_1^2)/E_1 + (1-v_2^2)/E_2 \,]\}^{2/5} \quad (10.10)$$

From the equations here and in Timoshenko and Goodier (1951), plots are presented in Fig. 10.2 for the normalized contact force P/C_2 vs. the normalized contact time t/C_1 for several velocities of the impacting sphere. C_2 is given by

$$C_2 = (4/3) \, C_1^{3/2} \, [(1-v_1^2)/E_1 + (1-v_2^2)/E_2 \,] \quad (10.11)$$

Hertzian Cone Fractures and Flake Initiations

Archaeologists and knappers referring to Hertzian fractures are usually aware, of course, of the differences between the classical Hertzian cone fractures and the fractures in knapping. Some of these are noted explicitly in Table 10.2.

Some Lessons of Interest

Considering Hertzian cone fractures may give us some ballpark feeling or understanding for knapping. Some of this was done in the pioneering efforts by Kerkhof and Müller-Beck (1969) and Speth (1972). Some of these and other considerations are noted here.

All or almost all factors relevant to Hertzian cone fractures are also of interest for Herzian flake initiations in knapping in a qualitative sense. Quantitatively, however, the factors can have drastically different effects in these cases. This is mostly because of the differences listed in Table 10.2. From Eq. (10.1) for the static case, the contact radius depends on the cube root of the applied force and of the radius of the sphere, as well as the properties of the materials involved. For flake initiations, common sense indicates that the contact area is expected to increase with the loading as well as the local curvatures of the flaker. From Eq. (10.2) it is evident that the modulus of elasticity E is much more important than the Poisson's ratio v. This will likely hold also for flake initiations.

Eq. (10.4) indicates the maximum radial stress, occurring at the contact circle, to increase with the load and to decrease with the contact radius. In a qualitative sense, one expects this to also hold for flake initiations. More relevant to Hertzian flake initiations, however, are the empirical observations for cone fractures that they originate at a slight distance outside the contact circle. This relates to the distribution of flaws. With Hertzian flake initiations, there is much variability in the location where the fracture originates. With flake initiations, the distribution of flaws is relevant in two dimensions – the "radial" as well as the "lateral".

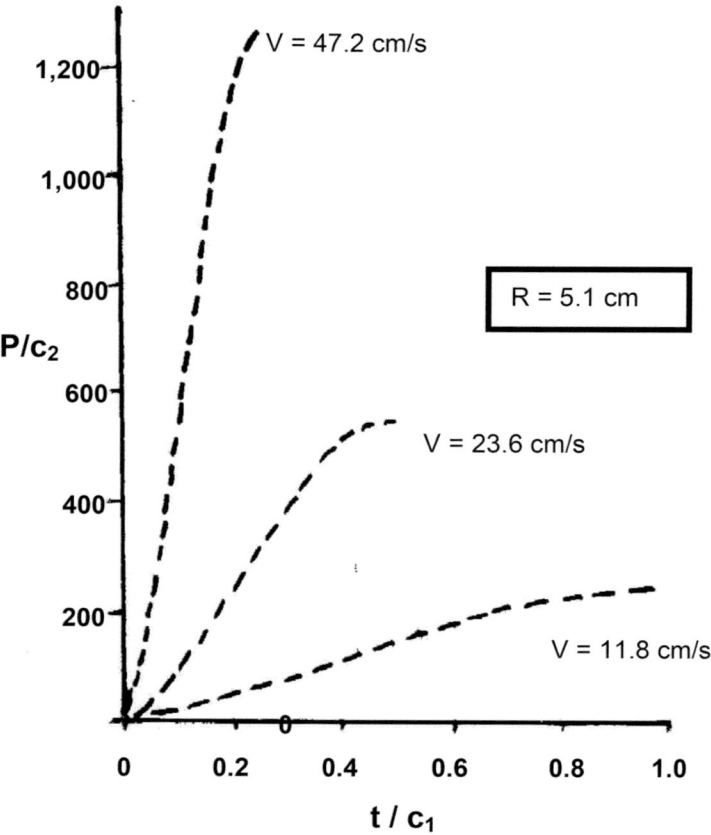

FIG. 10.2 FORCE VS. TIME FOR SEVERAL IMPACT VELOCITIES AND SPHERE RADIUS R = 5.1 CM..

Eq. (10.6) indicates a Hertzian cone crack to start extending from the ring crack into the body of the specimen only when a critical value of the force is reached. That value depends on the sphere radius times a material constant. In knapping, obviously a sufficiently high force needs to be applied for flake initiation, but further suggestions from the latter equation are not warranted in light of the differences noted in Table 10.2.

Eq. (10.7) indicates the cone angle as well as the diameter of the cone base to be independent of the sphere radius. This poses intriguing questions on Hertzian flake initiations in knapping.

For the dynamic case, Eq. (10.8), the increase in the interaction force with the sphere velocity is of obvious relevance to flake initiations. Its increase with the sphere radius is not as evident. Fig.10.2 indicates the variation of the normalized contact force with time for several velocities of the impacting sphere. Qualitatively, these are thought to be highly relevant to Hertzian flake initiations. Observations with percussor softness and speed in knapping, to be disussed, are rather interesting.

Contact Initiations

Contact initiations involving a single blow or force application, but with single or multiple contact, are considered in this section. Those associated with multiple blows are discussed in a subsequent section.

Wedging Initiations

For flakes with **wedging initiation (**Fig. 10.3), the terms "split cone" and "sheared cone" are used in Crabtree (1972). They characteristically have a flat surface and no bulb of force in the proximal region. Many ripples resembling concentric rings are also characteristic in such cases. Wedging initiation was already recognized by De Freminville (1914) as a sharp-contact initiated fracture.

Some mechanisms for the wedging action are discussed in Lawn and Marshall (1979: 71-77), Green (1998: 241) and Cotterell and Kamminga (1990: 141). Wedge initiations can occur in several ways. When a truly sharp contact is involved, there will be some locally inelastic deformation that can lead to wedging (Green 1998: 241). In such a case, it is the lateral crack system (Lawn 1993: 257) that leads to the flake initiation. According to Lawn and Marshall (1979: 76-77), most practical situations of particle contact are not ideally blunt or sharp. They can act initially as blunt, and then as sharp for subsequent wedging action. The wedging may be caused instead simply by some debris being pushed into a surface crack (Cotterell and Kamminga 1990: 141). It may also be associated with wedging action at locations of previous impact damage. Wedging initiations can be produced consistently by using a steel hammer with a wedge-shaped bit at a platform having a large edge angle. Wedging initiations are common in bipolar percussion.

TABLE 10.2 HERTZIAN CONE FRACTURES AND HERTZIAN FLAKE INITIATIONS: SOME DIFFERENCES

	Hertzian Cone Fractures	**Hertzian Flake Initiations**
Percussor Shape	Spherical	Various shapes of percussors & contact regions
Pressure Flaker Shape	Spherical	Various shapes
Flaker Material and Behavior	Elastic	Some non-elastic effects: Softening & denting of wood & antler flakers
Core Size	Semi-infinite or very large	Finite or small
Core Shape	Regular: half space or spherical	Very irregular
Contact Location	Away from all edges and boundaries	At or near an edge
Contact Area	Circular	Usually non-circular
Direction of Contact Force	Normal to surface contacted	Various directions
Fracture by Origin	With circular crack	Usually with no circular crack
Geometry at Fracture Initiation	Conical	Not conical
Supports at Core Boundaries	Not considered; Semi-infinite solid	Hard or soft supports
Reflections from Boundaries	Not considered (There are no reflections.)	Extremely significant in percussion flaking
Contact Region	Flat	Usually not flat

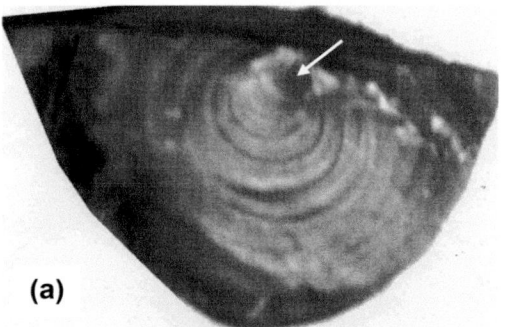
(a)

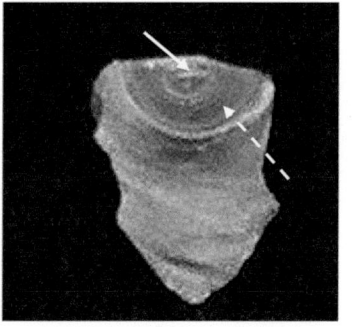
(b)

FIG. 10.3 FLAKE INITIATION BY WEDGING IN NORMANSKILL CHERT: SOLID ARROW IN BOTH CASES INDICATES A SPLIT CONE OR OTHER CONTACT FEATURE. IN CONTRAST TO THE PRONOUNCED RIPPLES IN (A), THE RIPPLES IN THE MORE CONFINED FLAT REGION IN (B) (DASHED ARROW) ARE SUBTLE. THE RIPPLES ARE ASSOCIATED WITH VIBRATIONS OF THE PARTLY DETACHED FLAKE, VERY DIFFERENT IN THE TWO CASES. THE MAXIMUM FLAKE WIDTH AND THICKNESS IN THE PROXIMAL REGION IS 8.5 AND 2.5 CM FOR (A) AND 5.1 AND 0.8 CM FOR (B).

Hertzian Initiations with or without a Cone-like Feature

The most common flake initiations in knapping are bending initiations and Hertzian initiations with or without cone-like features (Fig. 10.4). The changes from a bending to a Hertzian initiation are gradual, as are those from a Hertzian initiation with a cone-like feature to one without a cone-like feature.

From the classical Hertzian cone fractures it is recalled that the cone is formed when a crack extends inward from a ring crack at the circular contact area. When the contact area is not circular, it is not possible for a true cone to extend inward from it. In practical knapping situations, a contact area may locally resemble a circle. A cone-like feature can be manifested in such cases. Hertzian flake initiations are usually characterized by cone-like features adjacent to the platform edge. As a contact area in knapping deviates more and more from a circular one, a crack from near the edge of the contact area can extend inward without a cone-like feature. Although the maximum tensile stress is likely to be at the edge of the contact area, the Hertzian fracture may originate some distance outside it.

Full or partial ring cracks are manifested only occasionally in knapping. They are less likely to occur with smaller platform angles, when bending initiations for flakes are more likely. Stated differently, they are expected to be more likely with greater stiffness of the platform region. They have been observed in hardhammer percussion, and may be expected in indirect percussion when harder contact materials are involved. Their manifestation is conceivable in pressure flaking with some lever device to obtain a large enough contact force.

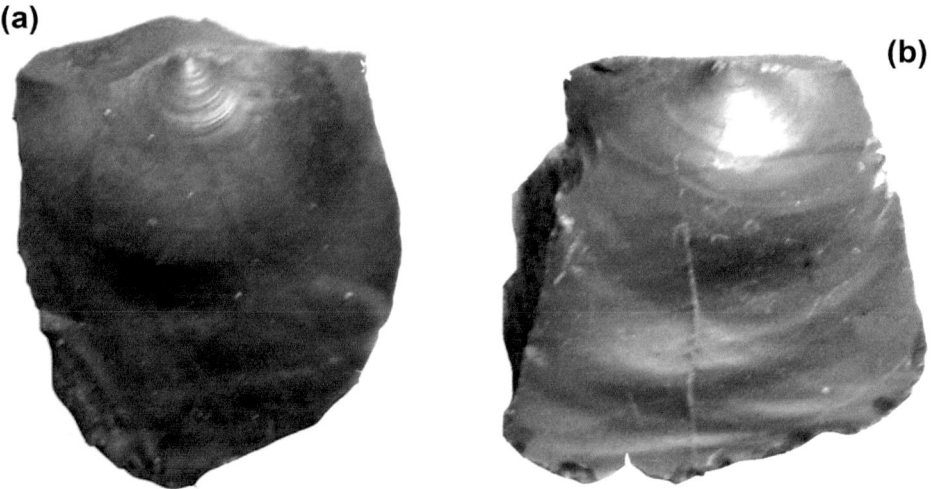

FIG. 10.4 FLAKES WITH HERTZIAN INITIATION IN NORMANSKILL CHERT: (A) A CONE-LIKE FEATURE WITH RIPPLES. A RING CRACK IS PRESENT ON THE PLATFORM. PROXIMAL WIDTH IS 5.7 CM. (B) THERE ARE THE PROXIMAL RIPPLES BUT NO CONE-LIKE FEATURE AND NO RING CRACK. THE HERTZIAN CONTACT FEATURE IS ELONGATED ALONG THE EDGE. PROXIMAL WIDTH IS 4.2 CM.

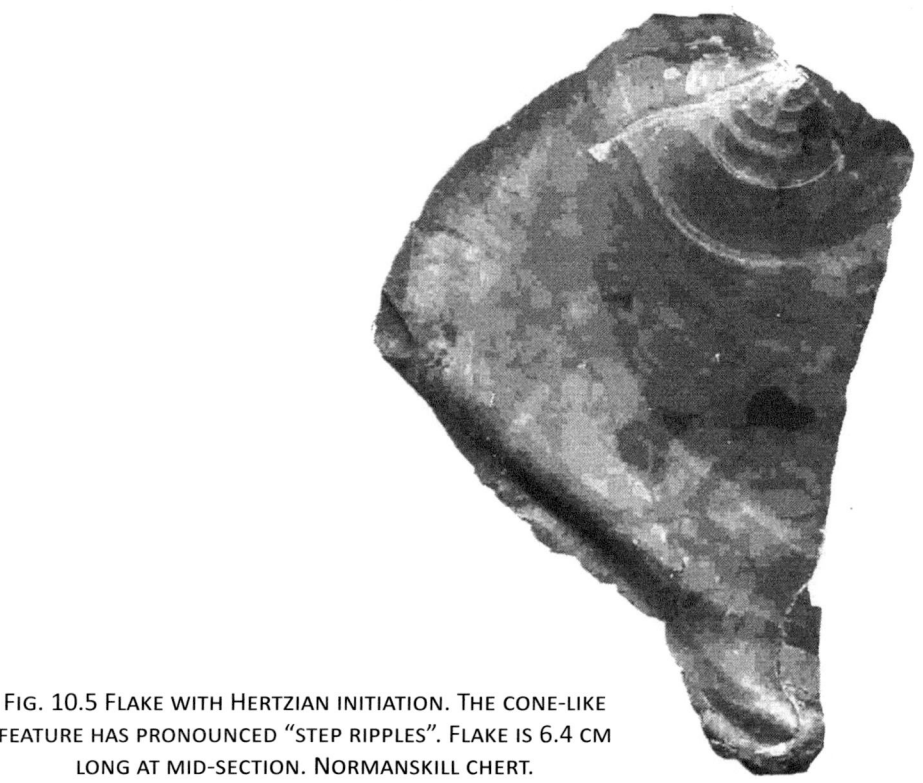

FIG. 10.5 FLAKE WITH HERTZIAN INITIATION. THE CONE-LIKE FEATURE HAS PRONOUNCED "STEP RIPPLES". FLAKE IS 6.4 CM LONG AT MID-SECTION. NORMANSKILL CHERT.

The cone-like features of Hertzian initiations often have significant ripples (Crabtree 1972: 45, Hayden and Hutchings 1989: Fig. 7) or step ripples (Figs. 10.4 and 10.5) from vibrations induced by percussion.

Combined Wedging and Hertzian Initiation

In very rare occasions, a wedging initiation occurs together with a Hertzian initiation (Fig. 10.6). In the figure, a partial cone-like feature is seen together with the rippled flat surface characteristic of a wedging fracture. The cone-like feature appears to be split. In this case, it is suggested that the wedging action causing the extension of a lateral crack may be such that the lateral crack runs through a cone-like feature, perhaps as it is being formed.

Multi-Contact Initiations

Flake initiations that have multiple fracture origins are occasionally encountered. Each of these may correspond to a Hertzian initiation, to a bending initiation or to their combination on the same flake. At least one of these partial fractures stops short, running into another partial fracture extending the length of the flake. It is surprising that often, especially in chert, no ridge (dividing line) is manifested between the two partial

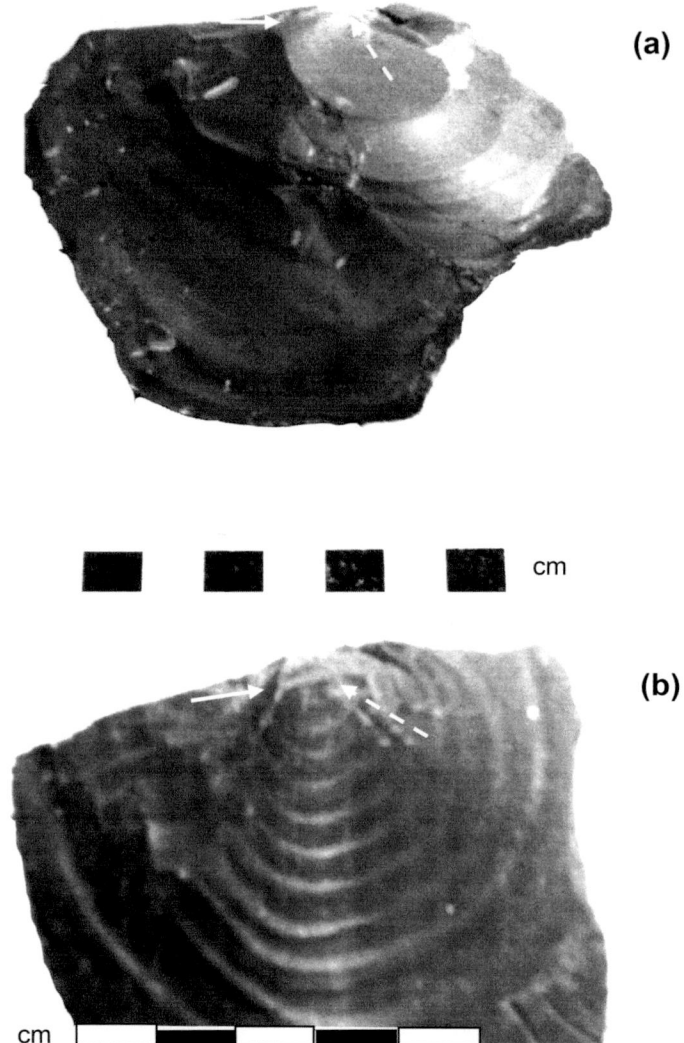

Fig. 10.6 Combined wedging-Hertzian initiations. The solid arrow indicates a partial cone-like or other Hertzian feature. The dashed arrow points to the "split" part of this feature. Nearly flat regions with ripples resembling circles are manifested in both cases. Though not evident in illustration (a), the flat region beneath the "split" Hertzian feature does have subtle ripples resembling circles. What is unusual for (b) is that the "nearly" flat rippled region is actually slightly concave in the longitudinal direction. Normanskill chert.

fractures. This suggests the tendency for an existing crack to attract another fracture running approximately parallel to it. The tendency appears to relate to the residual stress field ahead of the previous crack as the new one approaches it.

The principles related to each of the fracture origins of multi-contact initiations are akin to those considered for the respective kinds of single contact initiations. With multi-contact fracture initiations with biface thinning flakes, a very significant factor for their occurrence relates to the characteristics of the biface edge being flaked. As an extreme example, such initiations are unlikely with platform isolation.

Special Cases with Contact Initiation: Multiple Flakes and Wing Flakes

In percussion flaking, multiple flakes are occasionally produced by the same blow. These may appear to be "concentric", or they may be offset laterally.

Multiple Flakes without Lateral Offset

Multiple flakes without lateral offset, seemingly concentric, are discussed in Jelinek, Bradley and Huckel (1971). After a crack (corresponding to the ring crack of a Hertzian cone) forms at or just outside the contact area, an increase in the load can lead to another, additional contact zone and another crack (as if a concentric ring crack). Double flakes can be produced in this way. At least four such flakes from "concentric" initiations have been observed.

Multiple Flakes with Lateral Offset

Multiple flakes from the same blow are occasionally produced with their initiations offset laterally. These can be understood as multi-contact initiations, except that the fractures originating at the different locations usually do not run into each other. The timing for the fracture origins and their propagation is obviously an important factor. An irregular edge of a biface obviously promotes the manifestation of the multiple flakes noted.

Wing Flakes

When a percussion flake is detached, there are occasionally one or two narrow flakes or slivers extending along the upper edge of a flake (Figs. 10.7 and 10.8). Sometimes they turn at the laterally outermost platform corner to extend distally along the flake edge. They extend from the twist hackles near the cone-like or other Hertzian feature of the flake laterally and along the platform edge. Such slivers are termed **wing flakes** here. They leave evidence on a flake scar, but rarely on the detached flake itself.

A wing flake is in fact an extended lateral breakthrough of a twist hackle. The flake edge along the platform serves to guide the wing flake in a way similar to a ridge guiding a flake. As such it may be considered a hackle flake. Wing flakes were encountered frequently in punching flakes for square section axes.

146　Fractures in Knapping

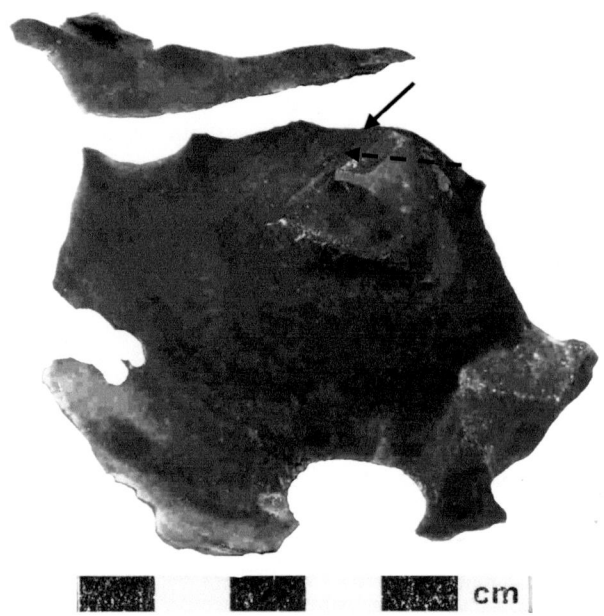

Fig. 10.7 A flake with a wing flake that was detached to the left side. Solid arrow shows the location of the Hertzian flake initiation; dashed arrow, the twist hackle from which the wing flake originated. Moose antler punch used. Texas flint.

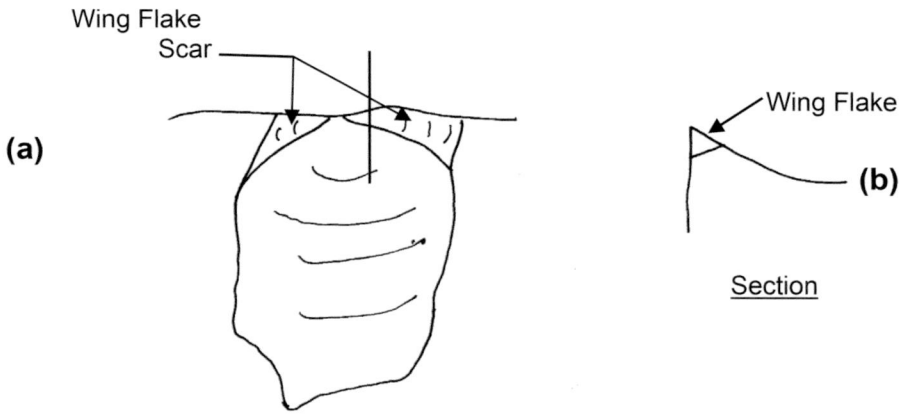

Fig. 10.8 A wing flake can drastically alter the edge angle for subsequent flaking, as seen in (b). A flake scar (2.6 cm wide) and wing flake scars are seen in (a). These are for the wider face of a square section axe.

The occurrence of wing flakes can be a great nuisance to a knapper, since it can significantly alter the edge angle (Figs.10.8). Such edge angle alterations can have adverse consequences, for example, when they occur with core rejuvenation flakes or with the flakes from the wider face of a square section axe (Vang Petersen 2008).

Non-Contact Initiations

A **non-contact initiation** is one in which the fracture origin is relatively far from the contact between the flaking implement and the core. The transition between these and the contact initiations is gradual.

Bending Initiations

Bending initiation is used here for non-contact initiations where the exterior platform angle is significantly less than 90°. These are non-contact initiations with significant bending. With a smaller platform angle, it is easy to visualize some bending occurring. With non-contact initiations there are lower stresses and probably bigger flaws at the fracture origins for flake initiations. Contact initiations involve higher stresses and probably smaller flaws. For example, if a knapper wishes to detach a longitudinal thinning flake from a biface with a given kind of edge preparation, use of a harder percussor will contribute to a greater local stress, thereby reducing the likelihood of accidental biface breakage, especially when no end support is used. Crabtree (1972: 75) refers to a flake with bending initiation as one showing a pronounced lip.

Non-Contact Initiation without Significant Bending

Non-contact initiations with a basic mechanism similar to bending initiation also occur occasionally when the exterior platform angle approaches or is roughly 90°. In such cases, with common sense judgement and by their appearance, it is difficult to think of the initiations as due to bending. It is appropriate to refer to such initiations as "non-contact initiations without significant bending," or simply as "non-contact initiations." Here these initiations are lumped together with bending initiations, recognizing the term is a misnomer. Here, such initiations are included under bending initiations or non-contact initiations (Table 10.1).

The basic mechanism is similar for the non-contact initiations with and without significant bending. This becomes evident in Chapter 12 from the results for a simplified two-dimensional model of a wedge loaded near its apex.

It is surprising to see the flake initiations with very large exterior platform angles. Yet they do occur. This was pointed out and an example of a Paleolithic blade with a platform angle of about 90° was shown to me by the late Joachim Hahn and Hans-Jürgen Müller-Beck (1978, personal communication). Relevant is a remark by Stephen Freiman, formerly with the National Bureau of Standards. He noted that a sliver or blade with a 90° exterior platform angle is occasionally produced accidentally from the corner of a prismatic specimen (with a square cross-section) during a compression test .In such cases, the likely occurrence of greater flaws at the two platform edges meeting at the corner is relevant.

Snap

Examples of special cases with non-contact initiation are noted here. Snap fractures occur in a special context. Sometimes referred to as a "half moon breakage", it is of particular interest for use-chipping (Ho-Ho Committee 1979: 133-135). Snap fractures are more likely with small edge angles (Chapter 12), and when the applied force is normal rather than parallel to the "plane" of the specimen. These fractures are characterized by the fracture surface being approximately normal to the two core surfaces.

Lateral Snap

A lateral snap is a transverse biface breakage due to a force application on its side rather than its end. The fracture origin may be at the edge or away from it. The fracture, usually accidental, is a bending break. The axial effects important for amputations are not significant here. Supporting one or both ends of a biface during knapping reduces the flexural movements, helping to reduce the hazard of a lateral snap. But a biface, especially a very thin one, may still break as a "beam on elastic foundation" (Hetényi 1946). In Chapter 13, the characteristics of transverse breaks from lateral snap are compared with those from a force applied at the end of a biface.

It is sometimes not possible to distinguish a lateral snap from an amputation. The bending stress associated with a lateral snap, for a relatively flat biface, is higher closer to the edge where the force is applied. This is not the case with amputation. With uniform distribution of flaws in the lateral direction, amputations are more likely to be more symmetrical than lateral snaps. A flake detached from the side of a biface may provide a clue. The origin of a lateral snap fracture is often a twist hackle produced during the flake detachment.

Amputation and Quartering

Quartering and usually amputation do not involve initiation of flakes as such. They are considered in Chapter 13.

Initiations with Multiple Blows

Unzipping

Flake initiation by unzipping is characterized by multiple impact sites. Returning from a trip to quarry Pennsylvania rhyolite, Scott Silsby and Jack Cresson had a huge flake (some 60 to 90 cm wide) with a platform well over 30 cm wide. Even though a steel mallet was used at the quarry, the platform width was rather unusual. The flake was produced by striking a number of times at different locations along a line roughly parallel to the inner platform edge of the prospective flake. Subsequently, Scott and Jack produced large flakes of rhyolite and New Jersey argillite by a similar technique, using very hard hammerstones. Only a few to quite a number of blows were used. The flake initiation in this technique is referred to as **unzipping**.

Fig. 10.9 shows a flake of New Jersey argillite "unzipped" with several blows. A single blow, though inadequate for the flake initiation, does introduce a significant flaw.

Subsequent blows will produce additional flaws for further weakening, more or less along the line of the multiple blows. The flaws, some with cone-like features, will interact and eventually connect to enable flake initiation. With unzipping flake initiation, smaller

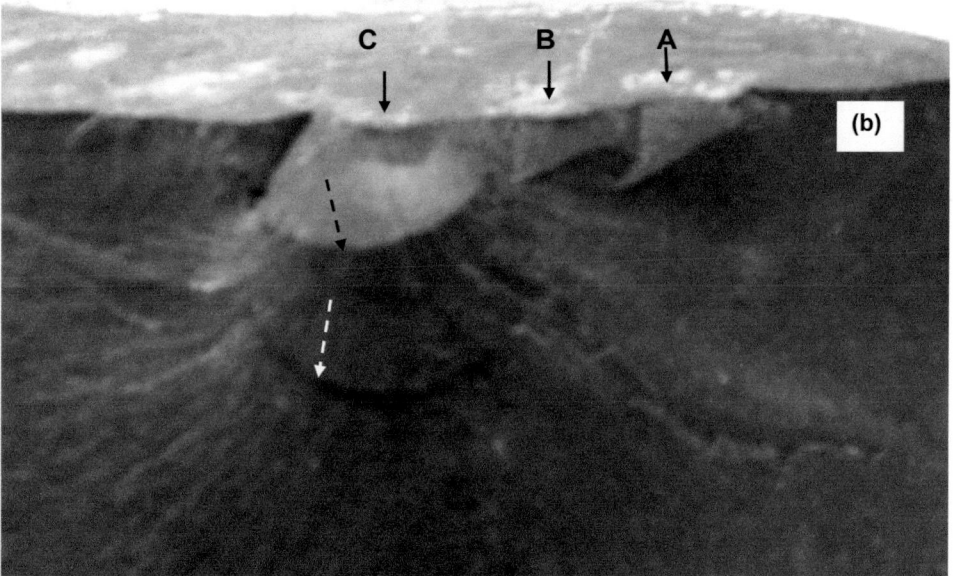

Fig. 10.9 Flake initiation by unzipping. The arrow in (a) corresponds to the arrow at C in (b). The core platform was struck a number of times with a very hard hammerstone, roughly along the line of the prospective flake edge. The biggest Hertzian contact fractures on the flake are by the arrows at A, B and C, with smaller ones elsewhere. The white areas on the platform to the left of C are additional impact sites. The fracture from C runs into that from B, and that from the latter runs into the fracture from A. Impacts to these three locations were not sufficient to release the flake along its platform. Additional blows were needed, as indicated by several arrest lines (as the dashed arrows in (b)). The many impact sites on the platform, with only some seen in (b), suggest a good number of blows were used. New Jersey argillite, flaked by Jack Cresson. Platform is 19.8 cm wide.

blows are needed to release the flake than would have been required for an initiation by a single blow.

Initiation with Pecked Platform

Pecking of force platforms for obsidian polyhedral cores was at times practiced in Mesoamerica (Flenniken and Hirth 2003: 98-107). This can introduce large flaws significant for flake initiation. The force required to detach a pressure blade from such a core can be significantly reduced. Fig. 10.10 shows the two surfaces by the proximal inner edge of a blade from the Otumba site in Mexico. Pecking and subsequent grinding of the platform is evident in the figure. On the inner (ventral) surface by the edge adjacent to a pecked platform, an irregular advance of the fracture is sometimes seen. The flaws appear to slow down or accelerate the progress of the crack along the blade platform edge, indicating that pecking does affect the fracturing for the flake initiation. According to experimental observations by experienced knappers, including Crabtree, Callahan and Flenniken, pecking does reduce the forces required.

Initiations with Pre-Cracking

For i**nitiations with pre-cracking,** cracks are introduced at an edge to reduce the force required for flake initiation. Such initiations are sometimes used by Langda knappers of Irian Jaya in making axes or adzes that have triangular cross-sections except near their bit (Schick and Toth 1993, Hampton 1999). This is seen in a film by Schick and Toth, with a knapper using multiple blows near the same location to detach a flake.

Other Cases

There are other cases in which multiple blows are used for flake detachment. For a biface thinning flake sometimes a single blow is not adequate, even for the flake initiation. A second blow often is. An arrest line as a kink in fracture profile is only sometimes manifested in such a case.

Effects of Cortex and "Layering"

The lithic materials of interest can have many different kinds of cortex with various effects. The calcareous cortex on flint nodules from limestone can vary greatly in thickness and mechanical properties. It can range from almost chalky to fairly hard, even for chert from the same source. This is true, for example, for the Cobden chert of Illinois. From a split Cobden nodule with a thick and fairly hard cortex, a series of percussion blades was readily detached all around. In general, a thick and soft cortex can make flake initiation difficult, tending to act as a sponge for percussion.

The cortex occasionally encountered on blocks of Normanskill chert provides a contrast. A thin cortex often has a high tensile strength, making it impossible or difficult at best to have a flake initiation from the cortical surface. This is reminiscent of unsuccessful attempts to initiate a flake from the coated back side of a mirror.

Knappers know that various surfaces of weathering cracks can hinder flaking across them. Solidified sediments filling such cracks usually do not present difficulties. However, most

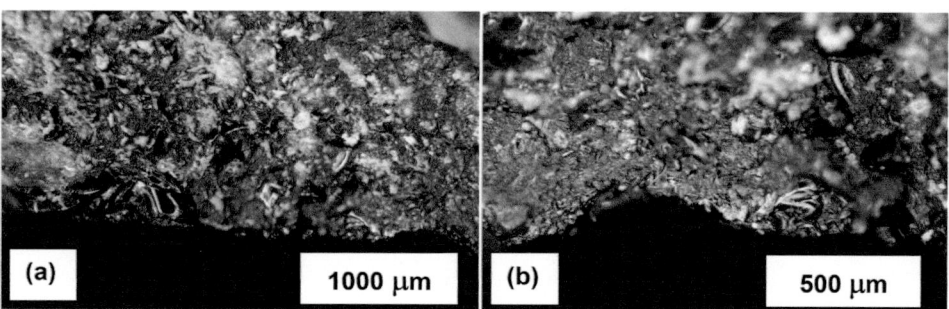

FIG. 10.10 GRINDING OVER PECKING ON A PLATFORM OF AN AZTEC BLADE FROM OTUMBA SITE IN MEXICO. THE ENLARGED VIEW IN (B) IS OF THE LOWER LEFT PART OF (A). PACHUCA OBSIDIAN.

weathering cracks in Normanskill chert are not filled in this manner. These present major problems in flaking, not only for flaking across them but also for flake initiations at some distance from the weathering cracks. Stresses from the blow at the striking platform are reflected in an adverse manner to hinder the flake initiation. In general, various kinds of stress wave reflections are expected to be relevant to flake initiation. After all, a stress wave traveling at some 5,000 m/s will have ample time to reflect from various surfaces during an impact.

Environmental Effects

Environmental effects are considered more generally in Chapters 3 and 8. External moisture, water and other liquids can affect fracture toughness of glass and other lithic materials. The physical-chemical process is enhanced at higher temperatures. The effects are expected to facilitate the initiation and slow propagation of fractures. However, if a specimen is allowed to be in a moist or wet environment without stress applied, then aging will occur to make fracture initiation more difficult. The two opposite effects have been explained by sharpening and blunting of microcracks. Flake initiations aside, wetting of a biface or a core surface can also affect flake detachment, but with a somewhat different mechanism (Chapter 3).

Percussor Softness and Speed

Some knappers use large wooden billets to flake rhyolite, argillite, quartzite and other tougher materials (Fig. 2.5b). It seems counterintuitive that softer, wooden percussors seem to work better with the tougher materials. Why should this be so? Suggestions are offered here.

A softer percussor can be useful not only for the detachment of a flake in general but also for its initiation. It is useful to recall that a flake initiation is defined here as the release of the proximal end of a flake rather than simply the start or extension of a microcrack. A softer percussor will make contact and have stresses distributed over a larger area with a biface or a core, in effect seeking a bigger flaw where the crack can start at a lower stress.

Another potential factor relates to the slower rate of load application associated with a softer percussor (Fig. 10.2). This slower loading rate has implications on the effects of stress wave reflections for flake initiations and crack advance more generally. These effects are necessarily tied with the timing for the various reflected stress wave arrivals. The stress wave velocities of interest are in the range of 3,000 to 6,000 m/s. Thus the time required for a stress wave to travel a distance of 5 cm and back, for example, is in the range of 0.03 milliseconds or less. For slower loading, weaker stress pulses have more time to have multitudinous reflections from a number of surfaces. For faster loadings, stronger stress pulses will have less time for this, and it is conceivable that they may thereby hinder flake initiation and the subsequent, early crack advance. Whether this in fact happens is yet to be demonstrated. The conceivable effect of less significant stress wave reflections with soft percussors, as well as slower blows was suggested by Matteo Cicotti (2011, personal communication).

Thirdly, it is conceivable that with a harder percussor there are higher local stresses that may introduce more inelastic behavior by the crack tip, increasing the associated process zone. Even glasses exhibit inelastic behavior near the crack front (Wiederhorn 1967). The concept of the associated process zone is well known, especially for metals (Broek 1978).

Knappers have observed that when a blow with a percussor does not detach or even initiate a flake detachment, then a slower blow with the same percussor will often do so. This may relate to the last two suggestions related to softer percussors.

The observation noted applies to direct as well as indirect percussion, for example when using an antler punch struck with a dogwood billet. A very gentle tap (with a slow blow) with the striker will often work much better than a hard (faster) blow.

Proximal Flake Features

Platform Characteristics

Platform Curvatures and Edge Angles

Platform characteristics are important for a blade core. With convex platforms, the edge angle usually exceeds 90°, thereby increasing significantly the force required for blade initiation. Control over the relative inward and outward force components is also diminished. These difficulties can be avoided with flat or concave platforms. The curvature of the top of a core platform can be modified by detaching platform rejuvenation flakes. Removal of most of a platform width in rejuvenation involves the risk of rounding the opposite platform edge. Removal of very short rejuvenation flakes, on the other hand, tends to lead to a convex platform or to developing a hump near the central region, especially with hinged or stepped flakes.

The flaking of the short face of a square section axe, as in Neolithic Denmark, provides an example of the significance of the platform curvature near the edge (Fig. 10.11). In learning to flake a square section axe, difficulties were experienced with the short side when using an antler but not a copper punch on the wider side. Realizing that the difference was due to more pronounced bulbs with the copper punch, the difficulties were overcome by using an antler punch with a less rounded tip.

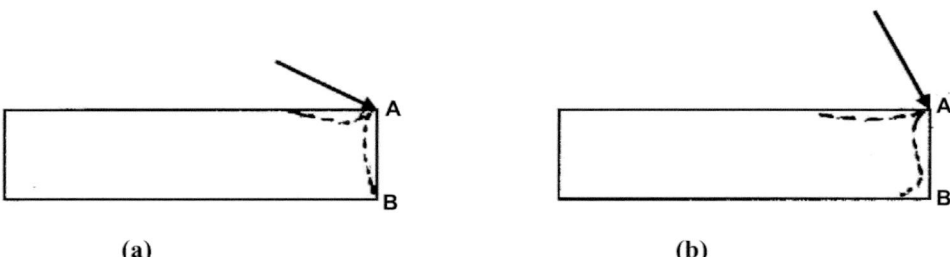

FIG. 10.11 SCHEMATIC OUTLINES FOR CROSS-SECTIONS OF A SQUARE SECTION AXE. FOR FLAKE REMOVAL FROM THE SHORT FACE AB, IT IS ADVANTAGEOUS OR EVEN NECESSARY TO APPLY THE FORCE IN THE DIRECTION SHOWN IN (A). IF THE FORCE IS APPLIED AS IN (B), THE FLAKE WILL TEND TO ROLL OVER AT B AS SHOWN. FOR PROPER FLAKE DETACHMENT FROM THE SHORT FACE, IT IS ADVANTAGEOUS TO HAVE A DEEPER POCKET FOR SEATING THE PUNCH, AS IN (A). AN ACCIDENTAL DETACHMENT OF A WING FLAKE (FIG. 10.9) FROM THE TOP SURFACE WOULD POSE DIFFICULTIES BY NEGATING THE BENEFIT OF A DEEPER POCKET.

Removal of Overhangs and Isolation

The detachment of a blade from a core can leave an overhang at the platform edge with an adjacent concavity. This difficulty is overcome either by seating the punch or pressure flaker sufficiently far back from the platform edge or by removing the overhang. Similar considerations are involved in the detachment of thinning flakes on a biface, for example.

With the chipping away of the overhang and often tiny chips to the sides, the isolation is often improved for the subsequent blade detachments. This reduces the forces required for the blade detachments. On bifaces, platform isolation and location of the edge with respect to the middle plane is done frequently.

Pecking and Grinding

Pecking and grinding are sometimes used in platform preparation (Hirth and Flenniken 2006). These processes have at least two effects. They reduce the slipping of the flaking tool on a blade core. In biface thinning, they allow for a better "bite" or "grab", especially when "sliding percussion" with a hammerstone is used. Pecking and grinding (Fig. 10.10) introduce cracks or microcracks which will reduce the forces required for flake initiation.

As already noted, the Langda axe makers of Irian Jaya (Schick and Toth 1993) sometimes used many blows apparently at the same location of the platform of the triangular-section specimen. Use of such multiple blows is analogous to pecking. Biface thinning may involve only slight to no abrasion or grinding along an edge. Abrasion may be parallel or normal to an edge. The direction of grinding or abrasion can have a significant effect on the strength of a specimen, observed to be 30% in an experiment with a diamond wheel on glass (Mecholsky, Freiman and Rice 1977).

Dorsal Ridges and Curvatures

Near the proximal end of a blade or flake, the presence or absence of a dorsal ridge, as well as its alignment with respect to the center of a flake is important for better control.

Ridges help to guide flakes. For flaking of a biface, there are alternative strategies for controlled flaking. In parallel diagonal pressure flaking (Nunn 2006), a knapper takes advantage of following the ridges. On the other hand, such ridges are not as important in collateral patterned pressure flaking.

Platforms aside, light abrasion has been used on the dorsal ridges of the prospective flakes for biface thinning by contemporary and prehistoric knappers in Europe and America. More severe abrasion, again by prehistoric as well as modern knappers, is often used on crested blades, probably for smoother stress flow (Collins 1999). The reason for the light abrasion on the biface ridges is not clear. Conceivably, it may be to reduce the effects of microcracks and thereby the likelihood of breakages by cracking from the outer to the inner face. Don Crabtree, when asked, said it was "for insurance."

Flake detachment from a surface with a dorsal concavity in the longitudinal direction poses difficulties. An "axial" ("inward") force component causes bending that tends to break a flake transversely. With sufficient flake thickness and by applying the force far enough behind the edge, the difficulty noted can be avoided. In this way, it is possible to flake across a surface longitudinally concave. Surface concavities can be reduced or eliminated by detachment of short and then gradually longer flakes.

Interior Platform Edge

The geometry in the longitudinal (along the flake "axis") and lateral directions is noted briefly for three of the basic flake initiation types.

Wedging Initiations

Flake initiations by wedging (Fig. 10.3) are characterized by a relatively flat region with ripples resembling concentric rings.

Hertzian Initiations

Hertzian initiations may be manifested with or without a cone-like feature (Fig. 10.4). The associated bulb may be pronounced or diffuse. Also, the platform interior angle may vary greatly. A lip is sometimes manifested with a Hertzian initiation.

Bending Initiations

With a bending initiation the interior platform angle of a lip varies laterally. It may not be 90° near the center. A bending initiation can rarely have a bulb, though a diffuse one, well below the contact region. Mist is manifested frequently on well-pronounced lips (Fig. 10.12).

Lips: Description and Meaning

In lithic technology literature, the term "lip" has been used to characterize the geometry at the platform interior edge (Crabtree 1972: 44,75; Odell 2004: 79; Hayden and Hutchings

FIG. 10.12 MIST AND HACKLE AT THE LIP BY THE RIGHT EDGE OF AN OBSIDIAN BIFACE THINNING FLAKE WITH BENDING INITIATION.

1989). Odell considers it to be the "protrusion of the edge of the striking platform over its contact with the ventral surface". Observations for the presence or absence of mist are most meaningful adjacent to the contact area for the force applied at the platform. In practice, a lip refers to the center of a cone-like or other Hertzian feature or, in its absence, to a location established by judgment from the center of the bulbar region and the platform configuration. A lip can sometimes be recognized visually or it may be identified by dragging a finger along the flake ventral surface towards the platform and feeling for it with a fingernail. Lips are more common on flakes with bending initiation, but they do occur occasionally with Hertzian initiations (Hayden and Hutchings 1989).

For the formation of a lip with bending initiations, the fracture may originate at one location near the center of the lip, to one side of it or, sometimes, there is more than one origin. Consider for a moment the case when the fracture origin is at the central location. With a bending initiation, the tensile stresses are high along the locations where the lip is formed. During and just after the fracture originates, the crack will advance rapidly in the lateral direction. In so doing, it can reach fracture velocities at or near its effective terminal velocity (Fig. 10.13).

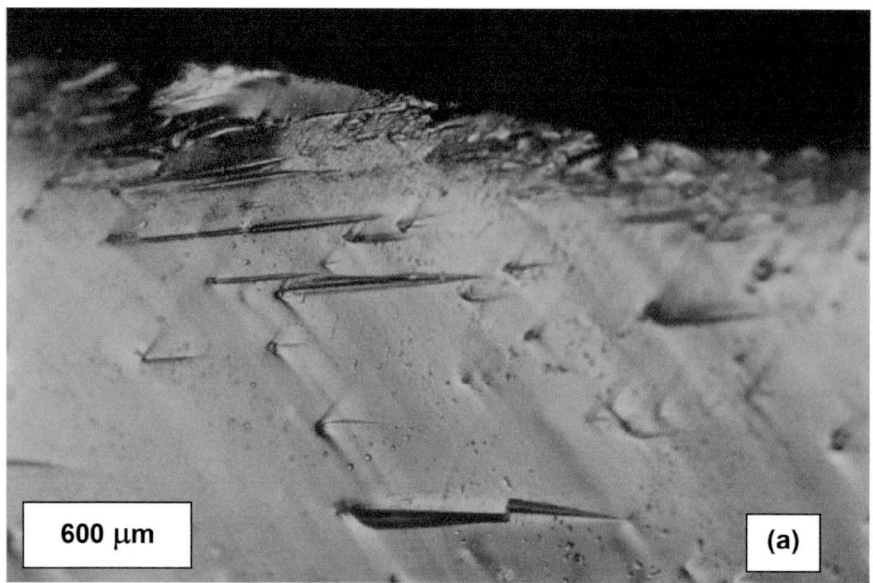

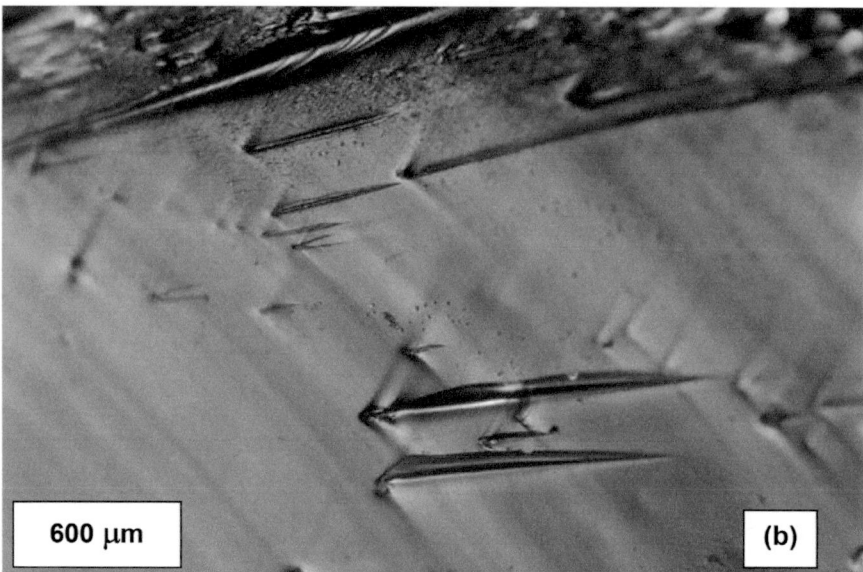

Fig. 10.13 Proximal region of the same flake (adjacent to its platform) produced by direct percussion, having a bending initiation. A mist-hackle region adjacent to the edge is conspicuous, especially in (a). These regions characteristically occur when the fracture velocity is close to the practical terminal velocity, as indicated also in this case by the gull wing angles. The reader can verify this approximately by recalling that $V_F/V_S = \cos$ (1/2 the angle between the gull wings). One needs to be cautious of the strong curvatures in this region. Still, it is evident that $V_F/V_S =$ 0.60+/- approximately.

The mechanism for the formation of a lip at such lateral locations is very different from that at the central region. By the origin near the central region, the fracture tends to propagate in the longitudinal flake direction. At the lateral locations, it tends to propagate in directions nearly parallel to the platform edge. This is seen by the mist patterns as well as the directions of the twist hackle tending to be parallel to the platform edge (Fig. 10.13). For the latter to form, there must have been some shear in the longitudinal flake direction. This shear is likely from the "axial" movement of the flake only partly detached laterally. Such movement also relates to the curvature of a lip at locations away from its central region.

Mist

With bending initiations, mist is often manifested near pronounced lips in percussion as well as pressure flaking. In all the cases observed, the mist regions are adjacent to the platform edge and well to the side from the center of the platform. The flake width along the platform edge was relatively large in all of the cases. Since most bending initiations involve bending indeed, the manifestation of mist in these cases is not surprising. After all, mist is observed frequently in accidental breakage of flakes and bifaces by bending.

Determined inspection is needed to find the mist regions, especially in chert. Observations of mist in obsidian were made by naked eye, verified with hand lens having a magnification of 20X or less. Microscopic inspections have revealed mist to be much more common than anticipated on obsidian flakes with bending initiations having a pronounced lip. In one selected sample, it was observed on about half such percussion flakes. For these, obsidian flakes with bending initiation were selected, and then only those having relatively large width along the platform. Recognition of mist on lips was more difficult, though it does occur, on flakes of chert or flint.

Wing Flakes

Wing flakes (Figs. 10.7 and 10.8), leave traces on a negative flake scar, but rarely on the flake itself. A wing flake is associated with a lateral breakthrough of a twist hackle by the cone-like or other feature of Hertzian initiation.

Bulbs

A bulb is usually seen below the cone-like feature of a Hertzian flake initiation. Bulbs are also manifested sometimes with Hertzian initiation without a cone-like feature. They even occur occasionally on flakes with bending and other non-contact initiations. A fracture surface tends to be normal to the maximum tensile stress. That is, it tends to extend along a compressive stress trajectory. Except in the proximal flake regions, the compressive stress trajectories tend to be parallel to the dorsal flake surface. With Hertzian cone fractures, the maximum tensile stresses cause the principal compressive stress trajectory to form a cone at an angle with the normal to the surface. Application of a force at an angle will change the direction of the compressive stress trajectories (Lawn and Marshall 1979; Quinn 2007: 4-39). The direction is also changed, for example, by having free surfaces on sides too close to the load. These and other factors will affect the direction of the stress trajectories even more at locations further from the load. The local effect of the load will be less there. A bulb is the manifestation of a fracture gradually outrunning the local effect of the load.

The diffuse, more subtle bulb or bulbar swelling occasionally seen with bending initiations of flakes, at some distance from the flake initiation region, indicates that the effect of compression from the "axial" or "inward" force component can still be significantly large after the flake initiation by bending. The "outward" force component associated with the bending initiation was apparently reduced upon flake initiation, perhaps simply by the increased lateral flexibility of the flake.

Why are some bulbs diffuse, others pronounced? Each of the four categories of variables for mechanical systems can affect the bulb characteristics. For example:

- Loading: An increase in the relative inward to outward force component tends to lead to a more pronounced bulb.
- Geometry: The use of a smaller, more rounded antler punch can lead to a more pronounced bulb. The core edge angle also relates to the bulbar characteristics.
- Support Conditions: A harder support for a core in percussion flaking can cause the axial force component to be amplified, as in the extreme case of bipolar percussion, and thereby cause a bulb to be more pronounced.
- Material Properties: The elastic properties of a flaking implement, as well as its inelastic behavior including denting, relate to the contact area during flaking. This can affect bulb characteristics. Poisson's ratio has been noted to influence slightly the angle of Hertzian cones (Kerkhof and Müller-Beck 1969). It may thus also affect bulb characteristics.

Bulbar and Other Hackle Scars and Flakes

Hackle flakes and scars, including bulbar scars, are associated with the lateral breakthrough of twist hackles. The extent of the breakthrough may be short or long in the lateral direction, initially approximately normal to the twist hackle. Readers who have tried their hand in knapping will find it useful to think of an analogy of the usual flake detachment with the hackle flakes. An increase in the relative outward (from the flake "plane") force component leads to shorter flakes in both cases. In some chert and other crystalline materials, an abrupt right angle break may even result.

An "inward" ("axial") force component contributes to a greater length for a lateral breakthrough. Bulbar scars usually have feathered terminations, but stepped and hinged terminations, and occasionally even overshots (Fig. 10.14) do occur. The manifestation of popouts is usually associated with the flakes of bulbar scars (Bordes 1970).

As always with flakes, ridges and higher topography are also relevant to hackle flakes. Though most frequent in a flake proximal region, hackle flakes do also occur elsewhere.

FIG. 10.14 A HACKLE SCAR ON A BULB, WITH THE ASSOCIATED OVERSHOT HACKLE FLAKE.

Proximal Chips

Some hackle scars, originating at twist hackles close to the force platform, are often seen to extend to the force platform. With obsidian, it is easy to verify whether this is indeed the case. In chert, such verification is difficult at best. Rarely, chips termed **proximal chips** here do originate at the force platform of a flake. They are caused by a force applied near the inner edge of a partly released flake (Tsirk 2010b). They are formed differently from bulbar scars and flakes.

Popouts and Stepouts

Popouts and stepouts are usually initiated in the proximal flake regions. Popouts are evident from the surface of a flake but usually not from a flake scar. The presence of stepouts or "incipient popouts" near a core platform can ruin the core.

There is a great variety of popouts, stepouts and their combinations (Chapter 13). Many illustrations appear in Eloy (1975 and 1980) and Tsirk (2010b). At their locations, the parent flakes are often broken.

Flake Surface Features

Fracture Directions

The most important directionality indicators for a fracture are twist hackles and wake hackles (a.k.a. tails) as well as Wallner lines and other ripples. Many of these markings are seen on obsidian surfaces. For fracture surfaces on many cherts, however, there are often large regions where none of these appear. In those regions, it can be difficult at best to establish the fracture direction. In some cherts, there are what appear to be incipient tails or twist hackles. Fracture directions are considered further in Chapter 13.

Ripple Configurations and Fracture Fronts

In general, ripples do not represent fracture fronts. For Wallner lines this is evident from the fact that they often cross each other (Fig. 10.13). Wallner lines are parallel to fracture fronts when the fracture velocity is very low, as with LIFMs (Chapter 8). They also represent fracture fronts when the source of the stress pulse was far from the fracture front.

Ripples, including Wallner lines, can still be used as evidence for the general progress of a fracture front. Wallner lines not parallel to the fracture fronts indicate the advance of the fronts in an exaggerated form. Fractures tend to advance more easily at ridges and locations of higher topography, so as to guide flakes. Other than geometrical effects may also facilitate fracture advance at particular locations.

Fracture fronts are perpendicular to twist hackles, tails and the bisectors of gull wings. Examples of estimated fracture fronts for the fracture surface of an accidental break as well as a flake surface are illustrated in Chapter 13.

An arrest line with real arrest does not necessarily represent a fracture front except at the very instant of the arrest, because the arrest often occurs at different times along the front. Evidence for this is seen occasionally by twist hackles upstream or downstream of some arrest lines not being normal to it.

Ripple Concavity

Wallner lines and other ripples are usually concave in the upstream direction, but not always. The mechanisms that can lead to Wallner lines or other ripples being at least locally convex in the upstream direction are associated with the following:

1. Variable thickness. The variability here and in the next three items refers to that along a transverse section of a flake (Figs. 10.15 and 10.16).
2. Variable fracture toughness.
3. Variable modulus of elasticity..
4. Variable residual stresses.
5. Effects of liquids, as with partial dry and partial wet fracture fronts (Tsirk 2012: Fig. 9).
6. Certain moisture effects, observed only in laboratory with Varner-Quackenbush scarps.
7. Wallner wakes. Wallner lines due to stress pulse source upstream of the fracture front.
8. Stress wave reflection from near a distal end of a flake.
9. A fractures starting from a circular crack around a cylinder, say.

Cases number 6 and 9 are not expected in knapping contexts. All the others have been observed in knapping obsidian, and at least the first four with chert. The fracture markings associated with case number 5, and usually also number 7, are observable with a microscope.

Ripples Related to Flake and Core Geometry

The leading and lagging parts of a ripple can, in principle, have a number of implications. Of the possibilities listed above, most can usually be ruled out easily. The leading and lagging parts of ripples can indicate variations in flake thickness in the transverse direction (Figs. 10.15 and 10.16).

Longitudinal variations in the thickness of a flake can also affect the fracture profile. Relatively sudden changes in flake thickness locally will affect the advance of a fracture in that vicinity, often manifested locally in the ripple configuration.

The effects noted above mean that the geometry of a core affects the flake accordingly. This is why a knapper pays much attention to the core geometry, modifying it after some flake detachments. Such modifications are one significant aspect for achieving greater control in knapping.

The ripple patterns on the flake scars of a biface or other core can indicate geometric characteristics of a detached flake that is no longer available.

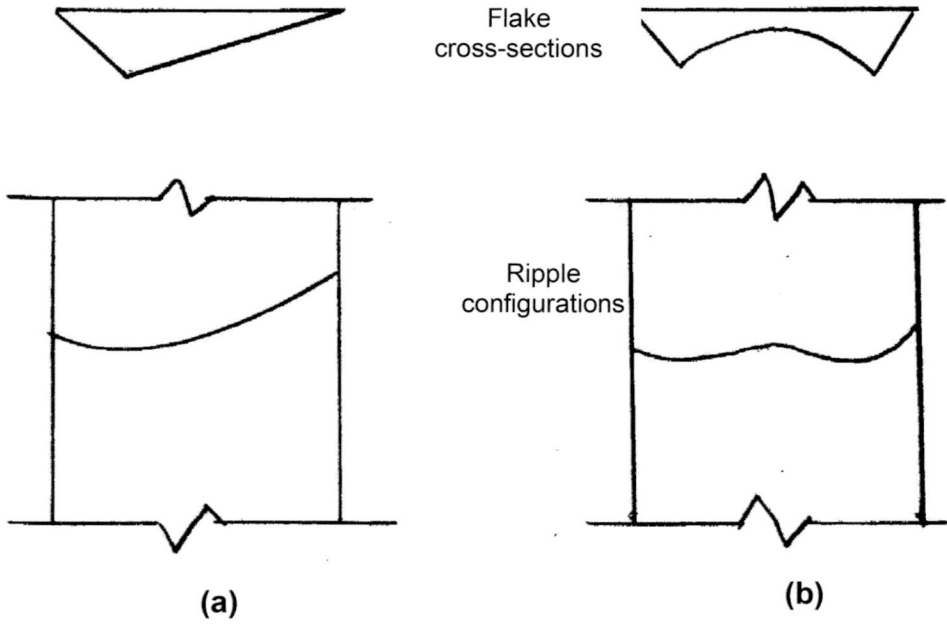

FIG. 10.15 VARIATIONS OF FLAKE THICKNESS IN TRANSVERSE DIRECTION AFFECTING THE FRACTURE FRONT AND RIPPLE CONFIGURATION. IN (B), IT IS PARTLY CONCAVE IN THE DOWNSTREAM DIRECTION. (ADAPTED FROM TSIRK 1981.)

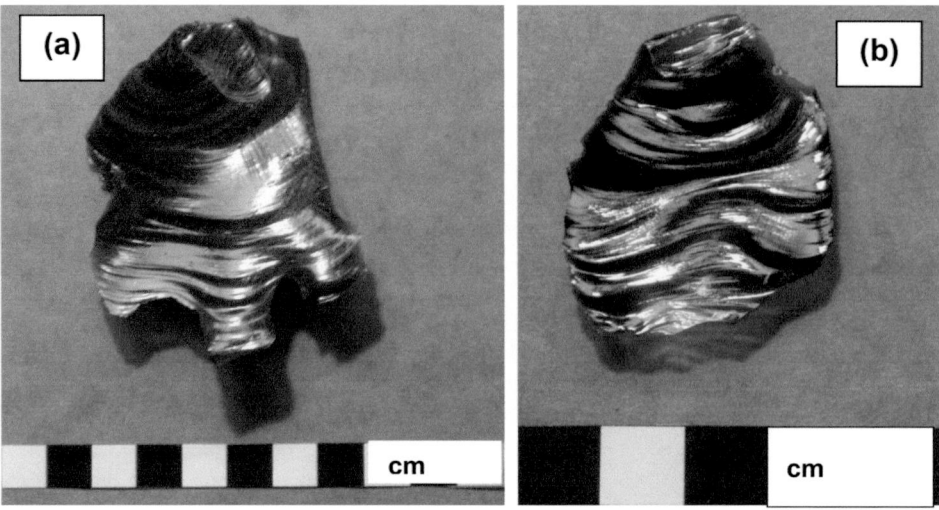

FIG. 10.16 THESE RIPPLE CONFIGURATIONS RELATE TO THE VARIATIONS IN FLAKE THICKNESS IN THE TRANSVERSE DIRECTION. (A) AND (B) ARE OBSIDIAN. (C) IS NORMANSKILL CHERT. (A AND B ADAPTED FROM TSIRK 2012: FIG 7)

Ripples at Inhomogeneities

Inclusions can affect the stresses at a fracture front. This is true for those on the fracture surface as well as those away from but close to it. Inclusions and other localized irregularities can thereby affect the ripple patterns. Even the detailed characteristics of gull wing ripples can provide information of interest.

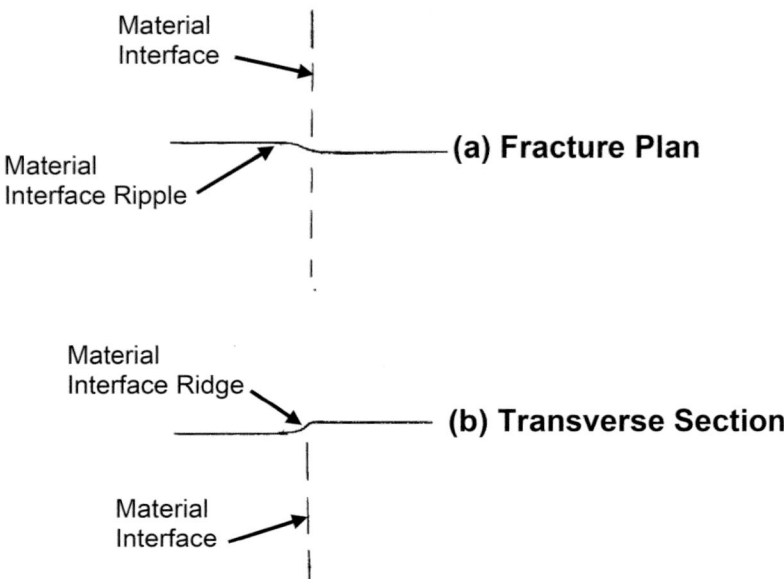

FIG. 10.17 MATERIAL INTERFACE MARKINGS: MATERIAL INTERFACE RIPPLE IN (A) AND MATERIAL INTERFACE RIDGE IN (B).

Occasionally, a chert may have a very different color locally which may relate to different mechanical properties. A ripple can sometimes be seen lagging locally at such an irregularity, due to differences in material properties. Most likely, the fracture toughness varied.

Especially in obsidians, there are often material interfaces with different colors to each side. Examples are the banded and the black-brown "mahogany" obsidians from Glass Buttes. It is of interest to know whether the materials meeting at an interface have different mechanical properties. Material interface markings (Chapter 8) can provide clues to this. Included among these are ripple irregularities at the interfaces termed "material interface ripples" (Fig. 10.17). However, ripple irregularities on a flake scar, together with other evidence, could indicate instead that the flake removed was split longitudinally (Fig. 8.3).

Why Ridges Guide Flakes

Even novice knappers know that longitudinal ridges or higher regions guide blades and other flakes. This relates to a fracture tending to lead at the thicker portions of a flake. Consider a blade, for example. The force applied for the blade production provides strain energy to the stone. As a crack extends, this energy is partly released and consumed by the process of fracture. As a blade bends, more strain energy must be stored in the thicker blade portions, thereby being more readily available for release and fracturing at those locations. This is an explanation for providing physical insight. A more theoretical explanation in terms of fracture mechanics is offered in Tsirk (1981).

Fracture Velocities

The fracture velocities V_F relative to the shear wave velocities V_S, V_F/V_S, can be determined from Wallner lines, at least for obsidian. The "knapper's speedometer" in Fig. 6.6 can provide rough estimates for the range of V_F/V_S from gull wings.

The variations in V_F/V_S for some flake surfaces are reported in Tsirk (1988). The partial fracture surface in Fig 5.10 is an exceptional case. It is for a black-brown "mahogany" Glass Buttes obsidian. The thick flake was produced with a hard hammerstone from a nodule having a very rounded striking platform. Some parts of the fracture surface on this flake were previously illustrated in Tsirk (1988 and 2012). The extensive and rather pronounced mist-hackle region indicates the fracture velocity V_F to be very high, close to its practical terminal value. Measurements of V_F/V_S were also reported in the 1988 article, with the highest value 0.58. With an assumed $V_S = 3,548$ m/s, this measurement gives $V_F = 2,060$ m/s.

The shear wave velocities for some obsidians and cherts are provided in Chapter 3. They range mostly from 3,520 to 3,576 m/s. For one black Glass Buttes obsidian, relatively free of inclusions, it was recently measured to be 3,552 m/s (Yasuda, personal communication, 2012). For some mist regions in intentional transverse breakage of this obsidian, $V_F/V_S = 0.62$ was obtained from gull wings, giving $V_F = 2200$ m/s.

I have not been able to measure V_F/V_S from gull wings on chert fracture surfaces. The markings on the cherts were rather ill-defined, unlike the crisp markings found in obsidians.

Mist and Related Markings

Mist and (velocity) hackle, mist lines, mist-hackle configurations, multiple tails and double tails resembling parabolas are rarely manifested on the surfaces of flakes produced in knapping. The last three markings have been observed only in obsidian.

General regions of mist and hackle are associated with greater surface roughness and more energy consumption than a mirror region. They are manifested with greater fracture velocity. Though quite common in accidental breakages, they have been observed very rarely on the surfaces of flakes produced in knapping.

General mist and hackle regions occur frequently near the lip of obsidian and occasionally chert flakes produced with bending initiations that have a pronounced lip (Fig. 10.13). In all such cases, the mist region was manifested at some lateral distance from the fracture origin for the flake, at or near the lip.

In a few cases, a general mist region was observed along the thicker edge of a flake. Mist lines are characteristically observed adjacent to a general mist region. Such locations have conditions close to but not quite ripe for general mist manifestation. It is some localized condition, such as a tail or a twist hackle, that contributes to the noted marginal condition to permit a mist line to form. In a few cases one or more mist lines were seen near a thicker flake edge without a general mist region.

Mist-hackle configurations and multiple tails were not observed in the above contexts. All of the fracture markings noted in this section were observed in one very exceptional case (Fig. 5.10). The paucity of observations on the noted markings in knapping lends support to the statement that the fractures in knapping are essentially subcritical rather than catastrophic.

Hackle Scars

Twist hackles and the narrow slivers referred to as "fracture lances" are well known (Sommers 1969). A "fracture lance" is formed as a lateral breakthrough with a twist hackle (Fréchette 1990), extending only a short distance from the hackle. Longer lateral breakthroughs form with bulbar scars commonly seen on the bulbs of flakes (Faulkner 1974). In both of these cases, there are hackle scars and hackle flakes. They are formed as extended lateral breakthroughs of a twist hackle at locations of higher contours, such as a bulb for example.

Hackle flakes and scars can be manifested also at locations other than the bulbs - in the proximal, distal and medial regions of a flake, as well as at flake edges (**ridge scars**). On a pronounces ripple in the distal region of a flake, a hackle flake (a **ripple scar**) extending over 6 cm from a twist hackle about 1.3 cm in length was seen, for example. Surprisingly, that ripple with the markings extended in the lateral direction on the flake. Fracture lances and bulbar scars are varieties of hackle flakes or hackle scars.

As a flake is detached, a ridge is usually formed along the lateral edges of the flake scar. There are often twist hackles, oblique to the fracture direction, that extend to these ridges. Hackle scars associated with such hackles are seen frequently along the edges of flake scars in obsidian as well as chert.

Ruffles

Ruffles (Chapter 8) on the surface of a flake or on a flake scar (Fig. 8.4) have the appearance of ripples in disarray. They are indicative of surface roughness on the dorsal face of the flake. A rough cortex on a nodule can lead to primary ruffles. These, in turn, can lead to less pronounced secondary ruffles on a subsequent flake.

Split Marks

Split marks (Chapter 8) on a flake scar manifested as a step, a ridge or as irregularities in ripples can provide evidence of the flake having been split longitudinally. Eamples of split marks are seen in Figs. 8.3 and 10.18. A split ridge can be seen on a cast of a Clovis point from Blackwater No.1 site (Fig. 1.3) and on another Clovis biface illustrated in Frison and Bradley (1999:54-55).

Tails and Incipient Tails

Tails (a.k.a. wake hackles) are rather common on obsidian fractures. The surface mismatch associated with a single tail may be formed when a fracture passes around

FIG. 10.18 SPLIT MARKS: SPLIT STEP (SOLID ARROW) AND SPLIT RIDGE (DASHED ARROW). ESOPUS CHERT.

or through an inclusion. With multiple surface mismatches, multiple tails may also be formed at an inclusion. Because of their appearance as well as formation mechanisms, tails have sometimes been referred to as fracture steps, a term quite descriptive for some twist hackles in chert.

With two (or three) tails at an inclusion, the fracture passes through the inclusion. As it does so, a translational and a rotational surface mismatch may result. The two outermost tails may form a fracture marking termed a "double tail" here (Figs. 5.9). It resembles what has been called a "fracture parabola" or a "Kies figure" (Fréchette 1990: 38, 41; Kerkhof 1970). The latter markings are formed quite differently in PMMA (Fréchette 1990: 41). In some materials, however, markings resembling fracture parabolas are said to be formed with the fracture apparently not running through an inclusion (Kerkhof 1970). Such markings have not been encountered in knapping contexts.

Determination of fracture directions is easy in obsidian but not in chert, as seen in Chapter 13. In chert, there are sometimes regions with tails or incipient tails. These can often be observed with optical microscopy not exceeding 100X. Such microscopic markings can serve as directionality indicators, though not as faithfully as twist hackles in obsidian.

11. Crack Paths and Flake Profile Features

Criteria for Crack Paths

For practical purposes in isotropic britle materials a fracture propagates in a direction normal to the maximum tensile stress, with contributions from modes II and III.

Crack Paths and Core Geometry

Even a novice knapper recognizes the profound effect of core geometry on a flake, especially in the vicinity of a prospective flake. It is on the suitable modification of this region that a knapper usually spends most time on.

Core geometry affects not only the crack path reflected by a fracture profile. It influences flake geometry in a three-dimensional sense, including its thickness, width, and flake edge angles. Not surprisingly, the geometry of a core and of a flake being detached play a significant role in the manifestation of fracture markings and other surface features on a flake (Chapter 10). Some of the effects of interest here were already discussed under "knapper's principles" (Chapter 2). These included the core geometry variation in the longitudinal and transverse directions of a prospective flake. The great effect of ridges and higher topography was considered in Chapter 10.

Unless a flake is too thick, the roughness of a core external surface leads to three-dimensional irregularities on a flake surface called here ruffles. It is not surprising that more significant irregularities on a core surface lead to greater flake surface irregularities, including profile features. Particular examples of this are the observations that a crack path is affected by the presence of previous step and hinge fractures, and by local concavities and protrusions in the core. Engineers sometimes use the term "stress flow" because of some similarities to flow of a liquid. Visualize the axial stresses in a blade being detached as it encounters a previous hinge (or a step) fracture. The "stress flow" is such that the compressive stress trajectories will bend outward at the hinge location. The thicker the hinge, the more will the stress trajectories be bent outward. This is why it is more difficult to remove the more pronounced hinges or steps. The bending of the stress trajectories also relates to a commonly observed tendency for "stacking" of multiple hinges or steps at the same location. One way to eliminate an existing hinge fracture is by removing a thick enough blade behind it, so that the crack extends along a stress trajectory not bent as much.

The deviations of a crack path at concavities and protrusions on a core surface can also be understood by considering stress flow and compressive stress trajectories. Protrusions extending over a small length in the direction of the fracture profile will have no significant effect on a crack path. As expected from stress flow, this is not the case for protrusions longer in that direction.

Crack Paths and Forces Applied

The effects of the forces applied and the core geometry are intricately combined. This will become more evident in Chapter 12. Crack paths depend on the location where the forces are applied and on the magnitude, direction and temporal variation of the forces. Reference is made here to the forces applied by a flaking implement as well as by the supports. The forces in knapping are considered more extensively in Chapter 12. Some considerations from a knapper's viewpoint were already discussed under "knapper's principles" (Chapter 2). Only some examples are noted here briefly.

The relative inward and outward force components can have several effects on a crack path. By an inward component we mean one in the direction of the flake length. An increased inward component can lead to a more pronounced bulb on a flake. This is observed, for example, in blade production by pressure as well as in collateral flaking of replicas of some Dalton points. Variation of the relative force components allows control over flake length. It has been observed in pressure flaking a point, for example, that increasing the outward force component can produce a shorter flake. On the other hand, avoiding an excessive outward force and maintaining an inward component is necessary for parallel flaking across the width of a biface.

The significance of supports is evident in many ways. Examples are the prevention of biface amputation by providing "axial" support at the far end as well as prevention of excessive overshots in edge-to-edge flaking (Chapter 13).

Interesting examples are seen in the constraint of movement during a flake detachment and in the support provided to the dorsal surface of a prospective flake. For flaking a biface to obtain a "crisp" central (longitudinal) ridge, it is advantageous to prevent rotation and to have no support at the dorsal face. Examples are the Eden point (Patten 1999:100) and perhaps the central ridge of the handle on a Danish dagger in preparation for its "stitching" (Apel 2001: Figs. 8.4 & 8.5).

Popouts and Related Fractures

Popouts and some related fractures are shown in Fig. 11.1. Compression lips, and their matching negative parts termed "compression curls" here, are common with bending breaks (Fig. 11.1c). The upper part of the flake in the figure resembles and may in fact be considered a stepout fracture with a short neck (stem). In both cases, a secondary fracture extended outward from the ventral face and then turned downward to form the lip (Fig. 11.1c) or neck (Fig. 11.1b). In lieu of a compression lip, a compression wedge and two compression curls (Fig. 11.1d) are sometimes formed instead. There is some similarity (the curls) but also an obvious difference (the branching forming the wedge) in these cases. The above figure, as well as some others in this chapter, are from Tsirk (2010b).

Compression Lips, Curls and Compression Wedges

A fracture extends along a compressive stress trajectory. In edge-to-edge flaking of a biface, for example, when support is provided to the opposite edge, the compressive stress trajectories run into the support, as does the crack, preventing an overshot (Silsby 1992, personal communication).

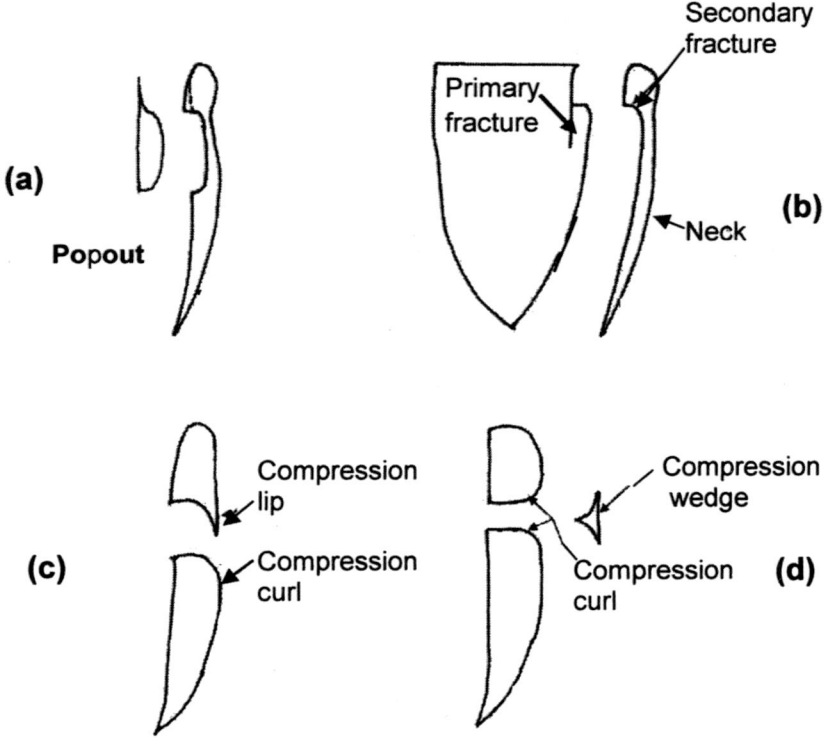

FIG. 11.1 POPOUT AND RELATED FRACTURES (SCHEMATIC): (A) POPOUT FRACTURE; (B) STEPOUT FRACTURE; (C) COMPRESSION LIP; (D) COMPRESSION WEDGE. (ADAPTED FROM TSIRK 2010B)

Consider the stress trajectories for bending of a slender prismatic specimen such as a blade. For the uncracked specimen in Fig. 11.2a, the tensile and compressive stress trajectories are parallel to the specimen edges. This is no longer true when the specimen is partly cracked as in Fig. 11.2b. The tensile stress trajectories must now bend downward to run around the crack, as shown schematically in the figure. Just ahead of the crack tip, the compressive stress trajectories (always normal to the tensile stress trajectories) would be divergent, curving to the left and right of the crack plane. At the extension of the crack plane itself, the compressive stress trajectory runs straight. Thus, when only bending is involved, a crack could extend (rarely if ever) straight down or curve to either or both sides. The latter possibility corresponds to the formation of a compression wedge (Fig. 11.1d) by branching.

It is unlikely for a crack to extend straight to the compression face without a lip. With the two divergent compressive stress trajectories noted above, the situation is directionally unstable. That is, the crack is most likely to veer to either side rather than extend straight. Furthermore, the case in Fig. 11.2 assumes there is pure bending, with no shear. Most practical knapping situations involve some shear as well. The effect of shear stress in lip formation is considered in Fig. 11.3 by reflecting on the nominal stress changes. With the

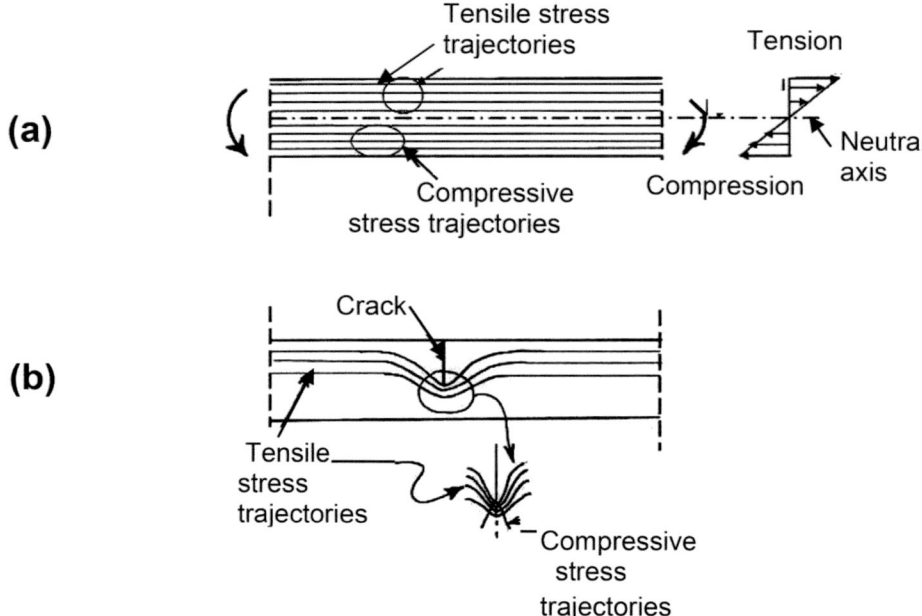

FIG. 11.2 NOMINAL STRESS TRAJECTORIES FOR BENDING OF AN UNCRACKED (A) AND PARTLY CRACKED (B) SPECIMEN (ADAPTED FROM TSIRK 2010B).

sense of the shear stress shown, the compression lip necessarily extends leftward as shown. This can be understood (See Fig. 11.3c) by noting that the shear stress is equivalent to some additional tensile stress in other than the horizontal direction, as shown. Thus, due to the shear, the direction of the maximum tensile stress and hence also the direction of the fracture surface is rotated clockwise. Thus the resulting fracture surface curls towards the direction shown in Fig. 11.3b.

A compression lip can curl to a particular side either due to shear in a particular sense or, in the absence of shear, due to the directional instability already noted. A compression lip extending to a particular side serves as evidence that either shear was absent or else acting in a sense consistent with Fig. 11.3b. In other words, a compression lip in a particular direction proves that shear in a sense inconsistent with Figures 11.3b and c was not present. The presence of a compression lip on a transverse break indicates that the break involved bending and that compression was on the side of the lip. The extension of the lip and its variability along the edge of the transverse break relate to the presence of axial compression and torsion, respectively.

In terms of their formation, it is important to distinguish a compression wedge (Fig. 11.1d) noted above from the lateral wedges occasionally encountered at the sides of bifaces and blades broken transversely by bending. The formation of the lateral wedges, well known to archaeologists (Pelegrin 1984: Figure 9 and 2013: Figs. 6 and 13), is usually preceded near the tensile face by mist, velocity hackle, and sometimes also aborted attempts at

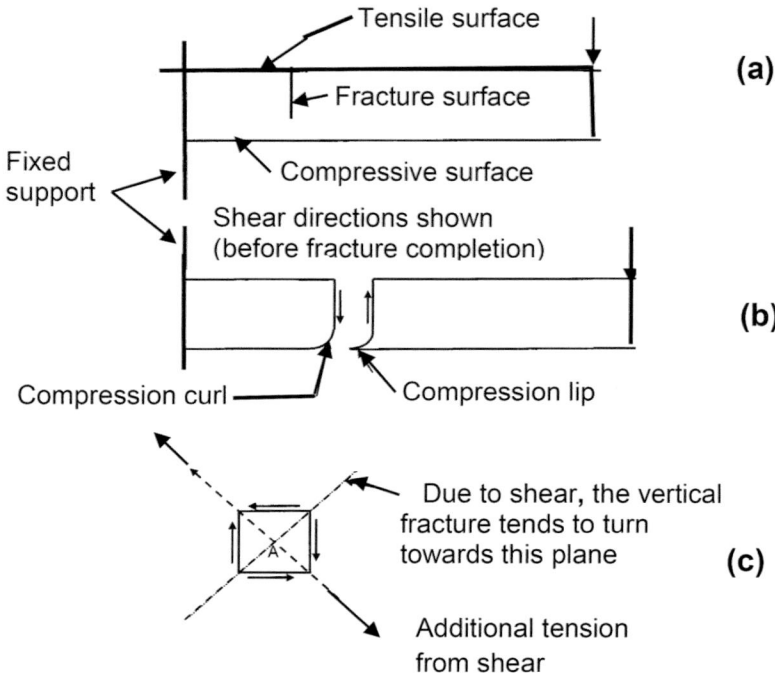

FIG. 11.3 EFFECT OF SHEAR ON THE DIRECTION OF THE COMPRESSION LIP: (A) CANTILEVER BEAM WITH SHEAR; (B) DIRECTION OF THE COMPRESSION LIP WITH THE SHEAR SHOWN; (C) EFFECT OF THE SHEAR STRESS AT AN ELEMENT JUST AHEAD OF THE CRACK TIP. (ADAPTED FROM TSIRK 2010B)

macroscopic branching, termed incipient branching here. All these features are associated with very high fracture velocity – over 2,000 m/s for some obsidians (Tsirk 1988: 67). In contrast, mist and velocity hackle have not been observed, nor are they expected, with the branching for the compression wedges. The fracture velocities in these cases are therefore lower. The formation of the compression and lateral wedges is associated with low and high velocity branching, respectively. Only three lateral wedges were encountered in this study with popout fractures produced by percussion flaking (Fig. 9b in Tsirk 2010b). Mist and velocity hackle, referred to simply as mist and hackle in the referenced figures, are considered in Quinn (2007) and Hull (1999). The term "mist hackle" is sometimes used for the two markings (Fréchette 1990: 26).

Step-In and Step-Out Fractures

Some stepout fractures have been included under "languette" in French by Bordes (1970) and Eloy (1975 and 1980). The terms "tongue" and "stemmed blade (languet)" have also been used. Stepout fractures here will include a class of fractures different from what has generally been considered under the terms noted above.

The early phases of stepout and popout fractures initiated in the proximal flake region are similar in terms of their appearance as well as formation. With both of these fractures, a

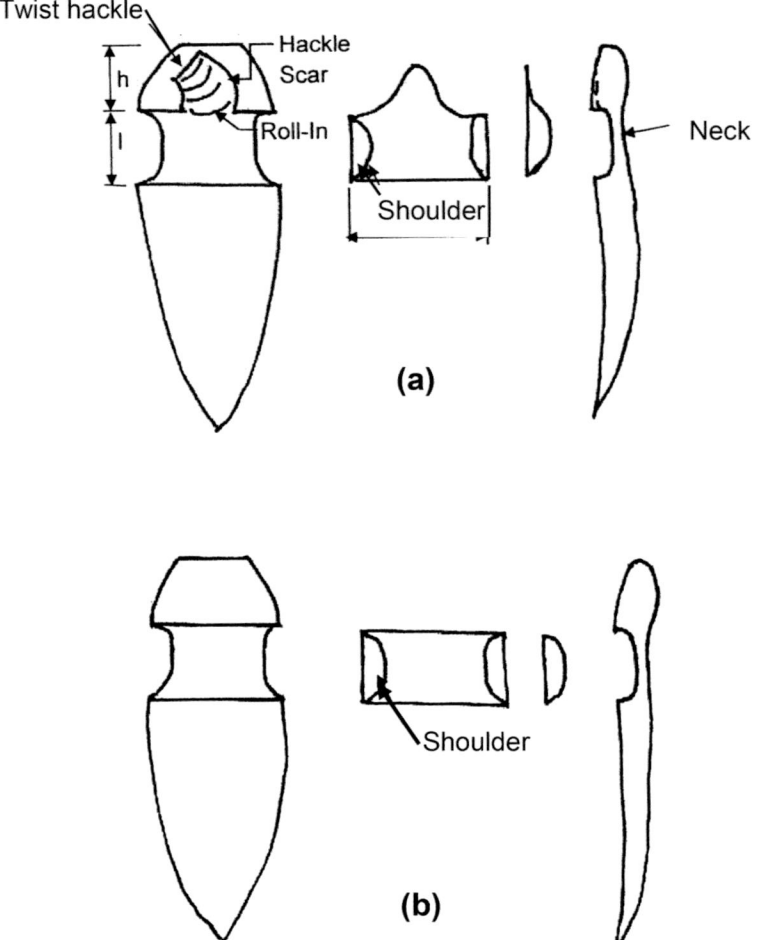

FIG. 11.4 REGULAR POPOUT FRACTURES WITH AND WITHOUT A ROLL-IN FROM A HACKLE SCAR. (ADAPTED FROM TSIRK 2010B)

crack extends outward from the ventral face and then downward approximately parallel to the flake dorsal surface. The outward extension may be gradual or abrupt as in Fig. 11.4a and (b). In this subsection, only the stepouts with the latter kind of outward extension is considered. Such an abrupt outward extension starts at the inner face as a tensile break from bending.

As discussed later, several kinds of detailed mechanisms may initiate a gradual outward extension. There are many intermediate cases between the idealized gradual and abrupt outward extension. Some of these may be viewed simply as transverse bending breaks initiated at large flaws.

The initial stepout phase with a crack extending outward from A at the inner face is shown schematically in Fig. 11.5a and b. The portion of the blade above ABC of Fig. 11.5a is shown again in Fig. 11.5b. Consider the nominal stresses at the section ABC as the crack extends outward. For the initial break to occur at A, the vertical stress there had to be tensile. This tension is the net effect of compression from the vertical load and bending from both the vertical and horizontal loads (Fig. 11.5a). As the crack extends outward, the size of the unbroken ligament (BC in Fig. 11.5b) decreases and the eccentricity e of the vertical load increases with respect to the centroid of that unbroken ligament. The nominal stress (+ for tension) at B is

$$\sigma_B = -\frac{P}{A} + \frac{Hh-Pe}{S} \tag{11.1}$$

where A is the area and S the section modulus for the cross-section of the unbroken ligament. For a trapezoidal section, with t = the thickness and α = the ratio of the shorter to the longer parallel side b, $A = (1+\alpha)$ bt/2 and $S = (1+4\alpha+\alpha^2)$ bh³/ $[12(1+2\alpha)]$. These expressions can also be used for a rectangle ($\alpha = 1$) and a triangle ($\alpha = 0$). Thus for a triangular section $S = bt^2/12$ and

$$\sigma_B = -\frac{2P}{bt} + \frac{12(Hh-Pe)}{bt^2} \tag{11.2}$$

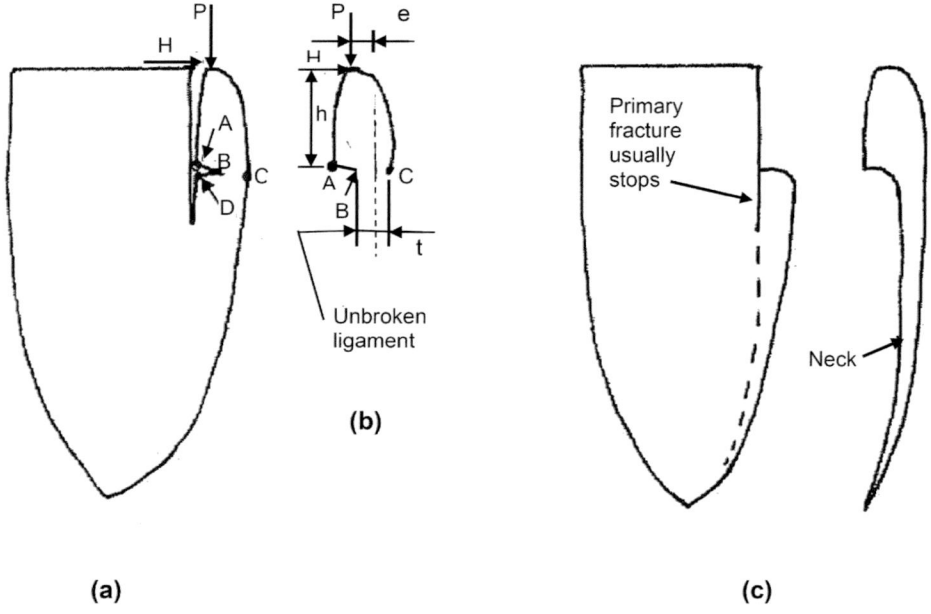

(a)   (b)   (c)

FIG. 11.5 FORMATION OF A STEPOUT FRACTURE: (A) INITIAL STEPOUT PHASE WITH CRACK EXTENDING OUTWARD (CASE WITH NO ROLL-IN); (B) FORCES CAUSING THE STRESS AT B BY THE UNBROKEN LIGAMENT, (C) A COMPLETED STEPOUT FRACTURE. (ADAPTED FROM TSIRK 2010B)

The horizontal force H provides the shear at the unbroken ligament. As seen from the above equations, for a small enough ligament, the nominal (net) vertical stress gradually decreases (from the tension when the crack started) and becomes compressive. The crack will not extend into the compression zone. In fact, several blades of transparent obsidian and industrial (soda-lime) glass have been observed that do not have a stepout or popout fracture but just a transverse crack extending partly through the blade. These observations are not surprising.

In a stepout fracture, the transverse crack (as AB in Fig. 11.5a) turns downward (parallel to the outer surface) due to adequate shear stress, just as in the case of a compression lip (Fig. 11.1c). In comparison to the usual compression lip from bending, the extension of the neck of a stepout is usually longer. The length of a blade with a stepout is often comparable to that of blades without a stepout from the same core (as in Fig.11.5c). The crack extension to form a relatively long neck relates to the presence of the axial compression (as from P in Fig. 11.5b). As already noted, a crack tends to run along a compressive stress trajectory. The length of the neck in a stepout fracture relates to the relative values of the outward and axial (horizontal and vertical in Figure 11.5, respectively) force components, as well as the initial thickness of the neck (as by the unbroken ligament BC in Fig. 11.5b). The shortness of a usual compression lip in bending relates primarily to the absence of significant axial compression. As already noted, stepout fractures may be viewed as transverse bending breaks with the presence of axial compression. A step fracture with a compression lip is in fact a stepout fracture with a short neck.

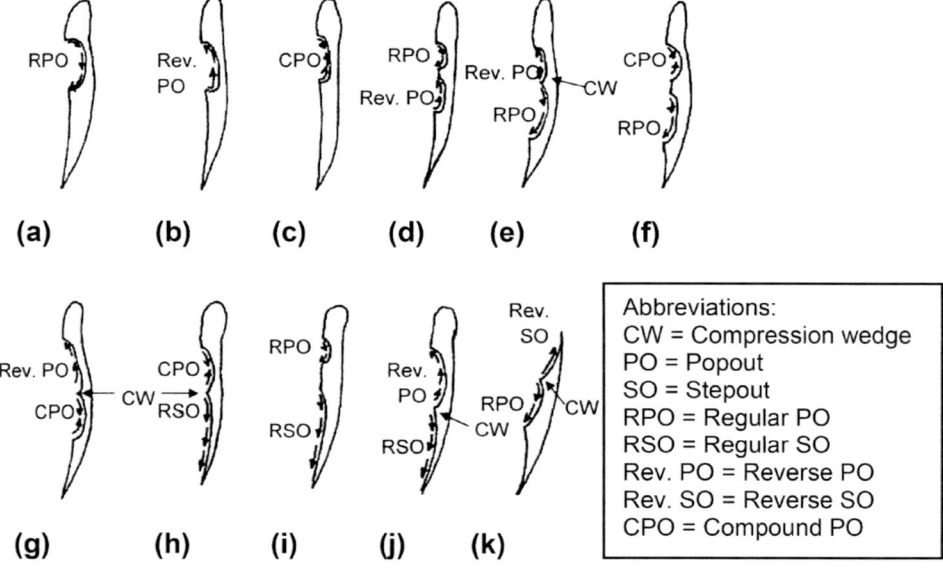

FIG. 11.6 SCHEMATIC PROFILES AND FRACTURE DIRECTIONS FOR POPOUT AND STEPOUT FRACTURES OBSERVED. (ADAPTED FROM TSIRK 2010B)

Stepout fractures are sometimes also produced at locations away from a flake proximal region (Fig. 11.6h and i). Reverse stepout fractures (Fig. 11.6k) may also occur, with the crack propagation towards a proximal region. The initial phases of all these stepout fractures are similar to those of the respective popout fractures. Occasionally **step-in fractures** are also manifested. Regular step-in fractures start at the dorsal face, extend inward and then downward. Flake dorsal convexity is often characteristic for such fracture regions.

With stepout fractures, the primary fracture usually stops a short vertical distance beyond the location of the outward extension of the secondary fracture. Occasionally, however, the primary fracture continues for the full length of the core. The two cases noted are depicted in Fig.11.5c by the solid and dashed lines, respectively. The extension of the primary crack depends partly on its timing relative to that of the secondary (the stepout) fracture.

Occasionally a fracture is arrested (or almost so) in the bulbar region. Upon re-starting, the primary fracture sometimes makes a sudden turn, leaving a kink in the fracture profile (Figure 11.7a). That kink is known as an arrest line (Fréchette 1990), a misnomer. Extending outward, the primary fracture can then turn and extend downward, sometimes for the full length of the core. The resulting flake is not to be confused with one resulting from a stepout, which can have a similar fracture profile. The latter is produced with an extension of a secondary fracture; the flake with an arrest line, with only a primary fracture. A factor involved with the formation of a stepout fracture is also operating in the latter case, to cause the outward turning of the fracture.

Incipient Breaks

In the formation of a step-out fracture as well as the earliest stage of a popout fracture, a crack originates at the ventral surface of a blade as a bending break and extends towards the dorsal surface. As it does so, the originally tensile stress at the inner surface and the unbroken ligament of the cross-section diminishes and gradually becomes compressive (Fig. 11.5). Further outward extension of the crack is thereby inhibited. It will stop or, with appropriate shear, turn downward. Such a stopped crack is referred to here as an **incipient break** (Fig. 11.7). It may indeed be viewed as an unsuccessful attempt in the formation of a step-out or popout fracture.

Popout Fractures

For some varieties of popout fractures, the term "nacelle blade" ("lame en nacelle" in French) coined by François Bordes (1970) has been used. The blade from which the nacelle piece was detached was called the parent blade ("lame mère" in French). In his study with prehistoric specimens, Eloy (1975 and 1980) notes that nacelle fractures are not at all rare. Nacelle blades are also considered in Texier (1984) and Hirth and Flenniken (2006). Instead of adapting the term of the above authors, "popouts" or "popout fractures" is used here for a broader class of fractures that includes the nacelle fractures considered by Bordes and Eloy.

Several different types of popout fractures, shown in Fig. 11.6, were observed. Including regular and reverse popouts, compound popouts, double popouts and various popout-

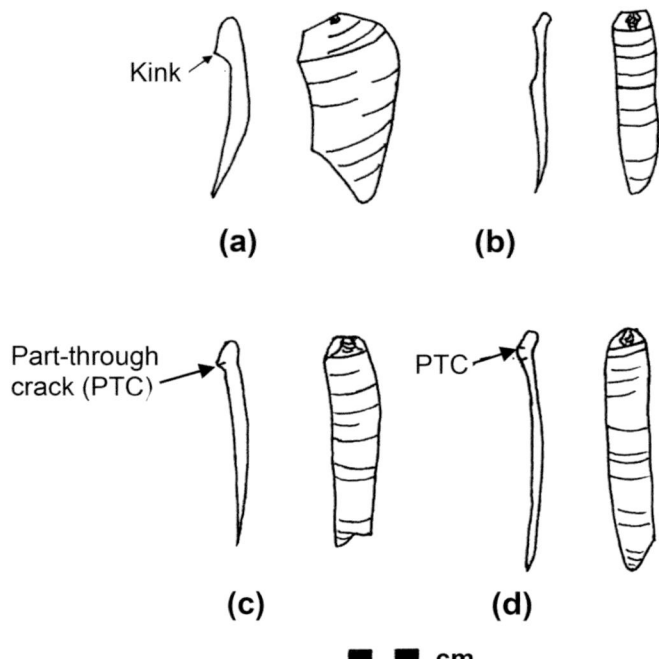

FIG. 11.7 INCIPIENT, QUASI-STEPOUT AND QUASI-POPOUT FRACTURES: THE KINKED PROFILE OF THE PRIMARY FRACTURE IN (A) RESEMBLES A STEPOUT FRACTURE. THE PRIMARY FRACTURE PROFILE IN (B) HAS SOME RESEMBLANCE TO A POPOUT FRACTURE. WITH THE PART-THROUGH TRANSVERSE CRACKS, (C) AND (D) MAY BE VIEWED AS INCIPIENT STEPOUT OR POPOUT FRACTURES. THE PRIMARY FRACTURE PROFILE IN (C) STARTS TO RESEMBLE A STEPOUT FRACTURE. (A) IS NORMANSKILL CHERT, OTHERS ARE OBSIDIAN. (ADAPTED FROM TSIRK 2010B)

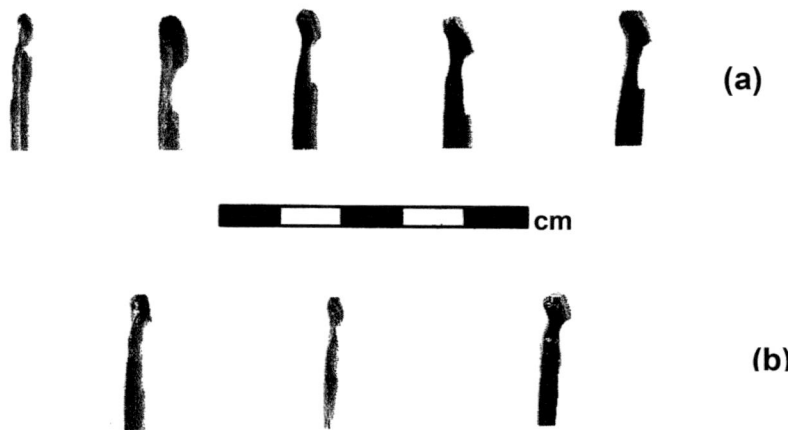

FIG. 11.8 PARTIAL PROFILES OF OBSIDIAN BLADES WITH DORSAL CONCAVITIES FOR (A) POPOUT FRACTURES AND (B) STEPOUT FRACTURES. (ADAPTED FROM TSIRK 2010B)

stepout combinations. The frequencies of occurrence for the basic types of popouts are considered in Chapter 13.

The initial phases of popout and stepout fractures are similar. A popout formation starts with a secondary fracture extending outward from a flake ventral surface. As with stepouts, this may occur abruptly or gradually (Fig. 11.4). The latter may involve a roll-in from a hackle flake. Most but not all popouts are initiated and occur near the proximal part of a flake.

On many of the blades and other flakes with popouts and stepouts, a dorsal concavity in the proximal region is conspicuous (Fig. 11.8). It is of interest to note that among the most recent blades produced from an aborted polyhedral core with a constricted platform there was a series of 13 consecutive blades that included 4 popout and 3 stepout fractures. The proximal dorsal surfaces of these flakes were concave.

Some of the profiles of popout and stepout fractures had no dorsal concavity in the proximal region near the roll-in for these fractures. Such absence was observed on 34% of the percussion blades, but rarely on pressure blades.

The formation of the observed popout fractures is viewed here as consisting of the following phases:

 – Initiation phase, with beginning of the outward extension;
 – Outward extension and the turning to vertical;
 – Vertical propagation;
 – The turning from the vertical, and inward propagation.

All popout fractures were initiated by a bending break or a secondary fracture turning outward from the ventral flake surface. Such bending breaks were observed in the proximal, medial and distal flake regions. Initiations by the secondary fractures, on the other hand, were limited to the proximal region.

Consider the next phase in popout formation. The outward extension and the turning to a vertical may be viewed as a bending break with the manifestation of variants of a compression wedge (Fig. 11.6e, g, h, j and k) or a compression lip (Fig. 11.1c). However, with popouts the latter features do not extend to and do not feather out at the dorsal flake surface. When they do, as in Fig. 11.6h to k, then they lead to stepouts rather than popouts. The direction of the shear stresses is important here in the same way as noted for the formation of compression lips.

Once the fracture has turned to the vertical, it will tend to extend in that direction, being parallel to the compressive stress trajectories. The turning from the vertical to inward propagation relates to bending stresses, to the vertical compressive stress and the shear stresses. These stresses will be considered further with the examples of a regular and a reverse popout. The terminal end of a popout is usually rounded, and may be viewed as a variant of a hinge termination of a popout flake, occasionally with a roll-out to the inner flake surface. Only rarely was the inward extension of a popout fracture tapered or feathered out gradually at the inner surface without a hinge.

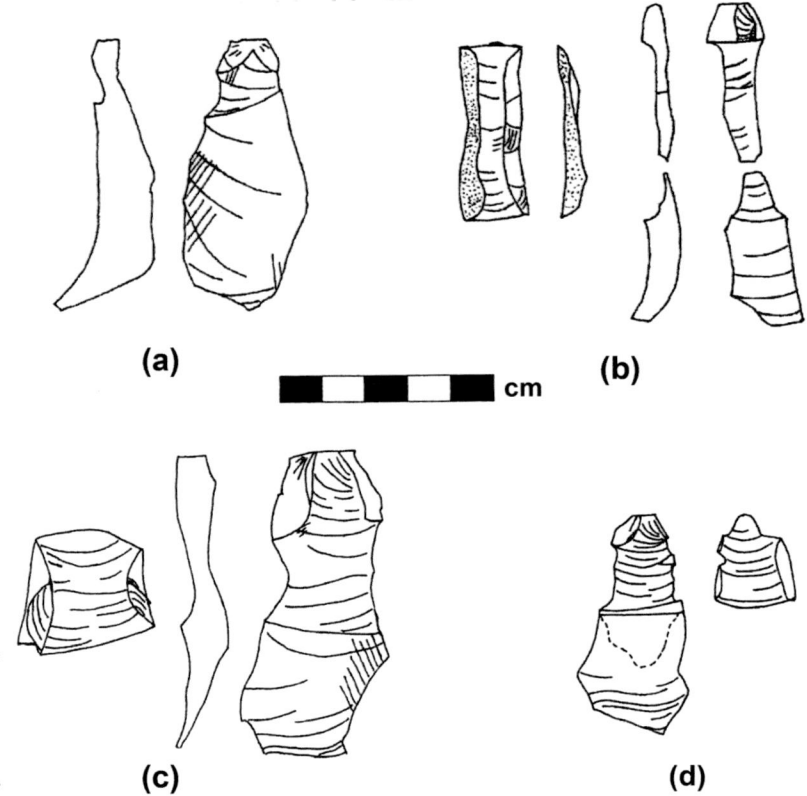

FIG. 11.9 REGULAR BUT UNUSUAL POPOUT FRACTURES FROM PERCUSSION, ALL INITIATING FROM A SINGLE HACKLE SCAR IN OBSIDIAN: (A) A POPOUT FRACTURE ON A VERY THICK FLAKE; (B) A VERY LONG (74 MM) POPOUT; (C) A THICK FLAKE WITH A MASSIVE POPOUT; (D) A DOUBLE-SIDED POPOUT FRACTURE BECOMING SINGLE-SIDED AND THEN AGAIN DOUBLE-SIDED. (ADAPTED FROM TSIRK 2010B)

The timing of the primary and the secondary fractures associated with popout formation is crucial, of course. In the case of a regular popout fracture, for example, the turning from the vertical to the inward extension of the crack can occur only if the primary fracture has already extended past its location. Some popout fractures initiating at a roll-in from a secondary fracture still have breakage from bending at its shoulders. Due to the roll-in acting as a large flaw, the breakage stresses at the shoulders are usually too low for the manifestation of mist and velocity hackle there.

Consider a regular popout fractures initiated with an abrupt bending break (as in Fig. 11.4b). At the location where such a popout fracture initiation occurs (as at A in Fig. 11.5 and 11.12), the inner face is in tension from bending . The partly detached flake tends to bend concave outward as indicated in Fig. 11.12a. When a bending break starts, the secondary fracture extends outward to initiate the popout formation. As the crack

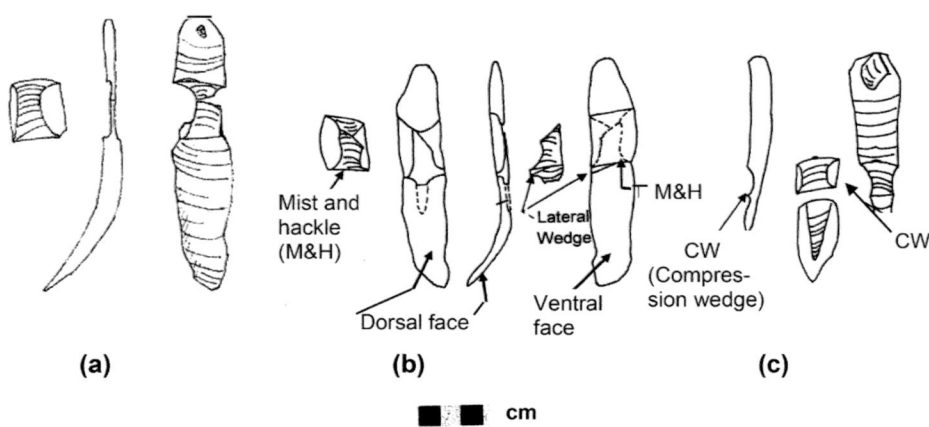

FIG. 11.10 REVERSE (A AND C) AND COMPOUND POPOUTS. (C) SHOWS A REVERSE POPOUT AND STEPOUT COMBINATION. ALL ARE OBSIDIAN, BY DIRECT PERCUSSION. (ADAPTED FROM TSIRK 2010B)

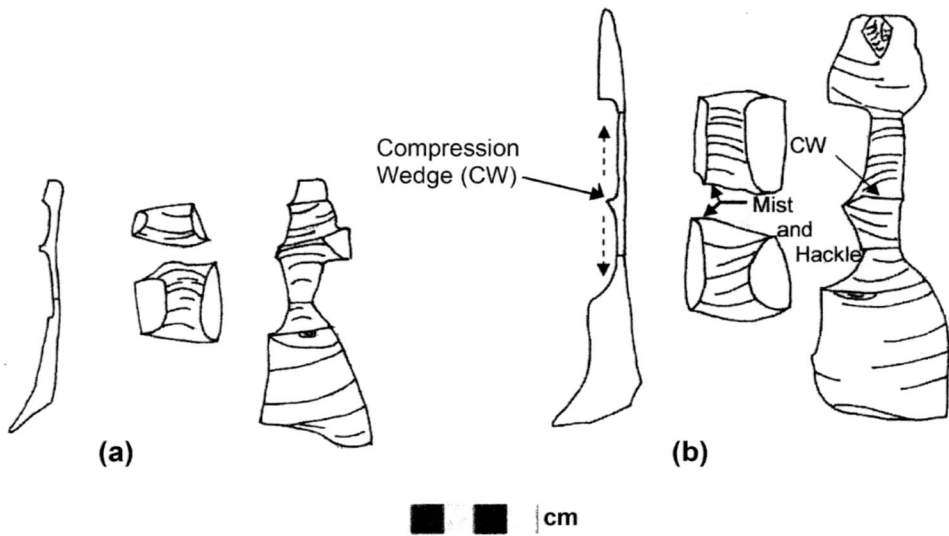

FIG. 11.11 DOUBLE POPOUTS. NOTE THE COMPRESSION WEDGE FROM WHICH THE REGULAR AND REVERSE POPOUTS INITIATE. THE DASHED ARROWS INDICATE THE FRACTURE DIRECTION. (ADAPTED FROM TSIRK 2010B)

extends outward, the eccentricity of the axial force increases on the unbroken ligament (See Equation 11.1 and Fig 11.5a and b). After the crack has extended sufficiently far outward, the vertical stress in the unbroken part of the blade will be only compressive for its full width (Fig.11.12b).

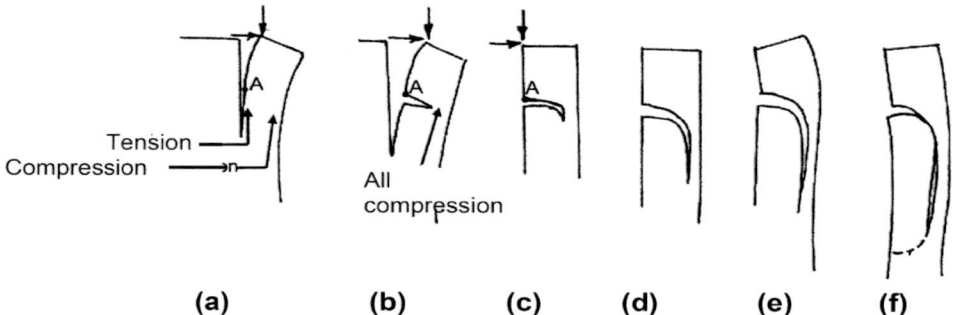

FIG. 11.12 FORMATION OF POPOUT FRACTURES. (ADAPTED FROM TSIRK 2010B)

FIG. 11.13 POPOUT FRACTURE ON AN OBSIDIAN BIFACE THINNING FLAKE (MAX. WIDTH ~8CM) AFTER A STUDY OF MANY POPOUTS AND OTHER FRACTURE SPECIMENS, IT BECAME APPARENT THAT INTRUSIVE HACKLE FLAKES (WITH HINGE TERMINATIONS) GRADUALLY "EVOLVE" INTO POPOUT FRACTURES. FIG. 11.14, AS WELL AS ELOY (1980), GIVE AN INDICATION OF THIS TRANSITION.

Before the crack stops, the outward shear (from the outward flaking force, as H in Fig. 11.5b) causes the initial curving (as with compression lips) until the crack runs parallel to the compressive stress trajectories from the axial force (Fig.11.12c and d). The axial force with its eccentricity contributes to the flake bending concave inward (See Equation 11.1 and Fig. 11.12e).

For the popout to form completely, the vertical crack has to turn back inward. With the flake bending concave inward, contact is established between the partly detached popout and the flake (Fig. 11.12f). The partly detached popout is thus being pushed inward and perhaps also downward. Frequently observed tiny edge chipping at the kinked shoulders of the popout parent flake serves as likely evidence for such contact. The inward push produces bending of the partly detached popout as well as shear on it. This causes the vertical fracture to turn inward to complete the popout fracture. The relation of the shear stress to the turning of a crack considered in Fig. 11.3c is also relevant here.

Similar reasoning can be used to suggest the mechanisms for the formation of other popouts (Tsirk 2010). A double popout, or a popout-stepout combination, is sometimes associated with the formation of a compression wedge, as in Figs. 11.6e, g, h, j and k. Compression wedges were observed to be associated with the formation of two double popouts and four popout-stepout combinations. Popouts have been observed on some core platform rejuvenation flakes and on biface thinning flakes (Fig 11.13). In his film "The Flintworker", Don Crabtree shows a popout on a biface thinning flake.

Fractures resembling the compression wedges with double popouts were already reported by de Fréminville in 1914. For example, Fig. 11.11b resembles his Fig. 9 (page 988) and the figures on page 1038, at least when viewed two-dimensionally.

Ripple Profiles and Kinks

The formation of ripples and kinks was discussed in Chapter 6. Considered in a static sense, a ripple may be viewed as a temporary loss and re-adjustment in the balance of the force components. As seen, they can be manifested due to a number of different causes. Always, however, their formation involves changes in the direction of the normal stress – a rotation about an axis parallel to the fracture front. That is, they are due to contributions from fracture mode II.

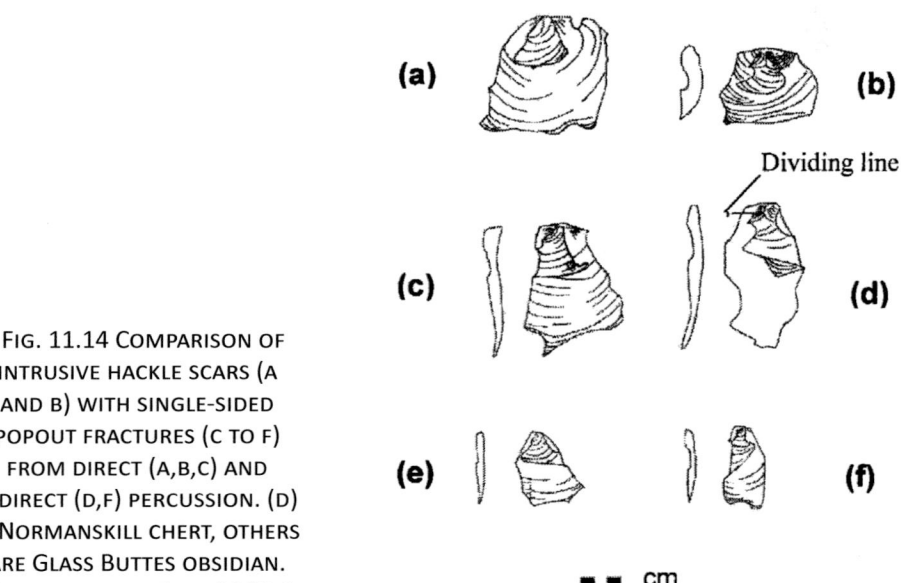

FIG. 11.14 COMPARISON OF INTRUSIVE HACKLE SCARS (A AND B) WITH SINGLE-SIDED POPOUT FRACTURES (C TO F) FROM DIRECT (A,B,C) AND INDIRECT (D,F) PERCUSSION. (D) IS NORMANSKILL CHERT, OTHERS ARE GLASS BUTTES OBSIDIAN. (ADAPTED FROM TSIRK 2010B)

From the above discussion it is evident that ripples by the distal end of a flake scar can be an indication of changes in a flake thickness along its length. A word of caution, however. In some "layered" obsidians, it has been observed that the amplitude of distal ripples is increased due to "layering" parallel or oblique to the fracture front.

Wavy Crack Paths

Wavy crack paths are sometimes encountered with thermal fractures. They can be seen on prehistoric bifaces (Purdy 1975: Plate 4b), as well as those from modern knapping (Fig. 3.5). The terms "crenated fractures" (Purdy 1975: Plate 4), "meander cracks" (Fréchette 1990: 43-46) and "oscillating cracks" (Bahat, Rabinovitch & Frid 2005: 99-100) have also been used for such wavy, sinuous, sinuous fractures.

In knapping contexts, wavy fractures have occurred in heat treating when the specimens are cooled too rapidly (Purdy 1975: 137 and Plate 4a). For example, this was encountered on a multi-colored Burlington chert from Crescent Quarry. Two of the chert and several quartzite bifaces were heat treated between two sand layers that were between two successive fires. The quartzite and one chert biface were removed and exposed to air shortly after the upper fire burned out. Only the chert biface fractured, with a wavy crack path (Fig. 3.5). The other chert biface was allowed to cool in situ before removal the next morning. It was heat treated successfully without fracturing.

The initiation of the thermal fracturing discussed is easy to understand. Consider a biface at a relatively high temperature that is suddenly exposed to air at room temperature. For the present purpose it is useful to reflect on the situation along a middle plane of the biface. Its parts closest to the biface edge will cool faster because of the greater surface area to volume ratio. Therefore the parts of the biface closest to its edge will want to contract more than its adjacent parts, introducing tension in the outermost part of the biface. With high enough tension, a fracture will occur. The above initiation mechanism is consistent with that for window panes that are heated by sun in its central region while its edges are cool (Fréchette 1990: 43). With rapid heating, fractures may initiate instead at locations away from an edge (Jones 2001, Tsirk 2003).

The picture is actually more interesting than suggested by the above discussion. In experimental research, crack branching is sometimes observed with thermal fractures (Fréchette 1990: Fig. 3.3, Bahat et al. 2005: 99, and possibly Purdy 1975: Plate 5). Also, the characteristics of the wavy patterns have been observed to change systematically (Bahat et al. 2005: 99-100). Unfortunately, some of the above experimental research has been on glasses with 0.1 mm (sic) thickness.

The fundamental reasons for the waviness of a thermal fracture as in Fig. 3.5 are suggested here. Basically, it relates to the differential stresses from the thermal effects inducing shears and the fracture orienting itself to minimize these shears. The self-relieving nature of the stresses and the differential cooling effects during the fracture also contribute to the "meandering" of the thermal crack. Such cracking is often characteristic but is not a proof of thermal fracturing according to Fréchette (1990: 43-46). In general, the relevant factors (Boley and Weiner 1960) include the following:

1. The geometry of the specimen;
2. The temperature differentials and their variation with time;
3. The coefficient of thermal expansion;
4. Thermal conductivity;
5. Specific heat;
6. The elastic constants;
7. Fracture toughness or strength.

It is relevant to note that the process is one with self-relieving stresses. To understand the formation of the wavy fracture paths, the analysis would have to be geometrically nonlinear.

It is not suggested that analyses with all these variables be considered to understand the wavy crack paths, although that would be possible by some numerical technique such as the finite element method. However, it is necessary to refer to the variables to explain the reasons for the different results in various experiments - using chert and quartzite, for example - with regard to fractures in heat treatment.

Flake Terminations

Five basic types of flake terminations are shown in Fig. 11.15. The first four of these are usually found in lithics literature. The fifth, blunt termination, has been added here. There are many variations of these basic types of terminations.

Feathered terminations, usually desired, are normally one aspect of flaking with good control. Ordinarily, the step and hinge terminations are knapping errors. The Mousterian resolved pressure flaking is an unusual example, from the Middle Paleolithic. It involved intentional use of step fractures. A **step fracture** (Fig. 11.15b) results when the fracture slows down or stops, and the flake then breaks transversely at or slightly behind the fracture front. On these transverse breaks, the fracture necessarily propagates from the ventral (inner) to the dorsal (outer) surface, as evidenced by the characteristic features of a bending break. Although the nominal bending stress at the inner surface is highest at the fracture front (where the fracture may have stopped), the stress intensity factor may be highest behind the front, depending on the flaws. A step fracture can occur, for example, when a fracture stops because of an inadequate "axial" force to advance it, and then the outward force component produces the bending break that forms the step.

A **hinge fracture** (Fig.11.15c) is usually formed with a continuous propagation of a fracture without arrest. The fracture changes direction and curls outward and usually at least slightly upward (occasionally then outward and downward again). It can occur when the inward force decreases too much, but not abruptly, relative to the outward component. Recalling the normality rule for fracture, the various crack paths observed at hinge fractures indicate that the normal stress directions must be changing for the crack to turn in various ways. The initial turning for a hinge can be viewed simply as a change in the relative inward and outward force components. But once a major turn in the fracture path takes place, the notion of the initial relative inward and outward components makes no longer sense. One needs to reflect on what is the normal stress with the changing surface

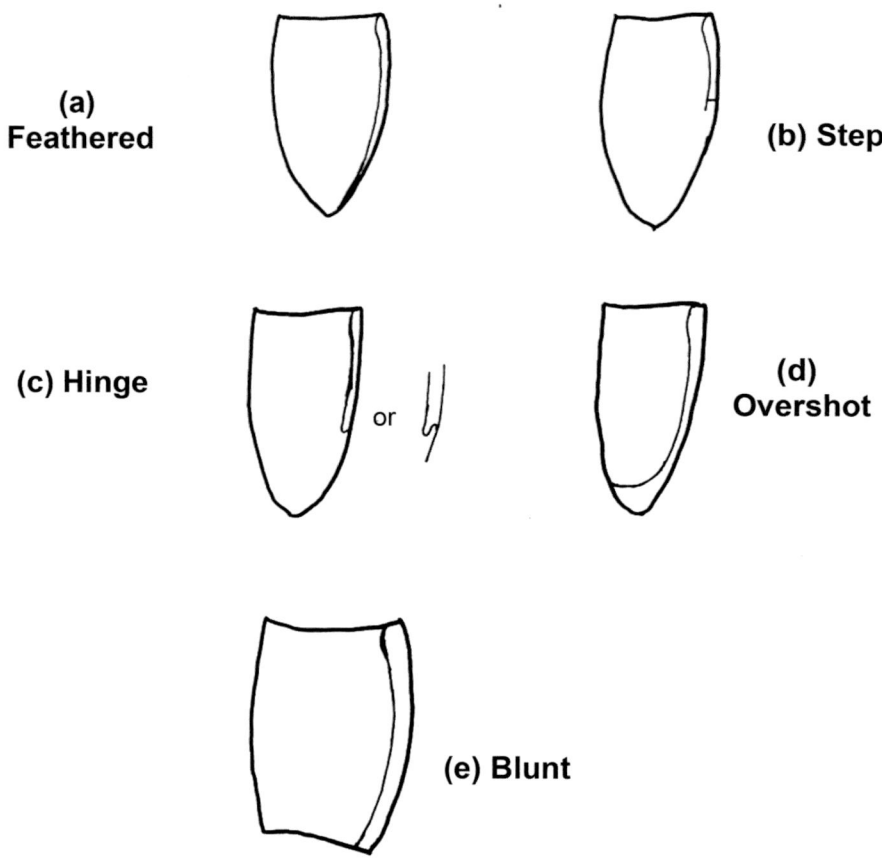

FIG. 11.15 FLAKE TERMINATIONS

orientation. Needless to say, the situation becomes rather complex. It is not surprising to see many variants of hinge fractures

An **overshot termination** is also referred to as an **outrepassé**, and the flake as a **plunging** flake. A necessary characteristic of an overshot is considered here to be the fracture changing direction significantly and curling inward, and sometimes then backward again. An overshot characteristically removes part of the opposite edge of a biface or the bottom of a core (Fig. 11.15d). Production and prevention of overshots on bifaces is discussed in Chapter 13. A bottom of a core is removed, for example, when a force is applied too much inward and too far from a platform edge. Attempts at fluting without supporting the far end "axially" will often lead to overshots. Flakes with slight overshots are intentional with Clovis biface technology (Frison and Bradley 1999). The terminations in edge-to-edge flaking could be overshots or they could be somewhere in the feathered-overshot-blunt termination group.

A **blunt termination** (Fig. 11.15e) is used for a termination in which the fracture runs to and exits a far face or edge of a core (or nodule or biface) without feathering or curling over. But it does remove at least some part of the far end or the opposite edge. Such a termination can occur, for example, when the force components on a thick flake are balanced in such a way that the flake thickness is essentially maintained in its terminal portions.

"Jacked" Flakes

When a hinge is being formed during a flake detachment, the very same force application occasionally "re-starts" the fracture again. A kink in the fracture profile is often seen in the vicinity of such a "re-start", to the sides of the hinge.

When a step and especially a hinge is produced accidentally, it can sometimes be removed completely or partly by indirect percussion, placing a punch at the location of interest. One is limited in the amount of outward force component that can be applied, especially with a step. With a hinge, this is easier. In these cases, one has two (or more) flakes, with a secondary flake initiation somewhere "in the middle" of a flake scar. I will refer to these secondary flakes as "Jacked flakes". They are named after the master knapper Jack Cresson, since I have seen him produce these more often than other knappers.

12. Forces in Knapping

The effects of a number of variables on the forces in knapping are considered in this chapter. The relative rather than the absolute values of the forces are considered for several reasons. In some cases, simplifications with idealized geometries and point or other loadings quite different from those in knapping are used. For analysis, this is done to make the problems tractable. In experimental research, such simplifications are used to facilitate interpretation of the results. The simplifications used not only make judgments regarding the absolute forces impossible. They also render comparisons for different simplifications difficult at times.

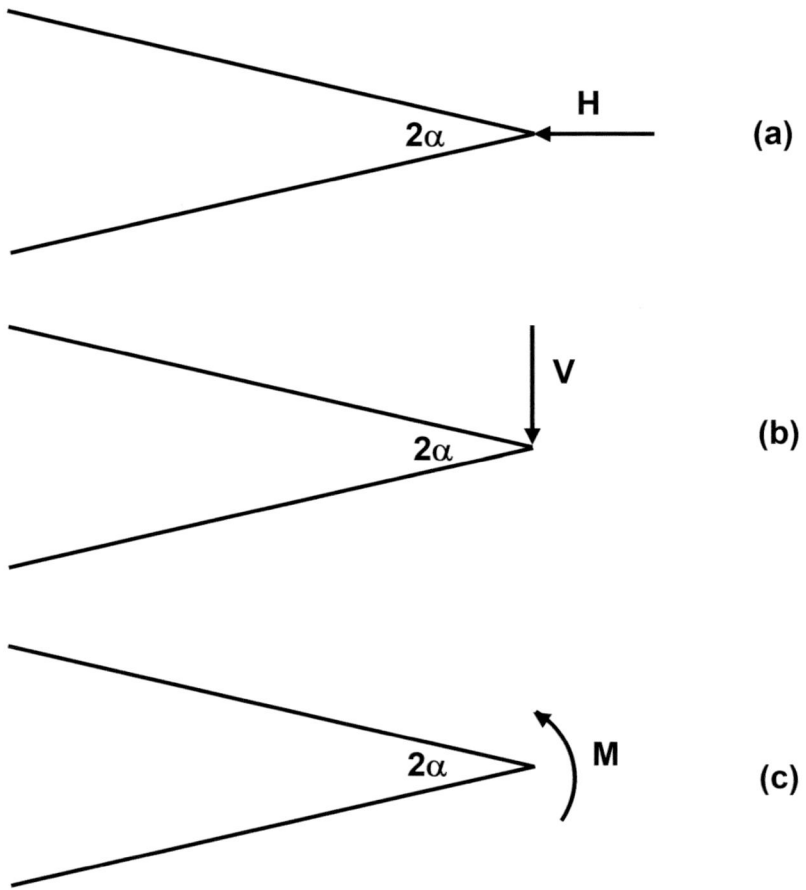

FIG. 12.1 WEDGE LOADED AT ITS TIP: (A) A FORCE APPLIED PARALLEL TO ITS MEDIAN PLANE; (B) A FORCE APPLIED NORMAL TO ITS MEDIAN PLANE; (C) MOMENT APPLIED.

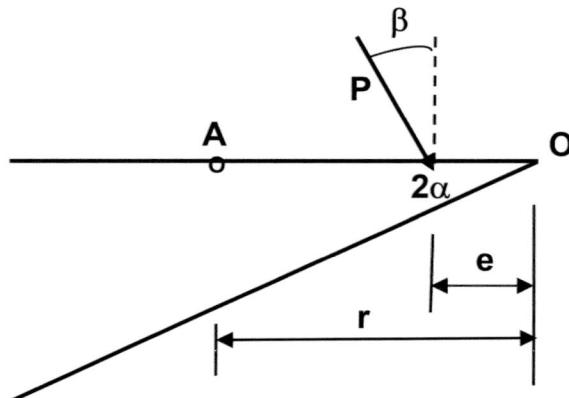

FIG. 12.2 WEDGE WITH A FORCE APPLIED IN AN ARBITRARY DIRECTION AT DISTANCE E FROM ITS TIP.

The discussions in this chapter are based on analytical results, controlled laboratory experiments, and judgments from experience in knapping. In all the cases, even if numerical values are presented, the results are qualitative approximations to actual situations in knapping.

Non-Contact Flake Initiations

For non-contact flake initiations, including bending initiations, use is made of the two-dimensional analysis in Timoshenko and Goodier (1951: 96-99) for a wedge of small thickness t loaded at its tip as shown in Fig. 12.1. By combining the results from these analyses, and making use of St. Venant's principle, Eq.12.1 is obtained. It is applicable for the more general case shown in Fig. 12.2 (Tsirk 1979).

$$P = \sigma_r\, r\, t\, \{[\cos(\alpha-\beta) \sin \alpha]/[\alpha-(1/2) \sin (2\alpha)] - [\sin(\alpha-\beta)\cos \alpha]/[\alpha+(1/2) \sin (2\alpha)] - (e/r)\, 2\cos\beta/[1-2\alpha\cot (2\alpha)]\}^{-1} \quad (12.1)$$

where P is the force applied at distance e from the tip, σ_r is the tensile stress at the upper face at distance r from the tip, with the angles α and β defined in Fig. 12.2. As seen from the latter figure and Fig.12.1c, the moment M is statically equivalent to Pe cos β. That is,

$$M = Pe \cos \beta \quad (12.2)$$

is applied at the wedge tip, whereas the force P is applied at a distance e from it. St. Venant's principle allows us to make the substitution in Eq. 12.2. In so doing, however, the results are valid only sufficiently far from the location where the substitution was made. In this case, "sufficiently far" means at a distance (r-e) >>e. That is, the results are valid at distances far enough from the force P. However, the results are also approximately correct even closer. As a rule of thumb, the results are expected to be accurate within 5% to 10% at distances greater than one to two times e from P.

Edge Angle and Core Geometry

For convenience, the normalized force P* is defined as

$$P^* = P/(\sigma_r rt) = (P/rt)/\sigma_r \qquad (12.3)$$

The variation of the normalized applied force P* with the wedge angle (2α), obtained from Eq. 12.1, is shown in Table 12.1 and 12.2. For various cases σ_r may be viewed as the tensile strength, assumed to have a constant value for the tables given. It is seen that a force needed for flake initiation increases very significantly with the wedge angle. Flake initiation becomes difficult or impossible for a large enough angle, unless there is a lower fracture stress – due to larger flaws. The figures provided also imply that the fractures originate at the same location A at distance r from the wedge tip. Results are provided for the case when P is at the wedge tip (e = 0) and at e = 0.30r. Although Eq. (12.1) is based on a simplified two-dimensional model, the results are relevant to blade cores. For biface edges they may provide some qualitative indications at best. Note that for e = 0 there was no need to invoke St. Venant's principle.

From the two-dimensional analytical model, it is impossible to see the effect of three-dimensional core geometry. The significance of the latter is evident to even a novice knapper. A knapper knows that less force is required in thinning a biface when the platforms are isolated. Essentially the same effect applies to blade cores. When viewed in the plane of the core platform, isolation of the ridge locations facilitates flake detachment by requiring smaller forces. This, of course, is based on judgment gained from knapping. In general, the numerical results presented are consistent with the expectations from the "knapper's principles" (Chapter 2).

TABLE 12.1 NORMALIZED FORCE VARIATIONS WITH WEDGE ANGLE FOR $\beta = 0°$ AND $\beta = 10°$ AND E = 0 AND E = 0.3R

Wedge Angle 2α (Degrees)	Normalized Force $P^* = P/[\sigma_r rt]$			
	$\beta = 0°$		$\beta = 10°$	
	e = 0	e = 0.3r	e = 0	e = 0.3r
10	0.005	0.007	0.005	0.008
20	0.021	0.030	0.020	0.029
30	0.048	0.070	0.046	0.065
40	0.090	0.132	0.083	0.117
50	0.149	0.223	0.136	0.194
60	0.231	0.356	0.205	0.295
70	0.345	0.551	0.297	0.433
80	0.505	0.845	0.419	0.623
90	0.734	1.311	0.546	0.806

Location and Direction of Force Application

Tables 12.1 and 12.2 indicate that more force is required when it is applied further from the wedge tip. Table 12.1 also shows that significantly less force is required when it has an outward component.

Platform Characteristics

For the analysis with the wedge and Eq. 12.1, the platform geometry between the wedge tip and the applied force is not important. That is, the results would be unaffected (Tsirk 1979). For a biface, however, the situation may be rather different, with the location of the force application shifting away from what is the upper surface for the wedge in Fig. 12.1. In such cases, the analysis by Eq. 12.1 is not applicable. Pecking and probably also grinding or abrasion (without pecking) of the platform by the force application will decrease the force required. They can also reduce the slippage of a pressure flaker or a punch and may thereby enable the use of a force with a greater outward component (greater β). As noted previously, the direction of grinding or abrasion can be significant. For greater force reduction, it should be parallel to the edge.

TABLE 12.2 FORCE VARIATIONS WITH DISTANCE FROM EDGE (R/E) FOR EDGE ANGLES 2α

Wedge Angle 2α (Degrees)	Normalized Force $P^* = P/[\sigma_r rt]$			
	e = r/2	e = r/3	e = r/4	e = r/5
10	0.0103	0.0072	0.0068	0.0064
20	0.030	0.031	0.028	0.026
30	0.100	0.074	0.065	0.061
40	0.193	0.139	0.123	0.114
45	0.258	0.184	0.161	0.150
50	0.335	0.237	0.206	0.191
60	0.556	0.379	0.326	0.302
70	0.913	0.590	0.501	0.460
80	1.531	0.912	0.759	0.690
90	2.755	1.437	1.159	1.038

Flaw Distributions

As already noted, a fracture originates where the combination of tension and a flaw create the worst situation. Leonardo da Vinci noted that longer wires are weaker. Chances are that bigger flaws are present in them. Pecking, abrasion and grinding can not only reduce the fracture stress, but also influence the location of the fracture origin. For example, pecking or abrasion of a platform at locations away from the applied force location can contribute to a non-contact, as opposed to a Hertzian flake initiation being likely.

Flaker Properties

When an applied force is more concentrated locally, having a smaller contact area, then the local tension in its vicinity is greater, but the tension away from the force is unaffected by it. For static and quasi-static considerations, this follows from St. Venant's principle. Consider a practical example for a dynamic situation. Suppose a long thinning flake is to be removed from the end of a biface without supporting the far end. To reduce the chances of breakage by amputation, it is better to use a harder percussor.

Contact Initiations

Much experimental work of interest has been done with sharp indenters and use of the concept of edge toughness. Use of sharp indenters always leads to the fracture originating at the location of the load. The use of such indenters produces the flaws for the fracture origins. Thus they do not provide indications for cases with non-contact, including bending initiations. The research on edge toughness has been with very small edge distances, usually less than a millimeter (Danzer, Hangl and Paar 2001, Morrell and Gant 2001). Extrapolations to larger distances as well as loadings with other than sharp indenters are expected to provide qualitative but not quantitative approximations for Hertzian initiations.

Location of Force Application

It is evident from knapping that the force required for flake initiation increases with edge distance d, the distance from a core edge to the location of the force application. Using a cylindrical core and laboratory testing equipment, Faulkner (1972) showed this to be the case.

For very small edge distances and usually sharp indenters, the research on edge toughness shows the load P to vary linearly (for many materials) with edge distance d for producing tiny chips from a square edge. That is

$$P = M^* d \qquad (12.4)$$

where the slope M^* is defined as the **edge toughness**. For the flakes in knapping, this trend is expected to hold approximately in a qualitative sense for larger edge distances and Hertzian initiations (Paar 1994:7-9). The research is seen as lending support to the conclusion from knapping noted above.

Direction of Force Application

There are many situations in knapping in which flake initiation is not possible without some outward force component. An example is the detachment of a blade from a blade core having an edge angle of about 90°, using the pressure flaking technique. It can be concluded that the magnitude of the force required for flake initiation is decreased if it is applied with a component towards the prospective dorsal surface. Faulkner (1972: 119-121) observed that it is also possible to detach a flake with an inward force component, but the downward force required is much greater. The results of Quinn and Mohan (2005) for edge-toughness tests are in agreement with this.

Edge Angle and Core Geometry

The observations from knapping indicate that with greater edge angles larger forces are required for flake initiation. In a qualitative sense, these observations are supported by the testing for edge toughness. An influence function $f(\alpha)$ is given in Paar (1994: 11) that gives the edge toughnesses and applied forces for any edge angle in terms of those for 90°. For example, it indicates that for 45° edge angle, about 29% of the force required for 90° is needed.

For specimens having rounding or a chamfer at the edge, the use of effective edge distances has been suggested in the edge toughness research by Danzer, Hangl and Paar (2001:50) (also Tsirk 1979: 88). It seems reasonable to use such approximations also with contact initiations.

Platform Characteristics

Experience from knapping indicates that less force is required, for example, at isolated platforms on bifaces and on blade cores. Although the term "platform isolation' is not used with blade cores, what is often done is in fact platform isolation when small chips are detached to define better the platform region over a dorsal ridge.

Suppose that a blade core platform has the shape of an elongated ellipse in plan. Such a case is in fact encountered when a rectangular shaped core is cut out for practicing blading. After removing a number of blades, starting at the corners, the platform may resemble an ellipse in plan. The locations with greater edge curvature on the plan of the platform, based on judgement, require less force for blade detachment. Pecking or abrading the platform surface will reduce the force requirements as well.

TABLE 12.3 COMPARISONS FOR CONTACT AND NON-CONTACT FLAKE INITIATIONS

No.	Item	Contact Initiation	Non-Contact Initiation
1	Force Increase with Edge Angle	Yes	Yes
2	Force Increase with Edge Distance	Yes	Yes
3	Force Decrease with Outward Force Direction	Yes	Yes
4	Initiation Type More Likely with Smaller Contact Area with Flaker	Yes	No
5	$\underline{P \text{ (for } 2\alpha = 45°)}$ $P \text{ (for } 2\alpha = 90°)$	0.29	0.16

Flaw Distributions

Fractures originate, we recall, where the combination of the tensile stress and a flaw create the worst situation. The location of a fracture origin relates, of course, to the distribution of flaws. This is one reason why non-contact initiations are more likely with larger contact areas.

Flaker Properties

By a flaker we mean here a hammerstone, a billet, a punch or a pressure flaker. Flakers associated with smaller contact areas during force application contribute to higher local stresses there. Flaker material hardness (meaning greater modulus of elasticity E here) and its geometry with greater curvatures contribute to that. Larger contact areas, on the other hand, contribute to lower localized stresses, with contact initiation less likely. Away from the contact region, the stresses would be unaffected by the above considerations. Therefore, non-contact initiations are more likely when larger contact areas are involved.

Contact and Non-Contact Flake Initiations: Comparisons

Some aspects of contact and non-contact (including bending) initiations, already considered, are compared in Table 12.3. The first three items have the same kind of effect for both of the initiation types. As noted in Item 4, the size of the contact area contributes to the likelihood of a particular initiation type. For non-contact initiation, the results in the table are based on Eq. (12.1). Those for contact initiation are based on the references cited. Most of them are based on use of hard indenters with laboratory equipment, very small edge distances and an edge angle of 90° (except for the first item). The very different basis for the results compared is reflected in the difference for the last item. For this item, the force P is acting normal to the surface ($\beta = 0$). For the non-contact initiation case, e = 0.300r (Fig. 12.2) was used.

Subsequent Detachment

After the flake initiation and the earliest phase of the flake detachment, the relative outward and inward force components are important in determining the fracture path. While a flake is being detached, its flexibility increases both in the axial and the transverse directions, more so for the latter. These changes in the flexibilities of the partly detached flake will alter the relative outward to inward force components. These relative force components can also be altered at will by a knapper to produce shorter or longer flakes. Even flakes that run the full length of a blade core or the full width of a biface can be produced by a knapper's control of the force components. Factors other than the relative force components are usually also important. In biface thinning, for example, the location of the edge relative to the middle plane is important, along with the roundedness of the edge from abrasion.

Once the detachment of a flake has started, it is generally not possible for a knapper to change at will the relative force directions in percussion flaking, except by rotation of the core. For assumed average fracture velocities of 50 m/s and 500 m/s, the time for the detachment of a 5 cm long flake would be 0.001s and 0.0001s, respectively. In pressure flaking, however, a knapper may have enough time to change the force directions once the flake detachment has started. After all, Crabtree (1968) was able to intentionally produce crack arrest during the manufacture of a blade from a polyhedral core, pressure flaking with a chest crutch. A knapper could, however, manipulate the relative force directions by his actions prior to the flake initiation, taking into account the expected changes in the flexibilities noted, sometimes together with the support conditions used.

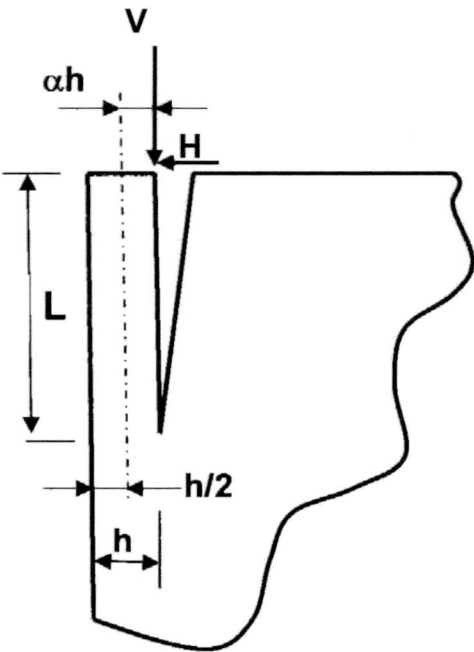

FIG. 12.3 A TWO-DIMENSIONAL MODEL FOR
ANALYSIS OF BLADE DETACHMENT FORCES
SUBSEQUENT TO THE INITIAL PHASE.

By controlling the relative outward to inward force components, a knapper can also cause a flake to have a feathered, hinged or a stepped termination. The latter case, for instance, involves an excessive outward force component. This was done, presumably, with the resolved flaking of the Mousterian culture.

Consider blade detachment subsequent to the earliest phase. In order for the crack to extend straight, parallel to the core surface, there needs to be a delicate balance for the two force components. The outward force component must gradually decrease. An idea of what is required can be obtained from approximate analyses for a two-dimensional case: Namely a thin plate, with the crack running parallel to the free edge (Fig. 12.3). Numerical results from such an analysis were presented in Cotterell and Kamminga (1987), and are shown in Fig. 12.4. The solid line in the figure is for the results to extend the crack straight, in fracture mode I. The mottled band is for Cotterell and Kamminga's result based on the changing stiffnesses as the crack extends. It uses the assumption that the direction of the flaker movement does not change during the flake detachment. The band corresponds to the flaker movement in the 0° to 60° range. It is not clear whether the assumption regarding the constant direction for the flaker motion is necessarily true.

The results from another analysis (Tsirk n.d.) are also shown in Fig. 12.4. It is for the same simplified two-dimensional model of Fig. 12.3 used by Cotterell and Kamminga (1987). This analysis is for an approximate extension of Thouless et al. (1987). The results from

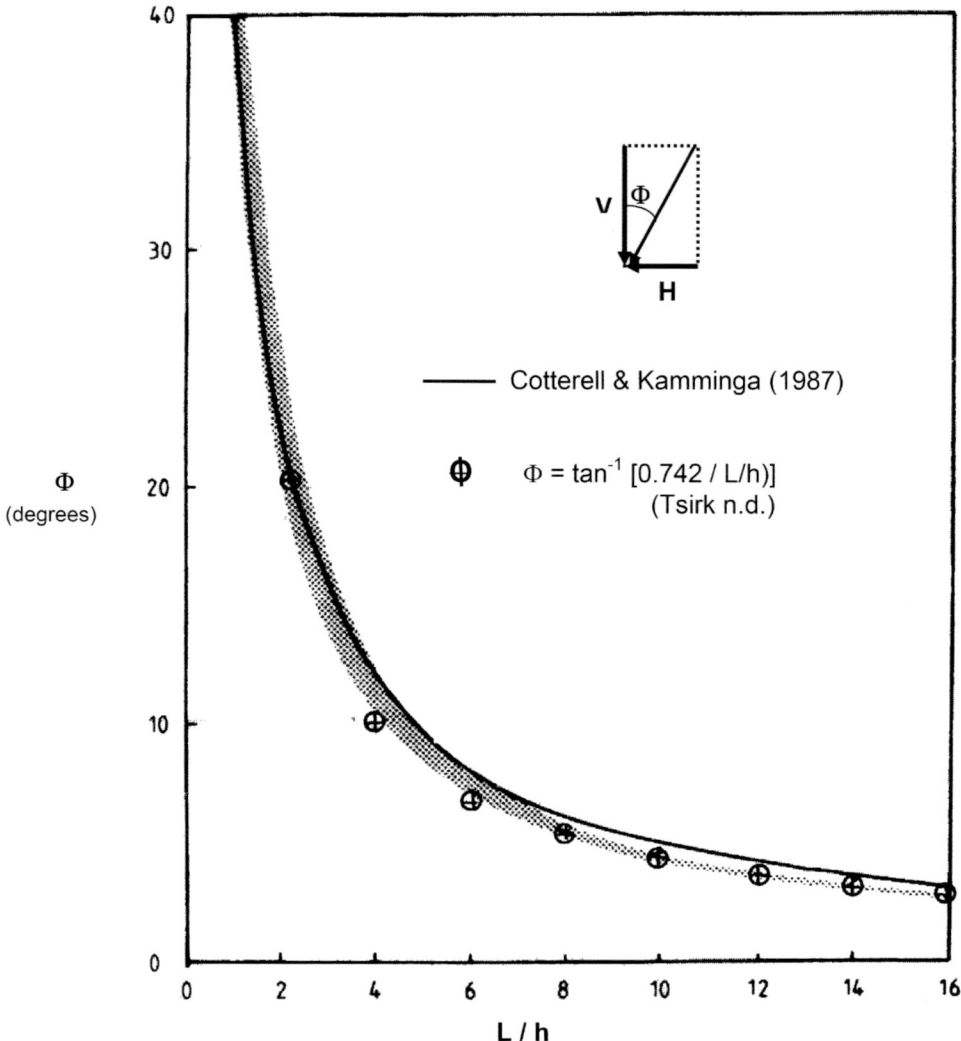

FIG. 12.4 VARIATION OF FORCES WITH LENGTHS OF THE DETACHED PART OF THE FLAKE.

the different analyses are rather close. The analysis of Tsirk (n.d.) led to the following expressions:

$$H/V = 0.742 / (L/H) \qquad (12.4)$$
$$H = 0.322\, h^{1/2}\, K_I / (L/h) \qquad (12.5)$$
$$V = 0.434\, h^{1/2}\, K_I \qquad (12.6)$$

where H and V are the horizontal (outward) and vertical (inward) force components, h is the "blade" thickness, L is the length of the blade already detached, and K_I is mode I stress intensity factor (Fig. 12.3). It is seen from the last equation that the axial force required for the extension of the crack is proportional to a "blade" width (normal to the paper, taken here as unity) and the square root of its thickness h. Furthermore, the analysis indicates it to be independent of the length L. These analytical results may be of interest for the production of long blades.

Cotterell and Kamminga (1987:698) state that "without this stiffness-control mechanism, flaking as we know it would be impossible", and that "flaked stone technology developed because basic flaking requires little skill." These statements reflect a lack of hands-on experience. Although core preparation and positioning of the flaker are important, the delivery of the forces is also significant. This is so with regard to their direction as well as magnitude over time (follow through and preform rotation, for example).

Direct Percussion

Percussor Characteristics

It seems counterintuitive that for tougher materials it is often advantageous to use a softer percussor. Wooden billets are sometimes used to work on various stages of biface thinning of argillite, rhyolite, quartzite and various other tougher stones. For example, billets of dogwood, boxwood and live oak work well. Smaller forces may be needed when using softer percussors and slower blows (See Chapter 10).

In the table for lithic grades (Fig. 3.1), Callahan also indicates "limitations of fabricators for secondary thinning." For the tougher materials, he shows wooden billets and no antler billets. Antler billets would wear out quickly or be ruined on the tougher materials. Interestingly, Callahan also indicates wooden billets for the lithic materials with least toughness. They could be used for thinning obsidian bifaces, for example, but there would be no advantage to using them. Antler billets and soft hammerstones would be better. This is consistent with Callahan's lithic grade scale.

The size of the contact area between a percussor and a core decreases with the hardness of a percussor, depending primarily on its modulus of elasticity. As already noted, this contributes to the frequency of Hertzian as opposed to non-contact fractures for percussion with harder percussors. It is also expected to lead to the bulbs being more pronounced. The geometry of a hammerstone can of course have effects similar to those discussed above.

Velocity of Blows

Decreasing percussor velocity, just as its hardness, increases the time of contact (Chapter 10). Conceivably, this tends to prevent stress wave reflections from hindering crack initiation and advance by having weaker reflections earlier rather than stronger ones later.

Indirect Percussion

Punch Characteristics

The geometry and material properties of a punch are important. By geometry is meant the length, diameter and end roundedness or other characteristic. For longer flakes or blades, punches cannot be too short. For heavier, wider and thicker blades or flakes, punches of adequately large diameter and density are desirable. The end geometry of a punch may relate to the task at hand. For heavier flakes, a more robust, well rounded end that will not split is more suitable. Such a punch is inadequate, however, for accurate seating on some flake scars, as with square section axes.

The material properties of punches are of considerable interest. Most significant are expected to be the effective modulus of elasticity in its axial direction, as well as the effective mass density. Punches such as soft antler that dent easily are not the best. They tend to soften the blows and require more maintenance. Materials that split or splinter easily, as some old antlers and wood such as live oak, are not desirable.

For the production of blades of obsidian and especially chert, dense moose antler works well. Smaller antlers of white tail deer work adequately for shorter blades. For obsidian blades, punches of dogwood, boxwood and live oak are suitable.

Questions regarding the material properties most desirable for punches, especially those of wood, are not well understood. To reflect on this point further, Table 12.4 lists some values for the modulus of elasticity and specific gravity for several woods. Copper, occasionally used for punches by contemporary knappers, is included in the table for comparison. Some deer antler, as well as steel are include for comparison as well.

It is of interest to note the longitudinal stress wave velocities in the table. Surprisingly they are very close for copper and the woods. During the impact in indirect percussion, the stress waves would have ample time to travel a number of times the length of a punch, say 10 cm long. A punch free at one end and fixed axially at the other has its fundamental natural frequency corresponding to the time it takes the stress wave to travel four times its length. Its natural frequency is the inverse of the period. The vibrations of a punch are expected to relate to the formation of some ripples. One may ask whether future research with ripples will yield information on flakers, punches or strikers.

TABLE 12.4 PROPERTIES OF SOME WOODS

Common Name	Species Latin Name	Specific Gravity	Modulus of Elasticity 10^6 GPa [10^6 psi]	Wave Velocity $c_o = (E/\rho)^{1/2}$ 10^3 m/s [10^3 ft/s]
Dogwood	Cornus florida	0.776	0.223 [1.54]	3.66 [12.0]
Live Oak	Quercus virginiana	0.955	0.284 [1.96]	3.72 [12.2]
Red Deer Antler	Cervus elaphus	1.5	7.40 [1.07].	2.22 [7.28]
Roe Deer Antler	Capreoius Capreoius	1.6	2.20 [0.319]	1.17 [3.85]
Copper	---	8.5	2.46 [17.0]	3.72 [12.2]
Steel	---	7.85	4.20 [29.0]	5.06 [1 6.6]

From a comparison of wood properties, the woods that seem to be especially desirable for punches do not seem tostand out from the others (See Chapter 2). The relevance of the geometry and density of punches is considered further in the next section in connection with the striker characteristics.

Striker Characteristics

The top of a punch is struck with a hammerstone, a wood or antler billet or other implement. The word "striker" is used here for such an implement. For smaller punches, it is convenient and adequate to use a smaller striker, which would be inadequate for larger and longer punches.

The relationship of punches and strikers is illustrated by the following experience with a stonemason. For re-pointing a masonry chimney, he was removing the old grout with a steel chisel and hammer. Occasionally he hit his knuckles with the hammer. When asked why he doesn't use a longer chisel, he said that he would then need a heavier hammer, requiring a greater effort. Since the material properties of steel are well known, it was easy to see whether the response made sense. For this an analysis was available for longitudinal impact on piles (Terzaghi 1961: 465-468, Love 1944: 431-435). Consider a pile of length L, supported at the base, impacted by a hammer (striker) of weight W_H with a velocity V. The weight of the pile (representing the punch) is

$$W_p = A L w \qquad (12.7)$$

A is the cross-sectional area of the pile, and w its density. With ρ its mass density and E its modulus of elasticity, the stress waves in the pile will travel with the velocity

$$c_o = (E/\rho)^{1/2} \qquad (12.8)$$

The ratio of the hammer weight to the pile weight is m

$$m = W_H / W_p \qquad (12.9)$$

If m > 5, then the maximum compressive stress at the base of the pile can be approximated as (Terzaghi 1961)

$$\sigma_{max} = E (1 + (V/c_o)) \qquad (12.10)$$

and the maximum force there is

$$P_{max} = A \sigma_{max} = A E (1 + (V/c_o)) \qquad (12.11)$$

Due to the hammer and pile weights, P_{max} varies as (1 +V/c). Examples are given below for several values of m.

m =	5	7	9	10	16	25
(1 + =	3.24	3.65	4.00	4.16	5.00	6.00

The comparison holds for any material, of course. According to this, the stonemason's response seems to make sense. For example, by reducing only the chisel length, if m changes from 10 to 5, then the force is decreased by 28%.

For the case when m < 5, the analytical results are presented in Love (1944). After the stress waves travel the length of a punch several times, there can be a temporary loss of contact. The results in Love can also be used to determine if and when this could occur. For the woods considered in Table 12.4, the stress wave would travel the length of a 10 cm punch in less than 0.00003 seconds!

Core Mobility

A number of questions on core mobility relate to the nature of supports.

Percussion Flaking

In principle, a contact force could be produced in percussion flaking without supports, with the inertia of the core. In practice, of course, a core must be supported somehow in percussion flaking. There are many ways for doing this. More flexible supports tend to reduce the force applied to a core. Some flexibility for a core support implies some mobility for it.

Core mobility not only tends to reduce the force applied. It also tends to change its direction, usually unpredictably, during the detachment of a blade or flake. It is necessary, or at least significant, to avoid core mobility – in particular, its rotation – in many situations. For example, production of blades from a blade core by pressure or indirect percussion is especially sensitive to core mobility. Using the punch technique for a square section axe (Vang Petersen 2008), especially for the narrow faces, is another example. If rotation is allowed, the punched flake tends to "roll" across and ruin the square edge at the far side.

Pressure Flaking

Pressure flaking a point to get a "crisp" central ridge, as on Eden points, is another example in which a rotation of the point is to be avoided. Allowing rotation would cause the flake to roll across the central region, ruining the crisp ridge. The situation here, as in some other cases, is analogous to that for the square section axes. It is very similar to establishing the central ridge of a Type VIc Danish dagger handle (Callahan 2000).

There are cases in which the rotation of a core (a point here) can be tolerable or even desirable. An example is the parallel, diagonal flaking for a point. In this case, the changes in the direction of the applied force are advantageous for the flake removals.

Supports

Distal

Distal supports in both "axial" and lateral directions can be important. In pressure as well as percussion flaking, axial supports at the far end or far edge can be used to facilitate edge-to edge flaking by preventing severe overshots. By providing a very hard "axial" support at the far end, the effect of the applied force is significantly amplified. Advantage of this is taken in bipolar percussion.

Lateral support at the distal end of a biface is often also important. When a flake is detached near the central region of a long biface while holding it "free hand", its ends will wobble due to bending accompanied by displacements out of the biface plane. Lateral support near an end will inhibit such a wobble, and decrease the danger of breakage.

Dorsal

Providing lateral support to the dorsal face of a prospective flake or blade is a common practice. This is done by use of fingers, the palm of the hand, the side of a thigh with leather padding or by other means. Such lateral support can prevent or reduce the lateral displacements of the flake while it is being detached. In so doing, it can reduce the danger of a flake or blade breaking. It can also lead to smaller reductions in the lateral (outward) forces in flaking. It is this mechanism that allows the flakes to run longer when lateral support is provided.

A biface is frequently supported on the palm of a hand or on a thigh with a leather pad. If the support is too flexible, a point in pressure flaking, for example, may break. The bending stress can be approximated by considering the point to be a beam and by using the theory for a beam on elastic foundation (Den Hartog 1952, Hetényi 1946). Assuming the point is rigid, the deflection under it will be uniform, as will be the reaction from the pad. Idealizing the situation as a two-dimensional model, with P the applied force normal to the plane of the point and L the length of the point, the bending moment is $M = PL/8$ and the bending stress is directly proportional to it. When the point is not assumed rigid, its flexibility can be taken into account (Den Hartog 1952: 159-160). The assumption of rigidity leads to excellent results when

$$\beta L < 1 \tag{12.11}$$

where
$$\beta = [k/(4EI)]^{1/4} \tag{12.12}$$

and E is the modulus of elasticity, I is the moment of inertia for the cross section assumed uniform along the length, and k is the foundation modulus in units of lbs/in/in = lbs/in² (kg/cm/cm = kg/cm³). The latter is a characteristic of the support.

Bipolar Percussion

An extreme case of a hard "axial" support is involved with bipolar percussion. To illustrate the basic principle involved, consider a long prismatic rod struck at one end and fixed at the other (Speth 1972, Kolsky 1963). A stress wave is reflected from a fixed end with the same sign, and from a free end with the opposite sign. Assuming that a core in bipolar percussion is represented by the rod, the compressive stress wave from the applied force travels towards the fixed end and is reflected there as compression. As a result, a compressive force with double the original magnitude can travel back towards the end where the force was applied. When the contact with the percussor is still retained, the loaded end tends to also act as a fixed end. Consequently, the stress wave may be reflected now with quadruple the original amplitude, and so on. It is the basic principle involved that makes bipolar percussion so advantageous. Eventually, there may be a loss of contact, and the increased compression can be reflected as a large tensile stress wave. Blade slicing is an example of the possible consequences (Chapter 13). The full picture is more complicated than the simplified considerations with the rod. The effects from the stress waves approaching the far end and those reflected from it are superimposed, taking into account the variations in time for each of them (See the references cited). The general mechanism for amputation is also applicable for the initiation of other fractures, as in quartering a large nodule of flint (Leakey 1953: Plate Ia) by striking it at a projection. For example, a large elongated flint nodule can be broken in two by striking it at one end.

A core in bipolar percussion is obviously not a prismatic rod. Therefore, the stress waves will not travel just "axially", and the amplification of stresses is not as simple as for a rod. Nevertheless, the basic principle and its consequences still hold, at least in a qualitative sense. Also, the practical situations are likely not to be axisymmetric. Therefore, bending may also be involved.

13. Breakage of Blades, Flakes and Bifaces

Axial Loads, Bending, Shear, Torsion and Their Effects

Consistent with the normality rule, a fracture surface will orient itself so as to minimize shear stresses (from mode II as well as mode III contributions). The surface of a blade or a biface break is not always normal to the long axis of the specimen. The general orientation of this surface can provide clues to the forces that were involved in the breakage. Oblique or skewed planar breaks, associated with tensile stresses normal to the surfaces, are caused by shear forces.

Instead of being flat, an oblique surface of a break may be curved or it may have a twist, due to torsion which can be introduced, for example, whenever an outward force is not applied symmetrically on a blade having a symmetric cross-section. With nonsymmetric cross-sections, torsion and twisting are produced when such a force component is not aligned properly. To avoid twisting, the resultant shear forces must pass through the shear center (a.k.a. center of twist).

The basic breakage patterns, as well as their details, relate not only to the shear forces and torsion but also to bending and axial forces. Shear forces and shear stresses have a significant effect on the fracture paths and details. Examples of such effects include compression lips and popout fractures, as well as twist hackles. Bending produces bending stresses that vary from the tensile to the compressive side. They, together with shear, are often associated with the curving of a fracture surface along that direction. (But see Chapter 11 on formation of compression wedges.)

It is of course not possible for an axial force to produce tension directly. Such tension is often produced by the reflection of a compressive force from a free surface. Amputation of a biface and the production of slices in blade breakage are examples with such tensile reflections.

Clues from Fracture Markings and Other Features

The utility of fracture markings and clues that may be obtained from them are indicated in Tables 4.3 and 4.4. The catalogue of fracture markings in Table 4.5 provides some reasons for their utility. For a better understanding of the markings, the reader is referred to Chapters 5 to 8.

A compression lip, unless it is very minute, indicates that the break occurred due to bending or that significant bending was involved. The side with the lip was the compression side. A mist pattern at or near the tensile edge provides supplementary evidence for this. Compression curls and compression wedges also indicate that the breaks were due to bending. The compression wedges from bending are associated with slow velocity branching, without mist manifestation. They should not be confused with the lateral wedges from high velocity branching that can occur in specimens subjected to bending or to axial tension only.

In principle, a mist pattern associated with a tensile edge of a blade break, for example, may be an indication that a tensile force in addition to bending was involved. In practice, however, this was not evident from the sample of mist patterns considered in blade breakage. Mirror-mist boundaries and mirror boundaries in general, are indicative of the fracture stress during the breakage (Chapter 7). Branching angles for lateral wedges relate to the state of stress for the break.

Some Fractures with Blades and Flakes

Splitting of Blades and Flakes

Flakes are occasionally split lengthwise during their detachment. This is of archaeological interest for technologies where the flakes were utilized. Even when the flakes are not available, evidence for their splitting is usually available from the split marks on the negative flake scars (Chapter 8). The split marks may be manifested as ridges, steps or irregularities in the ripples. Examples of split flakes and split marks are illustrated in Fig. 8.3. A split step or a split ridge manifested on a Clovis biface is illustrated in Fig. 1.3 and Frison and Bradley (1999: 54-55). Splitting of blades, though it does occur, is rare.

Step-In and Step-Out Fractures

The formation of step-in and step-out fractures is considered in Chapter 11. Step-out fractures are illustrated schematically in Figs. 11.1, 11.5 and 11.6. The neck of a step-out fracture is sometimes short, but extends occasionally the full length of a core (Fig. 11.1). With step-outs, the primary fracture usually stops near the step-out location. Occasionally, however, it extends the full length of the core (Fig. 11.5). A core being pressure flaked is sometimes ruined by short step-out fractures near the platform.

Dorsal concavities by the step-out location, though not necessary, will facilitate their formation. Although most common in the proximal region of a blade, step-outs also occur elsewhere. Those associated with a hackle flake (Fig. 11.4a), however, have been observed exclusively in the proximal regions.

Step-in and step-out fractures are of interest for breakages of the tips of projectile points (Kelterborn 2001, Cresson 2004). They can reflect the characteristics of a target.

Incipient Breaks

The formation of incipient transverse breaks of blades is considered in Chapter 11. Since they can be viewed as unsuccessful attempts in the formation of step-out or popout fractures, they may occur wherever step-outs can be expected. They have been observed rarely, and only in the proximal blade regions. The incipient breaks can be seen with difficulty, and only if one looks for them intentionally. Unless the material is translucent, they are visible only as hairline cracks on the blade ventral surface. The full extension of the incipient breaks into the blade was evident only in a few cases with industrial glass and translucent obsidian. Surprisingly, even a pair of close-by parallel incipient cracks was observed in a few cases (Fig. 11.7d). Even the ventral hairline cracks were observed very rarely in chert.

Popouts

The data here on popouts derive from observations in contemporary knapping. Popouts were observed most often on pressure blades, and frequently on punched blades. They were also encountered, however, with thin as well as very thick flakes in various contexts, produced by direct and indirect percussion. Intrusive, hinged bulbar scars gradually "evolve" into popout fractures with roll-in type initiations (Fig. 11.14). This was recognized by Eloy (1980),

The formation of popout fractures is discussed in Chapter 11, with a number of popouts illustrated. Observations are reported here, especially on the most common types of popouts. The occurrence of a greater variety of popouts, and more details on their formation and observation is considered in Tsirk (2010a).

The fracture profiles and fracture directions of most of the observed types of popout fractures are illustrated in Fig. 11.6. They are shown schematically, not to scale, in idealized form. Some of the cases are examples of popout-stepout combinations. Information on the flakes and popout fractures observed is provided in Tables 13.1 and 13.2.

The data base for the tables consists of accidental popout fractures on 122 blades and other flakes of obsidian (108), dacite (2), industrial glass (8) and chert (4) produced

TABLE 13.1 DIMENSIONS (MM) OF FLAKES WITH POPOUT FRACTURES

Column		1	2	3	4	5
Flaking Technique		Pressure Flaking	Indirect Percussion	Direct Percussion	Unknown Percussion	Total Percussion
Maximum Length	Range	41-142 n = 36	40-143 n = 49	51-128 n = 8	43-136 n = 12	40-143 n = 69
	Median	73.5	83	115.5	102.5	
	Mean	77.5	80.6	99.8	93.8	85.1
Maximum Width	Range	9-22 n = 44	15-67 n = 50	41-107 n = 8	16-48 n = 13	15-107 n = 71
	Median	13	28	59	29	
	Mean	14.2	29.7	63	32	33.9
Maximum Thickness	Range	2-8 n = 44	3-18 n = 49	5-32 n = 7	4-20 n = 12	3-32 n = 68
	Median	3	8	12	14	
	Mean	3.5	8.8	15.9	12.2	10.1

(Adapted from Tsirk 2010b)

TABLE 13.2 NONDIMENSIONAL POPOUT CHARACTERISTICS

Column No. Flaking Method		1 Pressure Flaking		2 Indirect Percussion (IP)		3 Direct Percussion- (DP)		4 Questionable		5 Both IP & DP	
		No.	%	No.	%	No.	%	No.	%	No.	%
Material	Obsidian	37	84.1	45	90.0	7	87.5	16	100.0	68	91.9
	Plate Glass	5	11.4	2	4.0	0	0.0	0	0.0	2	2.7
	Dacite	2	4.5	0	0.0	0	0.0	0	0.0	0	0.0
	Chert	0	0.0	3	6.0	1	12.5	0	0.0	4	5.4
	Total	44	100.0	50	100.0	8	100.0	16	100.0	74	100.0
Popout Type	Regular	42	95.5	38	76.0	8	100.0	12	75.0	58	78.4
	Reverse	1	2.3	8	16.0	0	0.0	2	12.5	10	13.5
	Compound	1	2.2	3	6.0	0	0.0	1	6.2	4	5.4
	Double	0	0.0	1	2.0	0	0.0	1	6.3	2	2.7
	Total	44	100.0	50	100.0	8	100.0	16	100.0	74	100.0
Lateral Extent	Double-Sided	39	88.6	41	82.0	5	62.5	14	87.5	60	81.1
	Single-Sided	5	11.4	9	18.0	3	37.5	2	12.5	14	18.9
	Total	44	100.0	50	100.0	8	100.0	16	100.0	74	100.0
Popout Start Location	Proximal	43	97.7	36	70.6	7	87.5	11	73.3	54	73.0
	Medial	0	0.0	11	21.6	1	12.5	4	26.7	16	21.6
	Distal	1	2.3	4	7.8	0		0	0.0	4	5.4
	Total	44	100.0	51	100.0	8	100.0	15	100.0	74	100.0
At Start of Popout	With Roll-In	43		32	64.0	7	87.5	7	53.8	46	64.8
	With No Roll-In	1		18	36.0	1	12.5	6	46.2	25	35.2
	Total	44	100.0	50	100.0	8	100.0	13	100.0	71	100.0

(Adapted from Tsirk 2000b)

in contemporary knapping by pressure flaking (51) and indirect or direct percussion. Columns 1 to 5 of the tables refer to the knapping technique used for the flakes. Column 4 includes the specimens for which the technique used, either direct or indirect percussion, was uncertain.

Several different types of the popout fractures (Fig. 11.6) were observed. With the regular and reverse popouts (Figure 11.6a and b), the fracturing is in the distal and proximal directions, respectively. A compound popout (Figure 11.6c) involves bi-directional fracturing for the same popout. A double popout (d to g in the figure) includes two separate popouts on the same flake. Various popout-stepout combinations (h to k in the figure) can involve different kinds of popouts and stepouts. The frequencies of occurrence for the four basic types of popouts are indicated in Table 13.2.

Most but not all popouts are initiated and occur near the proximal part of a flake. Table 13.2 provides information on the locations where the popouts started. All popouts with a roll-in from a hackle flake or a proximal chip start, of course, near the proximal end of a flake. The popouts for all but one pressure blade were in the proximal region.

Most of the profiles of popout and stepout fractures indicate a dorsal concavity in the proximal region near the roll-in for these fractures. However, they were absent on 34% of the percussion blades, but rarely on pressure blades. All popout fractures were initiated by a bending break or a secondary fracture turning outward from the ventral flake surface. Such bending breaks were observed in the proximal, medial and distal flake regions (Table 13.2).

In all but one case, the secondary fractures responsible for the popout initiations were associated with hackle scars, usually included under bulbar scars in literature. In one case, the secondary fracture was a proximal chip extending from the platform. The one or two hackle flakes usually extend as a relatively thin chip more or less parallel to the ventral surface, but then they turn gradually towards the dorsal surface, as a roll-in. That is, the outer surface of the hackle flake (towards its dorsal surface) appears to roll into the thickness of the flake. A roll-in of a hackle scar is due to bending of the flake, with tension at its inner face (Fig. 11.12). A dorsal concavity can increase this tension significantly.

The aforementioned roll-ins were observed to involve either one or two hackle scars or a hackle scar formed by two of them merging. Although hackle flakes are usually thin, they may occasionally be so thick as to remove part or essentially all of a bulb (Fig. 11.9c). All the observed popout initiations away from and occasionally those within a flake proximal region are due to a bending break showing an abrupt break tending to be at 90 degrees with the flake ventral face (Fig. 11.4b).

The terminal end of a popout is usually rounded, and may be viewed as a variant of a hinge termination of a popout flake, occasionally with a roll-out to the inner flake surface. Only rarely was the inward extension of a popout fracture tapered or feathered out gradually at the inner surface without a hinge. The popout fractures initiating at a roll-in from a secondary fracture still have breakage from bending at its shoulders. Due to the roll-in acting as a large flaw, the breakage stresses at the shoulders are usually too low for the manifestation of mist and velocity hackle there. This was the case with all the popouts from pressure flaking. For the popout fractures with a roll-in initiation from indirect percussion, only one out of 30 specimens exhibited mist and velocity hackle. Of the 21 indirect percussion popouts with the abrupt bending initiation (no roll-in), however, mist and velocity hackle was observed in 8 cases.

A double popout, or a popout-stepout combination, is sometimes associated with the formation of a compression wedge (Figs. 11.6). Compression wedges were observed with the formation of two double popouts and four popout-stepout combinations.

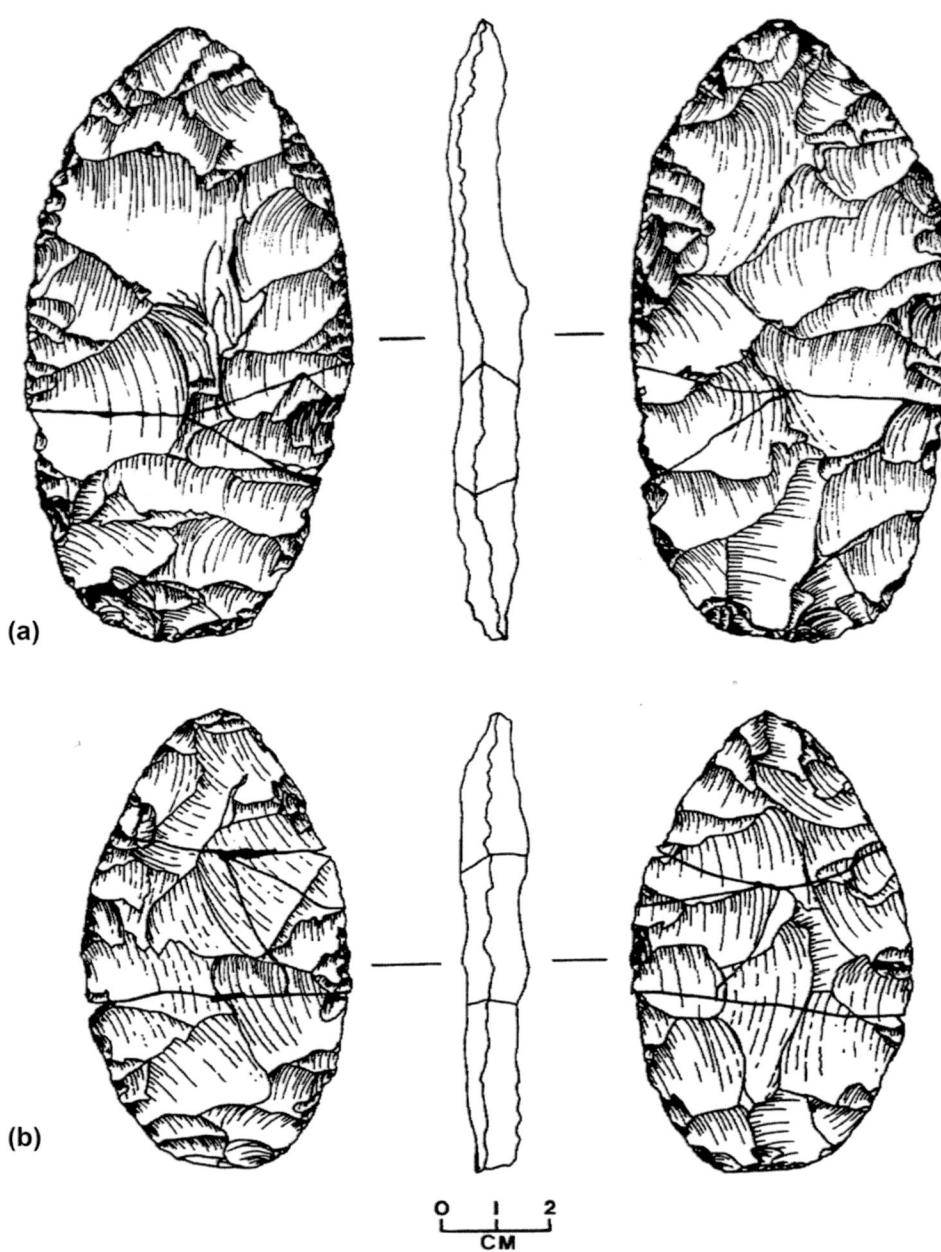

Fig. 13.1 Broken bifaces from the Caradoc Site, from the late Paleo-Indian ritual artifact deposit. Bayport chert. (From Fig. 2.8 in Ellis and Deller 2002, with permission)

Some Fractures with Bifaces

Bifaces are a major constituent of prehistoric lithic industries, especially in North America. Their breakage at various stages - from rough-outs or blanks to finished points – is encountered frequently. For example, it is quite common to see broken, usually thick bifaces at prehistoric quarry sites such as at Glass Buttes in Idaho and Flint Mine Hill in New York. Accidental biface breakages occur during their manufacture and use. Experiments on projectile point breakage during impact have been made by Kelterborn (2001) and Cresson (2004). On rare occasions, a biface breakage may be intentional, as in "killing" of an artifact for use with burial goods or for other ritual purposes (Ellis and Deller 2002) (Fig. 13.1). (See also Pelegrin 2013.)

The discussions of biface breakage in this chapter rely to a large extent on observations from contemporary knapping. The quantified results presented and the illustrations provided are for a set of nearly 700 biface breakages (Table 13.3) encountered since 1974. These included the amputations and the breakages associated with overshots, to be discussed. In addition to the categories of biface breakage considered here, not surprisingly there were a number of rather unusual breakages. One such example is illustrated in Fig. 13.2.

TABLE 13.3 BIFACE BREAKAGES CONSIDERED

Pressure Flaking	Direct Percussion	Material	Totals
117	293	Obsidian	410
20	257	Chert	277
137	550	Totals	687

FIG. 13.2 A NORMANSKILL CHERT BIFACE BROKEN ACCIDENTALLY DURING MANUFACTURE. IT IS SURPRISING THAT THE FLAKE (TOP) IS UNBROKEN. IT STARTED OUT AS A THINNING FLAKE FROM THE BASE (SEE THE SKETCH). THEN A CRACK FROM THE BENDING BREAK OF THE BIFACE EXTENDED UPWARD TO MEET THE OTHER SURFACE AND TURN RIGHT.

Overshots and Edge-to-Edge Flakes

Overshot flakes, or simply overshots, are also known as plunging and outrepassé flakes (Figs. 13.3 to 13.5). They do not necessarily lead to biface breakage or rejection. And they are not necessarily accidental. An example of a severely overshot flake is shown in Figs. 13.5. Because of the severe nature of this overshot, the biface was ruined, considered broken by the very removal of the overshot. Intentional use of slightly overshot flakes, however, may provide an efficient means of thinning a biface (Stanford and Bradley 2012). In such cases very little, if any, of the opposite edge is removed. These may be considered to be edge-to-edge flakes. Edge-to-edge flaking was used extensively for Solutrean and Clovis bifaces. Such flaking is illustrated for Clovis bifaces in Fig. 13.3 and on many of the plates (for example No. 1 to 6) in Frison and Bradley (1999).

It is impractical to provide a formal definition for overshot as opposed to edge-to-edge flakes without an overlap. For practical purpose, it will suffice to define an **edge-to-edge flake** as one that does not remove much of the opposite edge. If much of the opposite edge is removed, however, the flake is considered to be an **overshot** but not an edge-to-edge flake. For a flake to be considered an overshot here, its distal part will show significant curving due to the roll-in. Thus an edge-to-edge flake may or may not be an overshot, and vice versa.

An overshot flake can be produced intentionally by using a heavily ground striking platform set well below the center plane of the biface, and applying a force with sufficient follow through for its "axial" component. Overshot flakes can be avoided even in most of such cases by providing support to the opposite edge. This is part of the recipe for producing edge-to-edge flakes.

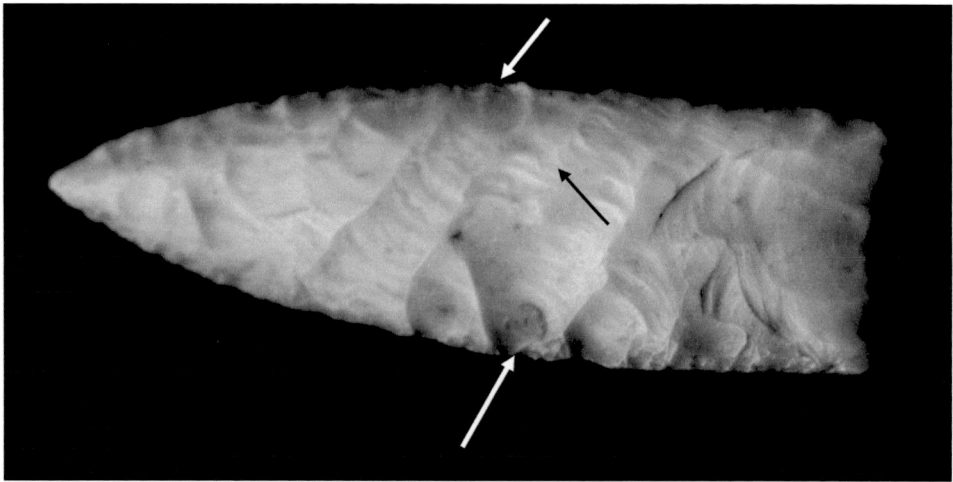

FIG. 13.3 OVERSHOT (WHITE ARROW) FLAKES ON A CLOVIS PREFORM FROM BLACKWATER NO.1. ONE OF THESE WAS SPLIT, AS BARELY SEEN BY THE SPLIT RIDGE (BLACK ARROW). (PHOTO OF PLASTIC CAST BY KRISTIAN METS)

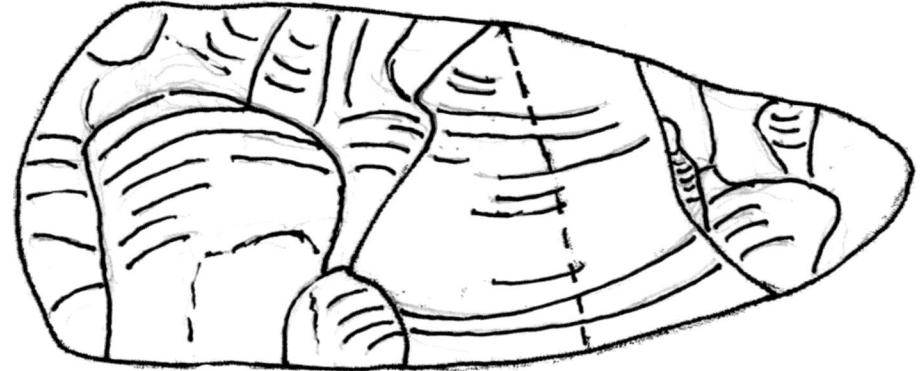

Fig. 13.4 Biface with a laterally overshot flake, ruined by the transverse biface break at the location of the overshot. Normanskill chert, direct percussion. Actual size.

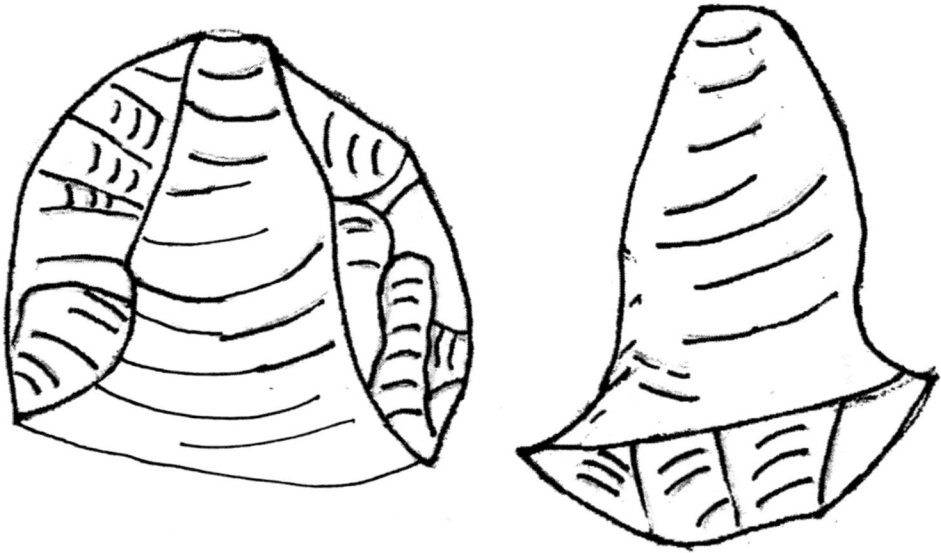

Fig. 13.5 Biface with a longitudinally overshot flake. Obsidian, direct percussion. Actual size.

Manifestation of mist on the surfaces of overshot flakes associated with biface breaks is rather unusual. That is because the break occurs gradually with a roll-in. Mist was observed in only one instance for the lateral (14) as well as for the longitudinal (16) overshots for obsidian. It is not surprising that the observed mist occurred to the side of the roll-in portion of the flake, from a bending break of the unbroken part. Mist, of course, is manifested more often on the transverse breakages of the overshot flakes themselves, as with other flakes broken by bending. Almost all of the overshot flakes noted were broken, in one case by longitudinal splitting. Only three (3) obsidian and one chert overshots remained unbroken.

Since all but one of the longitudinal overshots for obsidian extended the full width of the bifaces, they were really transverse breaks. For the lateral overshots, there are a few corresponding cases of transverse biface breakage in which the overshot extended the full length of the biface.

Surprisingly many transverse (including diagonal) breaks of the bifaces themselves were associated with lateral overshots. In all such cases for obsidian, these breaks originated at a twist hackle produced by the overshot.

Amputations

A biface break known as an amputation is illustrated in Fig. 13.6 and Crabtree (1972:34). It is encountered often when a biface with a strong platform is struck at one end while the other end is left unsupported. Amputations can be prevented by supporting the far end to reduce axial movement as well as wobble or out of plane movement.

An amputation is due to a combination of axial effects and bending. The bending is introduced essentially by the outward component of the applied force trying to rotate

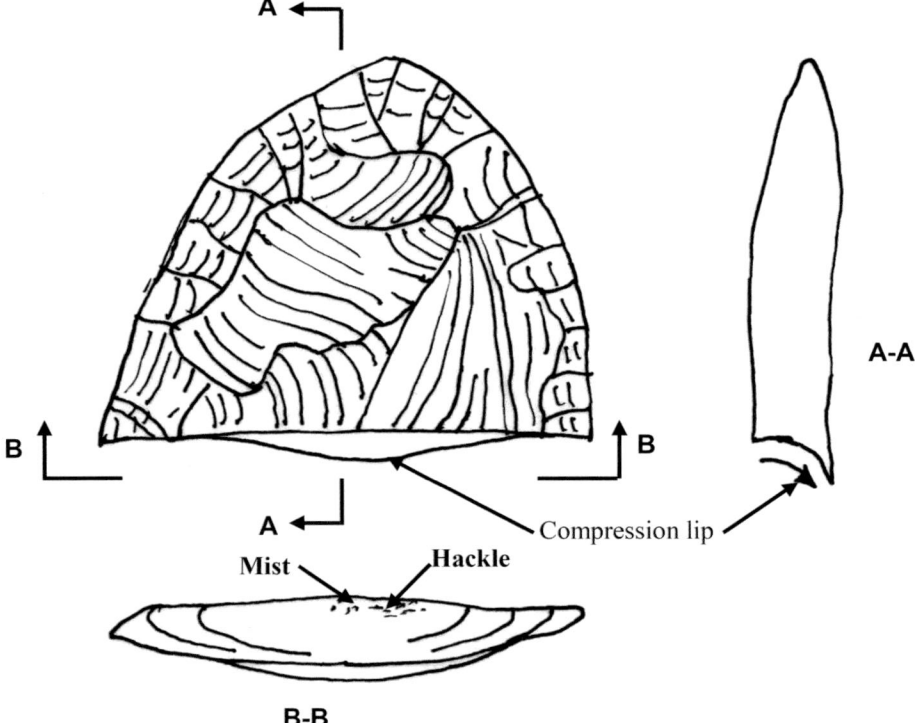

FIG. 13.6 SCHEMATIC ILLUSTRATION OF AN AMPUTATION FROM DIRECT PERCUSSION (TO THE UPPER END IN SECT. A-A). TENSION IS AT THE TOP SURFACE (IN SECT. B-B), AS INDICATED BY THE MIST-HACKLE AND BY THE COMPRESSION LIP. THE FRACTURE DIRECTION IS SHOWN BY THE ARROW IN SECTION A-A. OBSIDIAN. (SPECIMEN PO-159) WIDTH IS 67 MM.

the biface. The inertia force of the biface mass near the far end tends to counteract this rotation. Consequently, bending is introduced in such a way that the tension from it will be at the upper surface when the applied outward force component is downward. The curling part of the accidental fracture surface is a compression lip, indicating that bending was indeed involved.

The axial effects contributing tension to the breakage stress can be understood by reflecting on the situation in bipolar percussion, discussed in Chapter 12.

Transverse Breakages

Transverse breakages are usually due primarily to bending. But contributions from axial tension can occasionally be significant, as in amputations and slice formation.

Accidental breakage of blades and other flakes as well as bifaces usually occurs during their manufacture or use. Prehistoric blades were sometimes broken intentionally, to use the segments with or without hafting as knives, scrapers and other tools as at the Otumba site in Mexico. Rare, intentional breakage of bifaces was already noted (Fig. 13.1).

Fracture markings or features characteristic of breakage by bending often include compression lips, compression wedges, mist and hackle, incipient branching, branching and lateral wedges. These and really all the other fracture markings or features may provide clues of interest in lithic analysis. The examples considered here are from contemporary knapping unless noted otherwise. The biface breakages considered (Table 13.3) are for complete transverse breaks, with a crack extending through the specimen thickness. Other breakages with bending for blades and flakes may involve the step-in, step-out and popout fractures already noted.

Fracture Origins

Fractures originate where the combination of a flaw together with the stress create the critical condition. Consider first the bending breaks with blades. It has been observed that the fracture origin for blades broken during their manufacture is most often at the dorsal (outer) surface (Fig. 13.7), though it may occur also at the ventral (inner) surface. Rarely, a break may originate at an internal inclusion or other flaw. Occasionally it originates at an edge, perhaps more likely during its use.

During its detachment, a blade may be deformed by bending in single or double curvature as shown schematically in Figures 13.7. The lateral displacements shown in this figure are exaggerated. Due to bending, there is always tension on the convex and compression on the other side. Here the curvatures, of course, refer to those from bending. In the single curvature case, (a) in the figure, all of the partly detached blade is bent concave outward. With double curvature bending, (b) in the figure, the blade being detached is concave inward in the upper part (as at A) and concave outward in the lower part (as at B). A transverse break always extends from the tensile towards the compression side. Thus in part (a) of the figure and in the lower part (as at B) of part (b) of the figure, it would extend outward from the inner surface. A break in the upper part (as at A) of (b) in the figure, however, would extend from the outer surface inward.

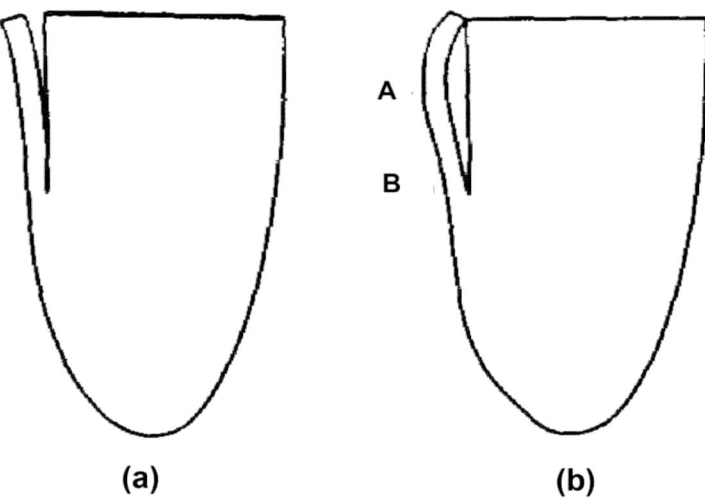

FIG. 13.7 BLADE DETACHMENT WITH (A) SINGLE AND (B) DOUBLE CURVATURE BENDING DEFORMATION. (ADAPTED FROM TSIRK 2009)

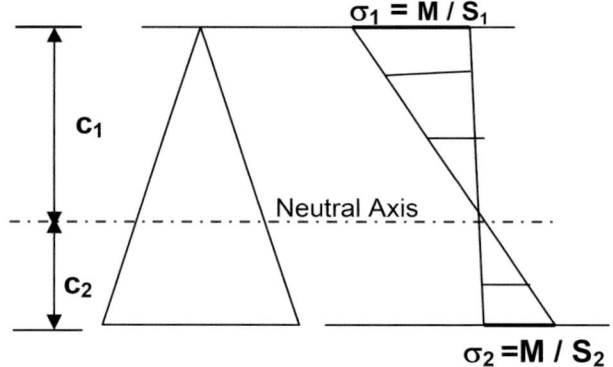

FIG. 13.8 STRESSES IN A BLADE WITH TRIANGULAR CROSS-SECTION FROM A BENDING MOMENT M.

Consider for a moment an idealized blade that is straight and prismatic. If the outward movement of the proximal blade end is negligible and the blade cross-section does not vary along its length, then the tensile stress near A is greater than by B. Also, the size of the tensile region near A (by the outer surface) is greater than that near B (by the inner surface). Assuming a uniform distribution of flaws, a transverse break near A is more likely than by B, especially when a core, and consequently a blade, is curved to start.

Transverse breakage in contemporary knapping is seen to occur much more often with inward than with outward cracking. Even casual observations without formal experiments will suffice to convince the reader. In a sample of 32 transversely broken pressure blades from a polyhedral core, all but 2 or 3 had inward cracking. It was also noted that outward

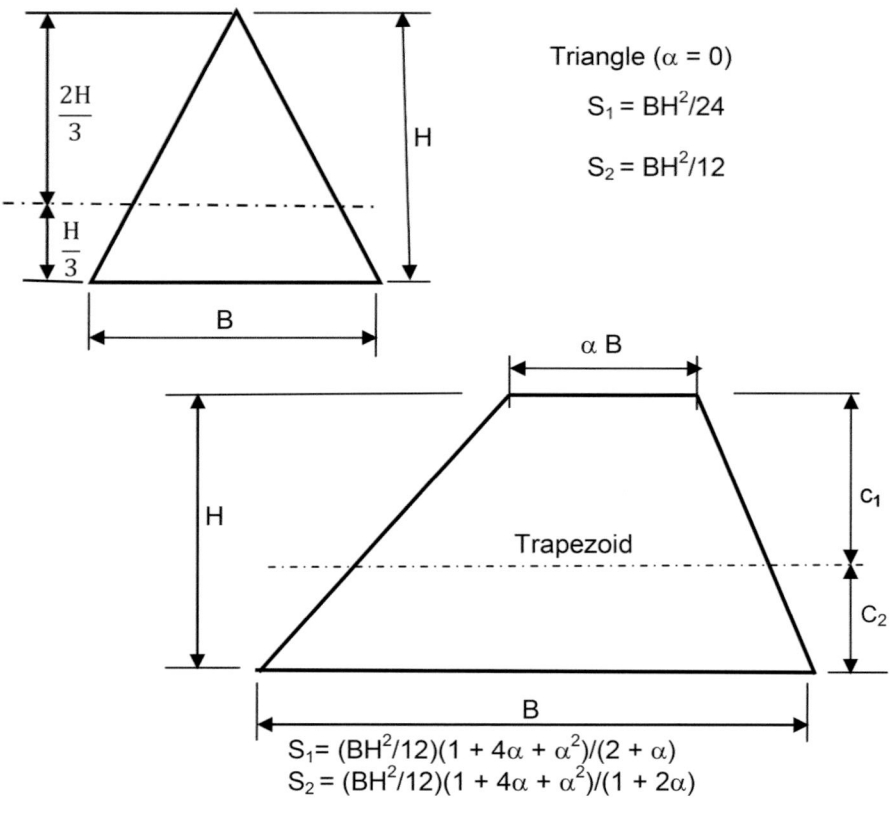
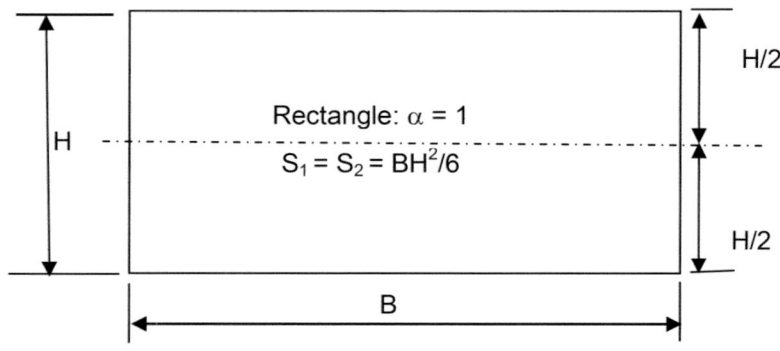

Fig. 13.9 Geometrical properties of triangular, trapezoidal and rectangular sections

blade breaks without step fractures do indeed occur. The surprising mechanism for this is considered in Tsirk (2009)

Intentional breakage of a blade with a triangular or trapezoidal cross-section is easier when the fracture originates at the outer face. This can be understood by considering the stress distributions in a blade (Fig. 13.8). The geometrical properties are provided in Fig. 13.9 for three hypothetical blade cross-sections - triangular, trapezoidal and rectangular. The neutral axis is seen to be closest to the inner surface for a triangle, at the mid-height for a rectangular and between these cases for a trapezoidal section. The stress is given by

$$\sigma = \frac{M\,c}{I} \qquad (13.1)$$

where M = the bending moment, I = the moment of inertia, and c = the distance from the neutral axis to the location of interest. A section modulus is defined as $S_i = I\,/\,c_i$. Consider the triangular section, for example. For the flat ventral surface, $c = c_2 = H/3$. For the apex at the dorsal surface $c = c_1 = 2H/3$. For the latter location, the stress due to a moment M would be twice as great as it would be for the flat ventral surface. Half as great a bending moment M would thus be required when the fracture is started at the dorsal surface. The difference would be smaller for trapezoidal blades. Clues for the location of a fracture origin for bending are obtained from the compression lip, the mist and hackle if present and various directionality indicators such as twist hackles, gull wings and other Wallner lines. A set of trapezoidal blade sections from the Otumba site is considered later.

Some of the characteristic features of transverse biface bending breaks are illustrated in Fig. 11.1 (See also Fig. 13.6 for a bending break from amputation.). Such breaks originate in a number of different ways. Frequently, the origin is at a flake termination, at a tiny twist hackle or a roll-in.

Fracture Directions

As already noted, the fractures for blades broken transversely during their manufacture usually originate at the outer surface and advance to the inner surface. As a fracture for a transverse break of a blade or a biface propagates across the thickness, it advances laterally, more so by the tensile face. The patterns for the fracture directions and fronts depend very much on the location of the fracture origin and, not surprisingly, on the overall geometry of the specimen and especially the fracture surface, the location of the applied force in case of a biface, as well as the sense of the moment from the applied load.

Fig. 13.10 shows examples of fracture fronts estimated from tails, twist hackles and gull wing bisectors on obsidian. Fracture directions are normal to the fronts. Fig. 13.10a is for the same accidental break as in Fig. 7.6, with mist-hackle at the upper left and right sides. Fig. 13.10b is for the surface of a thick flake, rather than an accidental break, produced by direct percussion, having a Hertzian initiation. As usual, the fracture fronts tend to lead at the thicker parts of a flake.

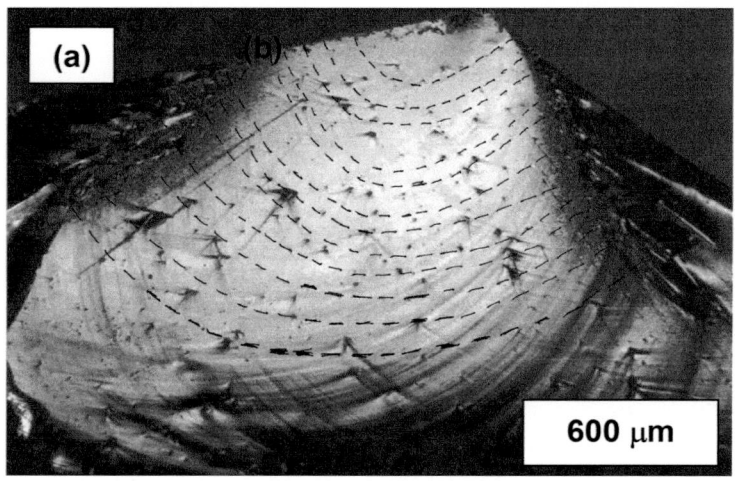

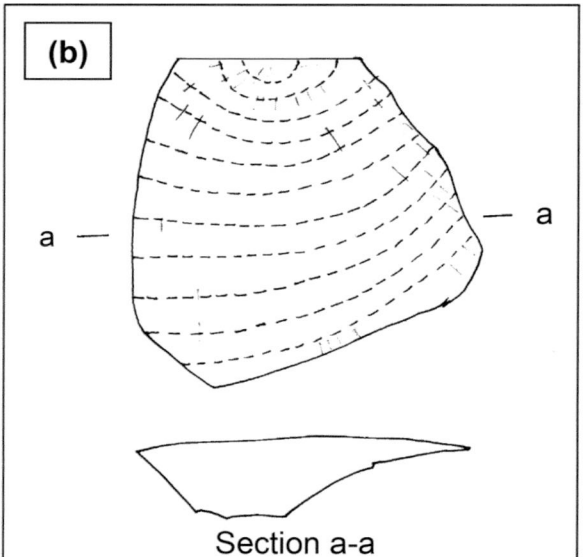

Fig. 13.10 Examples of fracture fronts (dashed lines) and fracture directions normal to them. Obsidian. Fracture direction downward. Flake in (b) 9.7 cm long and 2.7 cm wide. ((a) adapted from Tsirk 2012)

Compression Lips, Curls and Compression Wedges

These features are characteristic of breakage by bending (Fig. 11.1). Their formation is discussed in Chapter 11. The characteristic dimensions of the compression lips, curls and compression wedges are observed to vary significantly. The length of a compression lip (in axial direction) relates to the axial loading on the blade. With sufficient axial compression, a compression lip can grade into a step-out fracture. Variation of a lip length along the cross-section break relates to torsion.

For the blade breakages considered, compression lips were observed in almost all cases. In a number of cases, their length was very small. Compression wedges occurred less frequently. Compression wedges were also encountered with popouts and popout-stepout combination (Fig. 11.6).

For the biface breakages considered (Table 13.3), compression lips were observed less frequently, and compression wedges very seldom. These observations are seen as relating to the greater significance of shear forces in blade breakage (Fig.11.3). With bifaces as compared to blades, the compression lips are usually also shorter, often miniscule. The less frequent presence of axial compression with biface breakages is significant.

A feature seen occasionally with bifaces but not with blade breakages is a **tensile quasi-lip.** Occurring by the tensile face of a bending break, it is manifested when a partly detached flake at the tensile face of the biface has an overhang at the location of the bending break. It is characterized by an abrupt (about 90^0) angle of the "quasi-lip" with the surface of the tensile break, and thus easily distinguished from a compression lip.

Mist and Related Markings

For the set of transverse biface breakages considered, Tables 13.4 and 13.5 indicate the observations of mist and related markings, including the lateral wedges associated with crack branching, as well as the branching cracks on the tensile biface surfaces. Since the latter are extremely difficult to see and photograph, the frequencies noted in the table are no doubt the lower estimates. Such cracks are seen better in lighter colored materials, especially when they are at least slightly translucent.

As seen in Table 13.4, lateral wedges and other kinds of velocity branching (on the tensile surface) were not observed in pressure flaking. From the observation that mist is not all that rare in such cases, one does expect these features to be manifested occasionally also in pressure flaking. Even for the biface breakages by direct percussion, lateral wedges were produced rather seldom, around 2 to 4% of the cases. This is somewhat surprising in light of the frequent manifestation of mist and hackle (Table 13.5). Although mist, hackle and macroscopic branching (as for lateral wedges) have been observed to occur at very similar fracture velocities, manifestation of branching requires substantially more energy for crack extension.

Table 13.4 indicates that lateral wedges form with a wedge angle in the range of about 23 to 30 degrees, except for one case with a 38 degree angle approximately. In general, a branching angle relates to the state of stress (Preston 1935, Fréchette 1990:43-44). For a narrow strip of material, maximum branching angles of 45 and 15 degrees are expected for pure tension and twisting, respectively (Preston 1935). The idealized geometries and loadings considered in the cited literature are not involved in biface breakage. Those cases do not involve strips that are narrow, and bending rather than axial or in-plane stress is more relevant. Nevertheless, it is likely that the wedge angles in Table 13.4 relate to stresses from bending combined with twisting (Preston 1935). The single exceptional case with a wedge angle of 38 degrees may indicate that less twisting was involved in that case. Relevant is the fact that this particular break occurred when the biface was struck at its base with an antler billet.

It is noteworthy that lateral wedges were produced in cases with relatively flat bifaces. This is understood by considering the cross-section of a biconvex biface subjected to bending in its long direction. The bending produces tensile stresses at one of its surfaces normal to the section. These stresses are reduced significantly as one goes from the thickest part of the biface towards an edge. For a relatively flat biface surface, on the other hand, such a stress reduction does not occur.

TABLE 13.4 LATERAL WEDGES AND BRANCHING CRACKS ON BIFACE TENSILE SURFACE

	Pressure Flaking		Direct Percussion	
	Obsidian	Chert	Obsidian	Chert
Total No. of Broken Bifaces	117	20	260	220
With Lateral Wedge: No. [%]	0	0	5 [1.9]	8 [3.6]
Wedge Angle Range (degrees) Mean (degrees)	----	----	23 to 29 24.8	23 to 30* 26.5*
With Tens. Surf. Branch. Cracks: No. [%]	0	0	7 [2.7]	5 [2.3]

*There is one exceptional case with a wedge angle about 38 degrees.

TABLE 13.5 OBSERVATION OF MIST, HACKLE, MIST LINES AND PARABOLIC DOUBLE TAILS ON BIFACE BREAKAGES (No. & [% OF BIFACES])

	Pressure Flaking		Direct Percussion	
	Obsidian	Chert	Obsidian	Chert
Total No. of Broken Bifaces	117	20	260	220
Mist	28 [23.9]	3 [15.0] Perhaps 2 more: 3+2=5 [25.0]	114 [43.8]	102 [46.4]
Velocity Hackle	26 [22.2]	---	48 [18.5]	64 [29.1]
Mist Lines	25 [21.4]	0	20 [7.7]	0
Parabolic Double Tails	19 [16.2]	0	35 [13.5]	0

Mist, hackle, mist lines and multiple tails resembling fracture parabolas (a.k.a. so-called "fracture parabolas") were considered in Chapter 5. Observation of these markings for the set of biface breakages is indicated in Table 13.5. Mist lines and the so-called "fracture parabolas" have been observed only in obsidian.

The techniques used for the observations of mist and hackle are relevant. For all the biface breakages, observations were made by naked eye and by hand lens having up to 20X magnification. This was supplemented by binocular microscopic observation at 50X, and sometimes also 100X, but only for the pressure flaked obsidian specimens. With the microscope the observed frequency for mist increased by about 50% for pressure flaking. For the obsidian specimens from direct percussion, microscopic observation would no doubt have increased the frequencies reported for mist in Table 13.5. In comparing the frequencies in the table for obsidian breakages by pressure and percussion flaking, the differences in the observation techniques used should be kept in mind.

The recognition of mist was more difficult for chert than for obsidian. Use of magnification greater than the 20X used for the hand lens seemed to provide no advantage. Recalling that mist is really a kind of surface roughness, a comparison of different surface areas was essential. The greater magnification with a microscope did not seem to facilitate such comparisons for chert. Surprisingly, there were no significant differences in the observed frequencies for mist and hackle for several different lithic grades of Normanskill chert. It must be kept in mind that the assignment of the specimens to these lithic grades is, of course, highly subjective.

From Table 13.5 it is conspicuous for obsidian as well as chert that mist was observed much less frequently for the biface breakages by pressure flaking as compared to direct percussion. Intuitively, one might suspect this is because smaller forces were involved with pressure flaking. Since the strengths are presumably comparable, the difference is expected to be due to smaller widths of the pressure flaked specimens. The observations of mist increased with the width of the pressure flaked obsidian specimens at the break locations. Table 13.5 indicates that the frequencies for the occurrence of mist were fairly similar for obsidian and chert, for pressure flaking as well as for direct percussion.

Mirror boundaries are related to the breakage stress (through mirror constants). These have not yet been investigated (Chapter 7). For a given material, however, it is possible to evaluate the relative breakage stresses without knowing the mirror constants, using Eq. 7.2.

In contrast to the surfaces of flakes produced in knapping, mist and (velocity) hackle, mist lines, mist-hackle configurations and parabolic double tails are frequently manifested on the fracture surfaces of accidental breakages in obsidian. Of these, only mist and hackle have been observed with chert. These fracture markings were considered in Chapter 7 with illustrations. Additional illustrations appear in Figs. 13.11 to 13.13. Observation of these markings is indicated in Table 13.5 for a set of biface breakages. A similar comparison is not presented for blades. They are very much dependent on blade widths.

Most of the observations on mist and hackle have been in contemporary fractures from experiments. It is therefore relevant to note that the mist-hackle region is readily

Fig. 13.11 Mist and hackle at a transverse biface break from bending in direct percussion. Normanskill chert of medium grade. (a) More mist is seen at the upper part, closest to the tensile face. (b) is to the right of (a). Mist (left) and (velocity) hackle, seen as the more elongated features are indicative of fracture direction. (c) is to the right of (b). Macroscopic branching occurs at the right side of (c), with a lateral wedge manifested.

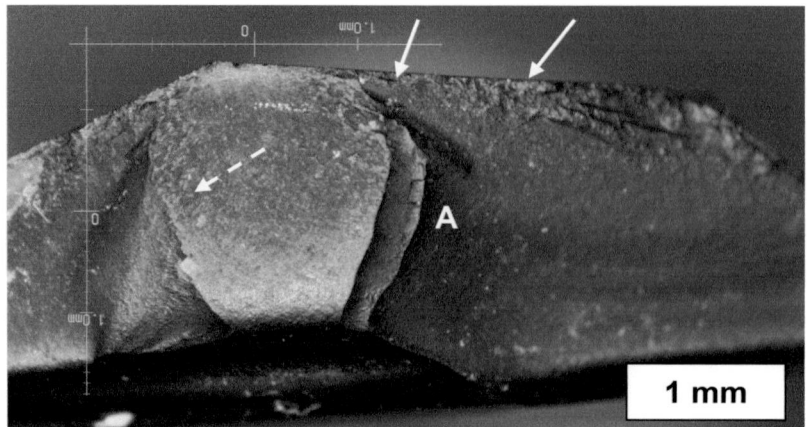

FIG. 13.12 MIST AND HACKLE (ARROWS) ON A SECTION OF A PREHISTORIC FLINT BLADE FROM THE 9TH MILLENNIUM B.C. IN ADDITION TO THE MIST-HACKLE BY THE TENSILE FACE AT THE TOP, AN INTRUSIVE MIST PATTERN IS ALSO MANIFESTED AT THE INTERIOR (DASHED ARROW). AN UNUSUAL HACKLE FLAKE SCAR IS SEEN LEFT OF A. THE LOCALLY CONCAVE REGION ON THE LEFT IS ANOTHER HACKLE FLAKE SCAR, FORMED WHEN THE LATERAL BREAKTHROUGH EXTENDED TO THE RIGHT. [SPECIMEN #4476-808 FROM THE PULLI SITE IN ESTONIA. PHOTO BY TARVI TOOME, COURTESY OF THE ARCHAEOLOGY INSTITUTE, TALLINN UNIVERSITY.]

seen in Fig. 13.12 for the fine-grained, high quality flint from an early Mesolithic site in Estonia. One anticipates that significant patination can obscure a mist pattern.

For obsidian, mist is observable even with fairly significant hydration. On a field trip to an archaeological site during the 1981 Symposium on Obsidian in Mesoamerica in Pachuca, Mexico, mist was observed on a number of archaeological specimens with significant hydration. Observation of mist in obsidian can of course be obscured to some extent by various surface alterations. On utilized blade segments, for example, residues from use or other causes can pose a problem. Alterations by forest fires, including vesiculation, can also affect a surface significantly (Steffen 2005). That mist patterns are quite observable, at least without vesiculation, is seen from a number of illustrations in the latter reference.

Their patterns aside, the manifestations of mist and hackle themselves are seen to be similar for transverse breakages of blades and bifaces. Examples of mist and hackle on experimental biface breakages by bending are seen in Figs.13.11 and 13.13 for a medium grade Normanskill chert. The figures are near the tensile face of each specimen. From (a) to (c) in Fig. 13.11, the surface roughness is seen to increase as one moves closer to the location of branching with the formation of a lateral wedge.

Fig 13.13 indicates a tendency for the velocity hackles to revert to twist hackles due to a contribution from fracture mode III. This tendency is also present on the blade fragment in Fig. 13.12, as by the arrows at the right. The raw material for this fragment, typical for

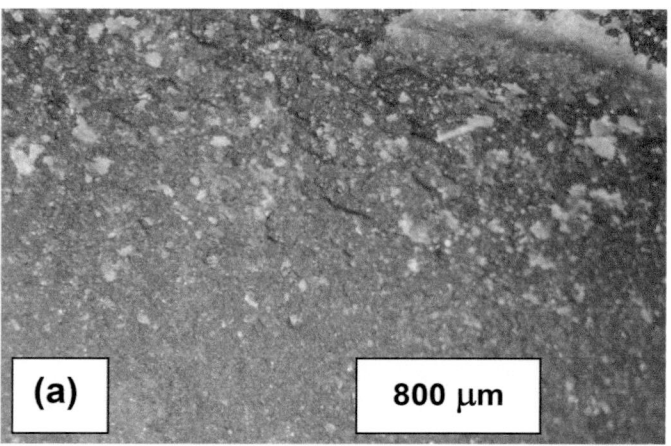

FIG. 13.13 MIST AND HACKLE AT A TRANSVERSE BIFACE BREAK FROM BENDING. NORMANSKILL CHERT OF MEDIUM GRADE. (A) MORE MIST IS SEEN AT THE UPPER PART, CLOSEST TO THE TENSILE FACE. (B) IS TO THE RIGHT OF (A), AND (C) IS TO THE RIGHT OF (B). HACKLE SEEN AS THE MORE ELONGATED FEATURES IN (B) ARE INDICATIVE OF FRACTURE DIRECTION. IN (B) AND (C), THE VELOCITY HACKLE IS REVERTING TO TWIST HACKLES WITH A CONTRIBUTION FROM FRACTURE MODE III. THE LATTER MARKINGS SERVE MORE CLEARLY AS DIRECTIONALITY INDICATORS.

the Pulli site, is thought to be from southern Lithuania or Belarus. The lateral breakthough for the twist hackle at the left, and perhaps also at the right, is seen to produce a locally concave region on the fracture surface. It is these lateral breakthroughs that led to the ridges or abrupt (laterally kinked) edges of the relatively flat central region. It was the ridge on the right side that facilitated the unusually long extension of the hackle flake just left of A (Compare with Fig. 12 in Tsirk 2012).

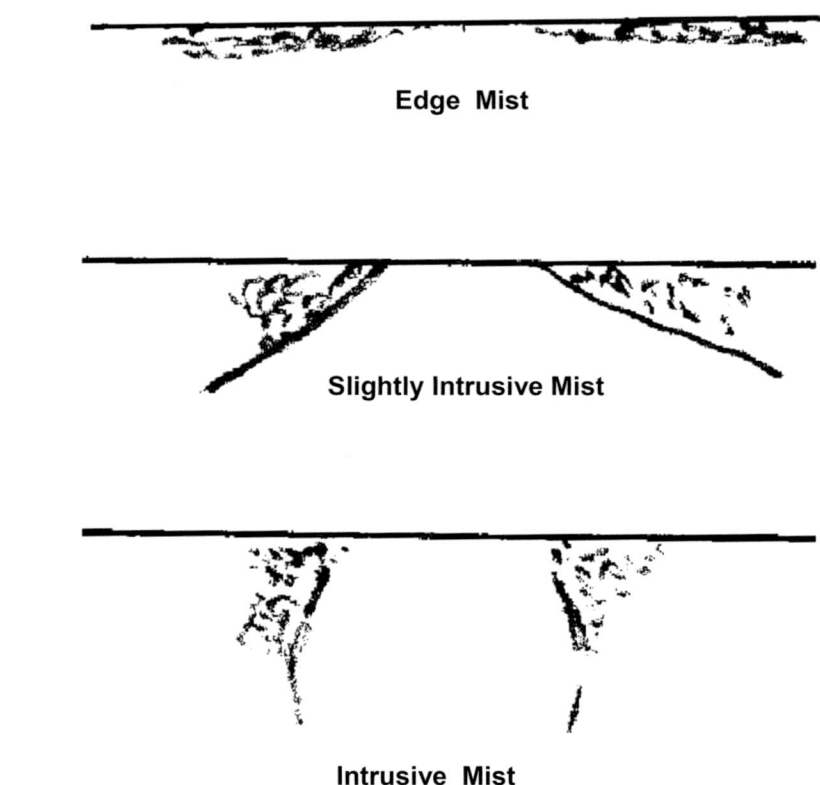

FIG. 13.14 SOME TYPES OF MIST PATTERNS

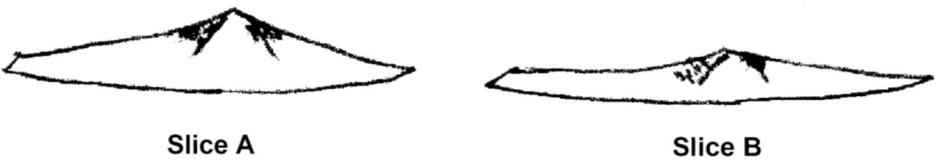

FIG. 13.15 MIST PATTERNS AT THE DOWNSTREAM FACES OF THE SLICES SEEN IN FIG. 13.16

BREAKAGE OF BLADES, FLAKES AND BIFACES 223

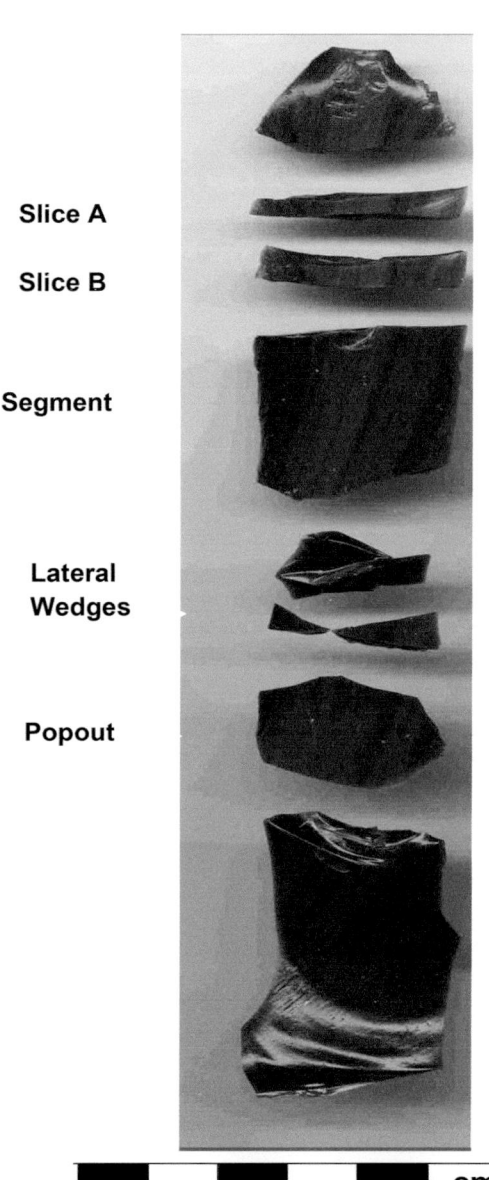

FIG. 13.16 MULTIPLE BLADE BREAKS WITH TWO SLICES. OBSIDIAN.

Some types of mist patterns near a flat surface of an accidental break are shown in Fig.13.14. With a convex rather than a flat surface, the pattern will depend on the surface geometry and the location of the fracture origin. For blade breaks in general the patterns may range from an edge mist to an intrusive mist. Twist hackles often occurring by the mist regions make the observation of the patterns unclear (Fig. 13.15). They are often also responsible for locally concave regions of a break surface, as in Fig. 13.12. The approximate mist patterns for the two slices in Fig. 13.16 are depicted in Fig. 13.15. The formation of these, to be discussed, involved extremely hard support for the core while the blade was being punched. Patterns of intrusive mist, in addition to "edge mist", were manifested at the breaks in Fig. 13.12 and 13.15. As a tentative suggestion, it may be asked whether hard supports together with a loss of contact at the platform were involved in both cases.

Branching and Lateral Wedges for Blades and Flakes

On a set of blade and flake breakages, branching was also observed, sometimes with lateral wedges from high velocity crack branching. All the obsidian specimens were blades, produced mostly by indirect percussion with an antler punch. Both blades and other flakes of obsidian and chert were involved. Several types of crack branching were seen, with single or multiple branches to one or both sides. Other types of lateral wedges and branching patterns are to be expected. Some branching patterns encountered in other contexts are noted in Bahat, Rabinovitz and Fried (2005).

Hairline cracks on the tensile surface (Table 13.4 for bifaces), very difficult to see, were identified on only one specimen. Lateral wedges and other kinds of velocity branching were not observed in pressure flaking.

Fracture Velocities

The fracture of a transverse break usually accelerates in the horizontal direction in the tensile zone by the tensile face. It reaches the practical maximum velocity near the mist-hackle region where it may branch at the start of a lateral wedge.

Proceeding from the tensile face towards the compressive face, the region initially in compression tends to inhibit crack growth. Crack velocities in through the thickness direction are therefore drastically smaller.

Location of Force Application

Bifaces broken transversely due to a force application at its end and sides show differences for the mist patterns manifested and for the locations of the fracture origin. When the force is applied at the end, the fracture origin can sometimes occur near an edge (13% observed), but usually it is near the center of a biface (56%). The mist configurations observed in such cases are usually (59%) double-sided, but may often be only single-sided (41%).

For biface breakages due to a force application at a side, on the other hand, the fracture origin is most often (45%) near the edge, but sometimes (12%) occurs near the center instead. In such cases the mist configuration is usually (87%) single-sided but may sometimes be double-sided (13%). The observations for direct percussion and pressure flaking, not surprisingly, were very similar.

The observations indicate that it is not possible to determine the location of a force application from the mist configuration or the location of the fracture origin. However, suggestions can be made in that regard as to the likely location of the force application. The above remarks are relevant to identification of a lateral snap (Chapter 10).

Some Special Breaks

Bowties

Lateral branching wedges from high velocity branching sometimes occur on two sides of a specimen, opposite each other. Occasionally the two wedges are connected by a small ligament at the center. The resulting piece resembles and is referred to as a **bowtie** (Fig. 13.17). I have encountered bowties with breakage of blades, but not with wider flakes or bifaces. Since paired lateral wedges are occasionally seen with biface breakage (Fig.13.18), one suspects that bowties may rarely occur also with narrow bifaces.

Breakage of Blades, Flakes and Bifaces 225

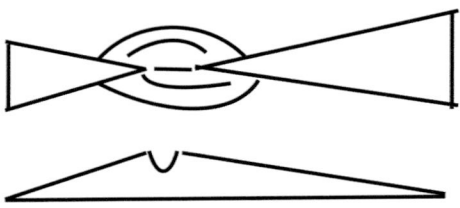

Fig. 13.17 Bowtie from blade breakage. Heat treated Arkansas novaculite. Twice actual size.

Fig. 13.18 A pair of lateral wedges on a Cobden Chert biface, broken accidentally during manufacture.

The manifestation of bowties should not come as a surprise. On a single lateral wedge, a compression lip or a compression wedge often occurs partly as an apparent extension of the lateral wedge beyond its apex, towards the center of the specimen. For a pair of lateral wedges opposite each other, such compression lip or compression wedge "extensions" can join to form a bowtie.

Slices

With blades, transverse breakages are occasionally seen in which the breaks are very close, with more or less parallel fracture surfaces creating a slice (Andrefsky 1998: 87). Two or three such breaks form one or two slices, respectively. It is characteristic of a **slice** that the distance between the adjacent break surfaces (the slice thickness) is small compared to the width of the blade. When the slice thickness is not small, then the terms segments and segmentation rather than slices and slicing are used here.

Observations were made on 13 cases of obsidian slices on blades (Table 13.6). Of these, two (No.12 and 13) are on pressure flaked blades, others on punched blades. One of

TABLE 13.6 OBSERVED OBSIDIAN SLICES

Ref. No.	Mist Pattern: Proximal Face Distal Face	Cross- Section	Longitudinal Region	Between Which Breaks	Over- shot?
1	No mist seen EM	~Triangular	Medial	Between 2 & 3	No
2	No mist seen EM	Triangular	Medial	Between 1 & 2 of 2	Yes
3	EM Very subtle EM	Trapezoidal	Medial	Between 1 & 2 of 2	Yes
4	No mist seen EM	Triangular	Proximal	Between 1 & 2	Yes
5	SIM EM	Trapezoidal	Prox. to Medial?	Between 1 & 2 of 2	No
6	EM – very faint EM – very faint	Triangular	Proximal?	Between 1 & 2 of 2	Yes
7	No mist seen No mist seen	Triangular	Proximal	Between 1 & 2 of 2	No
8	No mist seen EM	Trapezoidal	Proximal	Between & of 3	No
9	SIM EM	Trapezoidal	~ Medial	Between 1 & 2 of 3	Yes
10	All three faces: IM	Trapezoidal	Proximal (See Fig. 13.16)	Between 1&2 and 2&3 of 5	Yes
11	IM No mist seen	Trapezoidal	Proximal	Between 1 & 2 of 4	No
12	No mist seen EM	Triangular	Distal	Between 2 & 3 of 3	Yes
13	IM SIM	Trapezoidal	Distal	Between 2 & 3 of 3	Yes

Mist Patterns (Fig. 13.14): EM = Edge mist; SIM = Slightly intrusive mist; IM = Intrusive mist

the punched blades (No. 10) has a double slice (Fig. 13.16). The blade cross-sections are either triangular or trapezoidal resembling a triangular one. In all but one case (No. 11), the break extends from the outer to the inner surface. Mist was observed in almost all cases. The patterns ranged from edge mist to intrusive mist (Fig. 13.14 and Table 13.6).

The detailed mechanism for the formation of the slices is not clear. A number of mechanisms are conceivable, and several factors may be contributing. Some suggestions are offered here. There are several possible mechanisms for the occurrence of a single transverse break. It is the closeness of the two transverse breaks that is unique with slices.

Consider Fig.13.19, with a blade represented in an idealized fashion. Assume the blade is produced by percussion flaking. Although a single slice is considered, a similar discussion is applicable to the formation of two adjacent slices. The distal end of the partly detached blade in (a) is considered fixed. The blade is in compression, with compressive pulses propagating back and forth between the distal fixed end and the proximal end where the percussion impact is being applied. Suppose there is a temporary loss of contact at the proximal end, as indicated in (b). A compressive pulse propagating towards it will be reflected at the end that is now free as a tensile pulse propagating in the distal direction. This pulse could produce the transverse break a-a, as in (c). The same tensile pulse is reflected at the new free (the break) surface at a-a as a compressive pulse propagating leftward. The

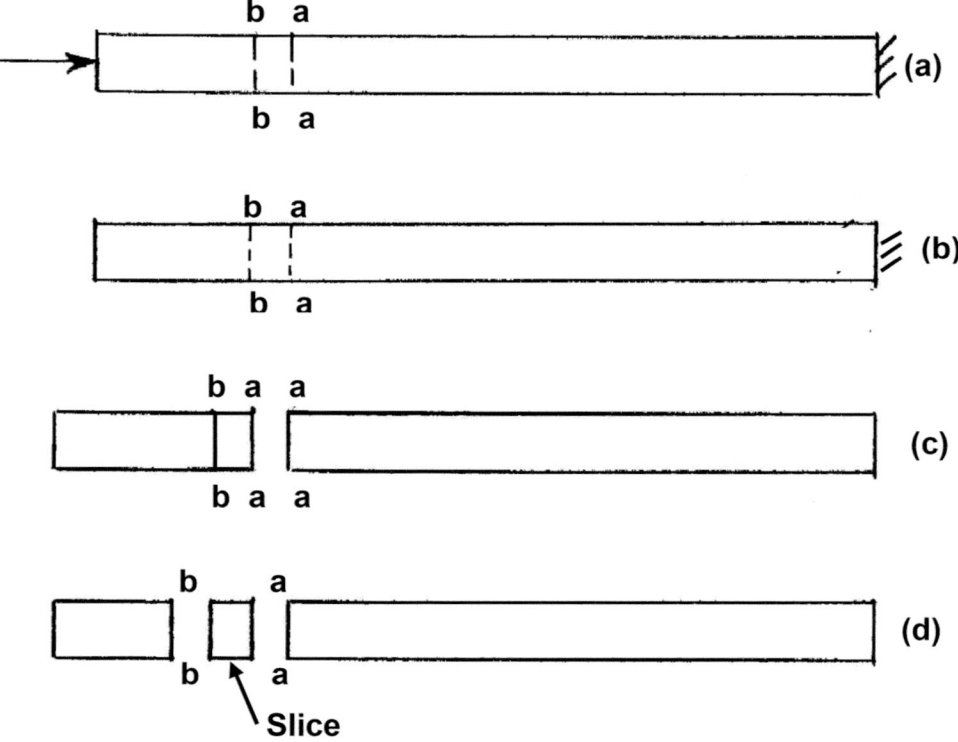

FIG. 13.19 SLICE FORMATION WITH LOSS OF CONTACT.

latter is reflected at the free proximal end again as a tensile pulse propagating rightward to possibly produce the second transverse break, at b-b as in (d). The process noted may be repeated in a similar fashion to produce a third transverse break and a nearby second slice. The only pair of adjacent slices encountered was observed in the proximal part of a blade, shown in Fig. 13.16. The formation of parallel transverse fractures is discussed in Kolsky (1963: 187) and Kolsky and Rader (1968). Solutions related to pile driving are available for an impact to one end of a column fixed at the other end, including considerations for loss of contact (Love 1944: 431-435 and Terzaghi 1961: 465-468).

The pair of adjacent slices noted above is from the production of a 10 cm long blade when the core was supported in a very unusual manner, on two short pieces of 2" by 4" wood on a concrete slab, with shod feet providing lateral stability. This unrealistic unreasonably hard support provided a greater amount of axial "fixity" and stronger reflections. A moose antler punch was used, with a dogwood billet as a striker.

Examples of the mist patterns observed on the transverse breaks for these slices are shown in Fig. 13.15. The mist patterns here are more intrusive than on most of the other slices. The interpretation of the patterns is not entirely clear, perhaps partly because of the triangular or trapezoidal blade sections and the crack starting at the outer face, the different locations of the fracture origins, and the frequent presence of twist hackles.

Now consider the case of a slice formed in the distal region of a blade being detached by pressure flaking. The discussion here is also applicable for percussion flaking. The distal end of this partly detached blade can be considered to be fixed in the axial direction by the core. As the blade detachment is completed, its distal end will become suddenly free and move in the distal direction, as in the case of releasing a compressed spring. As it does so, a tensile pulse is generated by this sudden release of compression. Various reflections of this pulse may conceivably relate to the formation of the slice in the distal region by pressure flaking.

In the above discussions, no mechanism for the formation of slices could be established. Only some suggestions about conceivable mechanisms were offered. The full picture is more complicated, with the various stress pulses being superimposed.

Some characteristics observed for the 13 obsidian slices mentioned are indicated in Table 13.6. All the blades for the table, except the last two, were produced by indirect percussion with an antler punch. The last two were pressure flaked. Slices may also occur, though rarely, with biface breakage (Fig. 13.20). Two proximal biface slices are shown in Nami (1997: Fig. 19D), produced during experimental fluting by direct percussion.

Segmentation

During an amputation or "end shock", a single piece of a biface near its end is broken off. A reflection of the compression as a tensile pulse from the unsupported, free end of the biface is the primary reason for this. Since the far end of a partly detached blade is not free, such a mechanism for blade breakage is not possible. Most blade breakages, usually

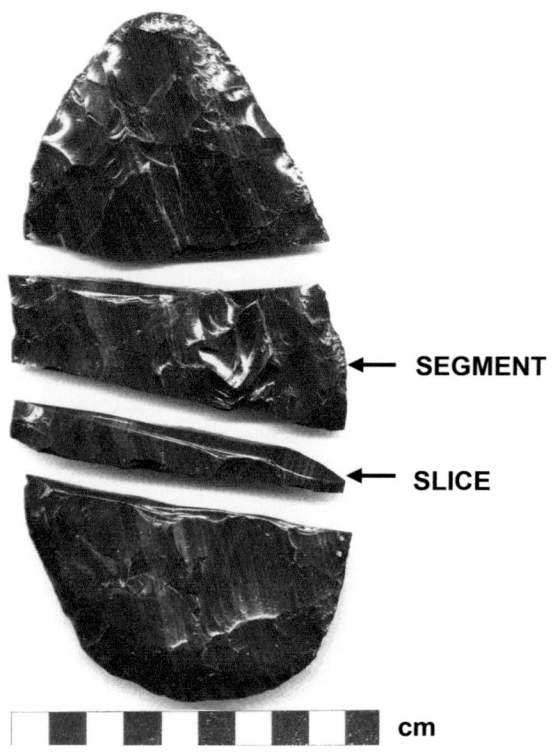

FIG. 13.20 SLICE IN BIFACE BREAKAGE. DIRECT PERCUSSION WITH ANTLER BILLET WHILE END SUPPORTED ON THIGH, APPARENTLY TOO LIGHTLY. GLASS BUTTES OBSIDIAN

resulting in two or three blade segments or fragments, are due to bending or bending combined with axial effects. Occasionally, a blade may be broken into several pieces due to reflection of stress waves when too hard a support is used. The blade breakage shown in Fig. 13.16 is rather unusual. The blade is broken into many pieces, including a segment and the two slices already noted. This obsidian blade was produced by indirect percussion with too hard a support for the core. An example of segmentation is illustrated in Andrefsky (1998: 87). He refers to segments as well as slices as "shattered flake fragments."

How can the formation of a segment be explained? A temporary loss of contact between the punch and the core could lead to the proximal end acting momentarily as a free surface, leading to strong tensile reflections from the top. These and subsequent reflections may conceivably lead to the first and subsequent fractures in segmentation.

The surfaces of the transverse fractures of essentially all segments have at least a slight compression lip, and often a thin linear pattern of mist along the tensile edge is present.

Both of these are indications that bending was involved. Especially with curved but usually also with straight blades, the break originates at the outer blade surface.

Aztec Appreciation of Mechanics

In many prehistoric societies, blades were often snapped into segments. Such segments were usually used as tools with or without hafting, as seen from the use-chipping and other use-wear indicators (Hayden 1979, Keeley 1980). Sometimes a series of such segments was even used to form an edge of a sword or a spearhead (Bicbaev 2010).

A bending moment for breaking a blade can be applied so as to produce tension either on the outside or inside surface. These correspond to curvatures from bending that are concave inward or outward, respectively. The fractures for the breakages extend respectively from the outer to the inner surface or vice versa. The fracture directions can be determined from fracture markings or other fracture features.

For a blade with a triangular or a trapezoidal cross-section, a smaller moment is required if it is applied so as to produce tension at the outer surface. For a rectangular cross-section, it would not make a difference. In general, the fracture stress σ is equal to the bending moment M_i divided by the section modulus S_i. That is (Eq. 13.1)

$$\sigma = M_i / S_i \tag{13.2}$$

where the subscript i is 1 or 2 for the outer or inner surfaces, respectively. The section modulus for some sections can be obtained from Fig. 13.9. In this figure, $\alpha = 0$ and 1 are for a triangle and a rectangle, respectively. From Eqn. 13.2,

$$M_i = \sigma S_i \tag{13.3}$$

and
$$M_2 / M_1 = S_2 / S_1 = (2 + \alpha)/(1 + 2\alpha) \tag{13.4}$$

which is 2 for a triangle and 1 for a rectangle. A plot of M_2 / M_1 is shown in Fig. 13.21. From this it is evident that a greater moment is required if applied to produce tension at the inner surface, especially if a cross-section is triangular.

A sample of Aztec blade segments from the Otumba site in Mexico was considered to see what percentage of the breakages originated at the outer surfaces. The blades were of Pachuca obsidian and had various cross-sectional geometries. For blades thicker than about 4 mm, advantage was taken of the smaller moment required with tension at the outer surface. In fact, for all the 25 blade fragments thicker than 4 mm at the break, the breaks were initiated at the outer surface. The Aztecs snapping the blades clearly had an appreciation of mechanics.

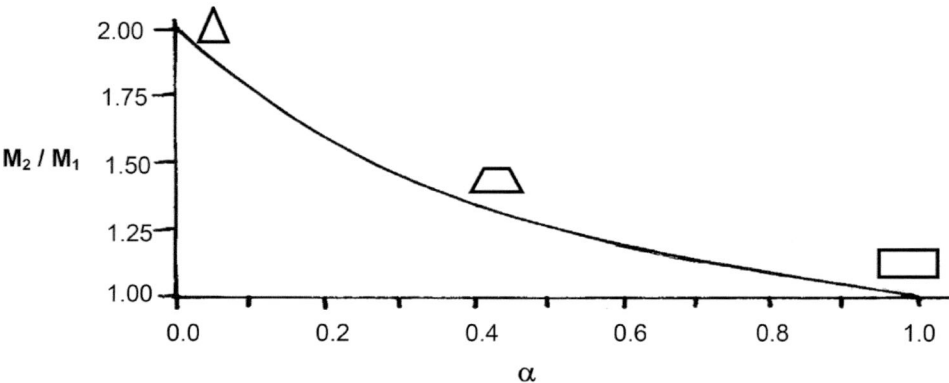

Fig. 13.21 Moment reduction vs. blade geometry when starting a crack from the outer face.

Concluding Remarks

Flintknapping, or simply knapping, has fascinated both craftsmen and scholars alike. Lithic artifacts often provide the primary source of evidence from an archaeological site. Lithic analysis involves an understanding of fracture mechanics and fractography. The principles hold for any application of fracture mechanics and fractography, including archaeology as well as industry. The practice of flintknapping relies on an intuitive understanding of fractures. It can therefore be rightly said that fractography has been practiced for at least 2.5 million years. A contemporary master in knapping has produced over a million fractures in his lifetime. An archaeologist may find over 10,000 fracture specimens among the artifacts from a single site. To a large extent, he relies on empirical rather than theoretical understandings of fracture. In contrast to industrial applications, it is the production rather than the prevention of fractures that is primarily of interest in archaeology.

It is not at all surprising that curiosity about knapping extends to experts in fracture mechanics and fractography. The first part of the book is intended to satisfy this curiosity, providing examples of prehistoric and contemporary knapping along with a discussion of knapping tools, techniques and materials. It is hoped that the book will serve as a "fractography bridge" between the applications in archaeology and other fields. Experts in fracture mechanics and fractography can benefit from the lessons from knapping.

Many fracture markings are considered in Part II of the book. The many types of markings and their names are provided to facilitate communication and interpretation of fractography with lithic artifacts. At times, the terms used for fracture markings on lithic fractures are consistent with fractography, as "twist hackles" for "fissures" that is more common in archaeological literature. Some terms used in archaeological literature are intentionally avoided. Such examples include "indenter" for a percussor or a pressure flaker and "waves of compression" for ripples. Many terms for fracture markings or features considered in the book are new to fractography, except for previous discussions by the author.

The terms "fracture direction" or "localized fracture direction" are used in the book to indicate the usual fracture direction, as indicated by twist hackles, for example. It has been convenient to also use the term "general fracture direction" (See Figs. 5.4 and 5.5), to indicate the "direction of flake detachment" extending from the proximal to the distal end of a flake, along its "axial" direction. It is most useful for a blade or a narrow flake. Twist hackles are usually not in the general fracture direction. The notion of a general fracture direction helps to interpret some fracture markings and features on a flake.

In Part III of the book, many fracture features of interest to knapping are considered. Ideally the objective here as well as in Part II of the book was to clarify and explain the mechanisms involved. Without that, the understanding of the fractures in knapping is necessarily incomplete. In experiments on knapping, replication is often equated with understanding. This is also done sometimes with sophisticated laboratory replications in fractography. Replications contribute significantly to understandings. However, they do not establish a causal relationship.

It is of interest to ask why a great variety of fracture markings and features is manifested in obsidian and not in industrial glasses such as window (soda-lime) glass. Several reasons can be suggested. First of all, obsidian includes various kinds of inclusions or irregularities not encountered in industrial glasses. These may be associated with residual stresses. It is the irregularities in obsidian that relate to:

- The parabolic double tails (Figs. 5.9 and 5.10) (so-called fracture parabolas) formed by a crack running through an inclusion;
- A tail (a.k.a. wake hackle) formed by a crack running around or through an inclusion; and
- Wallner wakes (Figs. 6.4 and 6.5) formed with a stress pulse source behind a fracture front.

The major reasons for the observed variability relate to knapping being done without laboratory controls on geometry, loading and boundary conditions. The fine laboratory research by Terry Michalske on liquid-induced fracture markings was on glass plates 3 mm thick and the research on oscillating (a.k.a. meandering, sinuous) cracks was with plates about 0.1 mm thick (Bahat, Rabinovitch and Frid 2005: 99-100). Such laboratory research can establish some basic principles, but it can limit considerations of variability, including those of the principles.

Glossary

aging	Increase in strength over time in the presence of moisture or a liquid and absence of stress.
amputation	Transverse biface breakage occurring far from the force platform due to bending combined with axial tension from stress wave reflections.
anisotropy	Not having the same property in any direction.
anvil technique	Direct percussion with the core supported on large stone anvil, and the blow struck not directly into the core.
argillite	A variety of metamorphosed shale or siltstone.
arrest line	A kink in fracture profile, which may or may not correspond to actual arrest. See also dwell mark.
bending	Deformation into a curved shape due to flexural stresses.
bending initiation	A non-contact flake initiation with significant bending.
billet	A club or rod of organic material (a.k.a. baton) used in flaking. May be used as a striker on a punch.
bipolar percussion	Direct percussion with the core supported on a large stone anvil and the blow struck directly into the core.
blade	An approximately parallel-sided long flake.
blunt termination	A flake termination at the far end of a core without feathering and without significant curvature near its end.
bowtie	A connected pair of lateral branching wedges resembling a bowtie.
branching	Forking of a crack. Usually occurs at high fracture velocity (V_F) as in the formation of lateral branching wedges. Can occur also at low V_F, as with compression wedges.
bridging	Impedance of crack growth by some particles (as inclusions) attached to each face of a crack.
brittle	Without inelastic behavior.
bulb	A feature resembling a swelling on a flake surface, usually manifested just below the cone-like feature of Hertzian flake initiation. May be pronounced or salient (a.k.a. diffuse).
bulbar scar	A.k.a. éraillure scar. A hackle scar on a bulb.
catastrophic fracture	A fracture that can propagate without an increase in load. Also known as critical or supercritical fracture.
cavitation scarp	A LIFM known as a scarp formed due to cavitation at an accelerating fracture front.
center plane	The mid-plane of a biface, halfway between the two faces.
chert	A crystalline rock consisting mostly of silica. Usually sedimentary. Used here to include flint.
compression curl	Negative scar of a compression lip or a compression wedge.
compression lip	The curling of the surface of a bending break near the compression face.

compliance	Flexibility.
compressive strain	Decrease in length per original length.
compressive stress	Compressive force per unit area.
compression wedge	The slow velocity branching and curling of the surface of a bending break near the compression face.
cone	Conical fracture surface of a Hertzian cone fracture. See cone-like feature.
cone-like feature	The proximal flake feature resembling part of a cone, seen usually with Hertzian flake initiations.
contact initiation	Flake initiation with fracture originating by the contact area with the load or beneath it. Hertzian initiation or wedging initiation.
core	A lithic artifact from which flakes are detached.
cortex	The outer surface of a core, which is weathered or has defects from other natural causes.
crack	A material separation by opening or sliding, without dividing the specimen into more than one piece.
crack extension force	Usually designated as G, it is the potential energy release rate per unit extension of the fracture and per unit length of the fracture front. (a.k.a. strain energy release rate).
crack path	The line on a fracture surface that follows the fracture direction.
crested blade	A blade with transverse flakes detached from its ridge before the blade removal.
critical stress intensity factor, K_{IC}	Fracture toughness. Stress intensity needed for crack growth.
deceleration scarp	A LIFM. See Table 8.2.
depletion band	A LIFM. See Table 8.2.
depletion scarp	A LIFM. See Table 8.2.
diagonal parallel flaking	The detachment of parallel flakes diagonally across the face of a point or a biface, usually by pressure flaking.
dilatational stress wave	See longitudinal wave.
directional stability	Ability of a crack to propagate along a particular path, characterized by the compressive stress trajectories not diverging.
direct percussion	A flaking technique in which the core is struck directly without a punch or other intermediary tool.
distortional stress wave	See shear wave.
dorsal surface	The outer surface of a flake.
double cantilever beam (DCB)	An often used test specimen with a crack near one end. It resembles a tuning fork, but instead of the space it has only a crack between the two arms.
double tail	Two tails extending downstream from the same irregularity, associated with two surface mismatches of three partial fracture fronts. See parabolic double tail.
downstream	The direction in which a fracture is propagating.
ductile	Behavior with relatively large amount of inelastic behavior.
dwell mark	A kink in fracture profile. See arrest line.

edge scar	A hackle scar manifested at the edge of a flake, along the ridge produced by flake detachment.
edge-to-edge flaking	Detachment of flakes all across the face of a biface without removing a significant part of the opposite edge. See overshot flakes.
elastic	Has two meanings: (1) Relative capability to deform elastically, as being more elastic (lower E) or less elastic (greater E); (2) Material response without inelastic behavior, with deformations vanishing upon unloading.
elasticity	It has two meanings, just as "elastic..
encounter scarp	A LIFM. See Table 8.2.
escarpment scarp	A LIFM. See Table 8.2.
éraillure scar	See bulbar scar.
feather termination	A flake termination with the thickness vanishing gradually to a sharp edge.
flake initiation	The release of proximal end of a flake.
flaw	A material irregularity.
flexibility Compliance.	A measure of displacement (or rotation) per unit load.
flint	A finer-grained variety of chert.
force platform	Surface on which a force is applied in knapping.
fracture	A material separation by opening or sliding, with or without dividing the item into more than one piece.
fracture marking	Marking on a fracture surface caused by the fracture that produced the surface.
fracture mode I	See opening mode.
fracture mode II	See sliding mode.
fracture mode III	See tearing mode.
fracture origin	The location where the fracture starts.
fracture parabola	A fracture marking resembling a parabola in fracture plan, due to a secondary fracture origin ahead of the primary fracture front, as in PMMA (Plexiglass). Also known as a Kies marking. Not observed in obsidian. See double tail and parabolic double tail.
fracture plan	Fracture surface as viewed normal to it
fracture profile	Profile section of a fracture along a fracture path. Not planar in general.
fracture toughness	Critical stress intensity factor K_{IC}.
Fréchette marking	Liquid-induced fracture marking (LIFM). See Table 8.2.
fundamental frequency	The lowest frequency of natural vibration.
fundamental natural period	The longest period of natural vibration. For axial vibration, it is four transit times for clamped-free rod, and two transit times for a free-free rod.
geometric nonlinearity	Characteristic of a system for which equilibrium cannot be considered based on original (undeformed) geometry, as a transversely loaded string.

gull wings	A pair of Wallner lines appearing as wings, usually short, due to the fracture front encountering an inclusion or other internal irregularity.
hackle	A linear feature in fracture plan, manifested due to overlapping of two partial fracture fronts, caused by rotation of the direction of the maximum tension about a line in the fracture direction (that is, Mode III participation). Not always in the fracture direction as usually with material interface hackles, hackle scarps and partition hackles.
hackle flake	Flake from an extended lateral breakthrough of a twist hackle.
hackle scar	The scar from a hackle flake.
hackle scarp	A LIFM. See Table 8.2.
hackle zig-zag	A LIFM. See Table 8.2.
heat treatment	Intentional thermal alteration of material properties by human activity.
Hertzian cone fracture	The classical Hertzian fracture of a spherical ball onto a half-space, with the ring crack and the cone.
Hertzian initiation	Contact flake initiation excluding wedging, in which the fracture origin is at or very near the load contact.
hinged termination	A flake termination having a 90°, 180° or various other turns.
homogeneous	Having the same properties throughout the specimen.
hydration	The chemical-physical alteration of obsidian, gradually penetrating deeper from the surface, depending on temperature, water content and obsidian chemistry.
incipient branching	Branching attempts most often manifested in accidental biface breakages by bending, near the tensile face. The attempts are unsuccessful because of the stress gradients in flexure.
indirect percussion	Percussion flaking in which a punch or other intermediary device is used that is hit by a striker.
inelastic	Behavior after which the material does not return to the original form.
inward force component	In the direction of the flake length (axial direction), used as an approximation for distinguishing the inward and outward force components in flaking.
Jacked flake	When a flake is unintentionally aborted by stepping or hinging, part of what would have been the distal part of the flake may remain on the core. Placing the broken proximal part of the flake back to its scar, and using it effectively as a punch that is struck by a percussor, the part downstream of the step or hinge may be removed. The latter is termed here a "Jacked flake".
isotropic	Having the same property in any direction.
kinked ripple	A ripple with an abrupt slope change (a kink) in fracture profile.
lateral branching wedge	See lateral wedge.
lateral snap	Transverse biface break due to force applied at its side.

lateral wedge	Seen in breakage of flakes and bifaces in bending, it is due to branching of the crack at high velocity by the tensile surface. To distinguish it from a lateral wedge produced by other causes, the term "lateral branching wedge" may be used.
LIFM	Liquid-induced fracture marking, a.k.a. Fréchette marking. See Table 8.2.
linear band features	A LIFM. See Table 8.2.
lip	The part of a platform overhanging the flake ventral surface. In fracture profile it is bounded by two surfaces, namely parts of the platform and the flake ventral surface.
liquid-induced fracture marking (LIFM)	A fracture marking due to the effects of a liquid, known also as a Fréchette marking. See Table 8.2.
liquid-induced hackle	A LIFM. See Table 8.2.
longitudinal stress wave	The primary or P-wave. Also known as a dilatational wave and irrotational wave.
material interface hackle	A hackle initiated at and extending along a materal interface.
material interface marking	Fracture markings manifested at the interface of two materials having different mechanical properties
material interface ridge	A fracture marking manifested as a ridge or escarpment along a material interface.
material transition ridge	A fracture marking manifested as a ridge or an escarpment along a material interface that is roughly parallel to a fracture front.
mirror A mirror region.	An optically smooth region between the fracture origin and the mist region.
mirror constants	Material constants relating the mirror radii to the fracture stress.
mirror radii	The distances from the fracture origin to the first onset of mist, velocity hackle and branching are the three mirror radii.
mist	Mist region, between the mirror and a velocity hackle region, having fine surface roughness. In obsidian, it has a dull misty or frosty appearance
mist-hackle	Fracture markings of the combined mist and (velocity) hackle regions.
mist-hackle configuration	A configuration characterized by the local enhancement of mist, mist and hackle or hackle due to the stress pulse generated when the fracture front encounters an inclusion or other irregularity. The formation of the configuration is analogous to Wallner lines, and to mist suppression configurations.
mist line	A narrow band of mist, hackle or their combination extending in the fracture direction. Within or near a

	general mist region, it trails a tail or twist hackle, or appears in lieu of them.
mist suppression configuration	A configuration characterized by the paucity of mist or velocity hackle due to the fracture front encountering an irregularity acting as an obstruction to the fracture propagation.
modulus of elasticity	Also known as Young's modulus, E. The material property defined as the ratio of stress to corresponding strain for elastic behavior.
modulus of rigidity	See shear modulus. Modulus of elasticity in shear.
multiple tails	Three or more tails extending downstream from the same irregularity, associated with surface mismatches of partial fracture fronts.
nominal stress	The stress in a specimen with the crack considered to be absent.
non-contact initiation	A flake initiation in which the fracture originates away from the contact area. Includes bending initiations.
nonlinear	Behavior for which superposition of results is not valid, encountered when inelastic behavior or geometric nonlinearity is involved.
normality rule	The premise that a fracture surface is normal to the maximum tensile stress.
normal stress	Stress acting perpendicular to an area.
obsidian	A volcanic glass, amorphous (noncrystalline).
opening mode	Fracture mode I, characterized by the surfaces moving apart as the crack extends.
orthotropic	The material properties being different in directions at right angles, as wood.
outrepassée flake	Overshot flake also known as plunging flake.
outward	Refers to the direction normal to a flake axis and towards its dorsal surface. For example, it is convenient to refer to inward (meaning here axial) and outward force components as approximations.
overshot	Also known as a plunging or outrepassée flake. A flake removing part of the opposite edge.
parabolic double tail	Two tails extending downstream from the same irregularity, associated with surface mismatches of the partial fracture fronts, and the outer two tails appearing as a parabola. As the fracture front passes the irregularity, there is a shift in the fracture plane.
partition hackle	A LIFM. See Table 8.2.
plunging	See overshot.
Poisson's ratio	The ratio of the lateral to longitudinal strain due to longitudinal loading.
popout	Also known as a nacelle flake, it is a piece removed from the ventral surface of a flake by secondary fracturing, having part of the dorsal surface at one or both of the lateral edges.
potlid	A flake, usually round, released from a specimen due to its heating, leaving usually a round pocket.

practical terminal velocity	The maximum fracture velocity observed in practice for a material, a fraction of the shear wave velocity, around 60% of it for some materials.
pressure flaking	Flake detachment by use of a force without percussion.
principal stress	The maximum (usually tension) or minimum (usually compression) stress at a point.
pronounced bulb	A bulb not as subtle as a diffuse bulb.
proximal scar	A tiny flake scar extending downstream from the platform and occurring on the main flake, not on its negative scar.
punch	An intermediary tool, such as an antler tine, used in indirect percussion by striking it with a striker.
punch technique	Indirect percussion technique as with a punch and a striker.
P-wave	See longitudinal wave.
Rayleigh wave	A surface wave, thought by some to limit the theoretical terminal fracture velocity.
rhyolite	An igneous rock that can resemble granite in composition, but has a finer texture.
ripple	A line or band in fracture plan, usually convex in fracture direction, with the appearance of a wave in fracture profile. Associated with fracture mode II participation.
ripple scar	A hackle scar manifested along a ripple.
ruffles	The ruffled ventral surface of a flake and the matching flake scar on the core having numerous irregular dimples, humps and multi-directional undulations.
shearing mode	Fracture mode II, also known as the sliding mode, characterized by the two surfaces sliding longitudinally past each other and normal to the fracture front.
shear modulus	Also known as the modulus of rigidity, G. The ratio of shearing stress to corresponding shear strain.
shear strain	The angular change (radians) of a corner of an originally (imaginary) square block. It is the shear deformation of the block without volume change.
shear stress	Stress acting parallel to a surface.
shear wave	The S-wave, also known as equivoluminal wave and distortional stress wave.
Sierra marking	A LIFM. See Table 8.2.
Sierra scarp	A LIFM. See Table 8.2.
slice	A segment of a blade or flake produced by two transverse breaks occurring close by with the segment length being small relative to the blade or flake width.
sliding mode	See shearing mode.
slurp scarp	A LIFM. See Table 8.2.
snap	A snap fracture, sometimes referred to as a "half moon breakage", is more likely to occur with small edge angles and when a force is applied normal to the surface. Of greatest interest for use-wear studies.

sonic modulation	Use of stress pulses at known but low frequency to induce ripples. See ultrasonic modulation.
split marks	Fracture markings from longitudinal flake splitting.
split ridge	A split mark formed with the fractures for the two flake parts near the split location propagating along different surfaces in the distal region.
split ripple	A split mark manifested as a ripple on a negative flake scar, having an irregularity or stopping abruptly at the split line.
split step	A split mark manifested as a step along the split line, with each flake part having a different thickness at the step location.
starvation band	A LIFM. See Table 8.2.
step fracture	A flake termination, occurring usually near the distal end of a core, with a 90° transverse break.
step-in	A fracture feature extending inward from the dorsal surface of a flake and then turning parallel to the ventral surface, usually in the distal direction. May be visualized as an extended compression lip at the inner face.
stepout	A fracture feature extending outward from the ventral surface of a flake and then turning in the distal direction. May be visualized as an extended compression lip at the outer face.
stepped cone	A cone-like feature with concentric looking kinked steps.
stiffness	A force or moment required for unit displacement or rotation, respectively.
strain	Deformation per unit value (as unit length)..
strain energy	Energy stored in a specimen due to stresses and strains in it.
stress	A force per unit area.
stress intensity factor	Designated as K with a subscript I, II, or III for the respective fracture modes. It indicates the intensity but not the distribution of the stresses by a crack tip.
stress wave	When there is a sudden change in loading, the effects will not be felt immediately at some distance. They will be transmitted there by means of stress waves.This is similar to the sound waves reaching us from an airplane.
St.Venant's principle	When a loading is replaced with a statically equivalent loading, then the stresses are unchanged at locations far from the location of the change.
subcritical	Not supercritical or catastrophic.
supercritical	A fracture is supercritical if it can advance without any load increase. Also known as catastrophic or unstable fracture propagation.
tail	The surface mismatch of this hackle is produced by a fracture front passing around, through or partly through an nclusion or other irregularity. Also known as a wake hackle.
tearing mode	Fracture mode III, characterized by lateral shearing parallel to the fracture front. Known also as anti-plane shearing mode.

tensile quasi-lip	Observed at the tensile face of a biface broken in bending, it is manifested when a partly detached flake on the tensile face overhangs at the side of the break surface.
tensile strain	Elongation per unit length.
tensile stress	Tension per unit area.
terminal velocity	The limiting fracture velocity, with reference to either the theoretical or practical maximum.
theoretical terminal velocity	The theoretical limiting value for the fracture velocity, thought to be the Rayleigh wave speed (close to the shear wave speed), that is never reached in practice.
thermal alteration	The change in material properties due to a temperature change, by nature or human activity.
twist hackle	A hackle in the fracture direction, due to rotation in the direction of the maximum tension about a line in the fracture direction (that is, Mode III participation).
ultrasonic modulation	Use of stress wave pulses at known frequency to induce ripples. Ripple spacing indicates the fracture speed, and ripple shapes in fracture plan indicate fracture fronts.
unzipping initiation	Flake initiation for which multiple blows are used to produce cone-like features along a "line". Some of the latter will interact to start the flake detachment and lead to flake initiation by "unzipping".
upstream	The direction from which a fracture is advancing.
velocity hackle	More pronounced surface roughness than for mist. When viewed by naked eye or at low magnification, a hackle region in obsidian appears as shiny and irregular. Often included with mist-hackle.
ventral surface	The inner surface of a flake.
vesiculation	The "puffing up" of obsidian due to fire effects, with flakes appearing as hardened sponges.
wake hackle	See tail.
wake scarp	A LIFM. See Table 8.2.
Wallner line	A ripple due to a stress pulse interacting with the fracture front.
Wallner wake	A Wallner line caused by a stress pulse having its source at the fracture surface behind the fracture front, due to secondary fracturing behind the front.
wedging initiation	Flake initiation from sharp contact. These have been referred to as "split cones" and "sheared cones". They are characterized by a strongly rippled flat region near the contact, and no bulb of force.
wing flake	A "sliver" extending laterally from a twist hackle by the cone-like feature usually seen in percussion flaking with Hertzian initiation. The "slivers" are detached from the core, thus leaving evidence on the flake scar but not on the flake itself.
workability	Ease of flake detachment.
Young's modulus	See modulus of elasticity.

References

Andrefsky, Jr., William
    1998   *Lithics: Macroscopic Approaches to Analysis,* Cambridge University Press, Cambridge.

Apel, Jan
    2001   Daggers: Knowledge and Power. The Social Aspects of Flint-Dagger Technology in Scandinavia 2350-1500 cal BC, Uppsala University, Uppsala.

Apel, Jan, and Kjel Knutsson (eds.)
    2006   *Skilled Production and Social Reproduction. Aspects of Traditional Stone-Tool Technologies,* Uppsala University, SAU Stone Studies 2, Uppsala.

Angier, Natalie
    2001   Sonata for Humans, Birds and Humpback Whales, *New York Times*, p. F5, January 9, 2001.

Bahat, Dov
    1977   Prehistoric Hertzian Fracture of Chert, *J. Mats. Sci.* 12(3): 616-620.
    1984   Fracture Interaction in the Gregory Rift, East Africa, *Tectonophysics* 104: 47-65.
    1991   *Tectonofractography*, Springer, Berlin.

Bahat, Dov, Avinoam Rabinovitch and Vladimir Frid
    2005   *Tensile Fracturing in Rocks. Tectonofractographic and Electromagnetic Radiation Methods*, Springer, Berlin.

Bauer, Ulrike
    1981   Condensation of Water Vapor on nFracture-Generated Glass Surfaces. Master's Thesis, Alfred University, Alfred.

Beauchamp, E.K.
    1995   Crack Front Stability and Hackle Formation in High Velocity Glass Fracture, *J. Am. Cer. Soc.* 78 (3) 689-697.
    1996   Mechanisms for Hackle Formation and Crack Branching, pp. 409-445 in *Fractography of Glasses and Ceramics III*, ed. by J.R. Varner and G.D. Quinn, The American Ceramic Society, Westerville.

Beauchamp, E.K., and B.A. Purdy
    1986   Decrease of Fracture Toughness of Chert by Heat Treatment, *J. Mats. Sci.* 21:1963-1966.

Beck, Benjamin A.
    1980   *Animal Tool Behavior: The Use and Manufacture of Tools by Animals*, Garland   STPM Press, New York.

Bertouille, Horace
    1989   Théories Physiques et Mathématiques de la Taille des Outils Préhistoriques, *Cahiers du Quaternaire* 15, Centre National de la Recherche Scientifique, Paris.

Beuker, J.R.
    1983   *Vakmanchap in Vuursteen: De Vervaardeguing en het Gebruik van Vuurstenen Werktuigen in de Prehistorie*, Museumfonds Publicatie 8, Assen.

Bicbaev, Veaceslav
    2010   Copper Age Cemetery of Giurgiulesti, pp. 212-224 in *The Lost World of Old Europe:The Danube Valley, 5000 – 3500 BC*, ed. by David W Anthony and Jennifer Y. Chi, Princeton University Press, Princeton..

Bilby, B.A.
    1980   Tewksbury Lecture: Putting Fracture to Work, *J. Mats. Sci.* 15(3): 535-556.

Blacking, John
    1953   Edward Simpson, alias 'Flint Jack' – A Victorian Craftsman, *Antiquity* 27: 207-211.

Blackwood, B.
    1950   The Technology of Modern Stone Age People, *Occasional Papers on Technology* 3, Pitt Rivers Museum, University of Oxford.

Boley, Bruno A., and Jerome H. Weiner
    1960   *Theory of Thermal Stresses*, John Wiley and Sons, New York.

Bonnichsen, Robson
    1974   Models for Deriving Cultural Information from Stone Tools, Doctoral Dissertation, Department of Anthropology, The University of Alberta, Edmonton, Alberta.

Bordaz, Jacques
    1969   Flint Flaking in Turkey *Natural History* 78: 73-79.
    1970   *Tools of the Old and New Stone Age*, Natural History Press, Garden City.

Bordes, François
    1968   *The Old Stone Age*, World University Library, New York.

Bordes, François, and Don E. Crabtree
    1969   The Corbiac Blade Technique and Other Experiments, *Tebiwa* 12(2): 1-21.

Bradt, Richard C., and Richard E. Tressler,
    1994   *Fractography of Glass*, Plenum Press, New York.

Broberg, K. Bertram
    1999   *Cracks and Fracture*, Academic Press, New York.

Broek, David
    1978   *Elementary Engineering Fracture Mechanics*, Sjithoff and Noordhoff, Alphen aan den Rijn.

Callahan, Errett
    1979   The Basics of Biface Knapping in the Eastern Fluted Point Tradition: A Manual for Flintknappers and Lithic Analysts, *Archaeology of Eastern North America* 7(2): 1-180.
    1985   The Flintknapping Industry of Eben-Emaël, *Quarterly Bulletin, Archaeological Societyof Virginia* (40) 2-3.
    1987   An Evaluation of the Lithic Technology in Middle Sweden During the Mesolithic and Neolithic, *Societas Archaeologica Upsaliensis Aun* 8, Uppsala.
    1996   The Bipolar Technique: The Simplest Way to Make Stone Tools for Survival, *Bull. of Prim. Tech.* 12:16-21.
    1999   Ishi Sticks, Iceman Picks and Good-for-Nothing Things: A Search for

Authenticity in Presure Flaking Tools, *Bull. of Prim. Tech.* 18: 60-68.
    2000   Experiments with Danish Mesolithic Microblade Technology, *Bull. of Prim. Tech.* 20: 62-68.

Chiu, W.C., M.D. Thouless and W.J. Endres
    1998   An Analysis of Chippiong in Brittle Materials, *Int. J. of Fract.* 90: 287-298.

Clark, J.G.D.
    1966   *Prehistoric Europe: The Economic Basis*, Stanford University Press, Stanford.

Clements, F.E., A. and Reed
    1939   "Eccentric" Flints of Oklahoma, *Amer. Ant.* 5(1): 27-30.

Collins, Michael B.
    1999   *Clovis Blade Technology*, University of Texas Press, Austin.

Cotterell, Brian, and Johan Kamminga
    1979   The Mechanics of Flaking, pp. 97-112 in *Lithic Use-Wear Analysis,* ed. by Brian Hayden, Academic Press, New York.
    1987   Formation of Flakes, *Amer. Ant.* 52(4): 675-709.
    1990   *Mechanics of Pre-Industrial Technology*, Cambridge University Press, Cambridge.

Cotterell, B., J. Kamminga and F.P. Dickson
    1985   The Essential Mechanics of Conchoidal Flaking, *Int. J. of Fract.* 20: 205-221.

Crabtree, Don E.
    1967a   Notes on Experiments on Flintknapping: 3. The Flintknapper's Raw Materials, *Tebiwa* 10(1): 8-24.
    1967b   Notes on Experiments on Flintknapping: 4. Tools Used for Making Flaked Stone Artifacts, *Tebiwa* 10(1): 60-73.
    1968   Mesoamerican Polyhedral Cores and Prismatic Blades, *Amer. Ant.* 33(4): 446-478.
    1970   Flaking Stone with Wooden Implements, *Science* 169: 146-153.
    1972   An Introduction to Flintworking, *Occasional Papers of the Idaho Museum of Natural History* 28, Pocatello.

Crabtree, Don E., and B. Robert Butler
    1964   Notes on Experiments on Flintknapping: 1. Heat Treatment of Silica Minerals, *Tebiwa* 7(1): 1-6.

Cresson, Jack
    2001   Wooden Billet Notes, *Bull. of Prim. Tech.* 22: 67-69.
    2002   Knapping Notes, *Bull. of Prim. Tech. 24: 82-83.*
    2004   Experimental Arrow Durability and Impact Test, *Bull. of Prim. Tech.* **28:** 68-70.

Danzer, Robert, Monica Hangl and Reinhold Paar
    2001   Edge Chipping of Brittle Materials, pp. 43-55 in *Fractography of Glasses and Ceramics IV*, ed. by J. R. Varner and George D. Quinn, The American Ceramic Society, Westerville.

Dauvois, Michel
    1976   *Precis de Dessin Dynamique et Structural des Industries Lithiques Préhistoriques,* Pierre Fanlac, Perigeux.

De Freminville, Ch.
    1914   Eclatement, *Revue Metallurgie* 11: 971-1056.

Den Hartog, J.P.
    1952   *Advanced Strength of Materials*, McGraw-Hill Book Co., New York.

Desrosiers, Pierre M.
    2012   *The Emergence of Pressure Blade Making from Origin to Modern Experiments*, Springer, New York.

Dibble, Harold L. and John C. Whittaker
    1981   New Experimental Evidence on the Relation between Percussion Flaking and Flake Variation, *J. Arch..Sci.*.6: 283-296.

Domanski, Marian, and John A. Webb
    1992   Effect of Heat Treatment on Siliceous Rocks Used in Prehistoric Lithic Technology, *J. Arch. Sci.* 19 (6): 601-614.
    2000   Flaking Properties, Petrology and Use of Polish Flints, *Antiquity* 74: 822-832.
    2007   A Review of Heat Treatment, *Lithic Technology* 32 (2): 153 -194.

Domanski, M., J.A. Webb, and J. Boland
    1994   Mechanical Properties of Stone Artefact Materials and the Effect of Heat Treatment, *Archaeometry* 36 (2): 177-208.

Domanski, Marian, John Webb, Robert Glaisher, Jan Gurba, Jerzy Libera and Anna Zokoscrelna
    2009   Heat Treatment of Polish Flints, *J. Arch. Sci.* 36(7): 1400-1408.

Ellis, H.H.
    1944   *Flint-Working Techniques of the American Indians: An Experimental Study*, Lithic Laboratory, Ohio State Museum, Columbus.

Eloy, L.
    1975   La Fracture Dite 'Segment de Lame en Nacelle:' Son Mechanisme, Ses Variantes, Ses Rates, *Bulletin de la Société Préhistorique Française*,72:18-23.
    1980   Etude Complémentaire sur la Fracture Dite 'Segment de Lame en Nacelle:' Son Mechanisme, Ses Variantes, Ses Rates, *Bulletin de la Société Préhistorique Française*, 77:70-75.

Faulkner, Alaric
    1972   Mechanical Principles of Flintworking, Ph.D. Thesis, University of Washington, Pullman.
    1974   Mechanics of Eraillure Formation, *Newsletter of Lithic Technology* 2(3): 4-12.

Finnie, I., and S. Swaminathan
    1974   The Initiation and Propagation of Hertzian Ring Cracks, pp.231-244 in *Fracture Mechanics of Ceramics 1: Concepts, Flaws and Fractography*, ed. by R.C. Bradt, D.P.H. Hasselman and F.F. Lange, Plenum Press, New York.

Flenniken, J. Jeffrey
    1978   Reevaluation of the Lindenmeier Folsom: A Replicative Experiment in Lithic Technology, *Amer. Ant.* 43: 473-480.

Flenniken, J. Jeffrey and Kenneth G. Hirth
    2003   Handheld Prismatic Blade Manufacture in Mesoarmerica, pp. 98-107 in *Mesoamerican Lithic Technology: Experimentation and Interpretation,"* ed. by Kenneth G. Hirth, University of Utah Press, Salt Lake City.

Fonseca, J.G., J.D. Eshelby and C. Atkinson
    1971   The Fracture Mechanics of Flint-Knapping and Allied Processes, *Int. J. Fract. Mechcs* 7: 421-433.

Forrest, A.J.
    1983   *Masters of Flint*, Lavenham Press, Lavenham.

Fréchette, V.D.
    1965   Characteristics of Fracture-Exposed Surfaces, *Proc. Bri. Ce. Soc.* 5: 97-106.
    1984   Markings on Crack Surfaces of Brittle Materials: A Suggested Unified Nomenclature, pp. 104-107 in *Fractography of Ceramic and Metal Failures*, ed. by J.J. Mecholsky, Jr. and S.R. Powell, Jr., *ASTM Special Technical Publication* 827, American Society for Testing and Materials, Philadelphia.
    1985   Fracture of Glass in the Presence of H_2O, *Glastechn. Ber.*, 58 : 125-9.
    1990   *Failure Analysis of Brittle Materials*, The American Ceramic Society, Westerville.

Freiman, S.W.
    1980   Fracture Mechanics of Glass, pp. 21-78 in *Glass Science and Technology, Vol. 5: Elasticity and Strength of Glasses*, ed. by D.R Uhlman and N.J. Kreidl, Academic Press, New York.

Frison, George, and Bradley, Bruce
    1999   *The Fenn Cache: Clovis Weapons and Tools*, One Horse Land and Cattle Company, Santa Fe.

Gebel, Hans Georg
    1980   Eine Rezente Abschlagindustrie in der Region Hilvan/Südosttürkei, pp. 396-403 in *5000 Jahre Feuersteinbergbau: Die Suche nach dem Stahl der Steinzeit*, Ed. by Gerd Weisgerber, Rainer Slotta and Jürgen Weiner, Deutschen Bergbau-Museum, Bochum.

Goodman, Mary Ellen
    1944   The Physical Properties of Stone Tool Materials, *Amer. Ant.* 9(4): 415-433.

Gould, R.A.
    1971   The Archaeologist as Ethnographer: A Case from the Western Desert of Australia, *World Archaeology* 3(2): 143-177.
    1980   *Living Archaeology*, Cambridge University Press, Cambridge.

Gramlety, Michael
    1984   Mount Jasper: A Direct Access Lithic Resource Area in White Mountains of New Hampshire, pp. 11-21 in *Prehistoric Quarries and Lithic Production*, ed. by Jonathan E. Ericson and Barbara A. Purdy, Cambridge University Press, Cambridge.

Green, David J.
    1998   *An Introduction to the Mechanical Properties of Ceramics,* Cambridge University Press, New York.

Hampton, O.W. "Bud"
    1999   *Culture of Stone: Sacred and Profane Uses of Stone Among the Dani*, Texas A&M University Press, College Station.

Hayden, Brian (editor)
    1979   *Lithic Use-Wear Analysis*, Academic Press, New York.
    1987   *Lithic Studies Among the Contemporary Highland Maya*, University of Arizona Press, Tucson.

Hayden, Brian, and Karl W. Hutchings
    1989   "Whither the Billet Flake?" pp. 235-258 in *Experiments in Lithic Technology*, ed. by Daniel S. Amick, and Raymond P. Mauldin, BAR Intl. Series 528.

Heizer, Robert. F., and Theodora Kroeber (editors)
    1979   *Ishi the Last Yahi: A Documentary History*, University of California Press, Berkeley.

Hellweg, Paul
    1984   *Flintknapping: The Art of Making Stone Tools*, Canyon Publishing, Canoga Park.

Hester, Thomas Roy
    1973   A Supplementary Note on Flint-Chipping with the Teeth, *Newsletter of Lithic Technology* 2(1-2): 23.

Hetényi, M.
    1946   *Beams on Elastic Foundation: Theory and Applications in the Field of Civil and Mechanical Engineering*, University of Michigan Press, Ann Arbor.

Hirth, Kenneth G., Bradford Andrews and J. Jeffrey Flenniken
    2006   A Technological Analysis of Xochicalco Obsidian Prismatic Blade Production, pp. 63-95 in *Obsidian Craft Production in Ancient Central Mexico*, by Kenneth G Hirth et al., University of Utah Press, Salt Lake City.

Hirth, Kenneth G. and J. Jeffrey Flenniken
    2006   "Appendix A. The Analytical Categories for Xochicalco's Lithic Terminology," pp. 301-314 in *Obsidian Craft Production in Ancient Central Mexico*, by Kenneth G Hirth et al., University of Utah Press, Salt Lake City.

Ho-Ho Committee
    1979   Ho-Ho Classification and Nomenclature Committee Report, pp. 133-135 in *Lithic Use-Wear Analysis*, ed. by Brian Hayden, Academic Press, New York.

Holmes, W.H.
    1919   Handbook of Aboriginal American Antiquities, Part I, Introductory: The Lithic Industries, *Bureau of American Ethnology Bulletin 60*, Smithsonian Institution.

Hull, Derek
    1999   *Fractography: Observing, Measuring and Interpreting Fracture Surface Topography*, Cambridge University Press, Cambridge.

Hutchings, Wallace Karl
    1997   The Paleoindian Fluted Point: Dart or Spear Armature? The Identification of Paleoindian Delivery Technology Through the Analysis of Lithic Fracture Velocity, Doctoral Dissertation, Department of Archaeology, Simon Fraser University.
    1999   Quantification of Fracture Propagation Velocity Employing a Sample of Clovis Channel Flakes, *J. Arch. Sci.* 26 (12): 1437-1447.

Inizan, M.-L., M. Reduron-Ballinger, H. Roche and J. Tixier
    1999   *Technology and Terminology of Knapped Stone*, Préhistoire de la Pierre Taillée Vol.5, Cercle de Recherches et d'Etudes Préhistoriques (CREP), Nanterre Cedex.

Jelinek, Arthur J., Bruce Bradley and Bruce Huckell
    1971   The Production of Multiple Secondary Flakes, *Amer. Ant.* 36 (2):198-200.

Johnson, J.W. and D.G. Holloway
    1966   On the Shape and Size of the Fracture Zones on Glass Fracture Surfaces, *Philosophical Magazine* 14: 731-743.

Jones, Scott
    2001   Small-Scale Thermal Alteration: A Case Study and Experiments in Southeastern Archaeology, *Bull. of Prim. Tech.* 22:35-42.

Kalin, Jeffrey
    1981   Flintknapping and Silicosis, *Flintknappers' Exchange* 4(2): 2-9.

Kalthoff, J.F.
    1973   On the Propagation Direction of Bifurcated Cracks, pp. 449-458 in *Dynamic Crack Propagation*, ed. by G.C. Sih, Noordhoff International Publishing, Leyden.

Kanninen, Melvin F. and Carl H. Popelar
    1985   *Advanced Fracture Mechanics*, Oxford University Press, New York.

Keeley, Lawrence H.
    1980   *Experimental Determination of Stone Tool Uses: A Microwear Analysis*, University of Chicago Press, Chicago.

Kelterborn, Peter
    1984   Towards Replicating Egyptian Predynastic Flint Knives, *J. Field Archaeol. Sci.* 11(6):433-455.
    2001   Replication, Use and Repair of an Arrowhead, *Bull. of Prim. Techn.* 21: 48-57.
    2003   Measurable Flintknapping, pp.120-131 in *Mesoamerican Lithic Technology: Experimentation and Interpretation,"* d. by Kenneth G. Hirth, University of Utah Press, Salt Lake City.

Kerkhof, Frank
    1970   *Bruchvorgänge in Gläsern*, Deutsche Glastechnische Gesellschaft, Frankfurt.

Kerkhof, Frank, and Hans-Jürgen Müller-Beck
    1969   Zur Bruchmechanischen Deutung der Schlagmarken an Steingeraten, *Glastechnische Berichte* 42:439-448.

Knutsson, Kjel
    1988a   Patterns of Tool Use: Scanning Electron Microscopy of Experimental Quartz Tools, *Societas Archaeologica Upsaliensis, Aun* 8, Uppsala.

Kolsky, H.
    1960   *Stress Waves in Solids*, Dover Publications, New York.

Kolsky, H., and D. Rader
    1968   Stress Waves and Fracture, pp. 533-569 in *Fracture: An Advanced Treatise, Vol. l: Microscopic and Macroscopic Fundamentals,* ed. by H Liebowitz, Academic Press, New York.

Kroeber, Theodora
    1969   *Ishi in Two Worlds: A Biography of the Last Wild Indian in North America*, University of California Press, Berkeley.

Lawn, Brian
    1993   *Fracture of Brittle Solids*, Second edition, Cambridge University Press, Cambridge.
    1998   Indentation of Ceramics with Spheres: A Century after Hertz, *J. Am. Cer Soc.* 81(8):1977-1994.

Lawn, B.R., and D.B. Marshall
    1994   Indentation Fractography, pp. 1-35 in *Fractography of Glass*, ed. by Richard C. Bradt and Richard E. Tressler, Plenum Press, New York, 1994.

Leakey, L.S.B.
    1953   *Adam's Ancestors: The Evolution of Man and His Culture*, Harper and Row, New York.

Leeuwerik, J. and F. Schwarzl
    1955   Morphologische Studie Van Het Breuk Verchijnsel, *Plastica*, 8: 474-479.

Lewis Johnson, L.
    1978   A History of Flint-Knapping Experimentation, 1838-1976, *Current Anthropology* 19(2): 337- 372.

Luedke, Barbara E.
    1992   An Archaeological Guide to Chert and Flint, *Archaeological Research Tools 7*, Institute of Archaeology, University of California, Los Angeles.

Mandeville, M.D.. and J. Jeffrey Flenniken
    1974   A Comparison of the Flaking Qualities of Nehawka Chert Before and After Thermal Pretreatment, *Plains Anthropologist* 19-64: 146-148.

Manghbabi, Murli H., Edward Schreiber and Soga Naohiro
    1968   Use of Ultrasonic Interferometry Technique for Studying ElasticProperties of Rocks, *J Geophys. Rers.* 73: 824-826.

Mason, H.J.
    1978   *Flint the Versatile Stone*, Providence Press, Ely, Cambridgeshire.

McCormick, N.J. and E.A. Almond
    1990   Edge Flaking of Brittle Materials, *J. of Hard Mats.* 1(1):25-51.

Mecholsky, J.J.
    1994   Quantitative Fractographic Analysis of Fracture Origins in Glass, pp. 37-73 in *Fractography of Glass*, ed. by Richard C. Bradt and Richard E.Tressler, Plenum Press, New York.

2001   Fractography, Fractals and Quantum Geometry, pp. 193-209 in *Fractography of Glasses and Ceramics IV,* ed. by James R. Varner and George G. Quinn, The American Ceramic Society, Westerville.

Mecholsky, J.J., S.W. Freiman and R.W. Rice
1977   Effect of Grinding on Flaw Geometry and Fracture of Glass, *J. Am.. Cer.. Soc.* 60: 114-117.

Mecholsky, J.J., and T.J. Mackin
1988   Fractal Analysis of Fracture in Ocala Chert, *Journal of Material Science Letters* 7: 1145-1147.

Michalske, T.A.
1979   Dynamic Effects of Liquids on Crack Growth Leading to Catastrophic Failure in Glass, Ph.D. Thesis, Alfred University, Alfred.
1984   Fractography of Slow Fracture in Glass, pp. 121-136 in *Fractography of Ceramic and Metal Failures*, ASTM Special Technical Publication 827, ed. by J.J Mecholsky, Jr., and J.R. Powell, Jr., American Society for Testing and Materials, Philadelphia.
1994   Fractography of Stress Corrosion Cracking in Glass, pp. 111-142 in *Fractography of Glass*, ed. by Richard C. Bradt and Richard E. Tressler, Plenum Press, New York, 1994.

Michalske, T.A., and B.C, Bunker
1987   The Fracturing of Glass, *Scientific American* 257: 122-9.

Miller, Tom O.
1979   Stonework of the Xêtá Indians of Brazil, pp. 401-407 in *Lithic Use-Wear Analysis*, ed. by Brian Hayden, Academic Press, New York.

Morrell, Roger
2005   Edge Flaking – Similarity between Quasistatic Indentation and Impact Mechanisms for Brittle Materials, pp. 14-22 in *Fractography of Advanced Ceramics II,* ed. by J. Dusza, R. Danzer and R. Morrell, Trans Tech Publications, Zürich.

Morrell, Roger, and A.J. Gant
2001   Edge Chipping – What Does It Tell Us? pp. 23-42 in *Fractography of Glasses and Ceramics IV,* ed. by James R. Varner and George D. Quinn, The American Ceramic Society, Westerville.

Nami, Hugo G.
1997   Investigaciones Actualisticos para Discuter Aspectos Tecnicos de los Cazadores-Recolectores del Tardiglacial: El Problema Clovis – Cueva Fell, *Anales del Instituto de la Patagonia 25: 151-186.*

Nunn, Greg
2005   *Replicating the Type IC Neolithic Danish Dagger*, DVD, Greg Nunn/Paleo Technologies, Castle Valley.
2006   Using the Jutland Type IC Neolithic Danish Dagger as a Model to Replicate Parallel Edge-to-Edge Pressure Flaking, pp. 81-113 in *SkilledProduction and Social Reproduction,* ed. by Jan Apel and Kjel Knutsson, Societas Archaeologica Upsaliensis, Uppsala.
2007   Using Soft Hammerstones, the Tool of the West, *Bull. of Prim. Tech.* 34:57-61.

Odell, George H.
    2004   *Lithic Analysis*, Kluwer Academis/Plenum Publishers, New York.

Paar, Reinhold
    1994   *Kantenfestigkeit von Hochleistungskeramik*, Diplomarbeit, Institut für Struktur- und Funktionskeramik, Montan-Universität Leoben, Leoben, Austria.

Parker, Arthur C.
    1925   The Great Algonkin Flint Mines at Coxackie, *Researches and Transactions of the New York State Archaeological Association*, Rochester.

Patten, Bob
    1999   *Old Tools- New Eyes: A Primal Primer of Flintknapping*, Stone Dagger Publications, Denver.

Pelcin, Andrew Walter
    1996   Controlled Experiments in the Production of Flake Attributes, Ph.D. Thesis, University of Pennsylvania, Philadelphia.

Pelegrin, Jacques
    1984   Système Expérimentaux d'Immobilisation du Nucleus pour le Déditage par Pression, pp. 105-116 in *Préhistoire de la Pierre Tailée: 2. Économie du Débitage Laminaire: Technologie et Expérimentation*, Cercle de Recherches et Étude Préhistoriques (C.R.E.P.), Presse de E. Durand, Paris.
    2003   Blade-Making Techniques from the Old World: Insights and Applications to Mesoamerican Obsidian Lithic Technology, pp.55-71 in *Mesoamerican Lithic Technology: Experimentation and Interpretation,* ed. by Kenneth G. Hirth, University of Utah Press, Salt Lake City.
    2013   Les Grandes Feuilles de Laurier et Autre Objets Particuliers du Solutréen: Une Valeur de Signe, Le Solutréen...40 Ans Après Smith' 66, Actes du Colloque de Preully-Sur-Claise, 21 Oct. – 01 Nov. 2007, *Revue Archéologique du Centre de la France* Supplement 47.

Poncelet, Eugene
    1958   The Markings on Fracture Surfaces, *Trans. of the Soc. of Glass Technology* 42, 279-88.

Pond, Alonzo W.
    1930   *Primitive Methods of Working Stone, Based on Experiments of Havlor L. Skavlem*, The Logan Museum, Beloit College, Beloit.

Preston, Frank
    1926   A Study of the Rupture of Glass, *J. Soc. of Glass Techn.* 10: 234-269.
    1935   The Angle of Forking in Glass Cracks as an Indicator of the Stress System, *J. Am. Cer. Soc.* 18 (6):175-177.

Purdy, Barbara Ann
    1974   Investigation Concerning the Thermal Alteration of Silica Minerals: An Archaeological Approach" *Tebiwa* 17(1): 37-66.
    1975   Fractures for the Archaeologist, pp.133-141 & Plates 2–8 in *Lithic Technology: Making and Using Stone Tools*, ed. by Earl Swanson, Mouton Publishers, The Hague.

Purdy, B.A., and H.K. Brooks
    1971   Thermal Alteration of Silica Minerals: An Archaeological Approach, *Science* 173(3994): 322-325.

Quackenbush, C.L., and V.D. Fréchette
    1978   Crack Front Curvature and Slow Glass Fracture, *J. Am. Cer. Soc.* 61(9-10): 402- 4.

Quinn, George D.
    2007   *Fractography of Ceramics and Glasses, NIST Recommended Practice Guide,* Special Publication 960-16, National Institute of Standards and Technology, Washington, D.C.

Quinn, Janet B., James W. Hatch and Richard C. Bradt
    2001   The Edge Flaking Test as an Assessment of the Thermal Alteration of Lithic Material, Bald Eagle Jasper, pp. 73-85 in *Fractography of Glasses and Ceramics IV,* ed. by James R. Varner and George D. Quinn, The American Ceramic Society, Westerville.

Quinn, Janet B., and R. Mohan
    2005   Geometry of Edge Chips Formed at Different Angles, *Cer. Eng. Sci. Proc.* 26(2): 85-92.

Rice, Roy W.
    1984   Ceramic Fracture Features, Observations, Mechanisms and Uses, pp. 5-103 in *Fractography of Ceramic and Metal Failures, ASTM Spec. Tech. Pub. 827*, ASTM, Philadelphia.
    1988   Perspective on Fractography, pp.3-56 in *Fractography of Glasses and Ceramics*, ed. by J.R.Varner and Fréchette, V.D. The American Ceramic Society, Westerville.

Richter, H.G.
    1985   Crack Propagation in Glass Under Liquids in an Intermediate Range of Crack Velocities, pp. 219-229 in *Strength of Inorganic Glass*, ed. by Charles R. Kurkjian, Plenum Press, New York.

Richter, H.G., and F. Kerkhof
    1994   Stress Wave Fractography, pp.75-109 in *Fractography of Glass*, ed. by Richard C. Bradt and Richard E. Tressler, Plenum Press, New York, 1994.

Schardin, H.
    1950   Ergebnisse der Kinematografischen Untersuchungen, *Glastechn. Ber.* 23: (I): 1-10, (II): 167-179,(III):325-336.

Schick, Kathy D., and Nicholas Toth
    1993   *Making Silent Stones Speak: Human Evolution and the Dawn of Technology*, Simon and Schuster, New York.

Schindler, D.L., J.W. Hatch, C.A. Hay and R.C. Bradt
    1982   Aboriginal Thermal Alteration of a Central Pennsylvania Jasper: Analytical and Behavioral Implications, *Ame. Ant.* 47(3): 526-544.

Schönert, K., H. Umhauer and W. Klemm
    1969   The Influence of Temperature and Environment on the Slow Crack Propagation in Glass, pp. 474-482 in *Fracture 1969*, ed. by P.L. Pratt, E.H. Andrews, R.L. Bell, N.E. Frost R.W. Nichols and E Smith, Chapman and Hall, London.

Semaw, et al.
    1997   2.5 Million-year Old Stone Tools from Gona, Ethiopia, *Nature* 385:333-336.

Sheets, Payson D., and Guy R. Muto
    1972   Pressure Blades and Total Cutting Edge: An Experiment in Lithic Technology, *Science* 175: 632-634.

Shepherd, R.
    1980   *Prehistoric Mining and Allied Industries*, Academic Press, New York.

Shepherd, Walter
    1972   *Flint: Its Origins, Properties and Uses*, Faber and Faber, London.

Silsby, Scott
    1985   Rhyolite: Cultural Preference and Knapping Techniques, pp. 29-34 in *Ancient Man Information Exchange Vol.: New Light,* ed. by Stephen R. Porcelli, Tekakwitha Institute of Ancient Man, Springfield, VA, 1985.

Slotta, Rainer
    1980   Die Heutige Feuersteinindustrie von Eben-Emaël (Belgien), pp. 366-374 in *5000 Jahre Feuersteinbergbau: Die Suche nach dem Stahl der Steinzeit*, ed. by Weigerber, Gerd, Slotta, Rainer, and Weiner Jurgen, Deutschen Bergbau-Museum, Bochum.

Smekal, A.
    1950   Verfahren zur Messung von Bruchfortpflanzungsgeschwindigkeiten an Bruchflächen, *Glastechn. Ber.* 23(3): 57-67.

Sollberger, J.B.
    1985   A Technique for Folsom Flaking, *Lithic Technology* 1(1): 41:50.

Sollberger, J.B., and L.W. Patterson
    1976   Prismatic Blade Replication, *Amer. Ant.* 41(4): 517-531.

Sommer, E.
    1969   Formation of Fracture 'Lances' in Glass, *Engineering Fracture Mechanics* 1 (1): 539-546.

Speth, John D.
    1972   Mechanical Basis of Percussion Flaking, *Amer. Ant.* 37(1): 34-60.
    1974   Experimental Investigations of Hard-Hammer Percussion Flaking, *Tebiwa* 17(1): 7-36.
    1975   Miscellaneous Studies in Hard-Hammer Percussion Flaking: The Effects of Oblique Impact, *Amer. Ant.* 40(2): 203-207.
    1981   The Role of Platform Angle and Core Size in Hard-Hammer Percussion Flaking, *Lithic Technology* 10(1): 16-21.

Stanford, Dennis, and Bruce A. Bradley
    2012   *Across Atlantic Ice: The Origin of America's Clovis Culture*, University of California Press, Berleley.

Steffen, Anastasia
    2005   *The Dome Fire Obsidian Study: Investigating the Interaction of Heat, Hydration, and Glass Geochemistry,"* Ph.D. Thesis, Department of Anthropology, University of New Mexico, Albuquerque

Stocker, T.L., and R.H. Cobean
    1984   Preliminary Report on the Obsidian Mines of Pico de Orizaba, Veracruz,

pp. 83-96 in *Prehistoric Quarries and Lithic Production*, ed. by Jonathan E. Ericson and Barbara Ann Purdy, Cambridge University Press, Cambridge.

Takacs-Biro, C.
    1986   Sources of Raw Materials Used for the Manufacture of Chipped Stone Implements in Hungary, pp.121-132 in *The Scientific Study of Flint and Chert,* ed. by G. de G. Sieveking and M.B. Hart, Cambridge University Press, Cambridge.

Terzaghi, Karl
    1961   *Theoretical Soil Mechanics,* Wiley, New York.

Texier, P.-J.
    1984   Le Débitage par Pression et la Mécanique de la Rupture Fragile: Initiation et la propagation des Fractures, pp. 139-147 in *Préhistoire de la Pierre Taillée: 2. Économie du Débitage Laminaire: Technologie et Expérimetation*, Cercle de Recherches et Étude Préhistoriques (C.R.E.P.), Presse de E. Durand, Paris.

Thomsen, Erich G., and Harrietta H. Thomsen
    1971   Litho-mechanics and Archaeology, pp. 51-62 in *The Applications of the Physical Sciences to Archaeology,* ed. by Fred H. Stross, *Contributions of the University of California Archaeological Research Facility* 12: 51-62.

Thouless, M.D., and A.G. Evans.
    1990   Comment on the Spalling and Edge-Cracking of Plates, *Scripta Metallurgica et Materialia* 24: 1507-1510.

Thouless, M.D., A.G. Evans, M.F, Ashley and J.W. Hutchinson
    1987   The Edge Cracking and Spalling of Brittle Plates, *Acta Metallurgica* 35(6): 1333-41.

Timoshenko, S., and J.N. Goodier
    1951   *Theory of Elasticity*, McGraw-Hill, New York.

Tindale, Norman B.
    1985   Australian Aboriginal Techniques of Pressure Flaking Stone Implements: Some Personal Observations, pp. 1-34 in *Stone Tool Analysis: Essays in Honor of Don E. Crabtree,* ed. by Mark G. Plew, James C. Woods and Max G. Pavesic, University of New Mexico Press, Albuquerque.

Titmus, Gene L.
    1985   Some Aspects of Stone Tool Notching, pp. 243-263 in *Stone Tool Analysis Essays in Honor of Don E. Crabtree*, ed. by Mark G. Plew, James C. Woods and Max G. Pavesic, University of New Mexico Press, Albuquerque.

Titmus, Gene L., and James C. Woods
    2003   The Maya Eccentric: Evidence for the Use of the Indirect Percussion Technique in Mesoamerica from Preliminary Experiments Concerning Their Manufacture, pp. 132-146 in *Mesoamerican Lithic Technology: Experimentation and Interpretation, "* ed. by Kenneth G. Hirth, University of Utah Press, Salt Lake City.

Tixier, Jacques
    1972   Obtention de Lames par Débitage 'Sous le Pied', *Bull. Soc. Préh. Française* 69: 134-139.

Tomenchuk, John
    1985   The Development of a Wholly Parametric Use-Wear Methodology and Its Application to Two Selected Samples of Epipaleolithic Chipped Stone Tools from Hayonim Cave, Israel, Ph.D. Dissertation, Department of Anthropology, University of Toronto.

Trachman, Rissa
    1999   An Additional Technological Perspective on Obsidian Polyhedral Core Platform Rejuvenation, *Lithic Technology* 24(2): 119-125.

Trachman, Rissa M., and Gene L. Titmus
    2003   Pecked and Scored Initiations: Early Classic Core-Blade Production in the Central Maya Lowlands, pp. 108-119 in *Mesoamerican Lithic Technology: Experimentation and Interpretation,"* ed. by Kenneth G. Hirth, University of Utah Press, Salt Lake City.

Tsai, Y.M., and H. Kolsky
    1967   A Theoretical and Experimental Investigation of the Flaw Distribution on Glass Surfaces, *J. of the Mechs. and Physics of Solids* 15: 29-36.

Tsirk, Are
    1979   Regarding Fracture Initiation, pp. 83-96 in *Lithic Use-Wear Analysis*, ed. by Brian Hayden, Academic Press, New York.
    1981   On a Geometrical Effect on Crack Front Configuration, *Int. J. Fract.* 17 (6): R185-R188.
    1988   Formation and Utility of a Class of Anomalous Wallner Lines on Obsidian, pp. 57-69 in *Fractography of Glasses and Ceramics*, ed. by J. R. Varner and V. D. Fréchette, The American Ceramic Society, Westerville.
    1989   On Flaw Characteristics, Environmental Factors and Fracture Markings Related to Obsidian Flaking, pp. 137- 145 in La *Obsidiana en Mesoamerica*, ed. by Margarita Gaxiola and John E. Clark, Instituto Nacional de Antropologia e Historia, Mexico.
    1996   Hackles Revisited, pp. 447-472 in *Fractography of Glasses and Ceramics III,* ed. by J.R. Varner, V.D. Fréchette and G.D. Quinn, The American Ceramic Society, Westerville.
    2001   An Exploration of Liquid-Induced Fracture Markings, pp. 87-101 in *Fractographyof Glasses and Ceramics IV,* ed. by James R. Varner and George D. Quinn, The American Ceramic Society, Westerville.
    2003   Obsidian Fractures from a Forest Fire Zone in Santa Fe National Forest, Report No. 020607, Appendix B in *The Dome Fire Obsidian Study: Investigating the Interaction of Heat, Hydration and Glass Geochemistry(New Mexico),* by Anastasia Steffen, Ph.D.Thesis, Department of Anthropology, University of New Mexico, Albuquerque.
    2007   Liquid-Induced Fracture Markings: An Overview, pp. 79-91 in *Fractography of Glasses and Ceramics V*, ed. by James R. Varner, George D. Quinn and Marlene Wightman, The American Ceramic Society, John Wiley & Sons, Hoboken.
    2010a   Fracture Markings from Flake Splitting, *J. Archaeol. Sci.* 37 (8): 2061-2065.
    2010b   Popouts and Related Fractures, *Lithic Technology,* 35 (2): 1049-170.

2012   Fractography Lessons from Knapping, pp. 123-132 in *Fractography of Glasses and Ceramics VI*, ed. by James R. Varner and Marlene Wightman, The American Ceramic Society and John Wiley & Sons, Hoboken.

n.d.   An Approximate Analysis for Blade Production, Unpublished manuscript.

Tsirk, Are, and William J. Parry
- 2000 Fractographic Evidence for Liquid on Obsidian Tools, *J. Arch. Sci.* 27: 987-991.

Vaidyanathan, Swaminathan
- 1969 The Shaping of Brittle Solids, Ph.D. Thesis, Mechanical Engineering, University of California, Berkeley, University Microfilms, Ann Arbor, Michigan.

Vang Petersen, Peter
- 2008 *Flint fra Danmarks Oldtid*, Forlaget Museerne, Nationalmuseet, Copenhagen.

Varner, James R., and V.D. Fréchette
- 1971 Fracture Marks Associated with Transition Region Behavior of Slow Cracks in Glass, *J. Appl. Phys.* 42:1983.

Waldorf, D.C.
- 1993 *The Art of Flintknapping*, 4th edition, Mound Builder Books, Branson.

Wallner, H.
- 1939 Linienstrukturen an Bruchflächen, *Z. Phys.* 114: 368-378.

Watson, Virginia Drew
- 1995 Simple and Significant: Stone Tool Production in Highland New Guinea, *Lithic Technology* 20(2): 89-99.

Weiner, Jurgen
- 1980a Cakmak in Jahre 1980 – Eine Heute Noch Produzierende Flintmine in Nordwestanatolien, pp. 383-395 in *5000 Jahre Feuersteinbergbau: Die Suche nach dem Stahl der Steinzeit*, ed. by Gerd Weisgerber, Rainer Slotta and Jurgen Weiner, Deutschen Bergbau-Museum, Bochum.

White, J. Peter
- 1967 Ethno-archaeology in New Guinea, *Mankind* 6(9): 409-414.

Whittaker, John C.
- 1994 *Flintknapping: Making and Understanding Stone Tools*, University of Texas Press, Austin.
- 1996 Athkiajas: A Cypriot Flintknapper and the Threshing Sledge Industry, *Lithic Technology* 21(2): 108-120.
- 2001 Knapping Building Flints in Norfolk, *Lithic Technology 26(1): 71-80.*
- 2004 *American Flintknappers*, University of Texas Press, Austin.
- 2008 Turkish Flinty Mines, *Chips* 20 (2):5-9.

Whittaker, John C., Kathryn Kamp and Emek Yilman
- 2009 Cakmak Revisited,: Turkish Flintknappers Today, *Lithic Technology 34 (2): 93-110.*

Whittaker, John C., and Michael Stafford
- 1999 Replicas, Fakes and Art: The Twentieth Century Stone Age and Its Effects on Archaeology, *Am. Ant.* 64(2): 203- 214.

Wiederhorn, S.M.
- 1967 Influence of Water Vapor on Crack Propagation in Soda-Lime Glass, *J. Am. Cer. Soc.*, 50: 407-14.
- 1978 Mechanisms of Subcritical Crack Growth in Glass, pp. 549-580 in *Fracture Mechanics of Ceramics*, Vol. 4, ed. by R.C. Bradt, D.P.H. Hasselman, and F.F. Lange, Plenum Press, New York.

Zukas, Jonas A., Theodore Nicholas, Hallock F. Swift, Longin B. Greszczuk and Donald R. Curran
- 1982 *Impact Dynamics*, John Wiley & Son, New York.

Index

A

amputation 44, 128, 148, 168, 190, 200, 210, 214, 228, 232, Fig. 13.6

B

bipolar technique 21, 23, 25, 28, 34, 88, 140, 158, 199, 200, 211, 232, Fig. 2.7

bowties 224, Fig. 13.17

breakage 28, 41, 43, 73, 78, 79, 80, 88, 92, 94, 96, 98, 126, 130, 131, 147, 148, 157, 164, 178, 190, 199, 201, 202, 205, 207, 208, 210, 211, 212, 214, 215, 216, 218, 224, 225, 228, 229, 232, 236, 238

    bifaces 3, 4, 16, 21, 23, 28, 29, 34, 41, 47, 88, 94, 96, 127, 131, 153, 157, 170, 182, 184, 191, 195, 206, 207, 208, 210, 211, 216, 217, 220, 224, 236

    blades and flakes 2, 3, 7, 8, 10, 14, 19, 21, 25, 27, 31, 41, 43, 86, 87, 94, 96, 98, 111, 123, 131, 133, 150, 154, 163, 170, 174, 175, 176, 177, 191, 195, 196, 198, 202, 203, 205, 211, 212, 214, 216, 218, 220, 223, 224, 226, 227, 228, 230

C

catastrophic crack propagation 49

compression curls 168, Fig. 11.1

compression lips 134, 177, 180, 201, 211, 215, 216, Fig. 11.1

compression wedges 96, 134, 171, 181, 201, 211, 215, 216, 232, Fig. 11.1

concavity 27, 84, 153, 154, 177, 205

crack growth 130, 224, 232, 233

crack path 167, 168, 182, 233

crack propagation 49, 109, 130, 175

E

edge-to-edge flakes 208, Fig. 13.3

F

flake initiations 130, 132, 133, 136, 139, 140, 142, 147, 151, 152, 187, 233, Table 10.1

    bending 92, 95, 98, 133, 142, 147, 154-167, 187, 190

    contact 133

    Hertzian 139, Figs. 10.4 and 10.5

    multiple flakes 145

    non-contact initiation 147, 148, 157, 191, 192

    unzipping initiation 148, 149, Fig. 10.9

    wedging initiation 10, 133, 140,143,154, Fig. 10.3

forces in knapping 29, 133, 168, 186

fracture markings

    branching 41, 56, 60, 61, 92, 94, 95, 96, 97, 130, 131, 168, 169, 171, 182, 201, 211, 216, 219, 220, 223, 224, 232, 233, 235, 236

    gull wings 56, 57, 59, 61, Figs. 6.3 and 6.4

    hackles 31, 56, 60, 63, 64, 65, 66, 67, 68, 69, 74, 75, 79, 84, 88, 89, 92, 93, 101, 102, 104, 107, 120, 123, 129, 131, 145, 158, 159, 160, 165, 166, 201, 214, 220, 221, 223, 228, 235

    multiple tails 55, 57, 69, Fig. 5.9

    tails 58, 60, 63, 64, 68, 70, 165, 217, Fig. 5.1

    twist hackles 31, 60, 63, 64, 65, 66, 67, 68, 69, 74, 75, 79, 84, 88, 89, 92, 101, 102, 104, 107, 123, 129, 131, 145, 158, 159, 160, 165, 166, 201, 214, 220, 221, 228, Figs. 5.1. and 5.4

    velocity hackles 220, Fig. 7.2

    hackle scars 55, 58, 60, 63, 73, 158, 165, Fig. 5.14

    liquid-induced fracture markings

(LIFM) 54, 79, 89, 110, Figs. 8,6 to 8.9
material interface markings 103, Fig. 8.1
mirror 27, 40, 41, 56, 61, 92, 94, 95, 97, 98, 150, 164, 202, 218, 236, Fig. 7.2
mist 41, 44, 45, 56, 59, 60, 61, 63, 69, 70, 72, 73, 74, 80, 82, 85, 92, 93, 94, 95, 96, 97, 98, 99, 100, 101, 102, 130, 131, 135, 155, 156, 157, 164, 170, 171, 178, 201, 202, 205, 209, 210, 211, 214, 216, 218, 219, 220, 221, 222, 223, 224, 226, 227, 228, 229, 236, 240, Fig. 7.6
mist-hackle configuration 99, 236, Fig. 7.4
mist lines 93, 100, 101, 102, 164, 218, Figs. 5.10, 6.4 and 7.5
overview 54-62
parabolic double tails 55, 70, 71, 72, 73, Figs. 5.9 to 5.11
ripples 60, 66, 74, 76, 78, 79, 80, 86, 87, 88, 89, 90, 91, 92, 106, 107, 128, 129, 131, 140, 141, 142, 143, 144, 154, 159, 160, 161, 162, 163, 165, 181, 182, 196, 202, 238, 240
ruffles 78, 107, 108, 165, 167, 238, Fig. 8.4
split marks 106, 107, 165, 202, 238, Figs. 8.3 and 13.3
terminology Table 4.1
velocity hackle 92-95, Fig. 7.2
Wallner lines 60, 61, 78, 79, 80, 81, 84, 85, 88, 90, 91, 98, 99, 103, 116, 117, 123, 125, 128, 131, 132, 133, 134, 159, 160, 164, 214, 235, 236
Wallner mist-hackle configuration 98, Fig. 7.4
Wallner wake 85, 86, 240, Fig. 6.4
fracture modes 129, 132, 239, Fig. 9.1
fracture toughness 35, 36, 40, 43, 47, 48, 60, 103, 127, 129, 151, 160, 163, 234, Table 3.4
fracture velocity 48, 59, 63, 67, 77, 81, 84, 85, 86, 87, 90, 95, 96, 98, 109, 110, 123, 130, 156, 160, 164, 171, 232, 237, 238, 239, 240
examples 130
practical (effective) terminal 130
theoretical terminal 130

G

Gerzian knife 3, 4, 27, Fig. 1.4
Gunflints 7, Fig. 1.8

H

Hertzian cone fractures 136, 138, 139, 142, 157

K

knapping techniques 12, Figs. 2.5, 2.9 and 2.10
knapping tools 16
    antler billets 16, 17, 195, Fig. 2.1
    hammerstones 1, 17, 18, 21, 131, 148, 195, Fig. 2.1
    pressure flakers 18, Figs. 2.3 and 2.10
    punches 18, Fig. 2.2
    wood billets 16, Figs. 2.2 and 2.5b

L

lateral wedges 41, 131, 170, 171, 201, 202, 211, 216, 217, 223, 224, 225, Fig. 13.18

N

normality rule 129, 183, 201, 237

O

Overshot flakes 208, Figs. 5.14, 10.14, 13.4 and 13.5

P

popouts 158, 159, 175, 177, 179, 180, 181, 203, 204, 205, 216, Fig. 11.13

R

Raw Materials 31, 243, 253
    alteration 39, 44, 48, 235, 240

hydration 44, 45, 123, 252, 254
patination 45
thermal 39
vesiculation 32, 45, 220, 240
antler 1, 13, 16, 17, 18, 19, 20, 21, 22, 23, 25, 26, 36, 133, 141, 146, 152, 158, 195, 196, 197, 217, 223, 228, 229, 238
lithic materials 39, 40, 41, 44, 54, 110, 123, 131, 132, 134, 150, 151, 195
wood 8, 16, 18, 19, 20, 21, 25, 36, 141, 196, 197, 228, 237
ripple concavity 27, Fig. 10.16
ruffles 78, 107, 108, 165, 167, 238

S

segmentation 226, 229, Fig. 13.20
sledges 7, 9, 10, 50
slices 201, 222, 223, 226, 227, 228, 229, Figs. 13.16 and 13.20
sonic modulation 89, 90, 124, 238, Fig. 6.9
stepouts 159, Fig. 11.1
stress intensity factor 40, 79, 101, 103, 109, 128, 129, 130, 183, 194, 233, 234, 239
Subcritical crack growth 130
supports 38, 141, 168, 198, 223

T

termination 75, 101, 177, 183, 184, 185, 193, 205, 214, 232, 234, 235, 239
termination of flakes 75, Fig. 11.15
terminology 54, 115
thermal cracking 45, Fig. 3.5
thermal effects 39, 46, 126, 127, 182
constants 38, Table 3.3
treshing sledges 7, Fig. 1.9

U

ultrasonic modulation 88, 89, 90, 124, 238, 240, Fig. 6.8

W

wing flakes 74, 137, 145, 157, Figs. 10.7 and 10.8
workability 33, 35, 41, 43, 44, 47, 48, 240